American Hegemony in the 21st Century

For many years now debates over America hegemony and its supposed decline have circulated academic circles. The neo-Gramscians have greatly enriched our knowledge in this field, developing some key theoretical tools and concepts, yet ontological inconsistencies, notably the downgrading of structure, has meant their explanation of the dynamics of the contemporary world order remains somewhat incomplete.

In this book, Jonathan Pass aims to counter such oversights, drawing directly on the ideas of Antonio Gramsci (amongst others) to elaborate a more sophisticated, overtly materialist, theory of world hegemony, rooted in a critical realist philosophy of science. Through the lens of this *Neo* Neo-Gramscian (NNG), the book examines the complex interplay of internal and external social forces responsible for the evolving 'nature' of US hegemony, from its establishment in the 1940s, passing through its different stages of crisis and restructuring up to the present. China's spectacular rise undoubtedly constitutes a 'world event', but is it potentially a 'world hegemon'? The book seeks to shed some light on this question, analysing the economic and geopolitical significance of China's emergence and how it affects, and is affected by, both American hegemony and its own extremely delicate 'passive revolution' at home.

American Hegemony in the 21st Century presents a major contribution to International Relations, International Political Economy, Politics, and Philosophy and will be of interest to researchers looking for a more sophisticated and convincing analysis of the dynamics of the contemporary world order.

Jonathan Pass is Lecturer in International Relations within the Department of Public Law at Pablo de Olavide University, Seville, Spain.

Routledge Advances in International Relations and Global Politics

For information about the series: https://www.routledge.com/Routledge-Advances-in-International-Relations-and-Global-Politics/book-series/IRGP

American Hegemony in the 21st Century

A *Neo* Neo-Gramscian Perspective

Jonathan Pass

Routledge
Taylor & Francis Group

NEW YORK AND LONDON

First published 2019
by Routledge
52 Vanderbilt Avenue, New York, NY 10017

and by Routledge
2 Park Square, Milton Park, Abingdon, Oxon, OX14 4RN

First issued in paperback 2020

Routledge is an imprint of the Taylor & Francis Group, an Informa business

© 2019 Taylor & Francis

Library of Congress Cataloging-in-Publication Data
Names: Pass, Jonathan, author.
Title: American hegemony in the 21st century: a *neo* neo-Gramscian perspective / Jonathan Pass.
Description: New York, NY: Routledge, 2019. |
Series: Routledge advances in international relations and global politics; 142 | Includes bibliographical references and index.
Identifiers: LCCN 2018049150 | ISBN 9781138311060 (hardback) | ISBN 9780429459061 (ebk)
Subjects: LCSH: United States—Foreign relations—21st century. | World politics—21st century. | International organization.
Classification: LCC JZ1480 .P373 2019 | DDC 327.1/140973—dc23
LC record available at https://lccn.loc.gov/2018049150

ISBN 13: 978-0-367-66191-5 (pbk)
ISBN 13: 978-1-138-31106-0 (hbk)

DOI: 10.4324/9780429459061

Typeset in Times New Roman
by codeMantra

The Open Access version of Chapter 2 was funded by Universidad Pablo de Olavide.

Contents

List of Abbreviations

ACFTU	All-China Federation of Trade Unions
ADS	Asian Developmental State
AIIB	Asian Infrastructure Investment Bank
AIPAC	American Israel Public Affairs Committee
AMF	Asian Monetary Fund
ASEAN	Association of Southeast Asian Nations
BOP	Balance of Payments
BRI	Belt & Road Initiative
BRICS	Brazil, Russia, India, China, South Africa
CDB	China Development Bank
CDO	Collateralized Debt Obligation
CDS	Credit Default Swap
CEE	Central and Eastern Europe
CELAC	Community of Latina American and Caribbean States
CEO	Chief Executive Officer
CFR	Council on Foreign Relations
CGL	Confederazione Generale del Lavoro
CIA	Central Intelligence Agency
CLCM	Code of Liberalisation of Capital Movements
CMIM	Chiang Mai Initiative Multilateralized
CNOOC	China National Offshore Corp
CNPC	China National Petroleum Corporation
CPC	Communist Party of China
CRA	Contingent Reserve Arrangements
CSCEC	China State Construction Engineering Corporation
CSP	Center for Security Policy
CSSTA	Cross-Strait Service Trade Agreement
DPJ	Democratic Party of Japan
DWSR	Dollar-Wall Street Regime
ECFA	Economic Co-operation Framework Agreement
EEC	European Economic Community
EEZ	Exclusive Economic Zone
ERT	European Round Table of Industrialists

ETUC	European Trade Union Confederation
EU	European Union
FBI	Federal Bureau of Investigation
FDI	Foreign Direct Investment
FDR	Franklin Delano Roosevelt
FIOM	Federazione Impiegati Operai Metallurgica
FIRE	Finance, Insurance and Real Estate
FOS	Form of State
FPI	Foreign Portfolio Investment
FRG	Federal Republic of Germany
GATT	General Agreement on Tariffs and Trade
GDP	Gross Domestic Product
GFC	Global Financial Crisis
HB	Historical Bloc
HST	Hegemonic Stability Theory
ICC	International Criminal Court
IEA	International Energy Agency
IMF	International Monetary Fund
IOAF	Internationalization of American Finance
IOP	Internationalization of Production
IOS	Internationalization of the State
IPE	International Political Economy
IR	International Relations
ISI	Import Substitution Industrialisation
ITO	International Trade Organisation
JCS	Joint Chiefs of Staff
JINSA	Jewish Institute for National Security Affairs
KPD	German Communist Party
KMT	Kuomintang
LDP	Liberal Democratic Party (Japan)
LRBIO	Liberal Rule-Based International Order
LTCM	Long Term Capital Management Fund
MAD	Mutually Assured Destruction
MBS	Mortgage Backed Security
MIC	Military-Industrial-Complex
MNC	Multinational Corporation
MSRI	Maritime Silk Road Initiative
NAFTA	North American Free Trade Agreement
NATO	North Atlantic Treaty Organization
NDB	New Development Bank
NGO	Non-Governmental Organisation
NIE	Newly Industrialised Economies
NIRA	National Industrial Recovery Act
NLL	Northern Line Limit

NNG	*Neo* Neo-Gramscian
NPC	National People's Congress
NSC-68	National Security Council document, April 1950
NSS	National Security State
NSS-2002	National Security Strategy 2002
NSS-2010	National Security Strategy 2010
NSS-2015	National Security Strategy 2015
NSS-2017	National Security Strategy 2017
NTB	Non-Tariff Barriers
NUM	National Union of Mineworkers
NWO	New World Order
OBOR	One Belt, One Road Initiative
OECD	Organisation for Economic Cooperation and Development
OEEC	Organisation for European Economic Cooperation
OPEC	Organization of the Petroleum Exporting Countries
PAC	Political Action Committees
PATCO	Professional Air-Traffic Controllers Organisation
PBC	People's Bank of China (PRC's central bank)
PCI	Italian Communist Party
PLA	People's Liberation Army
PN	Prison Notebooks
PNAC	Project for a New American Century
PRC	People's Republic of China
PSI	Italian Socialist Party
RMA	Revolution in Military Affairs
RMB	Renminbi
RTA	Regional Trade Agreement
SALT	Strategic Arms Limitation Talks
SAP	Structural Adjustment Programmes
SCOA	Systemic Cycle of Accumulation
SEA	Single European Act
SEZ	Special Economic Zones
SIC	Security-Industrial Complex
SPA	Socialist Party of America
SRA	Strategic Relational Approach
SREB	Silk Road Economic Belt
SROP	Social Relations of Production
SCOA	Systemic Cycle of Accumulation
SOCOM	Special Operation Command
TB	Treasury Bonds
THAAD	Thermal High Altitude Area Defense
TINA	There Is No Alternative
TPP	Trans-Pacific Partnership
TNC	Transnational Corporation

TVE	Town and Village Enterprise
UN	United Nations
UNCLOS	UN Convention on the Law of the Sea
UNCTAD	United Nations Conference on Trade and Development
US	United States
USCC	United States Chamber of Commerce
USSR	Union of Soviet Socialist Republics
VPN	Virtual Private Network
WDPDC	Weapondollar-Petrodollar Coalition
WMD	Weapons of Mass Destruction
WO	World Order
WOT	War On Terror
WSTI	Wall Street-Treasury-IMF (Complex)
WTO	World Trade Organisation
WWII	World War Two
YMCA	Young Man's Christian Association

Introduction

For mainstream international relations (IR) theorists of the realist/neo-realist approach, states remain the principal actors in 'international society'. The position each one occupies in the hierarchically structured interstate system depends upon their relative power or "distribution of capabilities",[1] which, while taking into consideration population/territory size, resource endowment, economist strength, and political stability, remains determined in the final analysis, by military prowess. Since the global system lacks an over-arching political structure (i.e. a world government) to impose order, states' innate power-maximising (offensive realists),[2] or security-maximising (defensive realists)[3] propensities tend to reproduce the pervasive systemic anarchy.

Working within this framework, some international political economy (IPE) scholars, envisaged the possibility that such a Hobbesian 'perpetual war' scenario could be avoided if one state were to possess such enormous capabilities to exercise *hegemony* over the rest – understood as being analogous to 'dominance' – encouraging inter-state cooperation by providing 'common goods'.[4] Many mainstream American liberal internationalist scholars concurred with their realist counterparts on the validity of this 'hegemonic stability theory' (HST), reiterating the multiple universal benefits of the US exercising its power responsibly and underwriting a liberal international order, although often preferring 'leadership' to 'hegemony' and replacing 'coercion' with 'consent' and 'hard power' by 'soft power'.[5]

Whether from a realist or liberal perspective, debates over American hegemonic decline have been omnipresent in mainstream academic circles for over 30 years.[6] In the late 1980s, the focus was on the 'threat' posed by Japan, while at the turn of the millennium some identified the European Union (EU) post-euro launch, and later the BRICS (Brazil, Russia, India, China, South Africa) countries. These predictions all proved to be premature. As we approach the end of the second decade of the 21st century, however, there appears widespread agreement amongst IR scholars, economists, military strategists, and political pundits that American hegemony is on its last legs and we are witnessing a historic

DOI: 10.4324/9780429459061-1

power shift within the world order (WO) towards the People's Republic of China (PRC).[7]

The main aim of this book is to try to shed some light on this assertion, but whose conceptualisation of world hegemony differs considerably from those advanced by mainstream IR/IPE theorists. To achieve this objective, we considered it to be indispensable for carrying out three ancillary 'tasks':

1 Developing a novel theoretical framework capable of offering a more convincing conceptualisation of world hegemony and social change within the WO.
2 Utilising the theoretical framework to uncover the causes and expressions of the evolving nature of American hegemony, from its original establishment and passing through periods of crises and restructuring.
3 Examining the significance of the rise of China, its inter-relation with, and effect on, American hegemony, and set against the backdrop of its own on-going "passive revolution".

Roughly speaking task (1) corresponds to Chapter 1; (2) is tackled in Chapters 2, 3, and 4; and (3) is addressed in Chapter 5.

To complete the first of these tasks we have considered it appropriate to adopt a historical materialist perspective, drawing heavily on the work of Antonio Gramsci. This sparks two immediate reflections.

First, it may appear a rather arbitrary decision to construct a theory of world hegemony based upon the ideas of a Marxist philosopher/dissident commonly held to be more concerned with Italian history/class struggle than external relations. Second, explicit references to hegemony in Gramsci's *magnum opus*, the *Prison Notebooks* (PN), are rather fragmentary, scattered across the 2,000-page compendium of unpublished notes and essays produced during his incarceration.[8] Furthermore, the context in which the PN was written[9] and the fact that Gramsci was denied the basic luxury of being able to re-edit and systematise his thoughts poses challenges for the reader and has led to diverse and often erroneous interpretations of his ideas.

In order to clarify Gramsci's understanding of hegemony, it is expedient to follow his own methodological guidelines. In an essay entitled *Some Problems in the Study of the Philosophy of Praxis*, Gramsci urges scholars seeking "to study the birth of a conception of the world which has never been systematically expounded by its founder to reconstruct the process of intellectual development of the thinker in question in order to identify those elements which were to become stable and permanent"; to search "for the Leitmotiv, for the rhythm of the thought as it develops".[10] At the same Gramsci warned against turning a thinker into a prophet – a "shepherd wielding a crook"/"Messiah"[11] – but to utilise those key concepts and ideas in a modified form to help illuminate ongoing processes in the contemporary historical conjuncture.

Applying this methodology to Gramsci himself, Chapter 1 begins by briefly exploring the evolution of his political life prior to imprisonment, beginning with his arrival in Turin in 1913 – spanning the *biennio rosso* ('two red years'), the establishment of the *Partito Comunista Italiano* (PCI) and the rise of fascism (and the strategic debates this promoted within the PCI and Comintern) – until his imprisonment in 1926. Once incarcerated and forced to limit his energies to the purely intellectual, the nucleus of Gramsci's research project revolved around the question of why attempts to provoke a working-class revolution, and establish a socialist state in advanced capitalist countries had hitherto proved unsuccessful, despite orthodox Marxist theory. Gramsci ridiculed the naivety of Stalinist-inspired determinism, auguring the inevitable and terminal collapse of capitalism circulating the Comintern in the 1920s.

It was in this search to account for the structural vigour of capitalism that led him to develop a sophisticated *class-based* conceptualisation of hegemony, the establishment of which, he observed, passed through three temporally differentiated *relations of force*, or "moments of the collective political consciousness": the *first* refers to the "relation of social forces" (class relations); the *second* to "relation of political forces" (political/cultural hegemony); and *third* to "the relation of military forces" (politico-military capacity).[12]

These three *moments* of hegemony will be a constant touchstone throughout this monograph, as will his reconceptualisation of the state: the *integral State*. Related to the *second moment* Gramsci would also enrich political discourse with a whole new range of categories (e.g. *historical bloc, passive revolution, common sense, good sense,* and *organic intellectual*), helping renew and expand Marx's notion of ideology and with it, and implicitly, supply vital tools for the comprehension of the dynamics of the global system.

Indeed, a common criticism of Marxist thought is that it pays insufficient attention to the realm of ideas: the absolute dread of liberal idealism means its approach to language, culture, and ideology often digresses little from a deterministic reading of the base-structure paradigm. One of the paradoxes of Gramsci's imprisonment, however, was that it permitted him far more intellectual freedom from Stalinist orthodoxy than most of his left-wing contemporaries, and able to draw on ideas from non-Marxist thinkers in order to theorise on the 'bourgeois' theme of culture and assess its relevance for working class consciousness and subsequent political organisation.

Consistent with his own Giambattista Vico-inspired[13] "absolute historicism",[14] Gramsci deemed it possible that ideas may transcend their original socio-historical context if they remain relevant to the real world. Moreover, as Chapter 1 emphasises, he remained an unrepentant historical materialist, constantly referring to the political economy and acknowledging the primacy of production. All ideas had to be materially grounded to be politically relevant, coinciding with Marx and Engels' line of reasoning in *Theses on Feuerbach*.[15] This document, in fact, along with Marx's "Preface" to the *Contribution of the Critique of Political Economy*, was constantly cited throughout his PN, both forming the basis of Gramsci's particular 'philosophy of praxis'.

Finally, in response to the above Italian-centricism accusation, Chapter 1 underscores Gramsci's eminently international-orientated perspective. Faithful to his Marxist heritage he insisted that the same social processes occurred at both, and across, the national and international level, in keeping with a global capitalist system beset by uneven and combined development. Coinciding with Lenin, Gramsci considered the inter-state system as hierarchically structured, dominated by hegemonic powers, at the top of which could sit a "world hegemonic state".[16]

In the elaboration of the book's theoretical framework, Chapter 1 will also draw upon perspectives inspired by Gramsci, notably the so-called neo-Gramscianism, founded by Robert W. Cox who sought to update, systemise, and extend the activist's conceptual framework in order to analyse world hegemony in the late 20th century.[17] Top of Cox's agenda was to critique mainstream IR theory, held to be incapable of explaining structural transformation due to erroneous ontological suppositions and positivist epistemological underpinnings. As an antidote, he favoured a *critical theory* of IR: an historicist approach which emphasises the contingent and conjunctural nature of all contemporary social/power relations, dominant norms and practices, institutions, which includes states (or *state-society complexes*), and WOs, etc. By studying their origins and evolution, Cox held, it would be possible to ascertain if they were subject to change, and in the case of the WO, for example, identify those social forces likely to develop a project for a new and fairer WO in keeping with their stated emancipatory agenda.[18]

Broadly speaking, this book adheres to this historicist method. As Gramsci discerned

> [e]very historical phase leaves traces of itself in succeeding phases, which then become in a sense the best document of its existence. The process of historical development is a unity in time through which the present contains the whole of the past and in the present is realised that part of the past which is 'essential'.[19]

To understand the dynamics of contemporary US hegemony (Chapters 4 and 5) it is vital to study its origins and establishment (Chapter 2) and historical evolution (Chapter 3). Furthermore, as stressed in Chapter 1, the theoretical framework adopted here owes a huge intellectual debt to neo-Gramscian thought, elaborating key concepts and categories, shedding light on the dynamics of world hegemony, and exploring how historical national and transnational social processes have dialectically interacted with, and shaped, American hegemony.

Unfortunately, and despite their major contributions, neo-Gramscian theory, especially in its Coxian version, is guilty of ontological (and hence epistemological) inconsistencies. Their absolute aversion to any underlying 'logic' (e.g. a mode of production) results in them *historicising* structure, effectively reducing it to inter-subjective relations. As Chapter 1 indicates, this over-reliance on agency as a motor of change not only confounds the neo-Gramscian original critical theory objective, but significantly, given the objective of this book, signals a severance from their professed historical materialist perspective coupled with a tendency to depict hegemony in ideological/consensual terms (not unlike the liberals) and down-grade coercion. Hegemony, however, as repeated throughout this book, necessarily includes *both* domination/coercion and consensus/leadership. This incomplete reading of hegemony explains why some neo-Gramscian 'predictions' – the weakening of the state, the end of US hegemony, the consolidation of a transnational capitalist class – have proven rather premature.

To develop a more convincing – i.e. *structural* – theory of hegemony we return to Gramsci himself, reviewing his reading of the structure-agency debate which, in terms of meta-theory, is shown to be compatible with 'critical realist philosophy of science', first propounded by Roy Bhaskar.[20] Within Bhaskar's 'ontological stratification' model, Chapter 1 identifies Jonathan Joseph's 'materialist theory of hegemony' with its differentiation between 'structural' and 'surface' hegemony as the critical realist approach most closely resembling with Gramsci's understanding. It is this *emergentist materialist understanding of hegemony* which serves as the basis for the *Neo* neo-Gramscian (NNG) theoretical framework presented here.

We adhere to the classic Marxist line that the capitalist mode of production is inherently anarchic and unable to reproduce itself without state regulation and intervention, effectively underwriting the accumulation process. Nonetheless, the contradictory nature of the said process means capitalism is subject to perennial crises manifested in a tendency towards declining profit rates.[21] Although both part of the same historical process, Gramsci saw fit to distinguish between "conjectural" and "organic movements": the former resulting from immediate contingent triggers and the latter generated by long-term deeper structural causes.[22]

When a crisis hits, the capitalist state plays an important role in trying to lessen, delay, or counter its effects and restore profit rates over the medium-term (albeit before their inevitable subsequent decline). This can be done by injecting liquidity, redrawing space, serving as 'consumer of last resort' and restructuring social relations of production (SROP), often via coercive means. Since capitalism is necessarily global in its scope, crises traverse national borders. The 'justification' for a world hegemon – and the fundamental basis of its *intellectual and moral leadership* – we argue here, is its ability to carry out similar functions to those of the state but at the global level, underwriting a profitable regime of accumulation. This chimes with Giovanni Arrighi's *systemic cycle of accumulation* (SCOA) which we have incorporated into the book's NNG perspective.

The SCOA highlights the crucial role played by the hegemonic state in underwriting successive cycles of development, providing both international leadership but crucially a sufficiently large "container of power" for global capital to bury its surplus-value in. Capital's endless accumulation needs, Arrighi claims, has meant that every period of material expansion (David Harvey's *spatio-temporal fix*) has been bigger and more complex than the last, requiring an ever-larger 'container of power' and politico-military capacity to enforce the system. Particularly relevant to Chapter 3, the SCOA holds that eventually inter-capitalist competition will result in a *realisation crisis* (reflected in reduced profit rates) and a weakening of the hegemon's position, who may see out its 'autumn' years generating profits sitting atop a new *financialized* regime of accumulation, corresponding to Marx's shortened capital circuit M-M' (instead of the longer version M-C-M') before its eventual demise and the system is engulfed in chaos[23] tantamount to Gramsci's 'organic movement'.

While recognising the utility of the SCOA meta-narrative, we share the traditional Marxist view that history is not made by abstract models or theories but by real people, locked in real class structures and engaged in real class struggles. World hegemony, as both Gramsci and Cox have insisted, is class-based, emerging out of the hegemon's *historical bloc* (HB) and exercised primarily to forward those class interests but it has to guarantee sufficient benefits flow to foreign bourgeois classes (or at least to be perceived as such), albeit with coercion omnipresent. It is in this context – and following Gramsci's *three moments* template – that we analysed the establishment and evolution of American hegemony from the mid-1940s onwards (Chapter 2).

Since hegemony is understood as a social process emergent from underlying social structures, evidently shifts in the accumulation process will generate social forces predisposed to challenge dominant systems of governance. Chapter 3, for example, studies how, by the late 1960s/early 1970s, the internal contradictions of exercising world hegemony actually undermined the US-led regime of accumulation, manifested in declining profit rates, widespread economic and political malaise (at both national and international level), a serious loss of intellectual and intellectual leadership, and a growing inability to restrain friend and foe alike. The world, it seemed was undergoing an 'organic movement'. In the end, as Chapter 3 explains, class mobilisation helped to revitalise US hegemony; launching both a new regime of accumulation (neoliberalism/financialization) to restore profit rates and discipline subaltern classes (concomitant with the second stage of Arrighi's SCOA) and, no less importantly, the *Second* Cold War.

By the turn of the millennium, however, American hegemony once more was running out of steam. The Clinton-era globalization euphoria had started to lose its lustre, a victim of the underlying class contradictions afflicting neoliberalism/financialization, while Washington's desperate search for a legitimising hegemonic vision – *Grand Strategy* – to replace anti-communism had proved fruitless. Against this background, Chapter 4 studies the importance of the 'neocon shift' under George W. Bush (Bush II), focusing especially on the *War on Terror*. The chapter examines to what extent the *Bush Doctrine* constituted 'new imperialism', and therein a significant departure from hegemony and associated established practices of governance, as many IR scholars avowed. As part of this assessment, the Bush administration's policies will be compared and contrasted to those of his predecessors and immediate successor, Barack Obama.

In the end, rather than unilateralism, heightened militarism, loss of 'intellectual and moral leadership' or 'imperial overstretch', Chapter 4 questions if the *real* challenge posed to the US hegemony in the first decade of the 21st century was due to the bursting of the latest financialized asset-bubbles. The advent of the Global Financial Crisis (GFC) might have actually bolstered Washington's power in the short to medium term, but, we maintain, it revealed severe structural class contradictions of the neoliberal regime of accumulation which in the long-term indicated the US's growing inability to act as the 'consumer of last resort' let alone the global 'container of power'. The crisis of political legitimacy of neoliberalism – later personified in Donald Trump – was the basis of the loss of American 'intellectual and moral leadership'. If the SCOA was anything to go by, we were witnessing a Gramscian 'organic movement' and the advent of a period of global economic, political, and possibly military turmoil.

In his last major work, *Adam Smith in Beijing*, Arrighi concurs with mainstream contemporary IR theorists and media pundits in identifying the PRC as the most likely future world hegemon, but based on his own appraisal of the country's capacity to act as a 'container of power' (a consequence of its unique economic, demographic, political, and cultural characteristics).[24]

Chapter 5 is devoted to the "China Challenge", evaluating the importance of the emergence of the Asian power for the US hegemony through the NNG lens. Sadly, given the vastness of the topic and the space available, it has proven impossible to engage in an extensive study and address all of the facets of the Sino-American relationship, covering what it considers the most significant aspects.

The chapter begins by examining the economic and geopolitical effects of China's rise in developing countries and its neighbours. Pointedly for the US, market penetration has been accompanied by China engaging in multilateral institution-building, considered by Cox as a key indicator of incipient hegemony (the third of his "categories of forces"[25]) and consistent with Gramsci's *second moment*. In this context, the chapter will also weigh up the significance of arguably Beijing's most audacious bid for regional hegemony, and possible alternative to a US-led financialized world economy: the launching of the *Belt and Road Initiative* (BRI).

The complexities of Sino-American bilateral relations are then examined, as well as Washington's hegemonic strategy to deal with an ever-powerful 'contender state': a combination of evolving 'carrot-and-stick' measures, a central pillar of which consists of reminding Beijing of the one domain US hegemony still remains supreme – military capacity (Gramsci's *third moment*). Chapter 5, therefore, pays special attention to the US's containment strategy across the Asia-Pacific region, centred on those areas China considers most sensitive: its territorial unity and surrounding seas.

World hegemony, as reiterated throughout this book, depends upon social forces emanating outwards from within a country's HB. Whether China will be able to exercise said 'function', ultimately, is contingent on the dynamics of its internal class relations within the context of a hierarchically structured global capitalist economy. The final section of Chapter 5, therefore, explores the complexities of PRC's evolving, and contested, "passive revolution". In so doing it will dispute the claim made by Arrighi that the Chinese state – supposedly yet to convert itself into a fully capitalist state – is pioneering a progressive, egalitarian, and ecological model of economic organisation by fusing together market-based, non-capitalist development with Western-style capitalism in a neo-Smithian (from Adam Smith) Marxism.

Finally, one might pose the question as to why the book chooses to concentrate on China at the expense of other countries. What about the EU or Japan, have not they the 'capacity' to replace the US as the global hegemon too? As hopefully will become clear in the following chapters these options must be discounted, at least for the medium term. At this juncture, citing a few basic reasons will suffice.

First, both are firmly ensconced in US-sponsored security arrangements – the EU with NATO and Japan its Treaty of Mutual Cooperation and Security – with American bases located on their soil, which severely limits foreign and security policy independence. Even in the unlikely event that Washington would voluntarily forgo its "empire of bases",[26] Japan lacks sufficient military capacity to patrol the global capitalist system while the EU is beset by major internal divisions (e.g. foreign policy traditions and capabilities) and lacks a unified 'world view'.

Second, the EU's recent euro/sovereign debt crisis not only showed the degree of the region's integration into, and subordination to American finance hegemony (not in itself unique), but also revealed a continent beset by uneven development, economic inequality, and political fragmentation. The refugee crisis, Brexit, and the rise of right-wing popularism only reinforces this impression and belies the notion of a unified, integrated political space.

Third, the smallness of Japan's internal market – standing at around 127 million people (and the world's fastest ageing population) – coupled with its high propensity to save and low consumption levels makes it highly unlikely it would ever be able to offer global capital a sufficiently large 'container of power' to bury its surplus value. Increasingly dependent economically on its giant to the West, whose GDP surpassed its own in 2011 (after 40 years at the no. 2 spot), Japan presently faces numerous economic, political, and social challenges, not least what to do about its public finances (recording the world's highest rate of government debt to GDP).

Alternatively, one could suggest the book should contemplate the possibility that the next 'container of power' could consist of a group of countries: a multipolar world hegemon. Yet historically such arrangements have proven impossible; uneven development, geopolitics, and inter-state rivalry tending to undermine attempts at closer cooperation. The BRICS coalition is a case in point. Despite noteworthy policy and institutional initiatives aimed at challenging US-led financial order (see Chapter 5), the BRICS association, at least at the time of writing, has failed to develop into a coherent counter-hegemonic political force, remaining largely Sino-centric in its economic orientation.

As we discuss in Chapter 1, many neo-Gramscians would favour abandoning the idea of state-centric hegemony altogether, preferring to talk of a WO governed by a transnational capitalist class and including a transnational HB.[27] But such affirmations lack empirical evidence to support them, remain incongruent with the nature of the global capitalist system and drift into non-Gramscian territory, akin to Kautsky's ultra-imperialism.

Notes

1 Waltz (1979).
2 See Mearsheimer (1990) and Morgenthau (1993).
3 See Jervis (1978) and Walt (1987).
4 See, for example, Kindelberger (1973), Krasner (1978), and Gilpin (1987).
5 See, for example, Keohane (1984), Nye (1990), and Ikenberry (2011).
6 See, for example, Kennedy (1987) and Zakaria (2008).
7 See, for example, Goldman Sachs (2007) and Jacques (2009).
8 Arrested by Mussolini's fascists on 9th November 1926, Gramsci was sentenced to just over 20 years on the 4th June 1928 and died in hospital on the 27th April 1937.
9 Obstacles Gramsci had to overcome included poor health, limited access to books/writing materials, bad lighting, and heavy prison censorship.

10 Gramsci (1971), p. 382.
11 Gramsci (1995), pp. 54–8.
12 Gramsci (1971), pp. 175–85, p. 161.
13 Vico (1984).
14 Gramsci (1971), p. 465. At the risk of over-simplification, historicism is understood here as meaning that any society or period of history must be seen in terms of ideas contemporary to it. It is traditional to differentiate between two types of historicism: *austere* and *absolute*. According to Adam Morton "austere historicism" involves drawing a line under the past, asserting that all past forms have to be set within their particular historical context and are therefore meaningless outside this. "Absolute historicism", on the one hand, looks at "the peculiarities of history, to pay consistent attention to the specificities of historical and cultural conditions" while at the same time recognising that ideas/values etc. may remain relevant beyond the temporal/spatial context of their production. See Morton (2003), pp. 120–33.
15 In the second of the *Theses*, Marx and Engels declared: "The question of whether objective truth can be attributed to human thinking is not a question of theory but is a practical question. Man must prove the truth – i.e. the reality and power, the this-sidedness of his thinking in practice" Marx & Engels (2002).
16 Gramsci (1995), pp. 222–3; Gramsci (2007), Quaderni 2, p. 166.
17 Cox (1996a, 1996b).
18 Cox (1996a), p. 89.
19 Gramsci (1971), p. 409.
20 See Bhaskar (1986, 1998, 2008).
21 Marx & Engels (2010).
22 Gramsci (1971), p. 79.
23 See Arrighi (2010) and Arrighi & Silver (1999).
24 Arrighi (2008).
25 Cox (1996a), pp. 98–9.
26 Johnson (2004), pp. 151–85.
27 See for example Cox (1996a), Gill (1991), Overbeek & van der Pijl (1993), van Apeldoorn (2004), and Robinson (2005).

Bibliography

Arrighi, G. (2008), *Adam Smith in Beijing: Lineages of the Twenty-First Century*, London: Verso.

Arrighi, G. (2010), *The Long Twentieth Century: Money, Power and the Origins of Our Times*, 2nd Edn., London: Verso.

Arrighi, G. & Silver, B. (eds.) (1999), *Chaos and Governance in the Modern System*, Minneapolis: University of Minnesota Press.

Bhaskar, R. (1986), *Scientific Realism and Human Emancipation*, London: Verso.

Bhaskar, R. (1998), *The Possibility of Naturalism*, 3rd Edn. [orig. pub. 1979], London: Routledge.

Bhaskar, R. (2008), *A Realist Theory of Science* [orig. pub. 1975]), Abingdon, Oxon: Routledge.

Cox, R.W. (1996a), "Social Forces, States, and World Orders: Beyond International Relations Theory" [orig. pub. 1981], in Cox, R.W. and Sinclair, T.J. (eds.), *Approaches to World Order*, Cambridge: Cambridge University Press.

Cox, R.W. (1996b), "Gramsci, Hegemony and International Relations: An Essay in Method" [orig. pub. 1983], in Cox, R.W. and Sinclair, T.J. (eds.), *Approaches to World Order*, Cambridge: Cambridge University Press.

Gill, S. (1991), *American Hegemony and the Trilateral Commission*, Cambridge: Cambridge University Press.

Gilpin, R. (1987), *The Political Economy of International Relations*, Princeton: Princeton University Press.

Gramsci, A. (1971), *Selections from the Prison Notebooks of Antonio Gramsci*, Hoare, Q. and Nowell Smith, G. (eds. and trans.), London: Lawrence & Wishart.

Goldman Sachs. (2001), "Building Better Global Economic BRICS", Jim O. Neill, *Global Economics Paper* no. 66, November (available online at www.goldmansachs.com/insights/archive).

Goldman Sachs. (2007), "The N-11: More Than an Acronym", Dominic Wilson and Anne Stupnytska, *Global Economics Paper* no. 153, March (available online at www.goldmansachs.com/insights/archive).

Gramsci, A. (1995), *Further Selections from the Prison Notebooks*, Boothman, D. (ed. and trans.), London: Lawrence & Wishart.

Gramsci, A. (2007), *Quaderni del Calcere: Quaderni di traduzioni* (1929–1932), Cospito, G. and Francioni, G. (eds.), Rome: Istituto della Enciclopedia Italiana, Quaderni.

Harvey, D. (1982), *The Limits to Capital*, Oxford: Basil Blackwell.

Harvey, D. (2003), *The New Imperialism*, Oxford: Oxford University Press.

Ikenberry, G.J. (2011) *Liberal Leviathan: The Origins, Crisis, and Transformation of the American World Order*, Princeton: Princeton University Press.

Jacques, M. (2009), *When China Rules the World: The End of the Western World and the Birth of a New Global Order*, New York: The Penguin Press.

Jervis, R. (1978), "Cooperation under the Security Dilemma", *World Politics*, 30, no. 2, 167–214.

Johnson, C. (2004), *The Sorrows of Empire*, New York: Owl Books.

Joseph, J. (2002), *Hegemony: A Realist Analysis*, London: Routledge.

Joseph, J. (2007), "Philosophy in International Relations: A Scientific Realist Approach", *Millennium: Journal of International Studies*, 35, no. 2, 345–59.

Joseph, J. (2010), "The International as Emergent: Challenging Old and New Orthodoxies in International Relations Theory", in Joseph, J. and Wight, C. (eds.), *Scientific Realism and International Relations,* Basingstoke: Palgrave Macmillan.

Kennedy, P. (1987), *The Rise and Fall of the Great Powers: Economic Change and Military Conflict from 1500 to 2000*, New York: Random House.

Keohane, R.O. (1984), *After Hegemony, Cooperation and Discord in the World Political Economy*, Princeton: Princeton University Press.

Kindelberger, C. (1973), *The World Depression 1929–1939*, Berkley: University of California Press.

Krasner, S.D. (1978), *Defending the National Interest: Raw Materials Investments and Foreign Policy*, Princeton: Princeton University Press.

Marx, K. (1967), *Capital: A Critique of Political Economy*, Vol. 1, New York: International Publishers Company, Inc. [orig. pub. 1887].

Marx, K. & Engels, F. (2002), "Theses on Feuerbach", *Selected Works*, Vol. 1. (available online at www.marxists.org) [orig. pub. 1888].

Marx, K. & Engels, F. (2010), *Capital: A Critique of Political Economy: Volume III* (available online at www.marxists.org) [orig. pub. 1894].

Mearsheimer, J.J. (1990), "Back to the Future: Instability in Europe after the Cold War", *International Security*, 15, no. 1, 5–56.

Morgenthau, H. (1993), *Politics among Nations: The Struggle for Power and Peace*, New York: McGraw-Hill.

Morton, A. (2003), "Historicising Gramsci: Situating Ideas in and Beyond their Context", *Review of International Political Economy*, 10, no. 1, 118–46.

Nye, J.S. (1990), *Bound to Lead: The Changing Nature of American Power*, New York: Basic Books.

Overbeek, H. & van der Pijl, K. (1993), "Restructuring Capital and Hegemony: Neo-liberalism and the Unmaking of the Post-war Order", in Overbeek, H. (ed.), *Restructuring Hegemony in the Global Political Economy. The Rise of Transnational Neo-liberalism in the 1980s*, London: Routledge.

Robinson, W.I. (2005), "Gramsci and Globalization: From Nation-State to Transnational Hegemony", *Critical Review of International Social and Political Philosophy*, 8, no. 4, 1–16.

van Apeldoorn, B. (2004), "Theorizing the Transnational: A Historical Materialist Approach", *Journal of International Relations and Development*, 7, no. 2, 142–76.

Vico, G. (1984), *The New Science of Giambattista Vico*, trans. T.G. Bergin and M.H. Fisch from the third edition (1744) with the addition of "Practice of the New Science", Ithaca, NY: Cornell University Press.

Waltz, K. (1979), *Theory of International Politics*, New York: McGraw Hill.

Walt, S.M. (1987), *The Origins of Alliances*, Ithaca, NY: Cornell University Press.

Zakaria, F. (2008), *The Post-American World*, New York: W.W. Norton & Co.

1 A *Neo* Neo-Gramscian Reading of Hegemony

Antonio Gramsci's Conceptualisation of Hegemony

Antonio Gramsci's earliest influences were Italian, and of a predominantly liberal orientation – notably Giovanni Gentile, Benedetto Croce, and Luigi Pirandello – who impressed on him the importance of *culture* in political life. What leftist ideas he did harbour arrived via the socialist Antonio Labriola, whose work on the structurally exploitative relationship between the dominant industrial North and the subservient agrarian South made sense to a Sardinian native. Nonetheless, even this relationship tended to be analysed by the young Gramsci from an idealist-nationalist perspective.

Only on arrival in Turin, Italy's industrial capital, in 1913, did he become aware of the importance of: (1) *social class*, the basis of the complex inter-regional dialectic which actually underpinned the aforementioned North-South dichotomy; and (2) *political organisation*. Inspired by the 'adventurism' of Rosa Luxemburg and Karl Liebknecht,[1] Gramsci threw himself into political activism, joining the *Partito Socialista Italiano* (PSI) and writing regular columns and theatre reviews for the PSI weekly *Il Grido del Popolo* and the Turin edition of *Avanti!*, amongst other initiatives.[2]

For the three years following the Bolshevik Revolution – a period he later described as his 'voluntarist' phase – Gramsci, along with other PSI members, worked tirelessly to mobilise and consolidate the exploited classes into a 'collective will', *en route* to a 'revolution from below', compatible with the objectives of the Third International and guided by Karl Marx's *Theses on Feuerbach*[3] (prioritising action over theorisation). In an article entitled "The Revolution Against 'Capital'" in *Il Grido del Popolo*, on 5th January 1918, for example, Gramsci denounced the Mensheviks for their procrastination and adherence to deterministic "historical laws" of capitalist development and "raw economic facts"; one had to "live Marxism thought", understand it as "men in relation to another", not cling to some rigid interpretation of the "Master".[4]

This amounted to what posteriorly Gramsci termed the "philosophy of praxis": the fusion of theory (thought) and practise (deed), or "history

DOI: 10.4324/9780429459061-2

in action".[5] To that aim, and to raise working-class consciousness Gramsci co-founded the influential revolutionary journal, *L'Ordine Nuovo: Rassegna Settimanale di Cultura Socialista* in April 1919 which provided the most important ideological support for the Turin proletarian struggle, and was largely based on Soviet-inspired Factory councils, as opposed to traditional trade unions.[6]

The extent of urban and rural unrest in Italy during 1919–20 – its *biennio rosso* ('two red years') – appeared to indicate that revolution was within reach. From September 1920 to May 1921 the optimism began to seep away, however, as Gramsci came to comprehend the structural power of capitalism and the organisational weakness of the left (evident in the failure of the April 1919 'general strike' and the collapse of the Turin Factory Council experiment). Officially endorsed by Lenin,[7] Gramsci and fellow *L'Ordine Nuovo* members founded the *Partito Comunista Italiano* (PCI) to coordinate and organise the revolutionary forces.[8]

It was not just the Italian left that was undergoing a tactical revaluation. Three months after the German Communist Party had its 'adventurist' seizure of power, the 'March Action', unmercifully crushed by state coercive forces, Lenin announced the new official strategic line at the Third Congress of the Communist International (June–July 1921). Under the slogan "to the masses", communist parties everywhere were encouraged to exercise *hegemony* (understood as 'leadership with consent') over other rival left-leaning parties, trade unions, and working-class associations, in order to form a "United Front" to fight against capital.[9]

After years of internal opposition, the PCI finally succumbed, adopting the official United Front strategy in the spring of 1923.[10] Gramsci would spend his remaining years in liberty attempting to promote solidarity amongst left-wing/progressive factions, encouraging labour to set up factory groups, worker and peasant committees, drawing on many of the ideas developed in the *L'Ordine Nuovo* (which was actually revived in the spring of 1924),[11] and even helping to boost PCI membership.[12]

In its final important strategy statement before being driven underground by Mussolini, the PCI presented what was later known as the "Lyons Theses" at their Third Congress in Lyons (France), in January 1926.[13] In his intervention entitled "The Italian Situation and Tasks of the PCI", Gramsci for the first time discussed hegemon*y*, reiterating the critical leadership role of the PCI in organising and unifying the proletarian vanguard, working class and peasantry as part of a broad leftist anti-fascist/imperialist United Front.

Once imprisoned, and deprived the right of political activism, Gramsci directed all his energies to intellectual theorising: to "give a focus to (his) inner life", he confessed.[14] The fundamental research question he sought to answer was *why* it had been so difficult to build provoke a revolution in an advanced capitalist country. In doing so, Gramsci would reassess the naivety of his earlier 'voluntarism',[15] and develop a better understanding of the structural nature of capitalist power. The latter, he later reflected, lay behind the shift in official Comintern strategy from a "war of manoeuvre" in March 1917 to a "war of position" in March 1921,[16] resembling Marx's earlier call for a "Permanent Revolution".[17]

The greatest impediment to working-class emancipation, Gramsci had concluded in the Lyons Theses, was the resilience of the *modern state*: the key instrument of bourgeois class power. *State formation*, thus, occupied a central position in the *Prison Notebooks* (PN). Gramsci opens up his "Notes on Italy History", for example, with the line: "[t]he historical unity of the ruling classes is realised in the state, and their history is essentially the history of states and of groups of states", while lamenting "[t]he subaltern classes, by definition, are not unified and cannot unite until they are able to become a 'state'".[18] But what *was* the source of the modern capitalist state's on-going stability and resilience?

For Marx, the modern state was necessary capitalist, whose principal functions were to defend private property, guarantee accumulation, and maintain an exploitative class system. Nevertheless, the appearance of the state was based on two inter-connected fictional dichotomies – economic vs. political structures;[19] and state vs. civil society[20] – which were purposely designed to depoliticise the subaltern classes. The reality was, of course, that socialism could never be achieved via the ballot box within the confines of the bourgeois parliamentary system (returning to one of the central debates of the Second International). The central question remained, therefore, as to why the working classes would consistently support a political system which so clearly clashed with their objective class interests. To resolve this conundrum, Gramsci returned to the idea of hegemony.

Hitherto, his understanding of hegemony varied little from Lenin's United Front conceptualisation, reflected in the Lyons Theses. Years of arduous political struggle, however, made it clear that building working-class hegemony in an advance capitalist country would be no easy task. Any talk of proletarian emancipation required the prior examination of the underlying dynamics, structural stability, and self-reproduction tendencies of *bourgeois* hegemony. This divergence in focus meant Gramsci's reading of hegemony was far more complex than Lenin's, and drew upon sources from outside the classic Marxist tradition.

In this endeavour to comprehend power dynamics, he turned to "the most classic master of the art of politics", Niccolò Machiavelli,[21] whose recommendations regarding the founding of a new state seemed relevant to his own project. But instead of an elitist cabal leading social construction (Machiavelli's *Prince*), Gramsci envisioned a vanguard party, supported by the mass public consistent with the Lenin's United Front line: a *Modern Prince* (see below).

What particularly attracted Gramsci's attention was Machiavelli's depiction of the dualist nature of power, famously drawing on an analogy of the mythical Greek centaur ("half beast and half man") to illustrate how *consent* and *coercion* interplay.[22] For a state to be successful, Machiavelli declared, it was fundamental that the ruler not only maintain the prestige said office demanded, but that he works to gain the active consent of his subjects, including the establishment of a 'fair' legal and institutional framework, for "when a prince has the goodwill of the people he must not worry about conspiracies".[23] Where compliance of the dominated could not be guaranteed solely by consent, however, coercion was recommended (along with fear, deception, fraud, and bribery). Nevertheless, Machiavelli only considered the ruling class *truly* hegemonic to the extent to which they were able to control subordinate groups via the consensual aspect of power.[24]

From this, Gramsci interpreted that social groups manifested their supremacy in two ways: "domination" and "intellectual and moral leadership" (or "hegemony"). The former involved the liquidation or subjugation of opposition elements by coercion means ("even by armed forces"); the latter, however, saw elites directing "kindred and allied groups" consensually.[25] He illustrated this distinction historically, contrasting state-formation in late 18th-century France – led by a hegemonic "Jacobin" force – with that in mid-19th-century Italy (*Il Risorgimento*)[26] – exemplifying "domination without that of 'leadership'; dictatorship without hegemony".[27]

Gramsci also shared Machiavelli's assertion that not all "forms of state" (FOS) were the same: a lesson painfully learnt during the failed 'March Action'. A *war of movement* could never prosper in advanced capital countries such as Germany, he reflected from his prison cell. The underlying reason was the embeddedness of ruling class power across the "two major superstructural 'levels'": (1) "civil society", referring to the "ensemble of organisms" commonly termed "private"; and (2) "political society" or "the State".[28] Unlike in the East (Russia) where "the State was everything, civil society was primordial and gelatinous"; in the West (Germany) "there was a proper relationship between state and civil society", hence, "when the State trembled a sturdy structure of civil society was at once revealed". So even if the advanced capitalist state was breached it represented merely "an outer ditch" behind which "a powerful system of fortresses and earthworks," constituting civil society, would repel revolutionary action.[29]

Such affirmations have been seized upon by some leftists to question Gramsci's Marxist credentials. Arguably, the most celebrated is Perry Anderson's 1976 article in the *New Left Review*, which censured what it identified as important antimonies and idealist tendencies at the heart of PN. Thanks to the influences of Croce and Machiavelli, Anderson charged, Gramsci was guilty of philosophical dualism, reducing the social world to a series of simple dichotomies: state/civil society; political society/economic society, domination/hegemony, coercion/consensus, and war of movement/war of position.[30] This categorisation inferred that ruling class hegemony over subaltern classes within civil society was purely cultural, and could be overcome by a peaceful ideological 'war of position' within the framework of a capitalist state. Liberals and social democrats might share this view, along with Frankfurt School critical theorists and post-Marxists such as Ernest Laclau and Chantal Mouffe,[31] but it was a complete anathema for Gramsci and other Marxists.

To clear up this misunderstanding and fully appreciate the complexity of Gramsci's conceptualisation of hegemony, we must re-examine his reading of the *structure-agency* debate. A necessary starting point, here, is Marx's "Preface" to the *Critique of Political Economy* 1859, which Gramsci considered "the most important authentic source for the reconstruction of the philosophy of praxis" (i.e. hegemony),[32] and whose central message was "it is on the level of ideologies that men become conscious of conflicts in the world of the economy".[33]

Contrary to Anderson's intimations, Gramsci remained a life-long historical materialist, ridiculing Croce's "speculative philosophy" and overly idealist "ethico-political" account of history.[34] Numerous sections of the PN are dedicated to the study of capitalism, both at the national and global level (e.g. "Americanism and Fordism").[35] David Ricardo was praised for introducing "new methodological canons...developing the science of economics", notably the "discovery of the formal logical principle of the 'law of tendency' leading to the scientific definition of the fundamental economic concepts of *homo oeconomicus* and of the 'determined market'",[36] which he defined as "determined relation of social forces in a determined structure of the apparatus of production, this relationship being guaranteed (that is, rendered permanent) by a determined political, moral and juridical superstructure."[37]

Further manifestations of Gramsci's conceptualisation of structure-agency can be found in his analysis of the way hegemony was established via three temporally differentiated *relations of force*, or "moments of the collective political consciousness", which, given their key importance for this book, it is worth summarizing:[38]

1   The *first* "moment", the "relation of social forces", arises out of the "structure" and is "objective, independent of human will" and scientifically measurable. Each of these social classes engendered by the "material forces of production" carries out a particular "function" and occupies a "specific position within production itself": a "refractory reality". Hegemony "must necessarily be based on the decisive function exercised by the leading group in the decisive nucleus of economic activity".

2   The *second* "moment" (the "relation of political forces") constituted the mediating phase, where a group of people become aware of their common objective interests and form a self-conscious social

class. It consists of three "levels". The first and second levels are of an "economic-corporative" nature, where members of a certain professional group feel solidarity with other members, organising themselves collectively, and an awareness which subsequently develops into class consciousness. Critically at the third stage (or level), groups seek to "transcend the corporate limits of the purely economic class, and can and must become the interests of other subordinate groups too". Considered "the most purely political phase", this marked "the decisive passage from the structure to the sphere of the complex superstructures" and involved dominant groups not only "bringing about a unison of economic and political aims" (granting economic-corporative and political concessions), "but also intellectual and moral unity", framing all questions on a "universal plane". In this ideological struggle, the "hegemonic apparatus", including "organic intellectuals", was pivotal (see below).

3   The *third* "moment" ("the relation of military forces") consists of two different forms of oppression (the "military" level and the "politico-military" level) and "which from time to time is directly decisive" in the struggle for hegemony since historical development "oscillates continually between the first and the third moment, with the mediation of the second". The use of coercion remained fundamental to hegemony, along with "corruption/fraud" (see below).

From this it is evident that Gramsci considers the second ethico-political inter-subjective "moment" as *emergent* from (or rooted in) the first "moment", objective social relations. Indeed, the underlying objective in the PN was to analyse "how the historical movement is born out of the structure" manifested in "the formation of active political groups" and whether these groups are capable of bringing about social transformation and establish their hegemony.[39]

Bearing in mind these and other passages, it becomes clear that Gramsci conceived structure and agency as being: (1) ontologically distinct (the former existed independently of an agent's consciousness of it); (2) temporally differentiable (the former pre-existing the latter); and (3) inseparable (engaged in a dialectal materialist relationship, in which the latter served to reproduce or transform the former).

What Anderson did not fully appreciate, according to Peter D. Thomas, was that while Gramsci was drawing a "methodological distinction" between socio-economic relations (structure) and political, ethical, and cultural practices/relations (agency), there was also a "dialectical unity" between them, expressed in the "historical bloc" (HB) – "the complex contradictory and discordant *ensemble* in the superstructure is the reflection of the *ensemble* of the social relations of production".[40]

The same differentiation applied to the state. The traditional "organic distinction" was erroneous, in "effectual reality", Gramsci affirmed, "civil society and the state identify themselves".[41] Again, a methodological or analytical distinction was made, this time applied to the "two major superstructural 'levels'", due to the different "functions" they carried out. To 'civil society' corresponded the "function of 'hegemony', which the dominant group exercised throughout society"; 'political society', on the other hand, referred to "'direct domination' or command exercised through the state and 'judicial' government".[42]

But while Gramsci referred to the respective *functions* of 'political society' and 'civil society' he did not consider they occupied separate political *spaces*, purposely choosing to bracket each term within quotation marks to underscore the highly qualified nature of their separation when, in fact, they were intricately connected, engaged in a dialectical and non-exclusionary relationship.[43]

Gramsci was, in fact, forwarding a new and sophisticated conceptualisation of the state which Anderson, amongst others, failed to discern. This enlarged version – the "integral State" – was composed of "the entire complex of practical and theoretical activities with which the ruling class not only justifies and maintains its dominance, but also manages to win the active consent of those over whom it rules"[44] and amounted to "hegemony protected by the armour of coercion" or alternatively as "dictatorship + hegemony".[45] Any attempt at separating social forces within 'civil society' from power in 'political society' was futile. It is in this context that Gramsci's affirmation that "in actual reality civil society and the State are one and the same" can be better understood.[46]

This conceptualisation of the state has two important corollaries for hegemony. First, it makes it impossible to locate it *solely* in just one of the two superstructural "levels", but instead, "as a practice 'traversing' the boundaries between them…a particular practise of consolidating social forces and condensing them into political power on a mass basis – the mode of production of the modern 'political'".[47] As Thomas explains, "hegemony elaborated within civil society, also impacts upon that other superstructural 'level' of the integral state, 'political society or State'". This was unsurprising, he continues, "because political society itself and the power concentrated in it are integrally related to civil society and its social forces, as their mediated, 'higher' forms".[48] Hegemony thus tended to reproduce itself. Working as it does across both superstructural 'levels', it can bolster certain social forces within 'civil society' and their subsequent consolidation into a coherent 'political force', which, in turn, would then help reinforce (often by coercion) the position of said social forces within 'civil society', *ad infinitum*. At the same time, as noted in Gramsci's *first moment*, ethico-political hegemony was necessarily materially-rooted.

Second, and contrary to Anderson's dualist depiction, it was not a question of hegemony (consensus) *or* domination (force): coercion was implicit to hegemony, explicitly recognised in the *third moment* 'relations of forces'. Nor was its use just reserved for antagonists ("those groups which do not 'consent' neither actively nor passively"), but applied to society as a whole, even for allies, especially when "spontaneous consent fades away".[49] "The 'normal' exercise of hegemony on the now classical terrain of the parliamentary regime", Gramsci elucidated, "is character-ised by the combination of force and consent, which balance each other reciprocally, without force predominating excessively over consent". Furthermore, when it is used "the attempt is always made to ensure that force will appear to be based on the consent of the majority, expressed by the so-called organs of public opinion – newspapers and associations". Located between consensus and coercion was "corruption/fraud", re-sorted to in those circumstances "when it is hard to exercise the hege-monic function, and when the use of force is too risky".[50]

Coercion was not limited to 'political society' either. As a Marxist, Gramsci was also acutely conscious of the inherently conflictual class relationship between the bourgeois and proletariat within a capitalist mode of production. Market mechanisms, which liberals locate in 'civil society', were necessarily reliant on coercion (which Marx referred to as the "dull compulsion of economic relations"[51]), corruption and fraud, in order to extract the surplus value from workers. The state (in its 'political society' guise) played a vital role here in guaranteeing on-going capital accumulation, often resorting to coercive means within 'economy soci-ety' to protect private property, restore profit rates, discipline the subal-tern class, or help restructure social relations of production (SROP) etc. Even *laissez-faire* economics was "introduced and maintained by legisla-tive and coercive means".[52]

In short, consensus and coercion were dialectically integrated and op-erated right across the 'integral State' (incorporating the 'State' and 'civil society'), while Gramsci applies the term hegemony to refer to two dif-ferent moments,[53] thus:

$$Hegemony = Domination* + Hegemony**$$

* including coercion, corruption, and fraud
** 'political hegemony', 'hegemonic activity', or 'intellectual &
moral leadership' (or consent)

Another critical responsibility of the bourgeois state in civil society was its role as an "educator", to shape the "civilisation and morality of vast masses to the necessities of the continuous developments of the economic apparatus of production".[54]

Nevertheless, *the* principal means the hegemonic class sought to shape intersubjective forms of consciousness and thus exercise 'intellectual and moral leadership' was via the "hegemonic apparatus", alluded to above: a complex opinion-forming network of 'autonomous' clubs, associations and societies; the media; religious groups; educational organisations; and theatrical, literal, and general artistic circles, etc. within 'civil society'.[55] "The realisation of a hegemonic apparatus, in so far as it creates a new ideological terrain", Gramsci explained, "determines a reform of consciousness and methods of knowledge: it is a fact, a philosophical fact".[56] Cultural hegemony, he held, had to be exercised before the seizure of the state.[57]

This *hegemonic apparatus* was inseparable from a particular dominant social class (and its allies) who established it and is in turn whose class identity and hegemonic project were consolidated by it. For Thomas, the hegemonic apparatus was the "'class focused' complement to Gramsci's new notion of the state ('integral State')" such that if the latter

> seeks to delineate the forms and modalities by which a given class stabilises and makes more or less enduring its institutional-political power in political society, the concept of 'hegemonic apparatus' attempts to chart the ways in which it ascends to power through the intricate network of social relationships of civil society.[58]

In other words, it constitutes "the means by which a class's forces in civil society are translated into political power".[59] The social power (hegemony) in 'civil society' was, therefore, of an intangible nature and took a "diffused and capillary form", mediated through various organisations.[60]

The key 'institution' responsible for the formulation and diffusion of ideas within any society, and thus the construction of hegemonic apparatus, were the *intellectuals*.[61] Gramsci saw fit to distinguish between "traditional" and "organic" intellectuals, with the latter, emergent from, or allied to, a particular SROP, the most politically relevant.[62] The function of *organic* intellectuals was threefold: (1) consolidate a genuine class consciousness in a dominant social group; (2) assimilate and conquer the 'traditional' intellectuals;[63] and (3) galvanise support amongst the subaltern classes for the former's hegemonic project (and ideas, philosophy, and ethico-political-cultural values).

This then raised the issue of *language*: a critical element in any future philosophical struggle between competing hegemonies. Venturing into terrain later developed by post-structuralists such as Michel Foucault and Jacques Derrida, Gramsci held that language was not just a collection of words "grammatically devoid of content" but "a totality of determined notions and concept" which convey "a specific conception of the world",[64] and ultimately the medium through which class projects were consolidated. Though 'organic intellectuals' emerge in the history on the back of a particular economic structure they tend to use pre-existing social categories.[65] Language never keeps up with social transformation, remaining "metaphorical with respect to the meanings and the ideological content which the words used had in preceding periods of civilisation".[66]

The subaltern classes would, hence, have to develop their very own concepts freed from the historical baggage. Before the working class could do that, they had to overcome the single most important obstacle to their acquiring class consciousness (Marx's 'class for itself') – and the cause of their political inactivity – their uncritical acceptance of "common sense". *Common sense* was "a product of history", "the traditional popular conception of the world" and comprising of "beliefs, superstitions, opinions, ways of seeing and acting" expressed in conservative popular culture (e.g. customs, religious rituals etc.). Self-consciousness and political identity were the products of the historical process "which deposited in (us) an infinity of traces, without leaving an inventory", reducing the individual to "walking anachronism, a fossil." In order to develop "a critical coherent conception of the world", therefore, the subaltern class had to historicise its "common sense", to become aware that it was the product of historical processes.[67]

Instead the *new* 'organic intellectuals', emanating from within the ranks of the working classes, which would form the basis of a new type of political organisation and oppositional culture (the reason for the establishment of the factory council journal, *L'Ordine Nuovo*) replacing common sense with *good sense* (tantamount to a "critical understanding of self"[68]). This would require them nurturing their own *social myths*.[69] This was the role of the "Modern Prince": a new democratic revolutionary party, "the proclaimer and organiser" of this working class "intellectual and moral reform"[70] and helping fashion "the national-popular collective will towards the realisation of a superior, total form of modern civilisation".[71]

Although much of his political and intellectual life was focused on domestic affairs, Gramsci fully understood that the same social forces at play in the national sphere were also acting *internationally*. The bourgeoisie, after all, was an international class and "must necessarily wield across national differences" and pursue its class interests.[72] Though hegemonic projects began at the national level (consolidated in particular HBs) their perspective was necessarily international.[73]

In an early pre-prison article in *Avanti!* (26th June 1919) entitled "The Return to Freedom", Gramsci discussed capitalism as a "world historical phenomenon" and how "its uneven development means that individual nations cannot be at the same level of economic development at the same time".[74] It was this *uneven and combined development* of capitalism,[75] which made modern Italian state formation implicitly, at once both a national and international phenomenon: "the historical fact…cannot have strictly defined national boundaries, history is always 'world history' and particular histories only exist within the frame of world history".[76]

To the question: "Do international relations precede or follow (logically) fundamental social relations?", Gramsci responded that they necessarily followed, with innovations in the social structure modifying "absolute and relative relations in the international field", even the "geographical position of a national state". At the same time, however, "international relations react both passively and actively on political relations (of hegemony among the parties)." This complex interplay between "the relation of internal forces, international forces, and the country's geo-political position" was precisely because the class struggle was not merely a national phenomenon. Class relations within a hegemonic system at the state level were inextricably linked to relations between international social forces that "constitute the combinations of States in hegemonic systems". Intra-capitalist competition at the international level created "the same hierarchies and system of slavery as in the national sphere".[77]

Under this exploitative international division of labour, the "great" – or "hegemonic" – powers (e.g. Britain, Germany, France, and the United States), having all undergone a complete social revolution (consolidated in a new mode of production, SROP and FOS), were able to penetrate and appropriate the surplus value produced in weaker underdeveloped ones (e.g. Italy, Spain, and Russia).

Nevertheless, a degree of consensus did underpin this self-reinforcing *core-periphery* relationship[78]: a hegemonic power became the "chief and guide of a system of alliances and of greater and minor agreements", shaping the interests of peripheral states so these "concur in a decisive way to form a system and an equilibrium", to the benefit of particular internal factions,[79] and possibly provoking a "passive revolution" (or "'revolution' without a 'revolution'")[80] expressed in "Caesarism" and/or "trasformismo".[81] Ultimately, it was a global competition that drove the "impetus for progress", leaving peripheral countries little choice but to assimilate core countries' material and intellectual conquests.[82]

And, in what superficially appeared to be a concurrence with contemporary mainstream neorealism IR, Gramsci argued that the relative power a given 'integral State' occupied within the inter-state hierarchy (and hence its capacity to threaten, wage, and win war), could be "calculated", taking into account: (1) its "extension of territory"(including population); (2) its "economic power" (differentiating between "productive capacity" and "financial capacity"); (3) "military power" (and war-making ability); and (4) "the ideological position a country has in the world, in being a representative of progressive forces in history".[83] He also agreed with Lenin and Rosa Luxemburg that in its drive to overcome the "tendency of the rate of profit to decline" capitalism was likely to provoke imperial expansion and war between the great powers.[84]

In short, Gramsci made little conceptual differentiation between hegemony at the international level and hegemony at the national level; in both cases, it referred to the domination of a "hegemonic character" (a mixture of "direct domination and hegemony").[85] The uneven and combined development of global capitalism manifested itself in a hierarchical system of states, with the hegemonic states (in the plural) exercising significance over relatively weaker states:

> Just as, in a certain sense, in a given state history is the history of the ruling classes, so, on a world scale, history is the history of the hegemonic states. The history of the subaltern states is explained by the history of hegemonic states.[86]

Furthermore, Gramsci contemplated the possibility of a country becoming a "world hegemonic state" if it were able "to imprint upon its activities an absolutely autonomous direction which all other powers, great and minor, have to feel the influence".[87] The "global politico-economic system" of "Anglo-Saxon world hegemony", he observed, was bringing about the "colonial subjection of the whole world to Anglo-Saxon capitalism". Indeed, "colonial populations become the foundations on which the whole edifice of capitalist exploitation is erected".[88]

The Neo-Gramscian Perspective: A Brief Overview

The neo-Gramscian perspective will be forever associated with Robert W. Cox who, in a couple of pioneering articles and book,[89] drew on Gramsci's conceptualisation of hegemony to forward what he deemed a more convincing account of the dynamics of the international system than that offered by mainstream 'problem-solving' neorealist IR theory,[90] denounced for its epistemological and methodological defects and implicitly conservative orientation.[91] Alternatively, and more conducive to the furthering of social emancipation, Cox opted for an agency-focused *critical theory*, based on a historicist epistemology, which "does not take institutional and social power relations for granted but calls them into question by concerning itself with their origins and how and whether they might be in a process of changing". Not only were all truth historically contingent – "theory is always *for* someone and *for* some purpose" – but also any concepts used had to undergo continual modification to reflect the changing reality.[92]

Cox's epistemological differences with 'problems-solving' theories had deeper ontological roots, specifically regarding the structure-agency debate. While rejecting agency-based perspectives, such as idealism and pluralism, Cox was especially critical of structuralism (e.g. neorealism, world-systems theory, and structural Marxism) and their associated 'inner essence' or 'logic' (e.g. power-maximisation, division of labour, or capital), which he considered mitigated against social emancipation.[93] Critical theory required the elaboration of a structurally grounded, yet non-determinist, explanation of social change, and with agency very much at the forefront. Cox's solution was to *historicise* structure itself.

So-called "historical structures" are "a particular combination of thought patterns, material conditions, and human institutions which has a certain coherence amongst its elements" (see below). They constitute a non-deterministic "framework for action", imposing "pressures and constraints", which social actors could work with or attempt to resist but could not ignore. Moreover, even where agents are able to "resist a prevailing historical structure" they are obliged to 'buttress' their actions "with an alternative, emerging configuration of forces, a rival structure".[94]

As indicated, Cox held historical structures were formed by the reciprocal, non-determinist interaction of "three categories of forces (expressed as potentials)", namely[95]:

1   *material capabilities*: considered "productive and destructive potentials"; existing in both "dynamic form" as "technological and organisational capabilities" and in "accumulated form" as "natural resources" transferable by technology into "stocks of equipment" and thus "wealth".
2   *ideas*: which are divided into two types: (i) "intersubjective meanings", defined as "those shared notions of the nature of social relations which tend to perpetuate habits and expectation of behaviour" and are "broadly common throughout a particular historical period" (e.g. norms governing state sovereignty, diplomatic relations, etc.); and (ii) "collective images of the social order held by different groups of people" (e.g. with regards to the "legitimacy of prevailing power relations") "may be several and opposed", thereby creating the intellectual 'space' counter-hegemonic ideas.
3   *institutions*: understood as "particular amalgams of material capabilities and ideas", which they help shape. Institutionalisation stabilised and perpetuated a determined order, mirroring power relations at their launching, and nurturing "collective images" for their reproduction, while providing "ways of dealing with conflict so as to minimise the use of force". In time, however, institutions might "take on their own life", becoming "a battleground of opposing tendencies". Clear parallels exist between this *institutionalisation* and the third 'level' of Gramsci's *second moment*.

Cox then applied "the method of historical structures" to three particular *levels* or *spheres* of activity. Similarly, these three 'spheres' were engaged in a dialectical relationship with each other and represented schematically, in a triangular format:[96]

1   *social forces*: the principal collective actors "engendered by the production process", SROP, which encapsulate certain configurations of social class forces and operate within and across *all* spheres of activity;
2   *forms of states* (FOS): derive from Gramsci's 'integral State' concept, these are considered as historically contingent *state-society complexes* resting upon certain configurations of social-class forces as a result of internal political struggles. The state is thus the

condensation of hegemonic relations between dominant classes and subordinate class fractions and expressed in the establishment of an HB.[97]

3   *world order* (WO): defined as "the particular configuration of forces which successively define the problematic of war and peace for the ensemble of states", allowing critical theorists, such as Cox, to envision the possibility of other alternative forms of WO. "Order" here meant "the way things usually happen" (e.g. established practices), rather than the absence of 'disorder'.[98]

Although each of these 'spheres' was, in theory, made up of its own particular configuration of 'material', 'ideational', and 'institutional' forces, the reality was that none of these spheres existed in isolation but reciprocally interacted with the other spheres. "Changes in the organisation of production", Cox elucidates, "generate new social forces which, in turn, bring about changes in the structure of states; and the generalisation of changes in the structure of states alters the problematic of WO".[99]

World hegemony had its origins in "an outward expansion of the internal (national) hegemony established by a dominant social class". As a result of this internationalisation of domestic social forces "[t]he economic and social institutions, the culture, the technology associated with this national hegemony becomes patterns for emulation abroad", causing a restructuring of domestic SROP and associated HBs. Chiming with Gramsci, Cox affirmed that in peripheral countries this would most likely take the form of a 'passive revolution'.[100]

By promoting a particular accumulation regime through the WO, a would-be hegemonic class was consciously consolidating its position at both the national and international level. But there could be no hegemonic WO without both a global hegemonic class and tacit support of key classes/fractions of classes within the 'receiving states'.

Cox repeated Gramsci's idea that world hegemony was not just an inter-state relationship rather "an order within a world economy and dominant mode of production which penetrates all countries and links into the subordinate modes of production", connecting different social classes, establishing links and alliances between civil societies across national frontiers to form a "globally conceived civil society". "The historic bloc underpinning particular states", he explained, "become connected through the mutual interests and ideological perspectives of social classes in different countries, and global classes begin to form". World hegemony, thus, was, at once "a social structure, an economic structure, and a political structure" providing an institutional, moral and ideological context to mould thoughts and actions".[101]

World hegemony had to be 'constructed'. Cox essentially repeated Gramsci's *second moment* arguments that the would-be hegemonic state/ class had to exercise 'intellectual and moral leadership' over subordinates and frame its particular interests "in terms of universal or general interests."[102] The new WO established had to be acceptable to a wide range of very different 'state-society complexes', or at least the most advanced ones, who felt their interests were compatible with, and furthered by, said hegemonic power, with whom they enjoyed an 'equal' (i.e. not vertical/imperial) relationship.[103]

Extending his 'historical structures' model to the global level, the key mechanism for promoting, maintaining, or transforming a particular WO was the founding of *international organisations*. Operating predominantly on the basis of consensus, their essential function was to embody, promote, ideologically legitimate, and socially embed those universal rules, norms, practices, and values most favoured by dominant economic and social forces and with it expand said hegemonic WO.[104]

Importantly, and again following Gramsci, Cox emphasised how these international organisations helped to legitimate certain national policies/institutions and marginalise others, while seeking to assimilate oppositional tendencies through conceding economic-corporate concessions, opt-outs, and derogations from the norm.[105] Such a process was especially important in co-opting the political elite from peripheral countries *trasformismo*.[106]

By way of summary, one can affirm that world hegemony for Cox constituted a *historical fit*: an expression of broadly based consent manifested in the acceptance of ideas (collective image of WO and acceptance of associated norms) and participation in universal international organisations though underpinned by a configuration of material power. Though it might manifest itself in a hierarchical inter-state system, world hegemony remained a form of *class rule*: different nationally based social classes linked together by the dominant mode of production penetrating all countries in dialectical inter-relation with subordinate modes of production (and their respective SROP).

Combining his 'method of historical structures' with work carried out by the Braudel Annals School, Eric Hobsbawm, and world-system scholar Immanuel Wallerstein, Cox' identified just two periods of world hegemony: *Pax Britannica* (1845–75) and *Pax Americana* (1945–65).[107]

Cox dedicated much of his empirical work to analysing the establishment of American world hegemony in the post-war period. Through a process termed the *internationalisation of the state* (IOS), he explained how Washington set up a complex set of institutional "machinery" (e.g. United Nations, the Bretton Woods institutions, the Organisation for European Economic Cooperation/Organisation for Economic Cooperation and Development [OEEC/OECD], Marshall Plan, and the North Atlantic Treaty Organization [NATO]) to oversee the application of the system's norms, harmonise national policies, and "reconcile domestic social pressures with the requirements of a world economy". In essence, this meant helping the Western countries restructure their SROP (along Fordist lines),

HB and hence FOS (towards internationally orientated Keynesian-welfare states) compatible with the new US-directed system of global accumulation,[108] while at the same time, respected natural divergences – a compromise John Ruggie termed "embedded liberalism".[109]

Key in this process was the arrival of huge foreign (largely American) direct investment (and to a less extent expansion of international trade) from the early 1950s onwards facilitated by the above IOS, resulting in deeper international economic integration, or what Cox termed the *internationalisation of production* (IOP). Since the 1970s direct investment was being joined by portfolio investment, which together reshaped the dominant mode of production at the national level, mobilising social forces, which in turn provoked a dramatic reconstitution in traditional systems of governance.[110]

Indeed, a central thesis forwarded by neo-Gramscians is the idea that the transnational social forces unleashed by this globalization process (incorporating both the IOS and IOP) served to undermine both the post-war economic development model and US hegemony itself.

According to Cox, new transnational social forces and associated class struggles began to emerge from 1965 onwards. Consequently, it was "increasingly pertinent to think in terms of a global class structure alongside or superimposed upon national class structure". Situated at "the apex" of this "emerging global class structure" was the "transnational managerial class", consisting of transnational corporate executives and investors; the most internationalised branches of state government/bureaucracies (e.g. central bankers, finance and trade ministers, etc.); and heads of key international organisations and think tanks.[111] This new transnational class had developed "its own ideology, strategy, and institutions of collective action" now constituted, in Marxist terms, "a class both in itself and for itself", pursuing its own transnational agenda and ideological indoctrination via its chosen international institutional architecture (e.g. the World Bank, OECD, International Monetary Fund (IMF), etc.).[112]

The modern state, accordingly, was being transformed, with transnational and local levels competing with its traditional monopoly of authority and loyalty.[113] Replacing the post-war Keynesian welfare state was a weakened "hyperliberal" (neoliberal) state, little more than "transmission belts from the global into the national economic sphere",[114] and which "willy-nilly became more effectively accountable to a *nébuleuse* personified as the global economy"[115] (i.e. the transnational managerial class). The core was not completely devoid of conflict, but these were largely limited to tensions between transnational and national capital, and amongst sections of the subaltern classes.[116] The classic Westphalian inter-state WO has been superseded by a 'new medievalism' in what amounted to a 'transnationalization of the state'.

Despite their differences, all subsequent neo-Gramscians broadly share Cox's transnationalization thesis. Stephen Gill, for example, has carried out important work on the formal/informal socialisation processes promoted by fora such as the Trilateral Commission[117] and their role in nurturing a transnational "identity" and "shared consciousness" amongst the "members".[118] Coinciding with Cox, Gill has heralded the advent of a new self-aware transnational capitalist class, committed to "the progressive transnationalization and liberalisation of the global political economy".[119]

The emergent *nébuleuse*, Gill avers, is imposing its 'supremacy' (rather than 'hegemony')[120] over the lower classes via augmented surveillance measures termed "disciplinary neoliberalism",[121] which have been socially embedded through "the quasi-legal restructuring of state and international political forms" known as "new institutionalism".[122] *New constitutionalism*, Gill elucidates,, is "a doctrine and associated set of social forces which seeks to place restraints on the democratic control of public and private economic organisations and institutions",[123] that is "to remove or insulate substantially the new economic institutions from popular scrutiny or democratic accountability".[124] State autonomy, in effect, was being limited to those fiscal and monetary policies favourable to the unhindered transnational flow of global capital as articulated in the 'Washington Consensus', embedded in the newly restructured Bretton Woods institutions (i.e. WTO, IMF, and World Bank) and various regional integration processes.

Neo-Gramscians of the so-called *Amsterdam School*[125] have also been drawn to the process of transnational class formation within an emergent transnational civil society,[126] underscoring the importance of organisation channels such as corporate interlocks and elite socialisations in transnational forums and planning groups.[127]

For prominent 'Amsterdam scholar', Kees van der Pijl, the process of transnational capitalist class formation dates back long before the 1960s, being on-going in the "English-speaking West" since the 18th century onwards, nurtured by the web of *haute finance*, and expressed in "transnational imagined communities" such as the Freemasonry and later the Bilderberg Group and the Trilateral Commission. Taking inspiration in Cox's FOS classification, van der Pijl's model depicts a WO beset by a centuries-old conflict between "Lockean" and "contender"/"Hobbesian" 'state-society' complexes, currently manifested in their respective 'hyperliberal' and 'neo-mercantilist developmental' forms.[128]

According to van de Pijl, the 'Lockean states' represent "the true bourgeois political formation", consisting of largely self-regulating civil societies dedicated to "protecting private property at home and abroad".[129] As these merge, the contemporary world is increasingly resembling a "Lockean heartland" – a "free space for capital, created with the help of states but shielded from democratic politics",[130] with transnational class formation and the "international socialisation of state functions"[131] transgressing national border. This development has re-written international relations. The traditional forms of world politics, van der Pijl insists, have now been replaced by the "struggle for hegemony between fractions of the bourgeoisie, through which the general tendency of the transnational ruling class asserts itself nationally and between the different states within and outside the Lockean heartland".[132] 'Outside' lay the "contender states", characterised by a weak bourgeoisie class. Conforming to Gramsci's 'passive revolution' analysis, economic development in these countries is directed by a powerful "state class", who employs all manner of neo-mercantilist industrial policies to 'catch up' with the 'Lockean states'.[133]

Fellow Amsterdam scholar Bastiaan van Apeldoorn has similarly been drawn to the process of transnational capitalist class formation, but with special attention being paid to the transformation of European capitalism and consolidation of a *European* transnational HB within the heartland. According to van Apeldoorn, this was largely achieved through the deepening of regional integration from the 1980s onwards. According to van Apeldoorn, this process was driven by the competitive interaction of three rival 'hegemonic projects' represented by the transnational neoliberal 'globalists' (American and European transnational financial, industrial and service companies, with bases in Europe); the neo-mercantilist 'Europeanists' (regional-based/orientated European multinational industrial firms capital who feared falling competitiveness); and the supranational 'social democrats' (centre-left parties, transnational unions, and NGOs identified with Commission President Jacques Delores).

Despite the early victory of 'Europeanists', reflected in the quasi-neo-mercantilist Single European Act (1986), it was the 'globalists' faction, van Apeldoorn maintains, which eventually was able to exercise hegemony over the other rival projects manifested in the neoliberal nature of the EU from the Treaty of Maastricht (1991) onwards, and most clearly set out with the launching of the *Lisbon Strategy* by the European Council in March 2000 (later replaced by *Europe 2020* in 2010).[134] The variances between Anglo-Saxon neoliberalism and this EU-level version – termed *embedded neoliberalism* – van Apeldoorn ventures, is explainable as a direct consequence of the interaction of the original projects, and crucially the wide-ranging social and regional/national concessions conferred by the 'globalists', as befitting their hegemonic role.[135] Nonetheless, these differences within the Lockean heartland were not to be overstated, van Apeldoorn insists, recognising that by the Treaty of Lisbon (2009) 'embedded neoliberalism' was closely resembling its Anglo-Saxon counterpart.[136]

Towards a *Neo* Neo-Gramscian Perspective

We are indebted to neo-Gramscians for their ground-breaking research and for broadening traditional IR theory. The contributions include:

1   encouraging a re-reading of Antonio Gramsci's work
2   demystifying and broadening the definition of 'the state' (via Gramsci's 'integral State' version)
3   stressing the importance of the ethico-political/intersubjective realm within a theory of hegemony
4   forwarding a model for understanding the dialectical interaction between socio-economic and ideological-political factors at the national level
5   helping shed light on some of the important social forces underpinning, and institutional characteristics of, *Pax Americana*
6   clarifying the dynamics of the transnationalization process and specifically transnational class formation and the complexities of regional integration
7   elaborating a useful set of concepts and analytical tools for theory construction

Nevertheless, for all the fine work carried out by neo-Gramscians some key inconsistencies undermine their ability to provide a coherent explanation for the functioning and changing nature of the international system. The root of the problem is ontological: fundamentally Cox's original handling of the *structure-agency* debate.

As noted above, guided by his 'critical theory' objective to revitalise political agency,[137] Cox chose to *historicise* structure. These 'historical structures' were not "out there", constituting an objective reality, he claimed, but "intersubjective" and "socially constructed": "they become part of the objective world by virtue of their existence in the intersubjectivity of relevant groups of people"; 'the objective world of institutions is real because we make it so by sharing a picture of it in our minds'.[138]

In reducing structures to historically contingent *intersubjective* relations (human consciousness and practice), not only was Cox taking ideology and subjectivity as causal within the production and reproduction of WO (see below), but also crucially, he was denying any ontological difference between structure and agency ("structures are not in any deeper sense prior to the human drama itself" they "are not 'givens' (data), they are 'mades' (facts) – made by collective human action"[139]). Thus hegemony, as a particular historically defined structure internalised (though not necessarily consciously) by social agents, is defined as: "a structure of values and understandings about the nature of order that permeates a whole system of states and non-state entities" and is derived "from the way of doing and thinking of the dominant strata of the dominant state or states".[140]

As Margaret Archer has indicated, the main problem with this merging of the structure with an agency (i.e. 'central conflation')[141] is that it prevents any real dialectic interaction between the two and hence hindering practical research.[142]

Gramsci, we have seen, did consider structure and agency ontologically distinct, temporally differentiable but at the same time inseparable, locked in a dialectal materialist relationship with the other. This conceptualisation dovetails with Margaret Archer's *morphogenetic approach*[143] and Roy Bhaskar's *transformational model of social activity* (TMSA),[144] both situated within a *critical* (or *scientific*) *realist* philosophy of science. In order to further a better understanding of the social world (and hence function of hegemony), it is helpful to briefly underscore the main characteristics of critical realism which, in its 'under-labouring'[145] capacity as a philosophy of science (or meta-theory), is specifically designed to clarify key ontological and epistemological questions and thus facilitate theory construction.

Critical realism, according to its 'founder' Roy Bhaskar,[146] sought to reaffirm the primacy of ontology over epistemology after centuries of neglect. Drawing on Immanuel Kant and Louis Althusser, Bhaskar differentiated epistemologically between *intransitive* and *transitive* dimensions of science: the former referred to objects of knowledge external to us, the latter to our knowledge of said objects, which was filtered through our socially constructed cognitive framework (epistemological relativism).[147]

The reason for this intransitive-transitive incongruence, Bhaskar maintained, was that reality was hierarchically structured, divided into three vertically inter-related ontological *domains*, with higher levels *emergent* from, though not reducible to, their lower ones. At the 'base' were non-observable underlying generative or causal structures/mechanisms (the *real*) out of which arose 'intermediate' objective, subject-independent events (the *actual*), who then expressed themselves as observable/measurable experiences at the 'surface' level (the *empirical*).[148]

Importantly, in this *ontological stratification* model, none of the domains emerged at a 'higher layer' in their original form, modified as they were by the interaction of multiple, and often conflicting, emergent causal mechanisms operating within 'open systems'. Since underlying structures and processes (the 'real') are simply imperceptible at the surface level (the 'empirical'), those epistemological traditions which conflated 'reality' (ontology) with 'our conception of that reality' (epistemology) – be it by empirical measurement (i.e. positivism), or intersubjectivity (i.e. neo-Kantian interpretivism) – Bhaskar affirmed, were guilty of the *epistemic fallacy*. Statements about 'being' (ontology) could not be transposed into statements about 'knowledge' of being (epistemology).[149] Given ontological stratification, an underlying generative mechanism/causal law could only be deduced via retroduction,[150] a complex dialectical process of theorisation and study of events, involving a movement from 'concrete to abstract, abstract to concrete',[151] with the criterion for 'testing' the 'truthfulness' depending on its superior 'explanatory power' compared to competing hypotheses.[152]

Despite having no particular theoretical attachment critical realism was, as Jonathan Joseph noted, especially compatible with Marxism.[153] Marx subscribed to the depth ontology thesis,[154] his life's work was spent studying the underlying generative mechanisms of capitalism (and connected class domination), and how these found their expression in certain institutional (e.g. the state) and ideational (e.g. ideology) forms, resulting in the false separation between the economic and political spheres.[155]

It was in his quest to shed light on how social structures are reproduced and occasionally transformed within an overdetermined, ontologically stratified open system that Marxist thinker, Jonathan Joseph, drew on the structure-agency conceptualisations of Gramsci, Bhaskar, and Nicos Poulantzas. The resultant *materialist theory of hegemony*, serves as a touchstone for this monograph.

Hegemony, Joseph holds, has a 'dualist' nature, analytically differentiable between its *structural* and *surface* characteristics (albeit that both were engaged in a dialectical relation within an open system).[156]

The *structural* aspect, Joseph posits, carries out the key function of securing the reproduction of social structures pertinent to a particular mode of production. Importantly, such structural reproduction occurs predominantly unintentionally: unconscious practises by agents (e.g. going to work) serving to reinforce structure (e.g. capital-wage labour relations). That said, the complex emergent nature of the social realm means this process could never be taken for granted. The organisation and reproduction of capitalism, for example, depended on a wide range of overt political, economic, social, cultural, and juridical mechanisms, with the *state* absolutely pivotal here (hegemony, it will be remembered, operated both through and across the 'integral State').

Joseph's *surface* hegemony, or "political moment", exhibits clear parallels with Gramsci's *second moment*. Emerging out of structural hegemony (underlying forces and relations of production), here conscious dominant groups mobilise around *hegemonic projects* to conserve,[157] advance or transform particular political programmes via societal reorganisation (e.g. reforming class relations and building institutions). The aforementioned 'hegemonic apparatus' is crucial. Said 'projects' remain dependent on underlying structural hegemonic conditions, which strategically determine access to resources and the options available but are not mere functional expressions of it, however, enjoying their own set of mechanisms, properties, and powers, and hence expression/agenda. This lack of direct correlation means hegemonic projects (and associated modes of regulation, state strategies, etc.) may not fulfil the vital function of reproduction (e.g. capital accumulation) – or, in the case of a genuine transformational struggle, could actually seek to undermine it – engendering conflict, crisis, and potentially systemic change.

Ideas and culture, therefore, do enjoy a degree of autonomy, but for them to be politically relevant they would have to be integrated into a hegemonic project anchored in underlying forces/relations of production. "[I]deologies would be arbitrary and individual fancies without the material forces,"[158] Gramsci emphasised, whereas in reality, they are "real historical facts" and "instruments of domination".[159]

Once a critical realist philosophy of science is adopted, and specifically, the materialist theory of hegemony, the short-comings of Cox's original ontological position become only too evident.

Evidently, on a basic level, Cox was guilty of committing the "epistemic fallacy". The assertion that 'historical structures' can be inferred "from observable historical patterns of conduct"[160] involved collapsing ontology into epistemology. Generative mechanisms, as noted, lay at a different level from, and hence unobservable at, the surface empirical level. Cox's decision to define 'historical structures' in purely intersubjective terms, furthermore, was tantamount to 'central conflation', making it impossible to explore the interaction of structure and agency, and therein precluding any serious conceptualisation of social change, his original 'critical theory' objective.

And while claiming his critical theory was rooted in a production paradigm,[161] reiterated by fellow exponents,[162] it is very difficult to square Cox's method with that of Marx. Not only did he refuse to grant causal primacy to any one of the three "categories of forces" – material capabilities, ideas, and institutions – each one enjoying the same autonomy and generative capacity,[163] he denied capitalism constituted a single capitalist mode of production[164] or that it was driven by an underlying "logic" or set of "tendencies" external to agents' consciousness.[165] Instead, Cox along with many other neo-Gramscian opted to 'historicise' the economy,[166] locating causation in the "social context of production"[167] within a particular HB with the focus on how surplus was distributed (Weber) not how it was generated (Marx).[168]

The problem with neo-Gramscian historicism was that by abandoning 'deep structure' (Joseph's *structural* hegemony) they implicitly relinquished any possibility of theorising on the dynamics of global capitalism or class reproduction/formation. Instead of capital-labour class conflict constituting the motor of change (Marx), political mobilisation now depended upon intersubjective elements within unique HBs, each based on its own particular SROP and associated accumulation strategy. While such a method might have its virtues at the micro level for analysing the dynamics *within* a discrete HB, at the macro level it lacked the necessary tools to conceptualise systemic change *across* a large number of different HBs. Unfortunately, by assuming or simply ignoring, the capitalist mode of production neo-Gramscianism was not only forgoing any possibility of analysing its structural tendencies but implicitly any hope of transforming it, therefore, impeding the realisation of Cox's original critical theory objective.

Once capitalism's underlying contradictions are side-lined, neo-Gramscian accounts of WO transformation are forced to rely on the voluntaristic inter-subjective conjunctural level (Joseph's *surface* hegemony) in the form of top-down ideological 'hegemonic projects'.[169] It was not just the capital-labour conflict that was downgraded in the transnationalization thesis, therefore, but also coercion and power politics, signalling a departure from Gramsci and a slide into the 'methodological dualism' denounced by Perry Anderson (i.e. hegemony understood being consensual and located in civil society).

Even the Amsterdam School falls foul here. This is typified by van der Pijl's decision to classify the WO along a rather simplistic Cox-inspired 'ideal type' binary categorisation, contrasting Lockean state-society complexes (consensus, civil society-centred, 'transcendent comprehensive concept of control', bourgeoisie, self-regulating, transnational) with their Hobbesian antagonists (coercion, state-centred, national interest, state class, centralised administration, international).[170] Such dualism results in two over-exaggerations. On the one hand, it overplays the distinctions between the two FOS: Lockean states, for example, clearly exhibit many Hobbesian attributes (e.g. coercion, state regulation/intervention, etc.) and vice-versa. On the other hand, it overstates the degree of harmony within the 'Lockean heartland'. As Adrian Budd has discerned, the latter scenario of core states cooperating with each other for mutual benefit[171] gravitates dangerously close to Kautsky's ultra-imperialism.[172] And while much of his empirical analysis challenges such a view,[173] van der Pijl is at least guilty of inconsistency, contending elsewhere that: (1) transnational capitalist class hegemony (expressed in "transnational imagined communities"[174]) had effectively suppressed interstate rivalry and class conflict within the core;[175] (2) struggles for hegemony between bourgeois factions had now replaced struggles between states; and (3) "hegemonic control" was based on "frameworks of thought and practice", á la Cox.[176]

As already indicated in the review of Anderson's critique, the risk of depicting hegemony as a purely ideological phenomenon is that it implies that once the 'Modern Prince' had won the ideological battle within 'civil society' it could assume political power via the ballot box and embark on radical social transformation: a revisionist programme dismissed as naïve by Marxists such as Gramsci, who as observed, considered the modern state *the* key instrument of bourgeois power.

Unsurprisingly, the Coxian lack of ontological depth manifests itself in an inadequate theorisation of the state, depicted as: (1) an inter-subjective social relation, contingent on its particular HB;[177] (2) located 'external' to, and enjoying independence from, the economy[178] (again, implying political neutrality); (3) increasingly powerlessness within the global economy (accountable to a *nébuleuse*[179]); and (4) reduced to a "transmission belt"[180] between the national and international sphere.

The theoretical framework adopted in this book does not abandon neo-Gramscianism but seeks to give it a firmer ontological grounding. This must involve placing Gramsci back within the Marxist tradition where he belongs, not least in order to reaffirm hegemony's essential structural underpinnings, compatible with the *emergentist materialist* philosophy of science set out above.

Whilst neo-Gramscian analysis of transnational class formation has much to commend it, we remain unconvinced that this process is actually undermining the capitalist state,[181] which is vital for the reproduction of 'deep structure' and on-going capitalist accumulation. As studied in Chapter 3, the nurturing and on-going 'management' of neoliberal globalization relies heavily on the vital supporting role of states, not least Washington,[182] and often in an overtly coercive fashion.

Indeed, a direct corollary of the neo-Gramscian down-grading of the state's importance has been insufficient attention being paid to geopolitics, coercion, and militarism in theory construction. And yet, as Chapter 2 reiterates anti-communism, the construction of a 'national security state', the setting up of a global network of security umbrellas and military bases, and participation in over/covert military operation, were as much a part of *Pax Americana* as the Bretton Woods institutions and the Marshall Plan.

The uneven development of capitalism and the complex dialectical interplay of national and international social forces, as Gramsci observed, are reflected in a hierarchical system of competitive states. One thing is to assert US world hegemony promoted a degree of intra-core consensus and allay military conflict within the 'heartland' during and after the Cold War, quite another is to claim it all but eliminated inter-state rivalry altogether. As the subsequent chapters in this monograph will argue, tensions within the core have always existed, be they social, economic, political, military, or cultural, and not least within the European Union itself.

Having made the case for the restoration of the state to its key position within WO, it is fitting to conclude this chapter by examining a little further the role of the world hegemon within the global capitalist system. To do so, however, it is necessary to comment briefly on some of the latter's structural tendencies.

Although "driven by its perpetual thirst for endless capital accumulation"[183] capitalism is prone to internal contradictions and systemic crises. The classic Marxist accumulation circuit consists of two basic stages: first, the extraction of surplus value from labour (in the form of commodities or debt securities) generated in the production process; and second, the sale of said commodities (i.e. the conversion of surplus value into money) at a profit, articulated in Marx's systemic cycle of accumulation M-C-M'. A break-down in either of these stages – i.e. the inability either to extract sufficient surplus value or to sell the product profitably, the so-called *realization crisis* – would provoke a systemic crisis.

During such periods businesses might opt to hoard capital or to speculate in financial markets, using its "idle money" to generate "interest-bearing" or "fictitious money",[184] entitling the holder to some kind of future royalty or right to trade financial assets in the 'financial sector' expressed in Marx's shortened capital circuit M-M' rather than directly investing in the 'productive economy'.[185] While successful at de-valuing of 'constant capital'[186] and appropriating the assets of the lower classes, this new financial aristocracy did not manage to return the economy to its earlier productiveness.

Most Marxists follow Gramsci, Lenin, Hilferding, and of course, Marx himself, and identify 'overproduction/overcapacity' stemming from inter-capitalist competition as the underlying cause of these crises. Other motives have been cited, however. Rosa Luxemburg, for example, blamed 'underconsumption' (or lack of effective demand) a direct corollary of the exploitative nature the capitalist system,[187] while Giovanni Arrighi flipped Luxemburg's argument, highlighting certain circumstances of where the exploitation of labour is "too low"[188] thanks to the strength of institutionalised organised labour, producing a 'profit squeeze from below'. All agreed, however, that capitalism suffered a *tendency for the rate of profit to decline.*[189]

Contrary to arguments forwarded by teleological Marxists, this did not signal the end of capitalism as a mode of production since "permanent crises do not exist."[190] Marx himself acknowledged that this tendency could be "checked, retarded, weakened" by a series of "counteracting forces", which included augmenting labour exploitation, investing in new technology, declaring bankruptcies, accessing foreign markets, and for-mation of monopolies.[191] And again, concomitant with 'structural he-gemony', the state had a pivotal role here which including acting as a consumer of last resort, of which military and other "waste spending"[192] were particularly important.

According to David Harvey, one recurrent solution to falling profit rates has been for capital to keep moving. Continuing the work carried out by Marx, Lenin, Trotsky, Luxemburg, and Gramsci, amongst others, Harvey linked the reproduction of capitalism historically to uneven de-velopment and the 'creation of space': the demands of endless accumula-tion driving capital to seek out new, ever-larger areas into which it could bury its surplus. Harvey referred to this geographic restructuring as a *spatio-temporal fix* (henceforth referred as *spatial fix*),[193] with the word 'fix' carrying a *double* meaning.

On the one hand, the invested capital was 'fixed' in the land: embedded in physical (e.g. airports, roads, railways, and sewage systems) and social (e.g. labour processes, distributional arrangements, and education/health care systems) infrastructures in a given territory/temporal setting.[194]

On the other hand, to 'fix' (i.e. resolve) its need to guarantee continual accumulation capital was driven to, in the words of Marx "strive to tear down every spatial barrier...to exchange and conqueror the whole world for its market" and "annihilate this space with time" to create a new "geographical landscape...only to destroy it and rebuild a wholly different landscape at a later point in time" in a geographical variant of Joseph Schumpeter's process of "creative destruction".[195]

There was, therefore, an implicit tension between the double meaning of 'fix': between 'immobile' and 'mobile'. If capital did move to a new spatial configuration to bury its surplus capital it would leave behind "a trail of devastation and devaluation" in the region, undermining the value and associated monopolistic privileges embedded within the 'old' spatial fix. But if it did not, the accumulated capital would start to "be devalued directly through the onset of deflationary recession or depression".[196]

The relocation process thus was not a foregone conclusion. An impasse, or "switching crisis" could occur, where deeply entrenched "territorial alliances" within given social infrastructures put up resistance to "conserve privileges already won, to sustain investments already made... to protect itself from the chill wind of spatial competition".[197] Obviously, the stronger this territorial alliance (coinciding with Gramsci's HB) and more powerful the state, within the prevailing WO, the more likely such relocation could be delayed.

Arrighi incorporated Harvey's 'spatial theory' into his particular world-systems analysis which also drew on Gramsci, Marx, as well as Fernand Braudel, to elaborate his own *systemic cycle of accumulation* (SCOA).[198] Historically, the stages of global material expansion occurred due to "the emergence of a particular bloc of governmental and business agencies capable of leading the system towards wider or deeper divisions of labour".[199] In keeping with the materialist theory of hegemony set out above, the ability this "particular bloc" (situated within a dominant country) to launch a hegemonic project (*surface* hegemony) ultimately depended on underlying social forces (*structural* hegemony).

The consensual component of hegemony, it will be remembered, was activated when a dominant actor appeared to be operating in the general interests of the other. Given capitalism's crisis tendencies, a powerful state (understood in an 'integral' or 'state-society complex' sense) could exercise 'intellectual and moral leadership' over other states, were it to successfully underwrite a mode of regulation and regime of accumulation – conducive to its own capitalist model – which increased returns to capital invested in production and trade, and therein helped restore profit rates.

For Arrighi, this involved an implicit vertical relationship. A state could become 'world hegemonic' when it could credibly claim either: (1) "to be the motor force of general expansion of the *collective* power of rulers vis-à-vis subjects", or (2) "that the expansion of its power relative to some or even all other states is in the general interest of the subjects of all states".[200] Applying this logic specifically to American hegemony, Harvey considered it imperative that "sufficient benefits flowed to the propertied classes in enough countries to make US claims to be acting in the universal (read 'propertied') interest credible and to keep subaltern groups (and client states) gratefully in line".[201]

According to Arrighi's SCOA, every period of material expansion (Harvey's *spatial fix*) was marked by a "steady increase in the size, scope, and complexity of successive regimes of accumulation on a world scale".[202] Historically, each hegemon distinguished itself from the previous one by offering an ever-larger territorial *container of power* for capital accumulation – running from 13th-century Italian city states, Britain nation-state colonialism, to the continent-sized US[203] (and possibly now China[204]) – and boasting the sufficient politico-military power to enforce the system.

This roughly coincided with Hannah Arendt's assertion that: "a never-ending accumulation of property must be based on a never-ending accumulation of power...The limitless process of accumulation needs the political structure of so 'unlimited a Power' that it can protect growing property by constantly growing more powerful".[205] In a competitive, hierarchically structured inter-state system, therefore, the hegemonic state, is inevitably driven to extend, expand, and intensify their politico-military capabilities/reach in an attempt to regulate the capital accumulation and surplus value extraction process to its favour.

In this context, Harvey referred to "capitalist imperialism" (or "imperialism of a capitalist sort"), made up of a "contradictory fusion" of two components: (1) "the politics of state and empire", and (2) "the molecular processes of capital accumulation in space and time". Although ontologically distinct, each driven by its particular *logic of power*, be it *territorial* or *capitalist*,[206] they enjoyed a complex, dialectical relationship, albeit one in with the latter was dominant (differentiating capitalist imperialism from 'classic' imperialism). According to Arrighi, recourse to "the politics of state and empire" became particularly acute during periods of overproduction/overcapacity in the productive sector manifested in increasingly hostile inter-state competition and declining profitability. Considering Marx's systemic cycle of accumulation M-C-M' "a recurrent pattern of historical capitalism as a world system",[207] Arrighi claimed that in this context the incumbent hegemon will prefer to hold their capital in liquid form and generate profits purely from financial operations concurrent with Marx's M-M'.[208]

For Arrighi, this new phase of financial expansion – *financialization*[209] – portended a "signal crisis"[210] of both a regime of accumulation and its accompanying hegemonic system of governance. During this *belle époque* period 'politics and empire' also increased as did the hegemon's wealth and power, but this was only fleeting since the process of financialization tended to deepen rather than resolve the underlying over-accumulation crisis. Primarily, Harvey held, it offered financial means "to rid the system of overaccumulation by the visitation of crises of devaluation upon vulnerable territories", the "sinister and destructive side of spatio-temporal fixes" with the state entering into "an unholy alliance" with financial capital to form "the cutting edge of 'vulture capitalism'", involving "cannibalistic practices" and "forced devaluations".[211] Updating and amending Marx's original concept, Harvey termed this seizure of a set of devalued valuable assets (including labour power) at minimal costs *accumulation by dispossession*.

Unfortunately, history has shown that financial expansions are unsustainable, drawing in far more capital than could be profitably managed, generating speculative bubbles and crashes. To contain the possibility of global economic melt-down (or quell anti-systemic voices), it was essential that the hegemonic power be prepared to intervene by organising bail-outs for local/region crises, either directly or via allied institutions. Coercion was omnipresent, not least to quell possible domestic opposition to the massive redistribution of wealth towards the upper classes which financialization engineers. Nonetheless, in true hegemonic style, the new accumulation system had to be constructed with sufficient consent amongst the leading capitalist agencies.

Though Marx's aforementioned 'counteracting forces' could temporarily help to boost profitability, increasing turbulence in high finance and devaluing investments indicated the system was entering into its "terminal crisis".[212] Historically, Arrighi noted, the overaccumulation of capital in the hegemon led to the transfer of surpluses to the emergent centres of capitalist development in return for claims on assets or future incomes paid in the form of interest, profits, and rents. In the short term, these payments reinforced the incumbent's position, but eventually, the debtor-creditor relationship was reversed, with capital pushing for a new spatial fix of even greater scale and scope. The hegemonic transition process was characterised by inter-state conflict and even often war, as countries fought to prevent the devaluation of their capital, but eventually, the new *container of power* that emerged as the "headquarters" of the leading capitalist agencies prepared to launch a new SCOA.[213]

Notes

1 Throughout the Second International, an ideological debate raged within the Social Democratic Party of Germany (SPD) between the 'adventurists' and the 'revisionists', represented by Eduard Bernstein and Karl Kautsky.

2 In 1917, for example, he co-founded a short-lived *Il Club di Vita Morale* (the *Moral Life Club*), dedicated to political education, and sponsorship of proletarian culture amongst young socialists, and launched the newspaper *La Città Futura* (*The Future City*), submitting articles on subjects as diverse as

state formation in Italy, the reorganisation of society and capitalism during crisis, the Russian Revolution, and building socialism in Italy.

3 Marx & Engels (2002).

4 At the same time, Gramsci stressed: "if the Bolsheviks reject some of the statements of *Capital*, they do not reject its invigorating, immanent thought" Gramsci (1977), pp. 34–5.

5 Gramsci (1977), pp. 65–8.

6 Gramsci (1977), p. 99. Trade unions were denounced for their undemocratic and intrinsically capitalist nature. See Gramsci (1978), p. 76.

7 Lenin (1982), p. 251.

8 See Gramsci (1977), pp. 190–5.

9 Lenin (1982), Vol. 17, pp. 232–3, see also pp. 78–9.

10 Contributory factors include Gramsci undergoing a year of socialisation in Moscow; rising working class support for, and violent seizure of power by, the Italian Fascist Party; and the weakness of the Italian left Cammett (1967), p. 153.

11 Gramsci launched a new daily newspaper in February 1924, *L'Unità*, with the specific aim of incorporating the Southern peasantry into a class alliance with the Northern working-class movement: a constant political theme throughout his life, resurfacing again resurface again in the "Southern Question".

12 Cammett (1967), p. 169.

13 Gramsci (1978), pp. 464–512. The central debates arising out of this Congress regarding hegemony, class, power structures, regionalism, and uneven development in Italy would form the basis of Gramsci's final (though unfinished) essay as a free man in autumn 1926, *Some Aspects of the Southern Question*, which would constitute the first piece in the PN.

14 Gramsci (1971), p. xcii.

15 *L'Ordine Nuevo*, for example, was denounced for its innocence and programmatic vagueness. In his own defence, Gramsci admits that at the time simply "we wanted to act, to act, to act". Gramsci (1971). p. xxxvii.

16 Gramsci (1971), p. 120.

17 Gramsci (1971), pp. 242–3.

18 Gramsci (1971), p. 52.

19 See Marx (1967).

20 Marx (1999).

21 Gramsci (1971), p. 64.

22 Machiavelli (1981), Section XVIII, p. 99.

23 Machiavelli (1981), Section XIX, p. 105.

24 Machiavelli (1981), Sections XVII & XVIII, pp. 95–102.

25 Gramsci (1971), p. 57.

26 Gramsci (1971), p. 131, p. 109, p. 100.

27 Gramsci (1995), p. 350.

28 Gramsci (1971), p. 12.

29 Gramsci (1971), p. 238.

30 Anderson (1976), pp. 21–9.

31 Laclau & Mouffe (1985), Chapter 2.

32 Gramsci (1971), p. 46.

33 Gramsci (1971), p. 162.

34 Gramsci (1971), p. 162.

35 See for example Gramsci (1971), p.184, pp. 277–318, p. 410, pp. 425–72.

36 Gramsci (1971), p. 401.

37 Gramsci (1971), p. 410.

38 The following is taken from Gramsci (1971), pp. 175–85, p. 161.

39 Gramsci (2007), Quaderni 11, p. 1422.
40 Thomas (2010), pp. 41–83, p. 137, p. 366, p. 418.
41 Gramsci (2007), Quarderni 13, p. 1590.
42 Gramsci (1971), p. 12.
43 See Thomas (2010), pp. 170–71.
44 Gramsci (1971), p. 244.
45 Gramsci (1971), p. 263, p. 239.
46 Gramsci (1971), p. 160.
47 Thomas (2010), p. 194.
48 Thomas (2010), p. 194.
49 Gramsci (2007), Quaderni 12, p. 1519.
50 Gramsci (1971), p. 80f.
51 Marx (1967), p. 737.
52 Gramsci (1995), p. 261, pp. 243–4, p. 160; Gramsci (1971), p. 160.
53 Gramsci (2007), Quaderni 19, p. 1962.
54 Gramsci (2007), Quaderni 8, p. 37; Quaderni 13, p. 1566.
55 Gramsci (1996), pp. 52–3.
56 Gramsci (1971), pp. 365–6.
57 Gramsci (1971), pp. 57–8.
58 Thomas (2010), pp. 224–5.
59 Thomas (2010), p. 226.
60 Gramsci (1971), p. 110.
61 It was Croce's work on intellectuals which first inspired Gramsci to write press articles and launch various political journals – most notably *L'Ordine Nuovo* – with the specific aim of promoting "certain forms of new intellectualism" and determine "new concepts" for the subaltern classes. The failure of the workers to mobilise political forces and defend their 'objective' class interests during *bienno rosso* and the rise and installation of Mussolini's fascist regime, impressed on Gramsci the need to elaborate a more coherent theory on the *structural* importance of intellectuals within the "integral State". Gramsci (1971), pp. 10–11.
62 See Gramsci (1971), pp. 5–23 for his comments on "intellectuals".
63 Traditional intellectuals were those intellectuals who enjoyed great prestige in society and were made up of "ecclesiastics…administrators, scholars and scientists, theorists, non-ecclesiastical philosophers" who "think of themselves as 'independent', autonomous, endowed with a character of their own" when in reality they were derived from, and maintained links with, previous or present "'essential' social groups" (i.e. ex-*organic* intellectuals), which was reflected in their ideology. Gramsci (1971), pp. 5–9.
64 Gramsci (1971), p. 322.
65 Gramsci (1971), pp. 6–7.
66 Gramsci (1971), p. 450.
67 Gramsci (1971), p. 134, pp. 196–7, pp. 323–8.
68 Gramsci (1971), p. 333.
69 Drawing heavily on the work of revolutionary syndicalist Georges Sorel, Gramsci defined "social myths" as "a creation of concrete fantasy which acts on dispersed and shattered people to arouse and organise its collective will". These were essential not only as weapons for activists seeking to overthrow the old order but also a general analytical device applicable to diverse political situations. Gramsci (1971), pp. 126–30.
70 Gramsci (1971), pp. 132–3.
71 Gramsci (1971), p. 367, p. 324, p. 334.
72 Gramsci (1975), p. 105.
73 Gramsci (1971), p. 240.

74 Gramsci (1977), p. 69.
75 Though addressed by Lenin and Rosa Luxemburg, it is Leon Trotsky who is commonly identified as the first to analyse *uneven and combined development* and its effects on state formation. See Chapter 1 "Peculiarities of Russian Development" in Trotsky (2017) and Trotsky (1997).
76 Gramsci (1985), p. 181; Gramsci (1977), pp. 69–72.
77 Gramsci (1971), p. 116, p. 176; Gramsci (1977), p. 69.
78 This *core-periphery* conceptualisation of the global capitalist was further extended by Lenin-inspired IR theories such as *dependency theory* and *world-systems theory*, see Prebisch (1950), Frank (1967), and Wallerstein (1974).
79 The more the peripheral states' economic life is subordinated to the core, "the more a particular party will come to represent this situation and to exploit it", drawing support from international social forces to defeat the domestic opposition group. But while this "foreigner's party" sold itself as "the most nationalistic party", in fact, it did not represent "the vital forces of its own country" but rather "the country's subordination and economic enslavement to the hegemonic nations". Gramsci (1971), p. 59, p. 105, pp. 176–7; Gramsci (2007), Quaderni 13, p. 1563, p. 1597, p. 1629.
80 Gramsci (1971), p. 59. A 'passive revolution' occurred in a country where the bourgeois was too weak to exercise hegemony over the other classes, hence it was the state that "'led' the group that should have been 'leading' and was able to put at the latter's disposal an army and diplomatic strength". Gramsci (1971), p. 195.
81 *Caesarism* was a 'passive revolution' in which a charismatic figure intervenes to resolve a political stalemate between domestic social forces. *Trasformismo*, on the other hand, involves coalition-building by the ruling class extended to a wide range of social groups, though necessarily including the co-option of opposition (working class) leaders. Gramsci (1971), p. 58, pp. 219–23.
82 Gramsci (1971), p. 84, pp. 116–17.
83 Gramsci (2007), Quaderni 13, p. 1598. Gramsci drew on such "calculations", for example, to analyse the changing fortunes of the great powers following the First World War, more specifically the US's rising GDP and favourable Balance of Payments (BOP) position compared to that Great Britain and how "tacitly" the latter "had to acknowledge the supremacy of the United States". What was occurring, Gramsci insisted, was an international power shift; Europe had "lost its importance and world politics depends upon London, Washington, Moscow, Tokyo rather than the continent". Gramsci (2007), Quaderni 2, p. 168, p. 181.
84 Gramsci (2007), Quaderni 19, p. 2018.
85 Gramsci (2007), Quaderni 19, p. 1962.
86 Gramsci (1995), pp. 222–3.
87 Gramsci (2007), Quaderni 2, p. 166.
88 Gramsci (1977), pp. 69–93, p. 302.
89 See Cox (1996a, 1996b), Cox & Sinclair (1996c), and Cox (1987).
90 Most prominently Kenneth Waltz. See Waltz (1979).
91 Cox (1996a), pp. 91–2.
92 Cox (1996a), pp. 87–90.
93 Cox (1996a), p. 95.
94 Cox (1996a), pp. 97–8.
95 See Cox (1996a), pp. 98–9.
96 Cox (1996a), pp. 100–1. Cox acknowledges his intellectual debt here to E.H. Carr who he cited as being one of the first thinkers to adopt such methodological scheme.

97 The historical blocs, thus, are "the configurations of social forces upon which state power ultimately rests". Cox (1987), p. 105; Cox (1996b), p. 168, p. 174.

98 Cox explains in a footnote that the term "world order" is preferred to both "inter-state system" – as it is relevant to all historical period (e.g. pre-Westphalia) – and "world-system" – which he considered held a connotation of static equilibrium. Cox (1996a), p. 116.

99 Cox (1996a), p. 137.

100 Cox (1996b), pp. 136–7, p. 171.

101 Cox (1996b), pp. 136–7, Cox (1987), p. 7.

102 Cox (1996a), p. 99.

103 Cox (1996b), p. 136.

104 Cox (1996b), pp. 137–9.

105 It was in this context that Cox compared hegemony to a pillow: "it absorbs blows and sooner or later the would-be assailant will find it comfortable to rest upon." Cox (1996b). p. 138.

106 Cox (1996b), p. 139.

107 Cox (1996b), pp. 136–7.

108 Cox (1996a), pp. 108–9. See also Rupert (2000).

109 Ruggie (1982).

110 Cox (1996a), pp. 109–11.

111 Cox (1996a), p. 111; Cox (1987), p. 359.

112 Cox (1996a), p. 111.

113 Cox with Sinclair (1996c), pp. 305–8.

114 Cox. (1993), pp. 259–60.

115 Cox with Sinclair (1996c), p. 298. Cox defines *nébuleuse* as 'governance without government' – Ibid., p. 301.

116 Two main cleavages had emerged within industrial labour: (1) between "established" workers (relatively skilled, employed by large corporations enjoying stable employment) and "nonestablished" workers (non-stable unskilled jobs linked to decentralised production); and (2) amongst "established workers", between those employed "in the sector of international production" ("potential allies of international capital") and those working "in the sector of national capital" (considered "more susceptible to the appeal of protectionism and national...corporatism"). Cox (1996a), pp. 111–12.

117 Gill (1991).

118 Gill (1983), p. 261.

119 Gill (1991), p. 94; Gill (2008), p. 138.

120 'Supremacy' is preferred since the new transnational HB's domination is not based upon 'intellectual and moral leadership' (and hence hegemony) over subaltern groups. Gill (1993), p. 40.

121 Gill (1995), p. 411. Drawing on Max Weber, Emile Durkheim, and Michel Foucault, Gill understands discipline as combining "macro- and micro-dimensions of power", understood as "the structural power of capital; the ability to promote uniformity and obedience with parties, cadres, organisations, and especially class formations with transnational capital...; and particular instances of disciplinary power in a Foucauldian sense".

122 Gill (1995), pp. 411–12.

123 Gill (1993), p. 10.

124 Gill (1992), p. 165.

125 At the risk of over-simplification, this book separates the neo-Gramscians into two groups: the 'Coxians' (e.g. Adam D. Morton, Andreas Bieler, Stephen Gill, Mark Rupert, and William I. Robinson) inspired by Robert Cox,

and the 'Amsterdam School' (e.g. Kees van der Pijl, Bastiaan van Apeldoorn, Henk Overbeek, Marianne Marchand, and Otto Holman) which apart from Cox also draw directly on Gramsci and Marx.

126 See for example Overbeek & van der Pijl (1993).

127 See van Apeldoorn (2004), p. 159.

128 van der Pijl (1998).

129 van der Pijl (2006), p. 8.

130 van der Pijl (2006), p. xiv, p. 28.

131 A variation on Cox's IOS, van der Pijl (1998), p. 70.

132 van der Pijl (1989), p. 19.

133 van der Pijl (1998), pp. 80–4.

134 *Consilium* (2000).

135 Pride of the place was given to free trade, competitiveness, self-regulating markets, and supply-side economics, but references were made to the protection and promotion of European capital (for the 'Europeanists') along with certain minimal guarantees on social rights and cohesion (social democracy). See van Apeldoorn (2002), pp. 130–42; and van Apeldoorn (1998) pp. 17–38.

136 van Apeldoorn (2009).

137 Constructivism and post-structuralism are also guilty of this. Indeed, neo-Gramscian critical theory approach arose in the 1980s as part of a broad post-structuralist paradigm shift sparked by key socio-economic-politico-cultural developments (e.g. the expansion of neoliberal globalization, the end of the Cold War, the decline in the traditional left, and the explosion of social movements).

138 Cox & Sinclair (1996c), p. 149.

139 Cox (1987), p. 395.

140 Cox & Sinclair (1996c), p. 151.

141 Anthony Gidden's 'structuration theory' opts for a similar solution to the structure-agency dilemma. See Giddens (1984).

142 For Archer's critique of Gidden's structuration, see Archer (1990), pp. 73–84.

143 Archer (1995). According to Archer's three-stage *morphogenetic cycle* structural conditions (T1), pre-condition social interaction (T2) which leads to structural elaboration (*morphogenesis*) or reproduction (*morphostasis*) (T3), which in turn preconditions future interaction (T1) and the subsequent launching of a new morphogenetic cycle.

144 Bhaskar (1998). According to Bhaskar; 'Society is both the ever-present *condition* (material cause) and the continually reproduced *outcome* of human agency. And praxis is both work, that is conscious *production*, and (normally unconscious) *reproduction* of the conditions of production, that is society', pp. 43–4.

145 Bhaskar uses the term *under-labour* to refer to the accessory role played by philosophy, particularly ontology, in scientific development. Bhaskar (2008), p. xxxvi.

146 See Bhaskar (1986, 1998, 2008).

147 Bhaskar (2008), pp. 11–12.

148 Bhaskar (2008, pp. 2–3, pp. 46–7.

149 Bhaskar (2008), pp. 26–7.

150 Bhaskar (1978). See also Archer *et al.* (eds.) (1998).

151 Sayer (1994), p. 87.

152 Critical realists shunned predictions for context-dependent 'evidential statements' with regards to particular 'tendencies'. See Lawson (1997), p. 213, p. 243; Bhaskar (1986), p. 7, pp. 53–4; and Bhaskar, (1998), pp. 59–61.

153 Joseph (2007), p. 345.

154 "All science would be superfluous", he famously commented, "if the outward appearances and essences of things directly coincided". Marx, K. & Engels, F. (1966), *Capital: A Critique of Political Economy: Volume III*, London: Lawrence & Wishart, p. 817.

155 Yalvaç (2010), pp. 179–81.

156 The following description of Joseph's conceptualisation of hegemony is taken from Joseph (2002), pp. 128–33, pp. 210–13; and Joseph (2010), pp. 61–4.

157 This coincides with Gramsci's observation that: incurable structural conditions have revealed themselves (reached maturity), and that, despite this, the political forces which are struggling to conserve and defend the existing structure itself are making every effort to cure them, within certain limits, and to overcome them. Gramsci (1971), p. 178.

158 Gramsci (1971), p. 377.

159 Gramsci (1995), p. 395.

160 Gramsci (1995), p. 395.

161 Cox (1996a), pp. 95–7.

162 See for example Bieler & Morton (2001) and Morton (2007), pp. 129–31.

163 Burnham (2006), p. 70.

164 According to Cox, the capitalist mode of development had spawned *twelve* different modes of SROP, conceptualised as "monads": "self-contained structures" each with its own "developmental potential". Cox (1987), p. x, p. 4, pp. 32–4, p. 406, fn. 7.

165 Cox (1987), p. 396.

166 Andreas Bieler and Adam David Morton, for example, advocated 'Critical Economy', claiming "categories are always situated within historical circumstances and assessed within the particular context from which they derived". Bieler & Morton (2003). p. 481, p. 491.

167 Cox (1987), p. 11.

168 See Lacher (2008), p. 88.

169 Cox with Sinclair (1996c), p. 151, p. 245.

170 van der Pijl (1998), p. 84.

171 van der Pijl (1989), pp. 16–19.

172 Budd (2013), p. 79.

173 van der Pijl (2006), van der Pijl (2007).

174 van der Pij (1998), p. 98.

175 van der Pijl (2006), p. 28.

176 Van der Pijl (1989), p. 19.

177 Bieler & Morton (2001), p. 22.

178 Cox (1987), pp. 219–30, pp. 399–400.

179 Cox (1996c), p. 301. Cox defines *nébuleuse* as 'governance without government'.

180 Cox (1993), p. 260. See also Robinson (2003), pp. 45–6, p. 62.

181 Robinson (2005).

182 See for example Gowan (1999), Harvey (2003), Gowan (2009), and Panitch & Gindin (2012).

183 Harvey (2003), p. 101.

184 Peter Gowan defined "fictitious capital" as "money derived not from the past but from expectations that it will be validated by future productive activity", Gowan (1999), p. 10.

185 According to Peter Gowan the 'productive sector' was *determinant* "because it produces the stream of value out of which the money-capitalists in the financial sector ultimately gain their royalties directly or indirectly". The financial sector, on the other hand, however, was *dominant*, since "it decides *where it will* channel the savings from the past and the new fictitious

credit-money – who will get the streams of finance and who will not". Gowan (1999), p. 13 (original italics).

186 This was reflected in idle machinery, tools and technical equipment, abandoned factories, and empty office space.

187 Luxemburg (2003).

188 Arrighi (1978), p. 4.

189 Marx & Engels (2010). Chapters 2 & 13. Marx referred to the "law of the tendency of the rate of profit to fall" as "in every aspect the most fundamental law of modern economy, and the most important for understanding the most difficult relations".

190 Marx (1975), p. 497.

191 Marx & Engels (2010), Chapter 14, Section 1, Chapter 25, Section 5a.

192 Marx (2002), Chapter 15, part 2. See also Luxemburg (2003).

193 Harvey (1982).

194 Harvey (2003), pp. 99–100, pp. 115–16; Harvey (1982), p. 428–9.

195 Marx (2002), p. 155. Harvey (1982), p. 377. Harvey (2003), pp. 96–8, p. 101. According to Schumpeter, "spectacular prizes" (high profits) provided a constant incentive to innovate technology but also attracts market entrants which eliminated excess profits and inflicted widespread losses by destroying pre-existing productive combinations. See Schumpeter (1950), pp. 73–4.

196 Harvey (2003), p. 116.

197 Harvey (1982), p. 428–9, p. 435.

198 Arrighi (2010).

199 Arrighi (2005), p. 87.

200 Arrighi (2010), p. 31.

201 Harvey (2003), p. 40.

202 Arrighi (2010), p. 376.

203 Arrighi (2010), p. 223.

204 Arrighi (2008).

205 Arendt (1966), p. 143. Arendt was focusing on the accumulation of power/capital within states, while Arrighi studied the evolving system of states headed by the hegemon.

206 The former refers to the "political diplomatic and military strategies invoked and used by a state or some collection of states operating as a political power bloc as it struggles to assert its interests and achieve its goals in the world at large". The latter, on the hand, involved extracting resources by "exploiting the uneven geographical conditions under which capital accumulation occurs" ("the 'asymmetries' that inevitably arise out of spatial exchange relations")…"across and through continuous space, towards and away from territorial entities through the daily practises of production, trade, commerce, capital flows, money transfers, labour migration, technology transfer, currency speculation, flows of information, cultural impulses, and the like". This exploitation was "expressed through unfair and unequal exchanges, spatially articulated monopoly powers, extortionate practises attached to restricted capital flows, and the extraction of monopoly rents". Harvey (2003), pp. 26–7, p. 31.

207 Arrighi (2010), p. 6.

208 Arrighi (2008), p. 232.

209 Understood in its basic form as the capacity of the finance capital to take over and dominate, at least in the short term, all the activities of the business world.

210 Arrighi (2010), pp. 220–2.

211 Harvey (2003), pp. 134–6.

212 Arrighi (2010), pp. 221–2.

213 Arrighi (2008), pp. 233–4.

Bibliography

Anderson, P. (1976), "The Antinomies of Antonio Gramsci", *New Left Review*, I/100,5–78.

Archer, M.S. (1990), "Human Agency and Social Structures: A Critique of Giddens" in Clark, J., Modgil, C. and Modgil, S. (eds.), *Anthony Giddens: Consensus and Controversy*, London: Falmer Press.

Archer, M.S. (1995), *Realist Social Theory: The Morphogenetic Approach*, Cambridge: Cambridge University Press.

Archer, M.S. *et al.* (eds.) (1998), *Critical Realism: Essential Readings*, London: Routledge.

Arendt, H. (1966), *The Origins of Totalitarianism*, New York: Harcourt, Brace and World.

Arrighi, G. (1978), "Towards a Theory of Capitalist Crisis", *New Left Review*, I/111,3–24.

Arrighi, G. (2005), "Hegemony Unravelling-2", *New Left Review*, 33, 83–116.

Arrighi, G. (2008), *Adam Smith in Beijing: Lineages of the Twenty-First Century*, London: Verso.

Arrighi, G. (2010), *The Long Twentieth Century: Money, Power and the Origins of our Times*, 2nd Edn., London: Verso.

Bhaskar, R. (1978), "On the Possibility of Social Science Knowledge and the Limits of Naturalism", *Journal for the Theory of Social Behaviour*, 8, 1–28.

Bhaskar, R. (1986), *Scientific Realism and Human Emancipation*, London: Verso.

Bhaskar, R. (1998), *The Possibility of Naturalism*, 3rd ed. [orig. pub. 1979], Routledge, London.

Bhaskar, R. (2008), *A Realist Theory of Science*, [orig. pub. 1975]), Abingdon, Oxon: Routledge.

Bieler, A. & Morton, A.D. (2001), "The Gordian Knot of Agency: Structure in International Relations", *European Journal of International Relations*, 7, no. 1, 5–55.

Bieler, A. & Morton, A.D. (2003), "Globalisation, the State and Class Struggle: A 'Critical Economy' Engagement with Open Marxism", *British Journal of Politics and International Relations*, 5, no. 4, 467–99.

Budd, A. (2013), *Class, States and International Relations: A Critical Appraisal of Robert Cox and Neo-Gramscian Theory*, Abingdon: Routledge.

Burnham, P. (2006), "Neo-Gramscian Hegemony and the International Order", in Bieler, A. *et al.* (eds.), *Global Restructuring, State, Capital and Labour: Contesting Neo-Gramscian Perspectives*, London: Palgrave Macmillan.

Cammett, J. (1967), *Antonio Gramsci and the Origins of Italian Communism*, Stanford: Stanford University Press.

Consilium, "Presidency Conclusions: Lisbon European Council", 23rd–24th March 2000 (available online at www.consilium.europa.eu/en/).

Cox, R.W. (1987), *Production, Power, and World Order: Social Forces in the Making of History*, New York: Columbia University Press.

Cox. R.W. (1993), "Structural Issues of Global Governance: Implications for Europe", in Gill, S. (ed.), *Gramsci, Historical Materialism and International Relations*, Cambridge: Cambridge University Press.

Cox, R.W. (1996a), "Social Forces, States, and World Orders: Beyond International Relations Theory" [orig. pub. 1981], in Cox, R.W. and Sinclair, T.J. (eds.), *Approaches to World Order*, Cambridge: Cambridge University Press.

Cox, R.W. (1996b), "Gramsci, Hegemony and International Relations: An Essay in Method" [orig. pub. 1983], in Cox, R.W. and Sinclair, T.J. (eds.), *Approaches to World Order*, Cambridge: Cambridge University Press.

Cox, R.W. with Sinclair, T.J. (1996c), *Approaches to World Order*, Cambridge: Cambridge University Press.

Frank, A.G. (1967), *Capitalism and Underdevelopment in Latin America*, New York: Monthly Review Press.

Giddens, A. (1984), *The Constitution of Society: Outline of the Theory of Structuration*, Cambridge: Policy Press.

Gill, S. (1983), "Neo-Liberalism and the Shift Towards a US-centred Transnational Hegemony", in Overbeek, H. (ed.), *Restructuring Hegemony in the Global Political Economy: The Rise of Transnational Neoliberalism in the 1980s*, London: Routledge.

Gill, S (1991), *American Hegemony and the Trilateral Commission*, Cambridge: Cambridge University Press.

Gill, S. (1992), "The Emerging World Order and European Change: the Political Economy of European Union", in Miliband, R. and Panitch, L. (eds.), *The Socialist Register: New World Order?* London: Merlin Press.

Gill, S. (1993), "Epistemology, Ontology and the Italian School", in Gill, S. (ed.), *Gramsci, Historical Materialism and International Relations*, Cambridge: Cambridge University Press.

Gill, S. (1995), "Globalization, Market Civilisation, and Disciplinary Neoliberalism", *Millennium – Journal of International Studies*, 24, no. 3, 399–423.

Gill, S. (2008), *Power and Resistance in the New World Order*, 2nd Edn., Basingstoke: Palgrave Macmillan.

Gowan, P. (1999), *The Global Gamble: Washington's Faustian Bid for World Dominance*, London: Verso.

Gowan, P. (2009), "Crisis in the Heartland: Consequences of the New Wall Street System", *New Left Review*, 55, 5–29.

Gramsci, A. (1971), *Selections from the Prison Notebooks of Antonio Gramsci*, Hoare, Q. and Nowell Smith, G. (eds. and trans.), London: Lawrence & Wishart.

Gramsci, A. (1977), "The Revolution against 'Capital'", in Hoare, Q. (ed.), *Selections from Political Writings, 1910–1920*, London: Lawrence & Wishart.

Gramsci, A. (1978), *Selections from Political Writings, 1921–1926*, Hoare, Q. (ed. and trans.), London: Lawrence & Wishart.

Gramsci, A. (1995), *Further Selections from the Prison Notebooks*, Boothman, D. (ed. and trans.), London: Lawrence & Wishart.

Gramsci, A. (1996), *Prison Notebooks*, Volume 2, Buttigieg, J.A. (ed. and trans.), New York: Columbia University Press.

Gramsci, A. (2007), *Quaderni del Calcere: Quaderni di traduzioni (1929–1932)*, Cospito, G. and Francioni, G. (eds.), Rome: Istituto della Enciclopedia Italiana, Quaderni.

Harvey, D. (1982), *The Limits to Capital*, Oxford: Basil Blackwell.

Harvey, D. (2003), *The New Imperialism*, Oxford: Oxford University Press.

Joseph, J. (2002), *Hegemony: A Realist Analysis*, London: Routledge.

Joseph, J. (2007), "Philosophy in International Relations: A Scientific Realist Approach", *Millennium: Journal of International Studies*, 35, no. 2, 345–59.

Joseph, J. (2010), "The International as Emergent: Challenging Old and New Orthodoxies in International Relations Theory", in Joseph, J. and Wight, C. (eds.), *Scientific Realism and International Relations*, Basingstoke: Palgrave Macmillan.

Lacher, H. (2008), "History, Structures and World Orders", Ayers, A.J. (ed.), *Gramsci, Political Economy, and International Relations Theory: Modern Princes and Naked Emperors* (revised Edn.), Basingstoke: Palgrave Macmillan.

Laclau, E. & Mouffe, C. (1985), *Hegemony and Socialist Strategy: Towards a Radical Democratic Politics*, London: Verso.

Lenin, V. (1982), *Collected Works*, Volume 31 (available online at www.marxists. org) [orig. pub. 1922].

Luxemburg, R. (2003), *The Accumulation of Capital*, London: Routledge.

Machiavelli, N. (1981), *The Prince*, London: Penguin Classics.

Marx, K. (1967), *Capital: A Critique of Political Economy*, Vol. 1, New York: International Publishers Company, Inc. [orig. pub. 1887].

Marx, K. (1975), *Theories of Surplus Value, Part II*, Moscow: Progress Publishers [orig. pub. 1971].

Marx, K. (1999), *Critique of Hegel's Philosophy of Right* (available online at www. marxists.org) [orig. pub. 1843].

Marx, K. (2002), *Grundisse* (available online at www.marxists.org) [orig. pub. 1857].

Marx, K. & Engels, F. (2002), "Theses on Feuerbach", *Selected Works*, Vol. 1. (available online at www.marxists.org) [orig. pub. 1888].

Marx, K. & Engels, F. (2010), *Capital: A Critique of Political Economy: Volume III* (available online at www.marxists.org) [orig. pub. 1894].

Morton, A.D. (2007), *Unravelling Gramsci, Hegemony and Passive Revolution in the Global Political Economy*, London: Pluto Press.

Overbeek, H. & van der Pijl, K. (1993), "Restructuring Capital and Hegemony: Neo-liberalism and the Unmaking of the Post-war Order", in Overbeek, H. (ed.), *Restructuring Hegemony in the Global Political Economy. The Rise of Transnational Neo-liberalism in the 1980s*, London: Routledge.

Panitch, L. & Gindin, S. (2012), *The Making of Global Capitalism: The Political Economy of American Hegemony*, London: Verso.

Prebisch, R. (1950), *The Economic Development of Latin America and Its Principal Problems*, New York: United Nations.

Robinson, W.I. (2003), *Transnational Conflicts: Central America, Social Change and Globalization*, London: Verso.

Robinson, W.I. (2005), "Gramsci and Globalization: From Nation-State to Transnational Hegemony", *Critical Review of International Social and Political Philosophy*, 8, no. 4, 1–16.

Ruggie, J.G. (1982), 'International regimes, Transactions and Change: Embedded Liberalism in the Postwar Economic Order', *International Organisation* 36, no. 2, 379–415.

Rupert, M. (2000), *Ideologies of Globalization: Contending Visions of a New World Order*, Florence, KY: Routledge.

Sayer, A. (1994), *Method in Social Science: A Realist Approach*, 2nd Edn., London: Routledge.

Schumpeter, J. (1950) *Capitalism, Socialism and Democracy*, London: Harper & Row.

Thomas, P.D. (2010), *The Gramscian Moment: Philosophy, Hegemony and Marxism*, Chicago: Haymarket Books.

Trotsky, L. (1997), *The Third International After Lenin: The Program of the International Revolution or a Program of Socialism in One Country?* (available online at www.marxists.org) [orig. pub. 1928].

Trotsky, L. (2017), *The History of the Russian Revolution*; Vol. 1: *The Overthrow of Tzarism* (available online at www.marxists.org) [orig. pub. 1932].

van Apeldoorn, B. (1998), "Transnationalization and the Restructuring of Europe's Socioeconomic Order: Social Forces in the Construction of 'Embedded Neoliberalism'" *International Journal of Political Economy*, 28, no. 1, 12–53.

van Apeldoorn, B. (2002), *Transnational Capitalism and the Struggle Over European Integration*, London: Routledge.

van Apeldoorn, B. (2004), "Theorizing the Transnational: A Historical Materialist Approach", *Journal of International Relations and Development*, 7, no. 2, 142–76.

van Apeldoorn, B. (2009), "The Contradictions of 'Embedded Neoliberalism' and Europe's Multi-level Legitimacy Crisis: The European Project and its Limits", in van Apeldoorn, B., Drahokoupil, J. and Horn, L. (eds.), *Contradictions and Limits of Neoliberal European Governance: From Lisbon to Lisbon*, Basingstoke: Palgrave Macmillan.

van der Pijl, K. (1989), "Ruling Classes, Hegemony and the State System. Theoretical and Historical Considerations", *International Journal of Political Economy*, 19, no. 3, 7–35.

van der Pijl, K. (1998), *Transnational Classes and International Relations*, London: Routledge.

van der Pijl, K. (2006), *From the Cold War to Iraq*, London: Pluto Press.

van der Pijl, K. (2007), *Nomads and Empires*, London: Verso.

Wallerstein, I. (1974), *The Modern World-System, Vol. 1: Capitalist Agriculture and The Origins of the European World-Economy in the Sixteenth Century*, New York: Academic Press.

Waltz, K. (1979), *Theory of International Politics*, New York: McGraw Hill.

Yalvaç, F. (2010), "Critical Realism, International Relations Theory and Marxism", in Joseph, J. and Wight, C. (eds.), *Scientific Realism and International Relations*, Basingstoke: Palgrave Macmillan.

2 Construction and Projection of US Hegemony

Creating a New World Order: From 'One World' to 'Free World'

Prior to the Second World War (WII), and despite its evident economic and military prowess, the US's geopolitical priorities remained focused on its enlarged 'sphere of influence'. The State Department and even the powerful pro-international business think-tank, the Council of Foreign Relations, conceived of US foreign and economic policy in terms of a *Grand Area* encompassing the Western Hemisphere, East Asia, and the Pacific, as expressed in 1914 by then Assistant Secretary of the Navy, Franklin D. Roosevelt (FDR): "Our national defence must extend all over the western hemisphere, must go out a thousand miles into the sea, must embrace the Philippines and over the seas wherever our commerce may be."[1] Participation in the WWII,[2] however, caused a radical re-think in the American world view.

First, there was a strategic aspect. Protected by the Atlantic Ocean on one side and the Pacific on the other, the US was not only spared expensive war damage but could base its entire military strategy on an offensive tactics (increasingly based on air-power). It was the only country in WWII who could truly claim to have fought on a global scale: possessing the capabilities to project its power at great distances – either to the West (Europe) or East (Asia) – and facilitated by a global system of communication.

This had major effects on the 'formal' state structure. Thanks to the enormous logistics required, all departments of the state were involved in planning and coordination activities, though the key ones were the White House, the State Department, and the War Department. What set post-WWII apart from previous periods (with the possible exception of the American War of Independence) was that now the heads of the armed forces – the Joint Chiefs of Staff – occupied the upper echelons of power, enjoying a pivotal role in forming US policy, constituting an enduring transformation in American civil-military relations.

The US now possessed a global military-economic-political infrastructure, encompassing a worldwide network of military installations,

DOI: 10.4324/9780429459061-3

which elites were eager to take advantage of. At the front of the queue was American capital, which relished the possibility of tapping into hitherto inaccessible energy resources, minerals, and other raw materials. Increasingly, from 1945 onwards, Washington ceased referring to 'foreign policy' in favour of the broader, more militarised, *national security* policy, defined in 'global' terms. "It no longer appears practical to continue...hemispheric defence as a satisfactory basis for our security", army chief and Harry S. Truman's future Secretary of State, George C. Marshall, explained, "We are now concerned with the peace of the entire world".[3] The *Grand Area* thus expanded to take in Western Europe, the Middle East, and the former British Empire. The State Department now prioritised 'strategic' conditions and geopolitics alongside its traditional concerns for economics and diplomacy.

Fighting WWII, of course, also had major economic effects. The estimated $300 billion (over $4.1 trillion in present money) spent on equipping its military between 1941 and 1945 represented a massive boon for all productive sectors.[4] Between 1939 and 1945 the US GNP increased by two-thirds,[5] ending the war with almost two-thirds of the world's industrial production and over 70% of its gold.[6] The state became universally recognised as a key economic actor, not just in mobilising resources but even substituting for market processes via strategically planned debt-financed industrial policies: Keynesian-style 'pump-priming' universally credited with dragging the US out of the Great Depression. Truman's Secretary of Commerce, Averell Harriman announced in 1946: "People in this country are no longer scared of such words as 'planning'...people have accepted the fact that the government has got to plan as well as individuals in this country".[7]

All American capital did benefit but perhaps no group more than the industrial sector. In a speech delivered to the Army Ordinance Association in January 1944 Charles E. Wilson, president of General Electric and the vice executive chairman of the *War Production Board*, called for an "institutionalised war economy" and that every corporation should have a "liaison" representative with the military; binding businesses and the military together in single military-industrial-complex (MIC).[8] This semi-command economy – directed by corporate executives in liaison with military chiefs and paid for by the public – represented a significant shift away from traditional liberal capitalism.

Yet despite enjoying a position of relative power and security unparalleled in human history, *the* single most important challenge facing State Department planners and corporate leaders alike, one that would underpin all aforementioned geopolitical objectives, was *how* to sustain/increase present output levels. With the winding down of the war and declining sales, Washington was haunted by the real fear that systemic over-production/capacity and rising inflation could drag the US back into a depression. As early as 1943, a future Nobel Prize economist warned of the possibility that the US could experience "the greatest period of unemployment and industrial dislocation which any economy had ever faced".[9] The New Deal capital-labour compromise would simply collapse under the strain of class conflict.

Maintaining demand in the post-war period would require, at a minimum, a continued large export surplus and improved access to foreign markets (notably Britain, USSR, and China) as guaranteed under the Lend-Lease programme (1941–45). As Undersecretary of State Dean Acheson (later Truman's Secretary of State) put it to a special Congressional committe in 1944:

> The United States has unlimited creative energy. The important thing is markets. We have got to see that what the country produces is used and is sold under financial arrangements, which make its production possible...You must look to foreign markets.[10]

The future health of the national economy, therefore, was intricately connected to the on-going stability and continuing expansion of the global economy (Harvey's *spatial fix*), tantamount to President Woodrow Wilson's *Open Door*.[11] This, in turn, depended upon the US creating, in the words of Marx, "a world after its own image",[12] exporting the American capitalist model abroad, as it were. In reality, this had long been underway. The social forces emerging out of the US's huge economy of scale were dramatically shaping 'foreign' social relations of production (SROP) in accordance with Harvey's *capitalist logic of power* analysis.

By the end of the First World War, the American vertically integrated corporate model had already replaced the British (family) system of business enterprise as the dominant form of capitalist organisation.[13] But what truly transformed the capitalist world was when these corporations adopted Ford's revolutionary mass production methods and a scientific exploitation of the labour-force. For Gramsci, *Fordism* (or "Americanism") went beyond a shift in SROP; it constituted socio-political regime designed to nurture "a new type of worker and man" who accepted their subordinate, assimilating the corporate ethos in return for concrete benefits. This was achieved, in true hegemonic fashion, with the tempering of "compulsion" (heightened managerial control over the production process and intrusion into workers' private lives) with "persuasion and consent" (the promise of an improved standard of living, a degree of collective bargaining, and high wages). Not only would the latter offset political radicalism but higher wages (at least for the "labour aristocracy"), would help enable workers to purchase the goods they were making, therein helping offset capitalism's perennial over-production problem.[14] Throughout the 1920/30s the huge productivity gains meant Ford's regime was copied by the most important sectors of US industry, marking the emergence of a consumer society.[15]

Global competition meant the basic characteristics of Fordist mass production system – noticeably Taylorism – started to appear in core countries (e.g. UK, Canada, and Australia) and even the USSR (the basis of the Five-Year Plans) either by imitation of American foreign direct investment (FDI). In those countries beset by "antiquated economic and social basis", with a weak bourgeoisie, "Americanisation" could only be achieved by a 'passive revolution' (e.g. Italy under Mussolini).[16] Fordism evidently developed out of the US's unique social history, so its full socio-political regime, social institutions included, remained largely an American phenomenon in the 1940s.

Social forces also colluded to promote 'the American way of life' at the level of 'civil society'. Gramsci noted the American bourgeoisie sought to "impose a network of organisations and movements under its leadership"[17] such as the Rotary Club, and the Young Man's Christian Association (YMCA) to shape intersubjective forms of consciousness and make the world safe for expanding markets and foreign investment opportunities. The American culture industry was also having its influence felt. Nowhere was this more powerfully demonstrated, perhaps, than regards cinema: Hollywood projecting glamourous images of the joys of mass consumption and the American societal model in the most glamorous manner imaginable which, in tandem with a cutting-edge marketing and advertising industry, had a huge effect in stimulating foreign demand for US goods and services.

But these processes, however important, were *ad hoc* and uncoordinated. If American capitalism was going to avoid post-war depression and guarantee market access, and it was vital to launch a new US-centred regime of accumulation and institutionalise world hegemony. As Cox indicated, the best way to do was by setting up international organisations and agencies. It was time to resuscitate Wilson's *one world* liberal internationalism.

As early as the spring of 1943 Council of Foreign Relations directors, Hamilton Armstrong and Normal H. Davis forwarded a plan for a "supranational organisation" to Secretary of State, staunch free trade advocate, Cordell Hull.[18] State Department officials realised they had to sell the new international institutions to policy-makers and public alike as forming part of an ethical and moral crusade for the promotion of global peace.

In July 1943, the US State Department released the first draft of its "Constitution of International Organisation"; paying special attention to classic liberal ideals of 'peace', 'freedom', 'equality', and 'opportunities accessible to all'. In the following months, US officials worked to flesh out the composition of this 'United Nations' adhering to two basic tenets of the League of Nations: (1) a universally accessible organisation, composed of 'equal' sovereign states; and (2) a renewed dedication to peace and security for the resolution of armed conflicts, though this time, crucially, with an enforcer remit. In addition, the proposed entity would recognise 'self-determination' as a guiding principle of international law and a general commitment to human rights protection.

Unlike the League, however, the United Nations (UN) would be hierarchically structured. At the lower level, there would be a 'general assembly' of sovereign states, including many formal colonies, which would constitute an institutionalised forum for dialogue and problem-solving and, it was hoped, facilitate countries' economic integration into an open international economy and draw them away from pre-war ideas of spheres of influence or autarky. Real authority in the UN, however, would lie at the upper level – the directorate – built upon the wartime political-military "Grand Alliance" coalition of the 'big three' (the US, Britain, and the Soviet Union). Roosevelt's idealism was always tempered with a fair degree of realism when it came to power politics.[19]

Though the UN order was officially set up in a two-month period (25th April to 25th June 1945), culminating in its Charter launched at the San Francisco Conference, the fundamental decisions were taken at the Dumbarton Oaks Conference in September 1944 and at Yalta, February 1945.[20] In his classic study of the negotiations at Dumbarton Oaks, Robert Hilderbrand reveals that the main diplomatic challenge for the US was to try and convince the Allies of the benefits of the UN's universal structure when both Britain and the USSR were more interested in maintaining regional arrangements.[21]

London was understandably suspicious of Washington's internationalist ambitions, considering the UN's dual principle of self-determination/sovereign equality of states, like Lend-Lease conditions (see below), as directly aimed at dismantling the British Empire (and especially the British Free Trade Area), and thus undermining its leadership in Europe.[22] Instead, Churchill proposed dividing the UN into regional Councils (Council of the Americas, a Council of Europe, and a Council of East Asia) thus leaving South Asia, the Middle East, and Africa (i.e. most of the British Empire) unregulated.[23] After certain deliberation,[24] FDR rejected the latter's regionalist 'sphere of influence' suggestion as being incompatible with US long-term Open Door objectives.

The Soviet Union's regional concerns, however, were more focused on security, having suffered massive military and civilian deaths at the hands of the Germans, and suspicious of the Allies' reticence to open up a second front until 1944. Any post-war institutional arrangement, Stalin insisted, had to buttress the geopolitical security of the Soviet state. This involved having its 1939 recognised, the establishment of a series of 'buffer' states in Eastern Europe, and Germany neutralised and de-militarised,[25] to offset what it imaged would be a US-dominated Europe.[26]

At the Yalta Conference in February 1945, the basic outlines of the post-war period were laid out and the limits of US globalism were most clearly revealed. The UN would comprise of a Security Council, based on the 'Grand Alliance' but the Soviets would be granted regional security arrangement it demanded in Eastern Europe, reparations from defeated Germany and a veto in the Security Council (where it would be outnumbered by capitalist states). Not only had the Red Army liberated all of Eastern Europe from fascism, but most importantly, the US believed it still needed Soviet cooperation and power to defeat the Japanese and subsequently prevent the re-emergence of Germany or Japan in the post-war world. To clarify any possible doubts the new President, Harry Truman, dispatched his aid Harry Hopkins to Moscow in spring 1945 with the message that: "Poland, Romania. Bulgaria, Czechoslovakia, Austria (sic), Yugoslavia, Latvia, Lithuania, Estonia etc al (re-sic), makes no difference to US interests".[27]

Thus, when 46 countries sent delegates to San Francisco in April 1945 for the establishment of the UN, it was FDR's last Secretary of State, former Director of US Steel and Ford Vice-President, Edward Stettinius who banged out a final agreement with the other Great Powers at his penthouse in the Fairmont Hotel. Article 51 of the UN Charter on self-defence was kept purposefully vague, while the General Assembly would be stripped of any real significant policy-making competence, and power would remain squarely with the Security Council. It was tacitly agreed that the US would exercise hegemony over the Western Hemisphere and Western Europe, while the Soviets would be granted their security belt in Eastern Europe.[28]

Roosevelt's *one world* vision also came under attack from within the US where powerful conservative forces questioned whether such liberal idealism was conducive to US power projection in the post-war capitalist world order (WO). One of the central tenets of the UN, for example, the principle of absolute sovereignty, sat uneasily with Washington's desires to reorganise advanced capitalist states' SROP, form of state (FOS), and eradicate alternative development models. Thanks to WWII, after all, the US now had both the resources and capabilities to intervene wherever it chose. Second, vehemently anti-communist, this conservative 'coalition' harboured deep animosity to the inclusion of the USSR into any global 'community of states'.

The inflection point came with the successful testing of the nuclear bomb in New Mexico on the 16th July 1945. Another beneficiary of wartime military expenditure,[29] the Manhattan Project constituted "a new order in international relations,"[30] shifting the global balance of power dramatically. Truman immediately sought to renegotiate the terms of Yalta and the San Francisco Conference with Stalin. Churchill described Truman as "a changed man" at Potsdam in July 1945, who "told the Russians just where they got on and got off and generally bossed the whole meeting".[31] "From that moment", Churchill told the House of Commons, "our outlook on the future was transformed (...) we were in the presence of a new factor in human affairs, and possessed of powers which were irresistible".[32]

Opposed by most US military chiefs, the decision to drop the bomb on Hiroshima and Nagasaki was taken overwhelmingly for political reasons, to reshape the post-war geo-political WO. First, it would keep the Russians out of Japan, leaving the US as the sole occupying power, affording them absolute freedom to shape the country's reconstruction and base for American hegemony promotion in East Asia; second, Soviet cooperation was no longer required in Europe. Indeed, the nuclear show of strength was the backdrop for Washington to reverse many of the provisions agreed in Yalta with regards to Germany.[33] Anti-communist forces were gathering momentum.

Determined to intervene to support conservative forces in the Greek Civil War Truman acted on Dean Acheson's advice to "scare the hell out of the country"[34] delivering his famously doom-laden eponymous Doctrine speech to Congress on the 12th March 1947. Warning of the imminent dangers of the spread of communism through the Mediterranean, Truman pledged American support for 'free people' everywhere, converting George F. Kennan's 'containment policy' telegram into official State Department, despite the fact that the USSR was financially bankrupt and undergoing a rapid mass demobilisation of the Red Army.[35]

Debates over Washington's *Grand Strategy*[36] had been settled. In the clash between competing 'hegemonic projects' Roosevelt's inclusive liberal internationalist *one-world* vision, and its accompanying emphasis on self-determination, equality of states. and human rights, had lost out to Truman's regionalist *free-world* paradigm, with its stark choice between 'good' (the emancipated) against 'evil' (the enslaved). The 'friend-foe' ('self-radical Other') construction that had proven so successful throughout American history was back with a vengeance. While 19th-century continental expansion was justified as a fight against a national enemy – the Native American Indians – international expansion was now to be justified to US citizens and foreigner alike as a struggle against a global enemy – communism. It was just the Manifest Destiny myth transposed to the worldwide scale.[37]

Just four months later the National Security Act was signed in July 1947, representing a major reconstruction of the military and intelligence agencies. A new Department of Defense (under the Secretary of Defense) was created, while the Joint Chiefs of Staff structure (and Central Intelligence Agency – CIA) was recognised as vital and permanent part of the US foreign policy establishment, formally institutionalised within the National Security Council (which replaced the State-War-Navy Coordinating Committee).

This setting up of *national security state* (NSS) – or "garrison state"[38] – finally launched what American industrial corporations had long been demanding: a *permanent war economy* during peacetime, to stave off declining demand and profits.[39] It was a recognition that the civilian economy by itself would be incapable of generating sufficient national growth (and demand) by itself. Furthermore, the benefits of *military* rather than classic Keynesianism as far as large American capital was concerned, was that it did not 'crowd out' the private sector. A vision shared by hawkish Republicans, military chiefs, and intelligence services.

Ideologically the Cold War left societies with a stark choice. Inside the American-led 'free world' there was liberty, democracy, individual rights, peace, and prosperity; outside there was nothing but dictatorship, coercion, war, and poverty. Thus, though US hegemony was fundamentally expansive, concerned with promoting market access (the Open Door), and helping underwrite a regime of accumulation, it was always justified in narrow security terms as a defensive arrangement to protect national democracies. (Hobbesian) security rather than (Lockean) free trade became *the* ideological touchstone of American hegemony.

The conceptualisation of 'national security' was now limitless, and necessarily expansionist, just like the Frontier Myth it drew upon.[40] In its name, and in true Orwellian style, Washington could justify all manner of foreign military and covert operations abroad and establish its "empire of bases"[41] doted around the world closely matching Yale geostrategist Nicholas J. Spykman's "Rimland Theory" recommendations: world hegemony depended upon exercising military hegemony over the three key areas of wealth creation of Eurasia's 'maritime' rimland – Western Europe, the Middle East, and East Asia.[42]

Taking the 1945 Act of Chapultepec as its prototype,[43] Washington set up a whole series of collective defence arrangements to formalise its politico-military dominance over key regional powers. In terms of the most important centres of capitalism in Eurasia, Western Europe, and Japan, this found its expression in the North Atlantic Treaty Organization (1949) and the US-Japan Mutual Security Treaty (1951). Under these security umbrellas, the US would underwrite the respective regions' political stability and national security (i.e. protect them from the communist threat 'within' and 'without') in return for agreeing American bases on their soil and, tacitly, the abandonment of an independent foreign policy. This regional political alliance strategy represented the definitive blow for the authority of the UN and any dream of liberal universalism.

While American anti-communist discourse was popular with Western European capital – to which communism did genuinely constitute a threat in the immediate post-war period (see below) – the huge disparity between the US productive model and the decimated state of its own meant there was little political support for the Open Door. Apart from reconstruction priorities, Western Europe's developmental programmes were heavily reliant on state planning and macroeconomic management policies designed to prioritise full employment, economic stability, and protectionism. Accordingly, the fundamental objective of American state planners, especially from 1947 onwards, became the rehabilitation and reconstruction of other advanced capitalist states' economies, which given the acute post-war malaise, was enthusiastically received by most European economic and political elites.

But anti-communism was never just about legitimising the international projection of American hegemony and militarisation of the state, it was, first and foremost, about forwarding the class interests of *capital*. In the US, its fundamental utility was to attack and weaken the labour movement which had begun to threaten profit rates. Furthermore, the Roosevelt's New Deal historical bloc (HB) harboured strong isolationist tendencies, most notably amongst the unions, who opposed any international commitments that could jeopardise Keynesian demand management programmes to maintain full employment. It was fundamental to reconstitute the national HB.

Reconstituting the National Historical Bloc

Since the introduction of the National Labor Relations Act of 1935 (commonly known as the Wagner Act), sections of corporate America had launched a counter-offensive to claw back some of the New Deal gains won by the unions. Between 1937 and 1945 they fought and won a long series of legal battles in the Supreme Court to reduce the scope of permitted industrial action. Moreover, wartime was also used by companies to impose wage freezes and extract voluntary no-strike pledges from union heads while they recorded unprecedented profits. But labour did not take this lying down. Unhappy with stagnating wages, the no-strike pledges, working conditions and management-labour relations in general, around 6,770,000 industrial workers took matters into their own hands participating in a record-breaking 14,000 strikes during WWII.[44]

Capital-labour relations became even more fraught in 1946, by which time union membership had hit its all-time high, more than double its pre-WWII rate, representing around a third of all workers.[45] The unions staged a virtual general strike, demanding large wage increases to compensate for lost wartime earnings and the removal of no-strike clauses. The whole country was brought to a halt as workers in the industrial sector (e.g. miners, foundrymen, meat-packers, machinists, auto and electrical appliance workers, etc.) were joined by those in transport, communication, and public sectors (e.g. sailors, railroad workers, the teamsters, the longshoremen, telegraph workers, and teachers, etc.). The US Bureau of Labor Statistics qualified the first six months of 1946 as "the most concentrated period of labor-management strife in the country's history", estimating the number of strikers at around 3 million, rising to 4.6 million for the whole year.[46] Of particular concern to both corporate and union bosses was the increase in wild-cat (unauthorised) industrial action.

The labour movement, the White House maintained, was getting out of hand. Writing in his memoirs Truman explained, "it was clear to me that the time had come for action on the part of the government". After fact-finding boards set up to negotiate with strikers failed, the President authorised the direct seizure of the industries including the railways and the mines, and seeking injunctions against the unions. "We used the weapons that we had at hand in order to fight a rebellion against the government", he clarified. Apart from the United Mine Workers – who were fined $3.5 million – all the workers in the major industries did return to their jobs once their industries were seized, though not without securing an average 18% pay increase first.[47]

This horrified capital. Though under institutionalised Fordism wage rises could actually help bolster aggregate demand, American corporate leaders only thought in terms of mounting production costs. Already they had successfully lobbied the 'conservative coalition' which dominated Congress (made up of Republicans and Southern Democrats) to make sure that Truman's Employment Act (signed on 20th February 1946) only set full employment as an 'objective' rather than a formal commitment, as was originally planned, which represented yet another blow for classic Keynesianism.

With the Congressional elections in November 1946, an alliance between conservative groups launched a backlash against the working class, reviving Woodrow Wilson's *Red Scare* campaign to denounce unions, workers, and independents as 'communists', accusing them of the worst crime imaginable for a public brought up on Manifest Destiny: being *un-American*. The Republicans decided to run their entire campaign on an anti-strike/anti-communist line. "Had enough?" the Republican campaign slogan asked, referring to both the scale of nationwide industrial action as well as Truman's considered the inept handling of it, warning the public that they were now in the midst of a war: "Communism vs. Republicanism".[48] The campaign message and the Republican's pledge to cut organised labour's growing political and industrial power struck a chord with the general public. The Democrats lost control of both the House of Representatives and the Senate to the Republicans; their biggest defeat since 1928.

According to Founding Father, James Madison, foreign and domestic policies anyway were inseparable, and the "means of defence against foreign danger historically have become the instruments of tyranny at home".[49] Just nine days after Truman pledged to support for "free people" everywhere (12th March 1947), the President signed Executive Order 9835 authorising the Federal Employees Loyalty Act. This sought to uncover "disloyal persons" amongst Federal Government employees, sanctioning the dismissal of anyone believed to be conspiring with the Soviet

Union or guilty of so-called "Un-American" behaviour. Truman's Justice Department also instigated a series of prosecutions against alleged communist collaborators, including the famous Rosenberg trials.

Still, the Executive Order 9835 did not go far enough for capital. Arch-conservative Senator Robert A. Taft drafted a bill, the Labor-Management Act – universally referred to as the Taft-Hartley Act – which represented a major revision of the Wagner Act, and the most serious attempt of some 250 bills circulating Congress in 1947, to undermine worker militancy.

Dubbed the 'slave labour bill' by union leaders, the Taft-Hartley Act: prohibited jurisdictional strikes, secondary boycotts, closed-shops, and mass picketing; authorised injunctions for national emergency disputes; prevented unions from directly financing federal candidates in elections; and empowered the President to declare an 80-day "cooling-off period" before strike action could take place. Critically, and what would be one of the opening shots of the Cold War, communists or other radicals were barred from holding union office. Though Truman publicly opposed the bill, forcing the Congress to over-ride his veto, he nonetheless invoked it 12 times during his presidency to discipline unions/resolve labour disputes.

One of the clear objectives of the act was to strengthen the position of union leaders relative to their members, offering them certain institutional benefits while making them liable for not restraining/disciplining radical elements in their midst. By the end of 1947, thanks to the Taft-Hartley Act and a flood of other such legislation enacted by Congress, including the aforementioned National Security Act (which like Wilson's Espionage Act of 1917 introduced measures to monitor and discipline leftists), most unions had adopted a far more conservative position.

The outbreak of the Cold War, as expected, strengthened still further the position of the hawks within the State Department and the national security establishment *per se*. In what is now considered to be *the* official US Cold War statement, the then top-secret National Security Council official planning document, NSC-68, in April 1950, the new strategy of "roll-back" was announced. According to NSC-68, "the cold war is in effect a real war in which the survival of the free world is at stake," and the US had the "responsibility of world leadership" and the need to assert itself everywhere around the world.[50]

The militarisation of the state, of course, extended into American 'civil society', where citizens were to expect "a large measure of sacrifice and discipline" and "asked to give up some of the benefits they have come to associate with their freedoms", notable cutbacks in social programmes. Communism was not just an external threat, it operated *within* American society. In line with James Madison's thesis, NSC-68 declared the need for "just suppression" over institutions within civil society, notably the unions.[51] The CIO[52] underwent a de-radicalisation, beginning with the dismissal of any leaders suspected of being communist sympathisers and extending to the expulsion of militant left-wing unions or those who opposed the international projection of US hegemony and associated granting of Marshall Aid (see below).

But it would not be *all* stick for the lower classes. Ahead of the 1948 elections, Truman announced a series of progressive New Deal-type measures including the proposed repeal of the Taft-Hartley Act, the introduction of national health insurance, a public housing provision, and a civil rights programme which collectively would become known as the "Fair Deal" (set out in his January 1949 State of Union address). Unfortunately, for reformers within the Truman administration, the conservative coalition made sure this "Fair Deal" remained at the purely rhetorical level, except for the Housing Act of 1949.

With the introduction of the Taft-Hartley Act and adherence to US Cold War foreign policy objectives, the American trade union tradition laid to rest any fleeting pretensions it might have harboured of constituting a genuine class movement, especially once tripartite collective bargaining arrangements (involving capital, government, and unions) became fully institutionalised in the early 1950s. It was the Cold War, in essence, that finally stabilised Fordist SROP. Under this modified regime there was a general agreement that capital and labour had mutual interests in: (1) increasing productivity and increasing the standard of living of the workers; and (2) the state should regulate labour and industrial relations. Unions, hence, enjoyed the right to engage in collective negotiations as long as workers accepted their subordinate position within a for-profit capitalist system.

By the late 1940s, most mainstream unions in the US had signed binding contracts curtailing their right to strike in return for guaranteed employment and tangible improvements in their standard of living, and by the early 1950s, almost all industrial union contracts stipulated severe penalties for strikes, which left leaving only corporatist arbitration and mediation methods. In parallel, union leaders were assimilated into elite economic and political circles, enjoying the perks of travel, high wages and expense accounts, becoming became little more than CEOs of 'business unions' – which Gramsci had so vehemently attacked – politically conservative, selling labour at the highest price, while disciplining unruly rank and file.[53] Moreover, given the narrow bipartisan nature of American politics, the Democratic Party knew the union vote was guaranteed, hence having little incentive to shift leftwards.

And, so it was, that industrial unions took their place as subordinate members of the post-war American HB and willing supporters of Washington's declared anti-communist foreign policy agenda. It did not mean the end of sporadic incidents of labour unrest, however. But as in the early 1930s (and Italy in the 1920s), such industrial action would be most effective when unofficial and outside the recognised institutional framework.

Apart from de-radicalising the unions and hence reconstituting the SROP, the anti-communist crusade was also vital in galvanising support for American hegemony amongst the general public, and curtailing isolationist and protectionist preferences, Truman depicted the global 'war on communism' in Jeffersonian terms, as bringing 'good government' to the rest of the world. This legitimation was important because projecting and maintaining American hegemony would be a costly business paid for by a notoriously fiscally-conservative citizenry. The existence of an external threat was pivotal. As Hobsbawm noted: "[i]f America was not safe, then there could be no withdrawal from responsibilities – and rewards – of world leadership, as after the First World War".[54]

Yet ultimately the American post-war national HB could not be constructed *solely* on coercion or communist scapegoating. The key here was the promise of access to unprecedented affluence: "[t]he promise of democracy was that of plenitude".[55] Under collective bargaining arrangements, unionised industrial workers would be able to negotiate rising 'real' wages, linked to productivity growth and/or the cost of living, in addition to New Deal-sanctioned social insurance, pensions, and state aid. The Cold War pledge to labour was that only liberal capitalism could deliver individual rights, prosperity, and a better quality of life. Even Ford, that notoriously vehement anti-union company, accepted tripartism as an integral part of the Cold War American business model which was to be a beacon to the rest of the world:

> Right now the peoples of many nations are faced with a choice between Communism and Democracy…And they are looking to us for help and leadership. They are looking at the promise of individual reward that has stimulated American invention and business enterprise; at American technical progress which has performed miracles of mass production; at American workers free to organize, to bargain collectively with their employers…and constantly increasing real wages for shorter working hours.[56]

On the back of the post-war boom, institutionalised Fordism and a dramatically extended credit system, genuine mass consumer society was born, helping to hold disparate (white) social classes together within the American HB. Despite the fact that 20th-century business concentration had squeezed out many small businesses, reducing many capitalists to salaried employees, these could still be considered middle class, liberals argued, if the category was defined in terms of consumption of hitherto inaccessible goods and services (property) rather than *productive* property. Mass consumption represented the drive to 'democratise desire': a 'good life' based on material abundance available to all. It was in essence, the fulfilment of the American Dream,[57] a promise that would remain central to US hegemony.

So, by the late 1940s, the fundamental elements of a true HB were in place. Productive capital and moderate labour were institutionalised in corporatist structures within a Fordist accumulation strategy (SROP) and particular FOS – a *welfare-warfare* state. Holding the HB together was a unique American hegemonic culture based on liberalism, consumerism, and anti-communism. Its continual reproduction required access to foreign markets, (close to) full employment and sustainable high growth which in turn depended on the US exporting its socio-economic model abroad.

The essence of American post-war hegemony, in short, was driven by social forces emerging out of its evolving HB who attempted to realign the 'free world', if not exactly in its own image, then at least conducive to its interests. This necessary involved leading foreign capital into a new dynamic period of sustained accumulation.

Embedding American Hegemony in the European Core

According to Paul Nitze, assistant to Truman's Secretary of State, Dean Acheson, American foreign policy in the late 1940s was dominated by the belief that US interests and security had become "directly dependent on the creation and maintenance of some form of world order compatible with our continued development as the kind of nation we are."[58] Truman's abandonment of Roosevelt's 'one worldism' did not in any way imply the eschewing of international organisations *per se*, on the contrary, those geared to promoting the new liberal economic order (the Open Door) played a vital role in helping restructure other capitalist countries' SROP and FOS, compatible with Cox's analysis discussed in Chapter 1. The construction of this new, American-centred WO was completed, according to Nitze, by 1953.

Nominally this process of international institution-building was carried out within the context of the UN. Washington's blueprint for a global trading and financial system had been presented at Bretton Woods in July 1944, out of which were born: (1) the ill-fated International Trade Organisation (ITO) – a multilateral free trade regime; (2) the International Monetary Fund (IMF) – promoting monetary policy and currency convertibility; and (3) International Bank for Reconstruction and Development – commonly referred to as the World Bank, and charged with offering aid for reconstruction and balance of payment (BOP) problems.

The US elite remained divided regarding the exact nature of the post-war trade and monetary system, however. On the one hand, the State Department backed by Wall Street prioritised trade liberalisation, capital movement, and greater international monetary/fiscal discipline (i.e. a return to the gold standard). On the other hand, the Treasury Department and the New Deal coalition – the 'planners' – insisted on preserving a directing role for the state in the economy. Furthermore, there were many powerful voices in the Congress and even in the executive that remained wary of substantial financial commitments by the US to an institution over which it would not have full discretionary control.

British economist John M. Keynes believed that a compromise was possible between these two positions, proposing a 'Clearing Union' which while preserving national autonomy in economic policy (favoured by Europe and the Treasury Department) committed states to international cooperation arrangements, both in the creation of credit and in the avoidance of measures that would export inflation (reflecting the interests of Wall Street and the City of London). Moreover, Keynes' Clearing Union offered a solution to the perennial problem of BOP disequilibria by obliging not just the deficit countries, but also the surplus countries, to adjust their exchange rates. In addition, countries could settle outstanding balances or conduct international trade with a new supranational currency – *bancor* – whose value would be based on a basket of the major currencies.

Keynes' final plans were backed by Britain, Europe, the Commonwealth, and Latin America. Anticipating major trade surpluses, any forced revaluation of the dollar was unacceptable to Washington, however. US Treasury Department negotiator Dexter White rejected Keynes' proposal out of hand "we have been perfectly adamant on that point. We have taken the position of no, on that".[59] When the IMF was finally put into place in March 1946, it was not Keynes's 'internationalist' scheme that prevailed but White's 'hegemonic' version in which exchange rates were to be fixed onto the dollar (rather than bancor), convertible into gold at a fixed price ($35 per ounce); and loans from the Fund were made conditional upon the adoption of national economic policies facilitating a return to payments equilibrium. Nevertheless, some concessions were made to both Keynesians and Wall Street/the City.

First, aware that countries had low reserves of gold and foreign exchange and the currency convertibility was still a while off, the US agreed to introduce capital controls without which welfare-states were unsustainable. Keynesian economic theory, after, was all based on a relatively closed economy, where trade was considered a 'leakage' and free capital movement disruptive of governmental control of savings, investment, interest rates, and ultimately full employment.[60]

Second, although Wall Street and the City favoured returning to the gold standard, hegemonic ambitions and practicalities[61] induced the Treasury to adopt the more flexible (and as it turned out highly profitable) dollar-gold standard, which would, in principal, prevent excessive dollar printing while at the same time allow deficit countries to settle international balances in 'greenbacks'. Obviously, this meant that despite aforementioned restrictions on general capital flow, the US itself would have to allow a sufficient flow of dollars abroad to supply global *liquidity* (i.e. run a BOP deficit) in order to function as the global reserve currency, but at the same time would must maintain *confidence* in the greenback (i.e. run a BOP surplus). This quandary was known as *Triffin's Dilemma*.[62]

The agreement on global free trade was an even more complex issue. The proposed ITO aimed to regulate and reduce restrictions on international trade, while establishing global rules on tariffs, trade preferences, quantitative restrictions, subsidies, and raw material price agreements.[63] It drew upon two sources: the 1934 *Reciprocal Trade Agreements Act* and its famed "most-favoured nation" clause; and Article VII of the wartime Lend-Lease agreements with the Allies, which stipulated that any state receiving aid had to agree "to the elimination of all forms of discriminatory treatment in international commerce, and to the reduction of tariffs and other trade barriers".[64]

With regards to the rest of the capitalist world, the main concern centred on the timing and extent of liberalisation given the massive productive capacity of American manufacturing and agricultural sectors.[65] The US government ceded to European demands that trade liberalisation be postponed in the short term so as not to undermine domestic reconstruction exigencies.[66] In addition, and to the annoyance of Washington countries such as Britain and France still maintained preferential trade arrangements with their soon to be ex-colonies. Less developed countries too demanded trade concessions to aid development programmes.

Ironically, and despite government lobbying, American capital remained ambivalent on the virtues of full trade liberalisation. Apart from high-profile internationally orientated corporations, most US firms were domestically based and opposed to opening themselves up to foreign competition. Furthermore, even those firms that were export-driven remained sceptical that the ITO could guarantee foreign market access during the reconstruction period.[67] Domestic political concerns over the loss of national sovereignty and tensions between the executive and the Congress over who executed political competence in the area meant a comprehensive multilateral trade agreement was doomed.

Nevertheless, the American elite did agree that reciprocity and non-discrimination in trade relations could form a foundation for mutual benefits from international trade in a climate of on-going liberalisation.[68] These basic principles were generally acceptable to the rest of the world provided they were permitted certain opt-outs and a reasonable transition period to open up with domestic objectives and national sovereignty. Thus, the trade pillar of Bretton Woods was abandoned to be replaced by a watered down, derivative version – the General Agreement on Tariffs and Trade (GATT) – a set of rules and a sufficient basis for intergovernmental cooperation on trade. The first multilateral round under GATT took place in Geneva 1947.

But these trade debates were largely academic, at least in the short term. The extent of war-damage, the state of public finances, negative trade balances, and the desperate need for dollars, meant that no country could seriously contemplate making their currencies freely convertible, let alone liberalise trade. With the US committed to high levels of exports there seemed a little possibility that the so-called 'dollar shortage' would be solved any time soon. British Chancellor of the Exchequer, Hugh Dalton, complained in 1947:

> The Americans have half the total income of the world, but won't spend it in buying other people's goods or lending it or giving it away on any sufficient scale. The Fund and the Bank still do nothing. How soon will this dollar shortage become a general crisis?[69]

One other problem worrying the post-war European elite, eluded to above, was of a more political nature. When Churchill gave his famous "Iron Curtain" speech at Fulton, Missouri, March 1946, he was not just denouncing Soviet continental expansionism or upping the ante to secure Britain a huge post-war loan from Washington,[70] but expressing genuine class concern over the rising support for far-left political parties across Europe, markedly in West Germany, Italy, and France, a situation that would be magnified following the terrible harvest and appalling winter of 1946/47.

All Western European governments, ranging from the social democrat Left to the conservative Right, were vehemently anti-socialist/communist, and urged Washington to forward aid to help economic recovery and to stem this leftward shift. Truman's 'Doctrine' speech constituted the US's reply:

> [t]he seeds of totalitarian regimes are nurtured by misery and want. They spread and grow in the evil soil of poverty and strife. They reach their full growth when the hope of people for a better life has died. We must keep that hope alive.[71]

Less than three months later the Marshall Aid (or officially, the European Recovery Program) was announced.

In his speech at Harvard University, 5th June 1947, US Secretary of State, George Marshall, declared that "the US should do whatever is able to do to assist in the return of normal economic health to the world without which there can be no political stability and no assured peace", and while stressing that it was "not directed against any country, but against hunger and poverty, desperation and chaos" he set as its aim the establishment of "free institutions."[72] Drawing on a Council for Foreign Relations study entitled "Reconstruction in Western Europe", co-written by New York Lawyer, Charles Spofford and Chase Manhattan's David Rockefeller, the Marshall Plan, on a basic level, was an example of international Keynesian stimulation, designed to counter the leftward shift in European politics.

When addressing American business Marshall was more candid, justifying the foreign 'pump-priming' programme in more national self-interested terms: either as a way for the US to get rid of its present surplus production, or the need to build up future markets for its exports. Marshall told *US News*: "The real idea behind the program, thus, is that the United States, to prevent depression at home, must put up the dollars that it will take to prevent a collapse abroad".[73] If the Bretton Woods system was going to be a success, and the 'greenback' converted into the global currency/main form of global *liquidity*, it was vital that the US redistribute funds to resolve the aforementioned 'dollar shortage'. Not only would this help European economies recover and help curb political radicalism, but it would also offset US over-production by creating stable guaranteed markets abroad. The Marshall Plan other key long-term ambitions.

The Truman administration had the very real worry that European elites could, at any time, actually eschew American hegemonic multilateralism, restrict international trade and investment and opt instead for national/autarkic capitalism. Speaking in January 1948 Marshall urged decisive action: "it is idle to think that a Europe left to its own efforts in these serious problems of recovery would remain open to American business in the same way that we have known it in the past".[74] Indeed, excepting some sectors of large capital and high finance, the majority of European business leaders, politicians, state officials were sceptical about free trade, favouring national economic autonomy (which included preferential trade with their ex-colonies). As in the US, WWII vindicated the role of the state in the accumulation process, helping the private sector in numerous ways: undertaking those tasks not considered profitable; offering financial aid (e.g. subsidies, price support, tax reductions), and even nationalising key industries (e.g. coal, steel, automobiles), as in Britain, France, Italy.

The American New Deal FOS had its parallel in the European post-war *national welfare-state*. Although each had its own version, most Western European countries adhered to some variant of Keynesianism (using fiscal and monetary policy to manage aggregate demand and promote reasonably full employment and economic growth), the existence of a welfare state,[75] with trade unions institutionalised in collective bargaining arrangements, sometimes extending to the state (tripartite consultations). While the state in Europe remained capitalist, and therefore concerned with capital accumulation, the greater complex of its social history (e.g. the strength of the Left) meant market activity was embedded in a different socio-politico-judicial framework than in the US. The main objective of these welfare-nationalist states was to try to enhance the power of national capital and preserve some of the social commitments required for the reproduction of their respective HB, though always located within competitive global capitalist economy characterised by uneven development. The challenge for Washington was how to get European countries to adjust their economies so as to be compatible with the American capitalist model and hence US hegemony.

This is where the Marshall Plan comes in again. Its long-term objective was to provide the sufficient funds (a total of $13 billion of grants and low-interest loans), technological assistance, and incentives to stimulate reconstruction and enable state elites to modify their respective SROP, HB, and FOS, in line with the Bretton Woods framework. It was, in Gramscian terms, essentially a Europe-wide *passive revolution*. The US had already a template to follow. Under the terms of the Lend-Lease and Anglo-American Loan Agreement, Washington had tied aid to London to the latter meeting a series of tough conditions: high-interest rates, scrapping of import controls, dismantling its imperial preference system, and full convertibility of sterling. Similarly, Marshall Aid would only be given to countries that adhered to American stipulations and committed to an open and expanding capitalist world economy (the Open Door).

Following established practice, the first step was to incorporate countries into a multilateral institutional framework.[76] Hence, to receive funds from the European Recovery Plan the 17 participating countries had to first integrate into the newly formed Organisation of European Economic Cooperation (OEEC)[77] and negotiate with each other, and then collectively with the US, rather than on a bilateral basis. In accordance with Cox's international organisation analysis, membership of the OEEC would bestow benefits but at the same time delimit political options. Vital aid would be forthcoming in return for governments agreeing on a series of measures compatible with American capitalist model and the social transformation underway stateside. These measures included reducing trade barriers on goods and services *en route* to multilateral trading steps towards trade liberalisation; meeting Bretton Wood's monetary policy objectives (e.g. balancing budgets, possible devaluations, controlling inflation by limiting wage increases); and only permitting moderate (i.e. not communist or socialist) trade unions to form part of tripartite industrial relations negotiations.[78]

The Marshall Plan had huge symbolic value for US hegemony, reinforcing its *intellectual and moral leadership* over the European core. It was also largely successful in alleviating short-term resource shortages, opening markets for American businesses hit by chronic over-capacity, and setting in motion the desired social transformation. Unfortunately, it did not have much effect on the continent's economic growth, which remained sluggish,[79] nor did it resolve the 'dollar shortage' since so few dollars actually crossed the Atlantic.[80]

As Keynes had warned, any country printing the global reserve currency would have to run a large BOP deficit to stimulate global demand and assure international liquidity, but the US trade surplus with rest of the world showed little sign of relenting.

The turning point came with the heightening of Cold War tensions in 1949, following the proclamation of the People's Republic of China (PRC). In the context of the Korean War, the US launched a massive rearmament programme, almost quadrupling its military budget from $12.2 billion in 1951 to $46.3 billion in 1954 (constituting an astounding 70% of total federal expenditure).[81] It was only after Washington international Keynesianism (Marshall Plan) to international *military* Keynesianism – injected unprecedented liquidity into the global economy via direct military expenditure abroad and military aid to governments – that industrial production really took off in advanced capital countries and the 'dollar shortage' was reversed. It is no coincidence, Giovanni Arrighi notes that the so-called 'Golden Age of Capitalism' (1950 and 1973) coincides directly with the beginning and end of the Korean War and Vietnam War, respectively.[82]

No country benefitted more economically from this pump-priming than Japan, converted into the US's industrial base for both conflicts. Following the 'loss' of China, Tokyo became Washington's key ally in East Asia (the extreme of Spykman's Rimland), whose security it underwrote in return for permanent military bases and direction of its foreign policy. Due to the exigencies of rapid industrialisation Japan was permitted a higher degree of protectionism, restrictions on FDI, and state intervention than would be tolerated elsewhere, which included resuscitating the imperial-age vertically structured *zaibatsu* conglomerates in the form of *keiretsu* corporations. This mix of US military spending, protectionism, and preferential trade access to the American market would prove hugely successful[83] and provide a prototype developmental model to follow for other East Asian countries (see Chapter 3).

The final and definitive push in reconstituting Europe's SROP, HB, and accompanying FOS, however, would only take place with the large-scale global expansion of the American Fordist multidivisional administrative corporation.

Concerned about over-production and inflationary pressure, the Treasury Department had long been offering American businesses generous fiscal incentives to 'go global', but the latter were reticent, given the political instability, fragmentary nature, and size of foreign markets compared to the US. From the early 1950s, American multinational corporations (MNCs) did start to set up branches in Europe. The key here was the role of US institutions, notably the OEEC, which pushed European reconciliation and cooperation and lowered tariff barriers across the region, and NATO, which guaranteed their political and military protection.

The 'new American invasion' of Europe began in earnest, however, following the launching of regional integration projects, namely the European Coal and Steel Community (Treaty of Paris, 1952), but above all and the European Economic Community (Treaty of Rome, 1957), which dovetailed perfectly with Washington's desire to revoke Yalta and re-industrialise and re-integrate West Germany back into Europe.[84] The granting of full currency convertibility in 1958 and the adoption of the Code of Liberalisation of Capital Movements (CLCM)[85] by the newly enlarged OEEC (the OECD) in 1961, saw US FDI in the region rise from $1.7 billion in 1950 to $24.5 billion in 1970.[86] The arrival of capital-intensive industries and service providers (e.g. banks, law firms, advertising agencies, and consultancies) drew Europe further into American circuits of capital, compelling companies to restructure their business model along similar lines. US hegemony was always about 'creating a world in our image': getting the rest of the capitalist world to emulate your corporate model and associated business culture (e.g. management and accounting practices) was an essential part of that.

As economic growth increased, the post-war leftward thrust in European politics was stemmed. The boom of the 1950s was presided over, almost everywhere, by centre-right governments, reflecting the internal restructuring of countries' FOS (moving away from welfare-nationalist states towards more internationally orientated liberal states). This did not mean state planning or Keynesian demand management were abandoned but states now formed part of regional security alliances and their economies were more dependent on international trade and access to foreign resources.

Nominally, all the main social actors shared the same industrial paradigm: rising production, growing foreign trade, full employment, industrialisation, and modernisation involving government control and management of mixed economies. Under institutionalised tripartite collective bargaining arrangements all could be 'winners', it seemed: capital had its right to healthy profits recognised; privileged institutionalised industrial labour could enjoy production-related wage increases and fringe benefits, such as a welfare state; while the government got to guarantee capitalist accumulation *and* social stability via macro-economic demand management programmes, albeit within the constraints of a dynamic global economy. Moderate unions were led by conservative leaders well-versed in the importance of BOP considerations and the need to keep export industries internationally competitive.[87]

During the reconstruction period, the Bretton Woods objectives of trade liberalisation, currency convertibility, and BOP correction were adhered to only to the extent they were compatible with the Keynesian states' domestic commitments and macroeconomic management programmes, but as Cox indicated in Chapter 1 from the 1950s this IOS process gathered pace, reinforced by emergence of transnational economic structures, increased international trade, and a growing web of international economic interdependence amongst domestic firms (Cox's IOP).

This reciprocal relationship would find its political expression, as we saw in Chapter 1, in a modification of core countries' FOS (e.g. giving pride of place to the most internationalised branches of state government and bureaucracies), as they became "part of a larger and more complex political structure that is the counterpart to international production".[88] Leo Panitch and Sam Gindin summarised the change as "a state's acceptance of responsibility for managing its own domestic capitalist order in [sic] that contributes to managing the international capitalist order."[89] A good example of this how, from the 1960s, the advanced capitalist economies were also expected to engage in mutual consultation and criticism of each other's national monetary and trade policies in the different international organisation they were party to.

By the mid-1960s US hegemony was at its height. As reiterated throughout this chapter, the basis of American 'intellectual and moral leadership' as far as the capitalist class in the core were concerned, political stability and security guarantees aside, was Washington's capacity to underwrite a profitable regime of accumulation, which in this case involved privileged and non-reciprocal access to the US's vast and highly lucrative domestic market and war-time technology (e.g. electronics, jet aircrafts). American corporations, meanwhile, were now free to tap into markets and resources throughout Western Europe, Latin America, East Asia, and the Middle East, described by Dwight Eisenhower as the richest and most "strategically important area in the world."[90]

Under *Pax Americana*, advanced capitalist countries experienced a huge post-war boom between 1950 and 1973, a *belle époque* reflected in rapid industrialisation, record high rates of economic growth (with average annual increases in GDP standing at 4.9% in the 1950s and 1960s, compared to 2.6% for 1870–1913 and 1.9% for 1913–50) and soaring global trade (increasing on average, by 6% p.a. between 1948 and 1960, and by 8% p.a. between 1960 and 1973).[91] American cultural hegemony, transmitted through the hegemonic apparatus, found its expressions in multiple forms and mediums, especially potent in popular culture (e.g. film, television, music, theatre, literature, and fashion). Overwhelmingly, these cultural expressions celebrated (or at least reflected) the American market-place society of which the most potent image was of Eisenhower's "Consumers' Republic": a middle-class of material opulence and promise of social advancement and outward trappings of success: house, cars, refrigerators, TVs, telephones, and other consumer durables. For subaltern classes in the core capitalist countries, US's intellectual and moral legitimacy was indirect, dependent on increased standards of living, near full employment, and consumption of opportunities.

The reality, of course, was never so benign. Consistent with Gramsci's conceptualisation of hegemony, the US would never actually abandon recourse to *coercion* in order to persuade or subjugate both allied and antagonistic groups alike, be it at home or abroad. The militarisation of the American state not only afforded the MIC a level of economic and political power that even out-going president, Eisenhower saw fit to censure,[92] but conforming to Madison's truism it was increasingly projected into domestic 'civil society'. The Senate Select-Committee's Report of 1976, the so-called *Church Committee Report*,[93] indicated the extent to which the NSS, via the various intelligence agencies, used anti-communism as an ideological smokescreen to undermine civil liberties of a wide cross-section of political and social groups. 'Subversive' domestic elements, including civil rights/black activists (notably Martin Luther King, Malcolm X, the Black Panthers), leftists, 'rebel rousers', anti-war demonstrators, or feminists were all subjected to heavy surveillance operations and multiple 'dirty trick' campaigns to soil their public image.[94]

And not all capitalist countries fell under the spell of US hegemony. At the Bandung Conference, a group of newly decolonised "Third World" countries opted-out of the Cold War framework, opting for state-driven national economic policies – state import substitution industrialisation – under a different FOS – neo-mercantilist developmental state – to lead to a 'catch up' with the West and liberate themselves from 'free trade imperialism' and 'colonial oppression'.

Ultimately, Pax Americana would not work for everyone, nor would the US-led regime of accumulation bring an end to the class conflict or resolve the internal contradictions of capitalism. American hegemony was entering a period of crisis and restructuring, before emerging into a different form.

Notes

1 Dallek (1979), p. 9.
2 Like Woodrow Wilson before him Franklin D. Roosevelt knew the importance of entering WWII, however late, to "create the geopolitical basis for a post-war world order that they would both build and lead". McCormick (1995), p. 33. On this point, see also Hull (1948) and Kolko (1968).
3 Sherry (1977), p. 202.
4 Daggett (2010), p. 2.
5 van der Wee (1987), p. 30.
6 Hobsbawm (1994), p. 258, p. 241.
7 Maier (1987), p. 129.
8 Bellamy Foster *et al.* (2008)
9 Samuelson (1942), p. 51.
10 Cited in Williams (1959), pp. 235–6.
11 Frustrated by European colonial domination of foreign markets (especially China), President Wilson demanded equal access for American corporations and freedom of navigation of the seas: the 'Open Door'.
12 Marx & Engels (1992), p. 7.
13 See Arrighi *et al.* (1999), pp. 115–34. Examples include the New York Central Railroad, Union Pacific, Standard Oil, the Carnegie Steel Company, General Electric, Eastman Kodak, American Bell Telephone Company, International Harvester, Singer, Edison, Otis Elevator.
14 Gramsci (1971), pp. 302–9.
15 The Fordist production also created new 'white collar' occupations such as industrial managers, engineers, financial advisers, administrative and clerical workers, who thanks to a dramatic expansion of the credit system

('buy now, pay later'), were able not only to purchase the latest range of cars, electrical goods and domestic appliances. For more on Fordism, see Rupert (1995, 2000).

16 Gramsci (1971). p. 317.
17 Gramsci (1971), p. 286.
18 Burnett & Games (2005), p. 106.
19 Earlier in his Presidency FDR had authorised military and economic intervention in Mexico, Cuba, Nicaragua, and Haiti (whose constitution he even claimed to have written) to restructure unfriendly regimes.
20 Schlesinger (2003). According to Schlesinger, the creation of the UN was "from the beginning, a project of the United States, devised by the State Department, expertly guided by two hands-on Presidents, and propelled by US power". Ibid., p. 174.
21 Hilderbrand (1990).
22 According to Gabriel Kolko, Churchill was also heavily critical of the US for nominating its client-state China, under Chiang Kai-Shek, onto the UN directorate. Kolko (1968), pp. 266–7. Britain countered by forwarding France's candidacy, and even proposing the UK aid the latter's ailing Empire in Indochina to prevent American expansionism in Asia.
23 Hull (1948), vol. ii, p. 1640.
24 Initially, this was attractive to the US since it did not rule out intervention at both ends of Eurasia – e.g. Europe (Germany, bases on the Med) or East Asia (Japan, Korea, Formosa) – and helped them retain their control over Central and South America.
25 Dallek (1979), p. 351.
26 Hilderbrand (1990), p. 215.
27 Schlesinger (2003), p. 213, xvii.
28 Isaacson & Thomas (1986), pp. 275–6.
29 It represented the largest and most costly scientific-industrial project to date, unthinkable in peacetime, where such high public expenditure on new, extremely risky, the military technology could hardly be justified.
30 Hewlett & Anderson (1962), p. 276.
31 Alperovitz (1985), p. 199.
32 Churchill (1945).
33 Despite the fiery rhetoric, Washington generally did respect the Soviet's 'sphere of influence' in East Europe as agreed at Yalta, never intervening to support the various democratic forces/popular uprisings that took place in Czechoslovakia, East Berlin, Hungary, Poland etc., throughout the Cold War.
34 Milhalkanin (2004), p. 9.
35 Soviet post-war troop demobilisation occurred almost as quickly as the US. The Red Army was reduced from its peak in 1945 of around 11.3 million soldiers to 2.8 million by late 1948. Quoted in Odem (1998), p. 39.
36 Understood as a sufficiently coherent unifying ideological doctrine to assure long-term American 'intellectual and moral leadership'.
37 In an Editorial in *The New York Morning News* (27th December 1845) John L. O' Sullivan famously declared "the right of our manifest destiny to overspread and to possess the whole of the continent which Providence has given us for the development of the great experiment of Liberty and federated self-government entrusted in us". Quoted in McCrisken (2002), p. 68.
38 Lasswell (1941), pp. 456–68.
39 Melman (1974).
40 Turner (1983).
41 Johnson (2004), pp. 151–85.
42 Spykman (1944).

43 This later became the Treaty of Rio (1947). Since 1940, under Nelson Rockefeller, the Co-ordinator of Inter-American Affairs (later promoted to Assistant Secretary of State for Latin American Affairs), the US had signed a series of military-security alliance with Latin American governments committing itself to defend them from 'external aggression' (read, 'internal opposition'), in return for giving American corporations such as Standard Oil, Guggenheim, General Electric, AT & T and United Fruit, access to resources and markets. Eisenhower's Secretary of State, John Foster Dulles, an earlier critic of Rockefeller recognised the "incalculable value" of the latter's intervention, admitting to Rockefeller that, "If you fellows hadn't done it, we might never have had NATO". See Collier & Horowitz (1976), pp. 230–6, p. 174.

44 Zinn (2005), p. 390.

45 Mayer (2004), Figure 1.

46 Quoted in Siedman (1953), p. 235, p. 1.

47 Truman (1955), p. 498, 504.

48 One is reminded here of Theodore (Teddy) Roosevelt's reaction to rising industrial action and social unrest. A year before the outbreak of the Spanish-American War Roosevelt confessed to his friend: "In strict confidence...I should welcome almost any war, for I think this country needs one". Quoted in Rorabaugh et al. (2004), p. 449.

49 Barry (2011), p. 300.

50 Truman (1950).

51 Truman (1950).

52 The CIO would merge with the American Federation of Labor (AFL) to form the AFL-CIO in 1955.

53 Rupert (2000), p. 179.

54 Hobsbawm (1994), p. 235.

55 Zunz (1998), p. 75.

56 Ford Motor Company, quoted Rupert (1995), pp. 160–1.

57 *The* dominant American liberal myth which maintained that opportunities were available to all, independent of social origins: any poor immigrant settler could, through hard work, diligence, creativity could become wealthy. A perennial narrative in American public life, given its modern twist by renowned historian James Truslow Adams his book *The Epic of America* (1931).

58 Nitze (1959).

59 Skidelsky (2004), p. 672.

60 Later, in the 1960s, two IMF economists developed the Mundell-Fleming model which confirmed the *trilemma*. This asserted that governments and central banks overseeing open economies could not simultaneously: (1) fixed exchange rates; (2) independence in monetary policy, and (3) capital mobility. Only the two of these objectives were possible at the same time, the third necessarily undermining one of the other. Emphasis on free trade, exchange rate stability/convertibility and concessions to Keynesianism (point ii.) meant capital movements had to be sacrificed.

61 As Jan Toporowski explains: "Central banks without gold reserves could not return to the gold standard, and over four-fifths of the gold outside the Soviet Union was in the United States." Quoted in Saad-Filho & Johnston (2005), p. 107.

62 Triffin (1960).

63 Spero & Hart (1997), p. 50.

64 Notter (1949).

65 In the post-war period it has been estimated that 1/3 of all exports from major high-income countries came from the US. Kenwood & Lougheed (1992), p. 289.

66 Gardner (1981).

67 The US was especially sceptical about the commitment of the British to dismantle the imperial preference system. Gardner (1981), pp. 372–80.
68 Curzon & Curzon (1976), pp. 143–67.
69 Quoted in Wood (1986), p. 33.
70 The *Anglo-American Loan Agreement* was signed in July 1946 with the final payment made in December 2006.
71 Truman (1947).
72 Jay (2005), p. 243.
73 Quoted in Wood (1986), p. 36.
74 Marshall (1948).
75 Between 1946 and 1948, for example, Britain's Labour Party introduced a universal welfare system including the National Health Service, unemployment benefit, public pensions, and public education paid for by an institutionalised progressive taxation and redistributive policies.
76 Spero & Hart (1997), p. 55.
77 In 1960, the OEEC as renamed OECD and expanded to include the US, Canada, and Japan; all the major capitalist countries thereby reasserting their commitments to the new WO.
78 Hogan (1987), pp. 42–5.
79 De Long & Eichengreen (1993), pp. 189–230.
80 Receipt of Marshall Aid was largely tied to the purchase of American goods. In practice, this involved the US government paying American producers to ship the goods to Europe to be bought in local currencies.
81 Cox & Skidmore-Hess (1999), pp. 68–9.
82 Arrighi (2005), p. 15.
83 Japan's manufacturing output double from 1949 to 1953, reaching its peak growth level (14.6% p.a.) during 1966–70. Hobsbawm (1994), p. 276.
84 Within the US state structure, the State and Defense Departments, respectively, favoured plans for European integration, while the Commerce Department voiced its opposition.
85 The CLCM also forbade governments from discriminating against foreign corporations, offering them the same level of protection as their national counterparts.
86 Chandler (1978), pp. 127–8.
87 The role Keynesianism and tripartite corporatism played in guaranteeing both economic development and class harmony was celebrated in key "common-sense" texts such as Anthony Crosland's *The Future of Socialism*; J.K. Galbraith's *The Affluent Society*; Gunnar Myrdal's *Beyond the Welfare State*; and Daniel Bell's *The End of Ideology*.
88 Cox (1987), pp. 253–4.
89 Panitch & Gindin (2004), p. 42.
90 Cited in Spiegel (1985), p. 52.
91 Hugill (1995), p. 293, 286.
92 In his *Farewell Address* on the 17 January 1961 Eisenhower warned:

> The conjunction of an immense military establishment and a huge arms industry is new in the American experience. The total influence – economic, political, and even spiritual – is in every city, every state house, and every office of the federal government...In the councils of government we must guard against the acquisition of unwarranted influence, whether sought or unsought, by the military-industrial complex.
>
> Eisenhower (1961)

93 Created on 27th January 1975 by the Senate in wake of the Watergate scandal, the 11-member select committee (The Church Committee) with a supporting

staff of 150 was given the task of investigating the role of the intelligence services. Gaining access to hundreds of classified documents and interviewing 800 individuals and carried out 250 executive and 21 public hearings, the Church Committee published its 14-volume report in May 1976. See AARC Public Digital Library (1976).

94 According to the Church Committee, one of the intelligence services favoured tactics to discredit a 'subversive' activist was to use "cooperative new media sources" to place completely false stories in the press/TV/radio. The Report also acknowledged that by 1975 the FBI headquarters alone housed around half a million intelligence files on its nationals. Yet despite the 500,000 separate investigations carried out by the FBI between 1960 and 1974 on 'subversive' persons and groups not a single one was prosecuted after 1957. For its part the CIA opened and photographed the contents of nearly 250,000 first class letters between 1953 and 1973, producing a computer index of 1.5 million names, See AARC Public Digital Library (1976) "Book II: Intelligence Activities and the Rights of Americans", pp. 6, 16, 19.

Bibliography

AARC Public Digital Library (1976), "The Church Committee Reports" (available online at www.aarclibrary.org).

Alperovitz, G. (1985), *Atomic Diplomacy*, New York: Penguin.

Arrighi, G. (2005), "Hegemony Unravelling-II", *New Left Review*, 33, 23–80.

Arrighi, G., Barr, K. & Hisaeda, S. (1999), "The Transformation of the Business Enterprise", in Arrighi, G. and Silver, B. (eds.), *Chaos and Governance in the Modern System*, Minneapolis: University of Minnesota Press.

Barry, J.C. (2011), "Empire as a Gated Community: Politics of an American Strategic Metaphor", *Global Society*, 25, no. 3, 287–309.

Bellamy Foster, J., Holleman, H. & McChesney, R.W. (2008), "The US Imperial Triangle and Military Spending", *Monthly Review*, 60, no. 5 (available at monthlyreview.org).

Burnett, T. & Games, A. (2005), *Who Really Runs the World?* London: Conspiracy Books.

Chandler, A.D. (1978), "The United States: Evolution of Enterprise", in Mathias, P. and Postman, M.M. (eds.), *The Cambridge Economic History of Europe*, Vol. 7, part 2, Cambridge: Cambridge University Press.

Churchill, W. (1945), "Where Should We Fear For Our Future?" Speech delivered in the House of Commons, London, 16th August, *The Churchill Society* (available online at www.churchill-society-london.org.uk).

Collier, P. & Horowitz, D. (1976), *The Rockefellers, An American Dynasty*, New York: Henry Holt & Co.

Cox, R.W. (1987), *Production, Power, and World Order: Social Forces in the Making of History*, New York: Columbia University Press.

Cox, R.W. & Skidmore-Hess. D. (1999), *U.S. Politics & the Global Economy: Corporate Power, Conservative Shift*, London: Lynne Reinner Publishers, Inc.

Curzon, G. & Curzon, V. (1976), "The Management of Trade Relations in the GATT", in Shonfield, A. (ed.), *International Economic Relations of the Western World 1959–1971, Politics and Trade*, Vol. 1, Oxford: Oxford University Press.

Daggett, S. (2010), "Costs of Major U.S. Wars", *Congressional Research Service*, 29th June (available online at fas.org).

Dallek, R. (1979), *Franklin D. Roosevelt and American Foreign Policy, 1932–1945*, New York: Oxford University Press.

De Long, J.B. & Eichengreen, B. (1993), "The Marshall Plan: History's Most Successful Structural Adjustment Program", in Dornbusch, R. *et al.* (eds.): *Postwar Economic Reconstruction and Lessons for the East Today*, Cambridge: MIT Press.

Eisenhower, D.D. (1961), "Presidential Speech Archive: Dwight Eisenhower, Farewell Address (17th January) *Miller Center: University of Virginia*" (available online on millercenter.org).

Gardner, R. (1981), *Sterling-Dollar Diplomacy* in *Current perspective*, New York: Columbia University Press.

Gramsci, A. (1971), *Selections from the Prison Notebooks of Antonio Gramsci*, Hoare, Q. and Nowell Smith, G. (eds. and trans.), London: Lawrence & Wishart.

Hewlett, R.G. & Anderson, O.E. (1962), *A History of the United States Atomic Energy Commission, Vol. 1, The New World, 1939–1946*. University Park: Pennsylvania State University Press.

Hilderbrand, R. (1990), *Dumbarton Oaks. The Origins of the United Nations and the Search for Postwar Security,* Chapel Hill: University of North Carolina Press.

Hobsbawm, E. (1994), *Age of Extremes: The Short Twentieth Century 1914–1991*, London: Michael Joseph.

Hogan, M. (1987), *The Marshall Plan*, Cambridge: Cambridge University Press.

Hugill, P.J. (1995), *World Trade Since 1431: Geography, Technology and Capitalism*, Baltimore, MD: John Hopkins University Press.

Hull, C. (1948), *Memoirs of Cordell Hull*, New York: Macmillan.

Isaacson, W. & Thomas, E. (1986), *The Wise Men: Six Friends and the World They Made*, New York: Simon & Schuster.

Jay, A. (ed.) (2005), *Oxford Dictionary of Political Quotes*, Oxford: Oxford University Press.

Johnson, C. (2004), *The Sorrows of Empire*, New York: Owl Books.

Kenwood G.A. & Lougheed, A.L. (1992), *The Growth of the International Economy 1820–1990: An Introductory Text* (3rd Edn.), London: Routledge.

Kolko, G. (1968), *The Politics of War. The World and United States Foreign Policy, 1943–1945*, New York: Vintage Books.

Lasswell, H. D. (1941), "The Garrison State", *The American Journal Of Sociology*, 46, no. 4, 455–68.

Maier, C.S. (1987), *In Search of Stability: Explorations in Historical Political Economy*, Cambridge: Cambridge University Press.

Marshall, G.C. (1948), Address by George C. Marshall to Pittsburgh Chamber of Commerce, January 15th, 1948: "The Stake of the Businessman in the European Recovery Program", *Department of State Bulletin* 28, 447.

Marx, K. & Engels, F. (1992), *The Communist Manifesto*, Oxford: Oxford University Press.

Mayer, G. (2004), "Union Membership Trends in the United States", CRS Report for the Congress, Paper 174, Cornell University ILR School Digital Commons, 31st August (available online at digitalcommons.ilr.cornell.edu).

McCormick, T. (1995), *America's Half-Century: United States Foreign Policy in the Cold War*, Baltimore, MD: John Hopkins University Press.

McCrisken, T.B. (2002), "Exceptionalism: Manifest Destiny", *Encyclopedia of American Foreign Policy*, 2, 68.

Melman, S. (1974), *The Permanent War Economy: American Capitalism in Decline*, New York: Simon & Schuster.

Milhalkanin, E.S. (2004), *American Statesmen: Secretaries of State from John Jay to Colin Powell*, Westport, CT: Greenwood Press.

Nitze, P.H. (1959), "Coalition Policy and the Concept of World Order", in Wolfers, A. (ed.), *Alliance Policy in the Cold War*, Baltimore, MD: John Hopkins University Press.

Notter, H.A. (1949), *Postwar Foreign Policy Preparation, 1939–1945*, Washington, DC: U.S. Department of State, U.S. Government Printing Office.

Odem, W. (1998), *The Collapse of the Soviet Military*, New Haven, CT: Yale University Press.

Panitch, L. & Gindin, S. (2004), *Global Capitalism and American Empire*, London: Verso.

Rorabaugh, W.J., Critchlow, D.T. & Baker, P. (2004), *America's Promise: A Concise History of the United States*, Vol. II, Lanham, MD: Rowman & Littlefield.

Rupert, M. (1995), *Producing Hegemony: The Politics of Mass Production and American Power*, Cambridge: Cambridge University Press.

Rupert, M. (2000), *Ideologies of Globalization: Contending Visions of a New World Order*, Florence, KY: Routledge.

Saad-Filho, A. & Johnston, D. (eds.) (2005), *Neoliberalism: A Critical Reading*, London: Pluto Press.

Samuelson, P. (1942), "Full Employment after the War", in Harris, S.E. (ed.), *Post-war Economic Problems*, New York: McGraw-Hill Company.

Schlesinger, S. (2003), *Act of Creation: The Founding of the United Nations*, Boulder, CO: Midwest Book Review.

Sherry, M. (1977), *Preparing for the Next War: American Plans for Postwar Defense, 1941–1945*, New Haven, CT: Yale University Press.

Siedman, J. (1953), *American Labor from Defense to Reconversion*, Chicago: University of Chicago Press.

Skidelsky, R. (2004), *John Maynard Keyes, 1883–1946: Economist, Philosopher, Statesman*, London: Pan Books.

Spero, J.E. & Hart, J.A. (1997), *The Politics of International Economic Relations* (5th Edn.), New York: St. Martin's Press.

Spiegel, S. (1985), *The Other Arab-Israeli Conflict*, Chicago: University of Chicago.

Spykman, N.J. (1944), *The Geography of the Peace*, New York: Harcourt Brace & Company.

Triffin, R. (1960), *Gold and the Dollar Crisis: The Future of Convertibility*, New Haven, CT: Yale University Press.

Truman, H.S. (1947), "President Harry S. Truman's Address before a Joint Session of Congress", Yale Law School: The Avalon Project, 12th March (available online at avalon.law.yale.edu).

Truman, H.S. (1950), "A Report to the National Security Council – NSC-68", *Harry S. Truman Library & Museum*, President' Secretary's Files, Truman Papers, 12th April (available online at www.trumanlibrary.org).

Truman, H.S. (1955), *Memoirs*, Vol. 1, New York: Double Day & Co.

Turner, F.J. (1983), *The Significance of the Frontier in American History* (available online at www.gutenberg.org).

van der Wee, H. (1987), *Prosperity and Upheaval: The World Economy 1945–1980*, Harmondsworth, Middlesex: Penguin Books.

Williams, W.A. (1959), *The Tragedy of American Diplomacy*, New York: Dell.

Wood, R.E. (1986), *From Marshall Plan to Debt Crisis: Foreign Aid and Development Choices in the World Economy*, London: University of California Press Ltd.

Zinn, H. (2005), *A People's History of the United States*, New York: Harper Perennial Modern Classics.

Zunz, O. (1998), *Why the American Century?* Chicago: University of Chicago Press.

3 Crisis, Reconstruction & Reassertion of US Hegemony

Pax Americana under Threat

Declining American Power

As we have seen, anti-communism was the ideological glue that kept Pax Americana together: the basis of US *intellectual and moral leadership*. Washington represented the principal guarantor of international private property rights and on-going process of capital accumulation, establishing a global defence shield for a capitalist world under threat from Soviet/communist incursion, which usually transposed into disciplining opposition elements at home. As part of its 'war on communism' between 1948 and 1991, Washington spent an estimated $15 trillion or $342 billion p.a. (in constant 2004 dollars) on arms, military interventions (both overt and covert), military aid, and a massive bureaucratic security apparatus.[1] This military deficit-spending became structural to American hegemony by: (1) enabling vital state reconstruction both at home and abroad; (2) offsetting domestic industrial overcapacity subsidised scientific research in new technology which not only managed to keep the US at the forefront of modern weaponry (and hence *military* hegemony) but whose vanguard know-how was appropriated by the civil sector to develop new lucrative production lines (*economic* hegemony).

Officially, the US shunned Harvey's *territorial logic of power* (e.g. empire, colonialism, or intervention into over sovereign states), adhering to a Thomas Paine-inspired 'democratic republicanism' espoused by the "Founding Father" (territorially-defined, political community, represented by a small accountable government). The reality, of course, as we have seen, is that Harvey's two *logics* are inseparable. Indeed, conforming to the critical realist *ontological stratification model* set out in Chapter 1 it is best to conceptualise the *territorial* logic as being *emergent from* the *capitalist* logic. Arrighi's earlier observation on the more frequent recourse to 'politics of the politics of state and empire' during periods of overproduction/overcapacity was borne out by the American colonies' perpetual expansion westward followed by incursions into the Caribbean and Latin America. Historically, the solution squaring this

DOI: 10.4324/9780429459061-4

circle has been to justify US power projection in republican missionary terms: the country had a moral obligation, Thomas Jefferson insisted, to bring freedom and the 'good life' to foreigners and establish an "empire of liberty". The US, John Quincy Adams declared in 1821, "goes not abroad, in search of monsters to destroy...She is the well-wisher to the freedom and independence of all".[2] "American imperialism", Harold Innis summed up in 1956; "has been made plausible and attractive in part by its insistence that is not imperialistic."[3]

In the post-war European countries were pressed to decolonise in the name of self-determination, democracy, and universal civil and political rights, but this did not prevent Washington itself from resorting to the *territorial* logic of power as part of its 'war on communism'. Throughout the 1950s and 1960s, the State Department, the Pentagon, and the Treasury worked together with the various intelligence agencies (most notably the Central Intelligence Agency – CIA) to install or bolster the position of pro-Western authoritarian/dictatorial regimes, quell national independence movements, and overthrow (or at least fatally undermine) 'dangerous' governments throughout the periphery/semi-periphery.[4] In terms of 'officially recognised' wars, however, there were just two: the Korean War (1950–) and the Vietnam War (1954–75), which constituted such a political, ideological, military, and economic disaster for the US, it appeared to signal the beginning of the end for American hegemony.

On a domestic level, Vietnam threatened the stability of the historical bloc (HB). Public demonstrations opposing the war began as early as 1964 but shot up from 1968 Tet Offensive onwards, when an increasingly critical media began to report and relay images of the true horrors and scale of destruction.[5] Middle classes eager to avoid the extended draft joined students, peace activists, political liberals, civil/black rights campaigners, the New Left, feminists, environmentalists, and workers associations – unsurprisingly the very same groups targeted by the national security state (NSS), according to the Church Committee Report – to protest against both US militarism and imperialist interventions abroad and the lack of social justice at home. This upsurge of progressive political activism, fuelled by anger over the deeper underlying contradictions of American society – poverty, inequality, systemic racial discrimination/ ghetto-isation – greatly concerned conservative social forces, fearful it could consolidate into genuine counter-hegemonic HB (see below).

At the international level, the South East Asia campaign did untold damage to American 'intellectual and moral leadership'. Not only for the dubious nature of the conflict, destruction waged, and attrition tactics, but it shattered the myth of American military invincibility: a fundamental pillar of Pax Americana. Despite dropping more tonnage of high explosives on Indochina than during WWII (equivalent to 200 Hiroshima-type bombs) the Viet Cong could not be defeated.[6] For the very first time, serious doubts over Washington's *military hegemony* began to arise, specifically its ability to protect advanced capitalist allies against Soviet attack and impose order in the periphery, symbolised in their forced abandonment of Laos, South Vietnam, and Cambodia. Worse still, by 1969, the USSR had reached nuclear parity with the US, boasting around 1,000 intercontinental ballistic missiles: a state of MAD ('mutually assured destruction') now existed.[7] Furthermore, Moscow was determined to push ahead with an anti-ballistic missile system programme which would undermine Washington's strike capabilities and force them to embark on a new highly expensive arms race.

It was against the backdrop of this political military malaise Nixon was forced to extend the olive branch to Moscow, proposing the superpowers engage in Strategic Arms Limitation Talks (SALT), which began in November 1969 and concluded in May 1972 with the SALT-1 Treaty on limiting the development of anti-ballistic missile systems. This period of superpower *détente* reached its zenith with the signing of the "Helsinki Agreement", at the Conference on Security and Cooperation in Europe in 1975, which formally recognised the legitimacy of the USSR's hegemony over East Europe 30 years after Yalta.

A sign of its relative decline, *détente* would prove disastrous to US hegemony. Freed from the threat of imminent nuclear war (and the Hobbesian 'friend-foe' logic) the Allies were afforded a degree of foreign policy autonomy from Washington, which they had not experienced since WWII. At the front of the queue were hitherto 'client states' Japan and the Federal Republic of Germany (FRG). Uneasy at improving Sino-American relations under Secretary of State, Henry Kissinger's *rapprochement* initiatives, Tokyo proposed expanding bilateral trade relations with Moscow, seeking to gain access to the latter's energy, mineral, and agricultural resources, in exchange for capital, technology, and capital-rich manufacturing/consumer goods.[8] Similarly, West German Chancellor Willy Brandt launched *Ostpolitik*, re-establishing diplomatic links with its estranged Eastern bloc neighbours, and crowned with the ratification of the Basic Treaty (1972). In direct contradiction of the US-endorsed Hallstein Doctrine, Bonn formally recognised the East German sovereignty claim, and established obligations on all parties to seek non-violent means to resolve problems.

Transatlantic relations also hit a post-war low in the early 1970s. For the first time, in almost 30 years, Europe publicly chastised Washington for Vietnam, the demise of Bretton Woods (see below), its involvement in the Arab-Israeli war, while the European Economic Community's (EEC) rejected new General Agreement on Tariffs and Trade (GATT) proposals. Such was the extent of the rift that the Nixon administration felt it necessary to designate 1973 the "Year of Europe", with Kissinger subsequently calling for a "new Atlantic Charter", offering to update and reinforce the North Atlantic Treaty Organization (NATO), while at the same time warning the continent to keep European integration within an overall framework of order managed by the US rather than consolidating into a protectionist trading bloc.[9]

Liberalism was also coming under increasing attack in the semi-periphery and periphery. Drawing on Lenin-inspired *dependency theorists* such as Raul Prebisch, Hans Singer, and Andre Gunder Frank, the Non-Aligned Movement (evolving from the Bandung Conference) denounced the hierarchically structured nature of the international trading system. Thanks to the limited range and low value-added nature of their exports, that the argument ran, developing countries suffered a perennial worsening in their *terms of trade* (the ratio of the index of export prices to the index of import prices) relative to the rich North, to which they were economically dependent, while locked in a permanent state of under-development.[10] Finding institutional expression in the United Nations Conference on Trade and Development (UNCTAD), the solution proposed by the so-called G77 countries was the formation of commodity cartels in raw materials (e.g. such as coffee, cocoa, sugar, rubber, and tin), an endogenous economic growth model based upon *import-substitution industrialisation* (ISI), and by the late 1960s, the right to expropriate (i.e. nationalise) foreign-owned national assets on their soil.

Again, it was against the backdrop *détente* and perceived declining American power that Third World economic militancy reached its zenith. In 1974 UNCTAD called for a radical reconstruction of international trade via its *Declaration for the Establishment of a New International Economic Order*, approved by UN General Assembly on 1st May. Amongst its principal demands were: raising and stabilising commodity prices; reducing rich countries' tariffs; regulating and supervising the activities of transnational corporations; and recognising both countries' rights to choose own developmental model and sovereignty over resources.[11] This was followed in the same year in December by the *Charter of Economic Rights and Duties of States*, passed by the General Assembly 120 votes to 6 in December of the same year which specifically spelled out states' rights to nationalise foreign property. Though nothing legally binding would come of these specific initiatives – vetoed by both the UK and the US – they did worry State Department officials. Such economic nationalism not only hurt American MNCs it placed in grave danger the whole functioning of the multilateral liberal order (i.e. *en route* to the Open Door) which Washington had so lovingly nurtured. This was a direct affront to the US's hegemonic role as the global guarantor of international private property.

As far as 'hawks' in Washington were concerned, the US was 'losing control' of the Third World in the 1970s. In addition to the retreat from Indochina, the rise of nationalist movements throughout Africa, Central America, and the Middle East was overthrowing incumbent US-maintained regimes in the name of self-determination, the most significant being Ethiopia (1974), Angola (1975), Nicaragua (1979), and Iran (1979).

But the underlying problem behind the root of this political malaise ultimately was the US's relative *economic* decline: itself a direct corollary of the exercising of hegemony.

Thanks in no small part to American largesse (economic aid, military expenditure, technology transfer, FDI, privileged access to its internal market, etc.), Bretton Woods, political/military stability, and Washington's toleration of non-reciprocal trade practices, the core capitalist countries enjoyed a virtuous cycle of high productivity, high consumption, high investment, and high profits throughout the 1950s and 1960s.[12] Predictably, given the huge post-war disparity, by the mid-1960s the global centre of economic gravity had started to shift significantly. The uneven (and combined) character of capitalist development meant many advanced countries were accumulating capital at a far quicker rate than the US. Paralleling Pax Britannica in the late 19th century, the very process of exporting surplus capital and technology to other advanced capitalist countries inevitably resulted in the hegemon losing its absolute economic supremacy in the manufacturing sector. While outward dollar-denominated capital flows rose more than quadrupled between 1950 and 1966,[13] the US economy experienced slower growth than any other industrial economy except Britain.[14]

Leading the pack of 'catch up' states were Japan and the FRG, both blessed with an ample, well-trained, productive, and inexpensive/largely compliant work-force,[15] high levels of state intervention, and associated endogenous industrial development models which helped to nurture efficient export-orientated oligopolistic corporate sector. By the late 1960s, these oligopolies had seized a large market share in key industrial sectors, such as automobiles, steel, textiles, electronics, consumer durables, and machine tools; areas hitherto dominated by their American counterparts.[16] German and Japanese trade surpluses rose inversely proportional to the US,[17] where the rate of profits in manufacturing and business, in general, started to drop dramatically from 1966 onwards.[18]

In addition, Washington's 'go global' strategy had encouraged many corporations to set up abroad. As a part of the aforementioned internationalisation of production (IOP) process, American companies tripled their number of foreign branches in 15 years to around 23,000 by 1966,[19] creating an international web of foreign subsidiaries, outsourcing operations, and subcontracting arrangements. But what was good for US global hegemony and corporate profits rates was not necessarily good for its national economy. Since American MNCs were no longer exporting from the US, corporate profits accumulated in extraterritorial markets did not show up on the national balance of payments (BOP) statistics, unless they were repatriated, which for the first time in almost a century started to record a deficit.[20]

By the late 1960s, the US was also facing a ballooning federal budget deficit. On the credit side of the ledger, there were low receipts, due to declining tax revenue from MNCs abroad and domestic businesses at home; Kennedy-era tax cuts; and the Congress's reluctance to liquidate national assets or sufficiently increase the fiscal burden. The debit side of the ledger was dominated by Vietnam War costs,[21] but it was joined by "Great Society" programmes.[22] Between 1964 and 1969 President Lyndon B. Johnson effectively doubled public social expenditure, introducing a series of progressive measures designed to ameliorate somewhat the aforementioned contradictions afflicting American society, and with its help mollify growing 'bottom up' social discontent.

Refusing to choose between guns or 'butter Washington's' solution was to offload the adjustment onto the rest of the world: after all, that was the key benefit of *dollar-seigniorage*. Thus, while the Federal Reserve set about printing more dollars, foreign governments, central banks, and companies were coerced to accept them under threat of the US abandoning the gold standard. Washington, in effect, was exporting its own inflation,[23] converting national debt into world debt.[24] By the late 1960s, the 1940s 'dollar shortage' had turned into 'dollar glut' which began to flow back into the US aggravating demand-pull inflation still further.

The damage done to American hegemony was enormous, not just reducing global profit rates but gravely undermining the functioning of the Bretton Woods system itself, the very pivot of the liberal trading system. Since 1962 France had been periodically been requiring Washington to honour its Bretton Woods' commitment to exchange gold for surplus dollars; by 1967, these purchases augmented dramatically after Paris withdrew from the London Gold Pool in June 1967. The on-going pound sterling crisis (culminating in its 14.3% devaluation in November 1967) only increased pressure on the dollar. With gold pouring out of Fort Knox, Washington temporary suspended the London Gold Pool in March 1968. Between 1949 and 1971, official gold stocks dropped from $25 billion to $10 billion meanwhile US liabilities totalled $68 billion; Germany alone held enough dollars to exhaust Fort Knox (at $35 an ounce rate).[25]

Inevitably, Bretton Woods came under attack. The on-going IOP, the size of the Eurodollar market, and the associated increase in short-term transnational capital flows, blurred the distinction between 'productive' (i.e. for trade or productive investment) and 'speculative' financial flows: a separation which Keynes had considered vital for the survival of the gold-dollar standard. As a result, the scale of the cross-border flows of private capital seriously undermined the ability of governments and central banks to maintain their International Monetary Fund (IMF) sanctioned fixed exchange rates (see Mundell-Fleming model). Keynes' concerns about the functioning of a dollar-based international monetary system were vindicated, while the *Triffin's Dilemma* remained unresolved. With the pendulum swinging so far in the liquidity, Europe and Japan openly criticised Washington for its exporting inflation, twin trade, and budgetary deficits, with the US blaming the economic malaise on its competitors (noticeably FRG and Japan) for maintaining under-valued currencies and adherence to neo-mercantilist policies.

The reality was that the establishment of Bretton Woods system had never been universally popular, most markedly amongst conservatives and factions of financial capital based in Wall Street and the City (of London), who vehemently opposed the limitation on the international movement of capital,[26] considered so necessary by Keynes and reiter-ated by the Mundell-Fleming model. Little surprise that these same so-cial forces actively sought to undermine its functioning from the outset under Truman. Wall Street prevailing over the Truman administration to dilute the scheme's original 'financial repression' mechanisms and curtail governmental intervention in financial markets,[27] becoming key inves-tors in manufacturing enterprises, mortgage and credit markets, merg-ers, and bond dealing.[28] Consequently, financial firms' profits grew a lot faster than non-financial firms' profits throughout the 1950s and 1960s.[29] American banks, as observed, were key players in the *Americanisation* of European firms from the 1950s onwards, facilitating the explosion of US FDI on the continent, before offering their services to foreign firms too.

Similar lobbying was taking place in London, where investment bank-ers exhorted Whitehall to weaken exchange rate control regulations in order to set the City up as an off-shore dollar-based capital market centre for both Arab countries and socialist states (e.g. the USSR and China) which, for political reasons, were reluctant to bank in New York.[30] Thanks to the further loosening of capital controls in Western Europe and Japan at the end of the 1950s/early 1960s the City became the official home of the highly lucrative Eurodollar and Eurobond markets, which simultane-ously exposed it to the whims of American hegemony, since at any time Washington could decide to clamp down on its offshore banking sector. Yet far from disapproving of the Eurodollar market, the US Treasury tac-itly supported US banks setting up there, considering it advantageous as a way to: sustain the value of the dollar; reinforce the international prom-inence of its international banks; and provide European-based funds for the expansion of its MNCs (as part of Cox's IOP process). The power of financial (or money) capital, in short, was on the rise.

By 1971, Washington had drawn a line in the sand with regards to Bret-ton Woods, determined that the rest of the world should take the burden for currency re-adjustment.[31] Even talk of revaluing the other currencies and the subsequent floating of the Deutsche Mark was insufficient to stop the Nixon administration formally abandoning the dollar-gold standard in August 1971 before imposing price controls and a 10% import charge on goods from countries it considered guilty of exchange rate manipu-lation. Following this, *Nixon Shock* was another lukewarm attempt to rebuild Bretton Woods via the Smithsonian Agreement in December 1971 – involving a devaluation of the dollar by 7.9% and an increase in the dollar price of gold to \$38 – but by then financial capital had won the argument. The White House decided to follow Wall Street's advice and formally float the dollar in March 1973. This greatly angered Western Europe and Japan. As Treasury Secretary John Connally famously quipped during the Smithsonian meetings: "The dollar may be our currency, but it's your problem".[32]

Thus, by the mid-1970s US economic, political, military, and cultural hegemony appeared in crisis. The post-war Pax Americana system was being undermined by its own success and many internal contradictions. The very measures taken to launch/sustain hegemony were responsible to for undermining it, and clear conflicts existed between the US's 'global' role and certain domestic interests.

The root of the problem remained that the US-led regime of accumulation was moribund, afflicted by heightened inter-capitalist competition which manifested itself in systemic over-production/capacity in the productive/manufacturing sector worldwide. Worse still, this 'horizontal pressure' was aggravated by 'vertical pressure' (wage inflation), stemming from class contradictions at the heart of the Fordist-Keynesian developmental model.

Keynesianism Unravelling

As indicated in Chapter 2, under embedded liberalism arrangements Western (including Japan) capitalist states were afforded a degree of policy autonomy to achieve domestic goals, albeit working within important external constraints established under Bretton Woods and towards the Open Door. For roughly 30 years, policy-makers, business, and academics alike had largely shared the same Keynesian industrial paradigm; the state should assume a major managerial, entrepreneurial, and financial role in the direction of the economy in order to counter the markets' tendency towards disequilibrium while promoting industrialisation, improving productivity, nurturing economies of scale, and achieving full employment goals.

Fordist-Keynesian "common sense" held mass production required mass consumption, so demand had to be kept high. But aggregate demand management was a delicate balance: increases in real and nominal wages had to be offset by an increase in levels of production, consumption, and contingent investment strategies otherwise inflation would ensue. As Chapter 2 noted the state's key hegemonic role within Fordist/Keynesian was to broker a corporatist 'social contract', or *class compromise*, between capital and industrial labour analogous to Gramsci's *first* and *second* hegemonic *moments* with the latter offered rising wages, near full employment, access to a welfare state, and recognition of moderate (business) unions, who could participate in tripartite collective bargaining arrangements along with governments and business chiefs. In return, organised labour had to accept its subservient role within said HB and above all recognise capital's legitimate right to make sustainable profits (reflected in productivity-linked wages) and renouncement of any genuine class transformation.[33]

Keynesianism and associated embedded liberal arrangements are often interpreted by social democrats, even by some neo-Gramscians, as 'putting a brake' on capitalism when in fact it merely constituted a different, contingent, capitalist accumulation strategy. Concomitant with Joseph's *materialist theory of hegemony*, Keynesianism's utility depended upon its ability to reproduce social structures and guarantee on-going capital accumulation and profits for business. Wealth distribution towards the subaltern classes remained only a secondary objective, and then only because it was necessary to maintain high aggregate demand (to avoid overproduction and falling profit rates) and in order to promote social peace by assimilating the working class within the HB. In was in this context that capital, though reluctant at first, came to accept the collective bargaining "premised upon an acceptance of capitalistic control of the labour process (in the form of 'workplace rule of law') and the prioritisation of private profits as the primary social value".[34]

Moderate levels of cost-push inflation (i.e. wage-push) were always tolerated under the Keynesian development model, considered indicative of economic growth and as an almost inevitable consequence of tripartite corporatism. Nevertheless, if inflation was to drive the country into a BOP deficit and thereby undermine its stable exchange rate within the Bretton Woods systems, it was understood that the state would then apply suitably austere fiscal and monetary policies and, together with capital, seek to impose stricter income policies on unions and promote measures to increase the productivity.

During the 1950s and the early 1960s, labour's share of income in the core stayed constant: wages prevented from rising too much by high post-war unemployment, rural exodus, the baby-boom, and increased immigration (except Japan which preferred to outsource production to neighbouring low-cost countries). Yet by the mid-1960s the cheap surplus labour had started to dry up. With profit rates hitting unprecedented rates,[35] the key industrial unions did enjoy reasonable success in having their wage demands met. The Keynesian commitment to full employment had somewhat strengthened the working class' political position, who now no longer feared dismissal and a return to Marx's 'reserve army'. Indeed, sections of the core working class even began to question the fairness of production-index wages which maintained the existing distribution of surplus between capital and labour.

As US-generated demand-pull inflation (derived from dollar-printing) started to spill-over abroad, capital everywhere sought to augment labour exploitation by reorganising work practices (e.g. speeding up production lines), provoking clashes with more militant factions, who also complained wages were not keeping up with inflation.[36] Following the

May 1968 protests in France – where formal union membership was quite low (and communist party support relatively high) – workers staged the first-ever wildcat general strike. Labour militancy spiked in the US too, with a marked increase in non-official strikes, walk-outs, and absenteeism, with capital complaining that wages were rising faster than productivity.[37] It was not long before countries began to suffer cost-push inflation as well as the demand-pull variant.

In short, by the early 1970s, the capitalist world was suffering from a systemic inflationary cycle arising from a complex interplay between excessive dollar printing, "monopoly capitalism",[38] inter-capitalist competition, and the 'pay explosion': the US printing dollars to underpin hegemony (and counter inter-capitalist competition) generated demand-pull inflation which oligopolistic corporations passed onto consumers, leading to unions to demanding higher wages to compensate for declining purchasing power, which oligopolistic corporations once again offloaded onto the consumers, *ad infinitum* (the exact dynamics of this inflationary cycle depending on the class dynamics of each respective country's HB within the hierarchically structured global economy).

As a result of these circumstances most advanced capitalist countries experienced declining profit rates in the early 1970s relative to their peak in 1960–65,[39] with Anglo-Saxon corporations particularly badly affected, losing valuable market share to their emerging competitors (horizontal pressure), and subject to the most pronounced increase in wage bills (vertical pressure) as a direct result of the conflictual nature of their industrial relations model.[40] Resolving the situation was complicated. Capital had two responses.

Many core-based companies imitated the American template, seeking a *spatial fix* by setting up (or investing in) production processes and service providers outside their 'home state',[41] becoming more embedded in transnational circuits of capital (reinforcing the IOP). Concurrently, eager to attract mobile capital, governments reiterated their commitment to the OECD Code of Liberalisation of Capital Movements (CLCM), especially the clause guaranteeing equal levels of protection for MNCs, regardless of nationality (buttressing the internationalisation of the state – IOS). The fact that the dynamics of global capitalism appeared to be moving in the direction of the Open Door, the US's original objective, brought cold comfort amidst a systemic crisis, and declining profit rates.

The second option involved, more universal in its application, involved what Marx referred to as "increasing intensity of exploitation",[42] which involved: raising productivity (introducing new technology, speeding up production, and augmenting the working day); lowering costs (reducing wages and staff); and engaging in investments strikes and lock-outs. In the context of worldwide overproduction and high systemic inflation, however, such tactics failed to improve profitability rates, while undermining official established trilateral corporatist arrangements.

With declining real wages, worsening working conditions, and rising unemployment, workers began to lose faith in official channels, participating in more frequently in non-official industrial action and nominating more class-conscious shop-stewards to speak on their behalf.[43]

Given rising unemployment and the scale of social conflict Western governments then opted for an inflationary strategy (demand-pull), involving increased public spending and the extension of the welfare state, while simultaneously calling for wage and price controls. The *Nixon Shock*, however, marked the beginning of the end for Keynesianism, not least by provoking the 1973–74 OPEC price hike, commonly understood (see below for a different interpretation) as an attempt by dollar-dependent oil producers to restore profitability in light of high systemic inflation and a plummeting dollar.

Quadrupling oil prices now drove the advanced economies into a deep crisis with countries experiencing record inflation figures[44] and widespread industrial action. Most states now faced serious fiscal problems as high unemployment and low growth simultaneously reduced tax revenues and spiked social expenditure.[45] Worse still, traditional 'stop-go' tools no longer served. The arrival of 'stagflation' appeared to disprove the hitherto revered *Phillip's curve*. There simply was no unemployment-inflation trade off, Keynes's critics insisted, deficit spending only augmenting unemployment and inflation still further.

Support for the post-war 'social contract' – the unwritten constitution of the Keynesian-welfare state's HB – began to evaporate. Capital blamed stagflation on the greedy unions, collective bargaining arrangements, and the 'bloated' welfare-state. Amongst the most vocal critics were sections of financial capital, angry with low corporate profits, negative real interest rates, diminishing asset values, and reduced returns to equity. These were joined the so-called 'net contributors' to the welfare-state – small capital, private sector workers, and the middle class – who resented 'their taxes' being wasted on the 'undeserving'.

In this general malaise all Western governments from 1975 onwards (although more acute in Anglo-Saxon countries), sought to regain profitability by abandoning commitments to both full employment and indexed-linked salaries. Though the rhythm would vary across the core countries, mainstream unions found themselves increasingly left without a political voice, as their traditional allies – the social democratic parties – all began to eschew Keynesianism in favour of austere monetarist and fiscal policies once in government. US-led transnational business pressure groups such as the Bilderberg Conference and the Trilateral Commission (see below) also urged a return to pre-1945 liberal economic orthodoxy in order to raise profits.

Appropriately, Keynesianism's *coup de grâce* was delivered in the famous economist's home country, Great Britain, which was bordering on a fiscal crisis in 1975.[46] When the value of the pound started sliding financial capital seized its moment. *The Wall Street Journal* advised investors to ditch sterling under the headline "Goodbye Great Britain", the City, the UK Treasury, and the Bank of England – supported by the US Treasury, the Federal Reserve, and Wall Street – all demanded the British Chancellor of the Exchequer, Denis Healey, to go to the IMF and solicit a bank-bail. It would prove a historical moment.

The austere *structural adjustment programme* (SAP) imposed on the UK constituted the first time a major country had been subject to such conditionality since the late 1940s (e.g. Lend Lease and Marshall Plan). The terms of the SAP involved required Britain to completely restructure its economic developmental model (social relations of production – SROP and HB, included). Under this *passive revolution*, strict fiscal, monetary and social conditions would require, amongst other things, an end to the full employment commitment, a dramatic cut-back on the welfare state, a removal of capital controls, and the tackling of working-class militancy.[47]

Britain's 'humiliation' in 1976 represented a defining moment in the politics of globalization. Industrial capitalism had effectively accepted the argument that a finance-led accumulation strategy was the only way to beat inflation and restore their profits. Hence it was not just the university economics departments around the world that were set for a major paradigm shift; once Keynesianism was officially pronounced, a dead major societal change was launched across the advanced capitalist world. With certain irony, therefore, the first steps towards the neoliberal revolution in Britain – so closely associated with the figure of Margaret Thatcher – were actually taken by the Labour party.

The causes of the collapse of the post-war accumulation strategy as we have seen were multiple, complex, and interconnected. Nevertheless, at the very least it became evident that there *was* an implicit class conflict between capital and labour, contrary to Keynesian 'common sense'. During the post-war boom most social classes in the West experienced real income growth between 1947 and 1973 and despite the conservative nature of incomes policies, there was a partial 'socialisation' of wealth accumulation, with the richest top 20% of earners seeing their relative share of national income dropping in proportion to the rise of the poorest 20%.[48] Countering this tendency would become one of the main focal points for the class-based restoration of profitability as set out in the next section.

Financialization, Neoliberalism & the Restoration of Class Power

The New Dollar-Wall Street Regime

The temporary suspension of the dollar-gold standard, as noted, served immediate two connected national priorities: (1) affording the White House greater control over its management of domestic aggregate demand; and (2) using currency devaluation to bolster American industrial global competitiveness. The decision to formally abandon Bretton Woods in 1973, however, had a key long-term objective. The global capitalist system was beset by a *realisation crisis*. Conforming to Arrighi's systemic cycle of accumulation (SCOA) set out in Chapter 1, the US as the incumbent hegemon would seek to restore systemic profitability by launching a new state of financial expansion, *financialization*. Marx's shortened capital circuit M-M', and with its hope to reassert American hegemony.

Although the end of Bretton Woods was greeted with great enthusiasm from Wall Street the future of the greenback given the huge dollar overhang remained in doubt. It is in this context, Peter Gowan maintains, that the OPEC crisis can be understood. According to Gowan, US was pondering over how to get conservative OPEC countries (Saudi Arabia, Iran, Kuwait, Libya, etc.) to raise oil prices a full two years before the outbreak of the Arab-Israeli war (Oct 1973). The short-term objective of this classic piece of economic statecraft, Gowan hold (citing Nixon's then Ambassador to Saudi Arabia) was to damage the US's main industrial rivals, Gulf oil-dependent Western Europe (especially the FRG), and Japan, Gowan to the benefit of American exporters and energy corporations. The long-term aim, however, was to forward the interests of financial capital and critically Wall Street.[49] In a similar vein, William Engdahl quotes confidential documents, revealing how the banking elite of the Bilderberg Group met in Sweden in May 1973 to discuss the benefits for the financial (and oil) sector of a projected rise of 400% in the price of petroleum, this time six months before OPEC actually took the decision. A decision which he maintains was actively encouraged by Secretary of State, Henry Kissinger, albeit in a covert fashion.[50]

Whether or not Gowan and Engdahl are correct in their thesis or not, the US wasted no time in exploiting the OPEC crisis to the advantage of its financial sector. Washington negotiated a deal with Saudi Arabia offering them cut price Treasury Bonds, arms sales, and protection of oil fields (notably from Israel) in return to their insisting OPEC oil be purchased *exclusively* in US dollars therein maintaining high demand for the dollar internationally post-Bretton Woods.[51] The exact nature of this arrangement would be overseen by US-Saudi Arabia Joint Commission on Economic Cooperation – set up by Kissinger in June 1974 – and placed in charge of stabilising oil supplies and price.

What the Nixon administration realised was that oil-producing countries, with Saudi Arabia at the helm, would never be able to invest all the dollars they would receive within their economies. What better than investing their dollars in safe American assets (public debt, real estate, industry, infrastructure, company shares, etc.) and helping to refinance American current account deficit. Immediately, Nixon's Treasury Secretary, George P. Shultz abolished capital controls to ensure that these lucrative *petrodollars* would be recycled through Wall Street and their affiliates in London. Aware that this signalled the end of 'financial repression' make them even more reliant on the dollar and Wall Street, Western Europe and Japan lobbied to get these petrodollars funnelled through the IMF and other similar multilateral institutions but to no avail.

There were two other ways petrodollars were recycled through the US. One of these, as alluded to, was the commercialisation of its *arms industry* which Jonathan Nitzan and Shimshon Bichler, hold began in earnest following the Six Day War (1967). Thanks to privatisation, a permissive policy on mergers and acquisitions and increased internationalisation, a sector hitherto considered out of reach of commodification was converted into a highly competitive dollar-based global business.[52] As Arab-Israeli tensions increased the Middle East, with Saudi Arabia at the lead, was soon converted into the world's chief importer of arms, helping to recycle petrodollars back into Wall Street and its offshore dollar centre, the City.[53] There were now, Nitzan and Bichler opined, three very powerful sectors in the US with a vested interest in on-going political instability in the region: finance (the Treasury, Wall Street); military/defence (represented by the military-industrial-complex (MIC)); and energy (oil companies) – which they baptised the "Weapondollar-Petrodollar Coalition"[54] (WDPDC).

A second important way these petrodollars would be recycled through the US, according to John Perkin was via *infrastructure* projects. Washington, Perkins, held, pressured the House of Saud to use the interest received on its Treasury Bonds to launch a national multi-billion-dollar industrialisation, modernisation, and urbanisation programme (including military installations, port, power plants, airports, sewage works, desalination plants, waste management systems, etc) right across the Arabian Peninsula. The key condition was that they contract, and pay exclusively in dollars, American engineering, construction, and servicing companies, hand-picked by the US Treasury Department, such as Halliburton and Bechtel, whose new Vice-President in 1974 happened to be one George P. Shultz before returning as Reagan's Secretary of State.[55]

Petrodollarisation in short, was fundamental to the whole financialization project: linking dollar parity to petroleum demand, undermining 'financial repression', recycling global surplus though Wall Street and other key sectors, while granting Washington enormous autonomy over its monetary policy. It also buttressed American hegemony over the Middle East, especially Riyadh. Saudi Arabia was granted privileged ally status by Washington; its elite free to enrich themselves and have their national security guaranteed. In return, they accepted political subservience; as the critical OPEC swing state, they would have to raise or reduce global oil supplies (and thus the dollar price) according to its benefactor's wishes, recycling the dollars earned in American securities, goods, and services, and adhere to Washington's regional foreign policy objectives.

Nevertheless, whether this dollar-based international monetary system continued to function over the long-term would depend on the robustness and 'depth' of the US financial sector. In 1975, the US embarked on a different type of regulation erroneously termed a 'deregulation'. Wall Street's so-called "Big Bang" involved a number of key changes, most notably reversing New Deal rules setting brokerage fees and creation of the Commodity Futures Trading Commission both to regulate and actively a new market in highly lucrative financial instruments – derivatives – specifically designed by Wall Street to help international investors/traders reduce risk (or hedge) in this new age of volatile commodity prices, floating exchange rates, and political uncertainty. Such initiatives, again, served to lock foreign capital onto the American financial system, which, together with the removal of capital controls, proved pivotal for the subsequent internationalisation of the US bonds market and development of "Yankee Bond" (a dollar-denomination issued in the US by foreign companies and governments).

Moreover, and again contrary to mainstream discourse, this 'deregulation' would actually require *more* state intervention and cooperation. Following the hegemonic template, this meant more international institutionalisation. In 1974, for example, the central bank governors of the ten richest capitalist economies set up the "Basel Committee on Banking Supervision" extending the regulatory role of the state first expressed in the 1975 "Concordant". This recognised that supervisory responsibility for bank's foreign branches, subsidiaries, and joint ventures should be shared between host and parent (home) supervisory authorities.[56] The US Treasury also called for regular meetings between central bankers and finance ministers of the advanced capitalist countries – the so-called G7 (later extended to the G20).

Further extending financial capital's hegemony, the US Treasury secured a re-writing of the IMF's Articles of Agreement (1976) which, apart from legitimising the floating exchange rate system, obliged members to adhere to strict monetary discipline, specifically charging the IMF with the powers to monitor compliance. Peter Gowan describes the relationship between the dollar and Wall Street as both symbiotic and mutual reinforcing: what he refers to as the *Dollar-Wall Street-Regime* (DWSR), based upon three interconnected and self-reproducing attributes:

1   the dollar's prestige as the world currency (due to the lack of any serious alternative and the sheer quantity of greenbacks circulating the global system) meant the majority of countries still held the bulk of their foreign currency reserves in dollars and in Wall Street (or its subsidy, the City)
2   key commodities (e.g. oil and arms) were priced/traded in dollars, thereby boosting the size and turnover in the Anglo-American markets.

3   the resultant size, depth turnover, and reach of Wall Street as a financial centre (not least with its thriving derivative markets post-Bretton
Woods) increased investors/lenders confidence and thus the scale of
financial transactions, which in turn reinforced the prestige of the
dollar as an international currency.[57]

By integrating other countries onto its own financial system (the DWSR),
the US was granted enormous leverage over the entire global capitalist
system. The entire international monetary system was now based on a
fiat dollar, permitting the US to obtain all the benefits of seigniorage
while offloading the adjustment costs on to the rest of the world. Under this *pure dollar standard*, the US Treasury could unilaterally decide
the price of the greenback simply by raising the interest rate or printing
money. Devaluing the dollar, for example, would simultaneously reduce
foreign debt owed and boost export sales. Since the currency was not
backed by gold, running a BOP deficit was no longer a problem. This
meant, in essence, that the US could enjoy an interest-free loan from the
other countries.

Given the aforementioned general economic malaise in the early 1970s,
and especially the US's relative decline in industrial competitiveness
with respect to the other core countries (especially Japan and the FRG),
such a powerful monetary lever was a vital asset for Washington. "[T]he
basis of American hegemony was being shifted", Eric Helleiner opined,
"from one of direct power over other states to a more market-based or
'structural' form of power".[58] Significantly, now it was Anglo-American
private transnational banks and money-markets which controlled international financial movements and become the chief source of international credit rather than public central banks or Bretton Wood
institutions. Revealingly, the IMF's new extended mandate included no
measures for the supervision of international financial operators. As a result, even minor shifts in American financial markets would now dramatically affect the rest of the world's financial systems and exchange rates.
Once again, the net result was to bolster the US government's leverage
over international financial markets.[59]

A new stage of economic history had begun with financial capital institutionalising its hegemony over productive capital requiring serious
adjustment by the advanced capitalist states. But whether the DWSR was
successful or not, to restate an earlier point, would ultimately depend on
the US being continually able to attract foreign mobile capital (keeping
the Wall Street at the apex of global surplus value extraction). For this to
occur it was vital that Washington restore the dollar as a stable standard
of value and maintain a low inflation rate: something which had proven
highly elusive for successive administrations, damaging profit rates.

President Jimmy Carter brought in former Chase Manhattan Bank
Vice-President, and president of the Federal Reserve Bank of New York,

Paul Volcker, to head the Federal Reserve and resolve the problem. Drawing on the 'common sense' ideas of the Mont Pelerin Society (see below) Volcker adhered to a strict monetary policy: limiting the growth in the money supply and allowing the interest rate to rise to whatever level necessary to break inflation. Over the next 18 months the Fed continuously raised the nominal interest rate, from a base rate of 8% in 1978 to a peak of 21% in 1981, and remained high throughout the mid-1980s.

Known as the *Volcker Shock* this represented a dramatic about-face in US monetary policy. It was a highly *political* gesture, constituting an assault on what capital considered *the* principal cause of the dollar crisis and double-digit inflation rates: the Fordist-Keynesian HB. Even productive capital recognised its utility as a necessary class instrument to undermine labour power. This slashing of inflation and reduction of domestic economic and social costs was also applauded by American for exporters, potential losers under high-interest rates and a high dollar. In short, all domestic factions of capital tacitly acknowledged the legitimacy of financial capital's *hegemonic role* in reviving accumulation.[60]

The Volcker Shock was also generally well received at the international level, at least in core countries[61] whose political elite, corporate heads, and investors, appreciated the restoration of monetary discipline (and potentially profits) to the international financial sector. The size of the US economy, American corporate penetration of the core (via the IOP), and the latter's increasing integration into the American financial system meant the stability of the 'greenback' was not merely a national problem but pivotal to the well-being of the entire global capitalist system. Unsurprisingly, German and Japanese productive capital was amongst the most enthusiastic support of the Volcker Shock. It represented a downgraded version of Bretton Woods, but at least a strong albeit fiat dollar offered some form of stable reference point for long-term investment decisions.

As successful as the Volcker Shock was, *financialization* could not fulfil its 'historical purpose' until all constraints had to be removed on capital mobility and the FOS restructured. It was crucial to downgrade the hitherto privileged position of industrial labour within the HB.[62] The *neoliberal* revolution was merely the broader, more overtly political *hegemonic project* which had financialization at its core, and whose objective was identical: to *restore class power* and *create conditions* for further class formation.

Neoliberal 'Common Sense' & the Conservative Counter-Revolution

According to Cox: "The building of a new counter-hegemonic historic bloc is a long-term task for organic intellectuals working in constant interaction with the groups whose dissent from the established order makes them candidates for inclusion".[63] Though Cox's 'organic intellectuals' (like

Gramsci) were progressive social forces, the above quote does chime somewhat with the political struggle waged by the bourgeois anti-Keynesian
forces *within* the global hegemon from the 1950s onwards; desperate as
they were to win over 'traditional intellectuals', and help facilitate the restructuring of SROP and establish a new, in this case, neoliberal, HB.

Although Keynesian 'common sense' dominated US university facul-
ties and policy-makers centres from the 1940s, onwards a small but influential group of renegade liberal economists, led by Austrian philosopher
Friedrich von Hayek and including Ludwig von Mises, Karl Popper, and
Milton Friedman, still retained faith in the fundamental virtues of the
free market – *laissez-faire*, Say's Law and the Pareto-optimal included –
forming the Mont Pelerin Society in 1947. Government intervention was
not just highly inefficient and politically corrupt, von Hayek explained
in his *Road to Serfdom* (1944), it represented the greatest menace to private property and the competitive market and thus individual freedom
itself.[64] In 1950s, the Mont Pelerin Society set up its American base at the
University of Chicago – the so-called 'Chicago School' – where both von
Hayek and Freidman gave classes.

The nucleus of Friedman's monetarist theory was that demand-pull inflation was due to excessive monetary supply by governments and central
banks. Consequently, government deficit financing of the welfare state
and corporatist industrial relations were counter-productive, guaranteeing neither economic growth nor stability. Labour had to be flexible,
while managers should be afforded greater control over the production
process, free to restructure SROP, and adopt technological processes as
required. Behind Friedman's pseudo-scientific and mathematical models
lay clear class objectives. Market deregulation, low taxes, free markets,
privatisation, and dismantling of the welfare (though not the 'warfare')
state was clearly designed to augment exploitation and redistribute
wealth away from the subaltern classes towards capital.

As we saw in Chapter 1, the success of any particular hegemonic project (surface hegemony) depends on its connection to underlying social
structure (structural hegemony). During the Keynesian boom, these
'neoliberal' ideas remained fairly isolated from mainstream academia
and policy-makers in general, finding its principal source of financial
and political support amongst wealthy conservatives and Wall Street,
although various elements of the US *state-society complex* (e.g. the State
Department, USAID, the Ford Foundation) did finance various counter-hegemonic initiatives to alter 'common sense' in the periphery, most
notably Latin America, where dependency theory-inspired develop-
mentalist programmes threatened American investments.[65] Indeed, the
'Chicago Boys' would famously have their first chance to put neoliberalism in Pinochet's Chile following the CIA-backed *coup d'etat* in September 1973,[66] proving an unmitigated disaster except for the rich industrial,
financial, and landowning classes.[67]

The tide turned for the neoliberal hegemonic project in the late 1960s as US profit rates started to decline. Milton Friedman enthusiastically endorsed Nixon's entrance into the White House in 1969, especially once a few of his former Chicago Boys, notably George P. Shultz and Donald Rumsfeld,[68] were elected to cabinet posts. Despite the worsening economic climate, the Keynesian 'common sense' held firm. Friedman watched in dismay as Nixon introduced wage and price controls, dismissing him as "the most socialist of the presidents of the United States in the 20th century".[69] Nevertheless, as the 'organic crisis' dragged on into the early 1970s, an ever-larger section of the corporate and business world started to blame Keynesianism for their declining profit rates and complain that American society was afflicted by a deeper *ideological* malaise.

While *moral* conservatives lamented the loss of traditional family values (undermined by late-1960s hippy decadence) and worried about the repercussions of a general public ever-distrustful of mainstream politics/institutions (in the wake of Vietnam, Watergate, and the OPEC crisis), what really angered *economic* conservatives was the broad business environment in the US: what they perceived to be a society-wide entrenched anti-capitalist scepticism towards private enterprise and the profit motive – the very essence of "Americanism".[70] This was epitomised by the cover of *Time* magazine, on the 14th July 1975, showing Adam Smith posing behind the headlines, "Can Capitalism Survive?"[71]

It was in this context that American private capital began to organise, to act consciously as a *class*, what in Gramscian terms involved constructing an *hegemonic apparatus*: to create a "new ideological terrain".[72]

In 1972, the CEOs of the largest US corporations formed the Business Roundtable and together with the United States Chamber of Commerce and the National Association of Manufacturers launched a well-financed political lobbying campaign, mobilising a huge amount of campaign funds to pressure Congress, the media, and academia to promote neoliberalism and adopt a more pro-capital agenda.[73] Simultaneously, corporate cash poured into right-wing think tanks, be they well-established ones – such as the aforementioned Ford Foundation, the Hoover Institution, American Enterprise Institute, Center for Strategic and International Studies, National Bureau of Economic Research, and the Pew Charitable Trust – or new ones, such as the Heritage Foundation, the Center for the Study of American Business and the Cato Institute. The influence these business lobbies, think tanks, and foundations, and the impact it had on nurturing 'common sense' within civil society institutions, especially the media and key university economics departments and business schools, was substantial.[74]

Due to the on-going IOP process, it was not just the domestic arena that worried American capital. By the early 1970s, 300 American MNCs, including its seven largest banks, generated 40% of their annual profit from business operations abroad.[75] In 1973, key American economic and political elites led by Chase Manhattan Bank's David Rockefeller and Columbia University professor and State Department consultant, Zbigniew Brzezinski, set up the Trilateral Commission in 1973, which neo-Gramscian Stephen Gill considered a crucial moment in the transnational managerial class formation.[76]

The true political agenda of Trilateral Commission were made apparent in its 1975 Task Force Report, entitled "The Crisis of Democracy", specifically Chapter 3 on the "United States" written by renowned academic and Democratic Party defence consultant, Samuel Huntington. Expressing conservative 'common sense' Huntington maintained the underlying cause of the society's ills was the "dramatic upsurge of democratic fervour in America" during the 1960s, expressed in the huge growth of citizens participation "in the form of marches, demonstrations, protest movements, and 'cause' organisations", and "markedly higher levels of self-consciousness" amongst the racial minorities, students, unions demanding equality.[77] This "excess of democracy" meant Washington had to allocate more and more of the federal budget to social spending instead of foreign and security policy. Worse still, it had fuelled a lack of respect for authority amongst the public thereby producing problems of "governability". The antidote, Huntington held, was to set "desirable limits to the extension of political democracy."[78]

Important as these movements were in 'civil society' it was vital that neoliberalism exercise be adopted at the state level ('political society') in order to reconstruct capital-labour relations. The interim president, Gerald R. Ford, did go some way to ameliorate conservative factions when, acting on the Treasury's advice, he introduced severe austerity measures and refused to bail out New York City once it declared bankruptcy in 1975, representing the first serious neoliberal experiment in the West. The state of the economy and the Watergate debacle, however, meant it would be the Trilateral Commission-heavy administration of Democrat president, Jimmy Carter[79] which, despite its progressive campaign and affable 'down-to-earth Christian' image and upbeat popul11arist civil rights rhetoric, was the first one to embark on a concerned neoliberal agenda which included: amending the Internal Revenue Code via the Revenue Act of 1978 resulting in a slashing of income, corporate, and capital gains tax rates (to the benefit of the very wealthy); vetoing plans to increase public spending; effectively abandoning the commitment to full employment under the Full Employment and Balanced Growth Act of 1978; and embarking on business deregulation, reflected in the Airline Deregulation Act (removing price controls and slashing workers' salaries/benefits), and the Motor Carrier Act of 1980 (deregulation of the trucking industry). Indeed, it was Carter that named fellow Trilateral Commission member Paul Volcker as Federal Reserve chief to execute his eponymous "shock."

By that time, and with the country in a deep political, economic, and cultural malaise (expressed in Carter's "Crisis of Confidence" television address[80]) conservative social forces had rallied behind the Republican Party as the most appropriate vehicle to carry out wholesale economic structural change, the neoliberal 'Modern Prince'. In reality, little ideological difference lay between American mainstream parties, typical of an advanced bourgeois democracy,[81] but Republican Party happened to harbour the fiercest critics of Keynesianism and was greatly benefitted by the Supreme Court's 1976 decision to remove restrictions limiting corporations' contributions to political parties and *political action committees* (PACs) in the name of 'free speech', whose number unsurprisingly shot up. Governor of California, Ronald Reagan, was just one of many high-profile right-wing Republicans whose political careers had been sponsored by PAC funding and contributions from wealthy anti-Keynesian individuals.

The real challenge facing the 'New' Republican Party and connected social forces, however, was how to galvanise sufficient electoral support for what was in effect a rather narrow class agenda. As Gramsci declared, *political* problems can be more easily solved when they are disguised as *cultural* ones. The construction of a new neoliberal HB would involve a new hegemonic project appeal to cultural nationalism – *American exceptionalism* – those age-old 'common sense' foundational myths which were deeply imbedded in national popular discourse (e.g. Manifest Destiny, Frontier Myth, American Dream, City upon a Hill,[82] Chosen People[83]), Reagan projected hope and optimism; promising to return the US to its glorious (i.e. pre-Vietnam) past.[84]

Appropriately, the ideological inspiration behind this conservative shift would be yet another University of Chicago professor, Leo Strauss,[85] whose anti-New Deal agenda were first popularly espoused by GOP's 1964 presidential nominee, Senator Barry Goldwater, but which bore uncanny similarity to Huntington's "excessive democracy" thesis. Traditional 'American values' – religion, nation, family, and individual responsibility – argued the *neoconservative (neocon)* followers of Strauss, such as Irving Kristol and Norman Podhoretz, had been soiled by Keynesian-inspired 'dependency culture', immorality, feminism, atheism, 'liberalism', and excessive tolerance of lefties and foreigners.

Financed by PACs and aided and abetted by sympathetic right-wing media outlets (e.g. Fox News) the Republican Party launched a moral crusade against decadent 'anti-Americanism', targeting the unfairness of affirmative action (reflected in the Supreme Court's 1978 decision in *Regents of the University of California v. Bakke*, 1978) and the pro-abortionists (following *Roe v. Wade*). These 'common sense' messages were like manna from heaven to social conservatives, especially the Southern and Western white lower classes, traditionally considered Democrat voters, which Reaganite campaigners had targeted as vital to their electoral success. In parallel, the Republican Party started to officially endorse the growing Protestant evangelical movement. This mutually reinforcing relationship resulted in the formation of the Moral Majority, a New Christian Right political organisation which would constitute the ideological touchstone for Reagan's *neocon* revolution.[86]

Amongst the middle classes support for neoliberalism also began to grow, reinforced by the elite media. Reflecting the shift in the accumulation regime, the influential business press (e.g. the Wall Street Journal, Business Week, and Time Magazine) all changed their editorial line, denouncing the New Deal arrangements for stifling individual freedom, entrepreneurism, and commercialisation. The Public Broadcasting Service, meanwhile, contracted Friedman to extol the virtues of free markets an expensive ten-part television series of his book – "Free to Choose". Corporate money also flowed into erstwhile Keynesian university economics departments and business schools (e.g. Harvard and Stanford) indoctrinating future national and foreign elites in neoliberal economic 'common sense'.

Reagan's electoral victory in 1980, thus, represented just another step in a long process of consolidating the *political* project of neoliberalism (i.e. re-establish the conditions for capital accumulation necessary to restore class power). Characteristically, Reagan's Inaugural Address, on January 20th 1981, once again drew on classic American exceptionist rhetoric, setting out his administration's proposals for "an era of national renewal"; a "new beginning" for this "nation under God". Eschewing "inevitable decline", it was time to "dream heroic dreams" (making reference to fallen American soldiers, quite pertinently those in Vietnam) and become "a beacon of hope" for the world's repressed. But this was only possible if the US returned to its pre-New Deal socio-economic model (when "we unleashed the energy and the individual genius of man") and governmental intervention and red tape was at a minimum. Invoking classic liberal 'common sense', the federal government was not the *solution* to the problem, it was the *problem*.[87]

As both the Volcker Shock and Reagan's Inaugural Address indicated, tackling inflation remained the top policy priority – not least since it reduced the profitability of financial assets (and thus undermined foreign capital inflows and US hegemony – which, neoliberal 'common sense' had it, was largely a result of cost-push pressure from corporatist industrial relations. It was absolutely imperative to disenfranchise *organised labour*. Symbolism being so important, it was vital that this open class war be manifested itself in a direct *political* showdown with, and the defeat of, a key union, in order to appease capital and dismantle all Keynesian-style social solidarity.

While the Thatcher government purposely targeted the central pillar of the British labour movement, the National Union of Mineworkers, and key public-sector unions (e.g. National Union of Teachers), the Reagan administration launched its exemplary campaign against an unlikely middle-class union, Professional Air-Traffic Controllers Organisation

(PATCO), which had gone on strike in August 1981.[88] Nonetheless, the defeat of PATCO, like the miners' strike in the UK, was highly significant. Paul Volcker classified it as: "the most important single action of the administration in helping the anti-inflation fight,"[89] a position later reiterated by Federal Reserve Chief, Alan Greenspan, stressing that Reagan "gave weight to the legal right of private employers, previously nor exercised, to use their own discretion to both hire and discharge workers."[90]

This victory over organised labour, coming on the back of the Volcker Shock, was important in helping regain US 'intellectual and moral leadership', showing global capital that the American state would be the principal agency in restoring class power *en route* to a new profitable regime of accumulation. World hegemony, in short, began at home. American union membership and industrial sector real wages entered a long-term decline from which they would never recover.

Unsurprisingly, Wall Street and global financial markets reacted enthusiastically, especially once Chicago School-inspired *Reaganomics* was unleashed with its tight monetary policy, social spending cuts, deregulation, regressive taxation,[91] and privatisation of public assets (including the commodification of sectors of the welfare state) in line with Harvey's 'accumulation by dispossession'. Contrary to the free market discourse, Reaganomics actually sponsored less competition and consolidated monopoly power. Between 1980 and 1989, for example, there were just over 31,000 mergers worth some $1.34 trillion; with the FIRE (finance, insurance, and real estate) sectors seeing their share of total private investment double (reaching around 25%) between 1975 and 1990.[92] This was not the only area where neoliberal theory clashed with neoliberalism as a class project. Government spending on the welfare state, which transferred state funds to the subaltern classes was 'old thinking'; defence expenditure (military Keynesieniam) which redistributed wealth to upper classes was very much modern.

Indeed, like the restructuring of SROP under Truman, the breaking down of the Fordist-Keynesian HB under Reagan would take place against during a period of heightened tensions and fear of communist expansion. Strong parallels exist between this so-called *Second* Cold War (1979–85) and the *First* Cold War (1947–53).[93]

As in the 1940s, Washington would revert to a massive deficit-funded arms race to stimulate domestic industries businesses and promote technological advances, increasing military spending from $171 billion in 1981 to $376 billion in 1986.[94] The money would be poured into the Defense Advanced Research Projects Agency, which brought bringing together elite university research centres, private laboratories, and corporations, in order to develop new capital-intensive technologies for the military (e.g. missile technology, electronics, semiconductors, materials science, information technology, and nuclear physics) but whose discoveries would also have an important commercial application and help to compete with the Japanese (e.g. computers, high definition TVs, etc.).

Well-connected MIC defence contractors such as Boeing, Northrop, Martin Marietta, Grumman, Lockheed, and General Electric obviously welcomed military spending being restored to levels not witnessed since the Korean and Vietnam Wars.

Furthermore, the launching of the Second Cold War helped to consolidate the New Right HB, and therein marginalise left-leaning liberals. Not only were conservatives, especially the religious Right, innately anti-communist, but by setting up high-tech industries and military installations in the southern and western States – the traditional home of Republican voters – they would now develop a vested *material* interest in (not just ideological identification with) the MIC and NSS.

In addition, high deficit spending would inevitably raise the national budget deficit. This provided a convenient fiscal excuse for the government to drastically cut back on the welfare part of the Keynesian welfare-warfare state, slashing social benefits and attacking those 'work-shy' unemployed (according to Friedman, unemployment was always voluntary) and 'welfare queens'.

But the launching of the Second Cold War had clear *international* objectives too.

Reassertion of American Hegemony

"Relation of Military Forces"

As constantly reiterated throughout the book, Washington's military pre-eminence remains absolutely pivotal to US hegemony. Pax Americana, as shown, was underwritten by a basic agreement: the US would establish and maintain a series of security umbrellas to protect Europe, Latin America, and/or Asia from communist incursion (and internal uprisings) in return to the foreign dominant capitalist classes accepting American leadership on trade and financial matters within the context of the post-war accumulation model.[95] Evidently, this was based on a double assumption that: (1) the communist threat was real; and (2) the US alone possessed the resources to keep it at bay.

The Vietnam War, we have seen, gravely undermined US military hegemony. First, by shattering the myth of American invincibility and laying bare its strategic short-comings; and second, by leaving the US so economically and politically exhausted that it felt obliged to engage in East-West peace talks (*détente* and SALT I), which in turn lessened the Allies' need for Washington's protection. The perceived waning of American power, as noted, manifesting itself in numerous and important ways, ranging from an escalation of transatlantic tensions augmented, the concern of growing Soviet nuclear capabilities, hitherto 'client states' West Germany and Japan exercising economic and political independence, and the Third World slipping out of control.

In short, by the late 1970s there was a wide-ranging consensus on Capitol Hill on the need to reverse *détente* and reassert US dominance. Despite Carter's acclaimed 'peace initiatives'[96] and 'ethical' post-Vietnam pledge to place ethics and human rights at the heart of American foreign policy, his presidency retained familiar 'hawkish' aspects: the domestic defence budget was augmented; client state dictators continued to be bankrolled (e.g. El Salvador, the Philippines, Nicaragua, Haiti, and Indonesia); the Islamic fundamental *mujahideen* militants in Afghanistan received an estimated \$3.5 billion[97] large financial aid and advanced weaponry from Washington and Riyadh via the Zia dictatorship in Pakistan to fight the USSR;[98] and Saddam Hussein's Iraq was encouraged and supported in its war against Iran (following the latter's Islamic Revolution).

The neocons within Reagan's New Right HB – especially those with links to the WDPDC – urged winding back the clock and revert to the same Hobbesian 'friend-foe' strategy which had served US hegemony so well. The new president needed little prodding. Cramming his first administration with members of the newly revived Committee on the Present Danger, including Cold War warrior Paul Nitz (author of the infamous NSC-68) hired as chief political advisers in strategic foreign policy planning, Reagan launched the *Second* Cold War against the 'evil empire' with gusto. Like their domestic counterparts, the international objectives of the Second Cold War were to further class power and restore corporate profitability. These were broadly two-fold.

First, the rising of East-West hostilities gave the Reagan administration the perfect alibi to expand military and covert operations in the Third World. Under the *Reagan Doctrine* Washington pledged to 'rollback' alleged Moscow-backed 'communist regimes' – i.e. those nationalist/left-leaning governments throughout Africa, Asia Latin, and America who refused to open up their markets to American corporations and opted instead to pursue their own independent economic development models (under import substitution industrialisation – ISI). Reagan's favourite conservative think-tank, the Heritage Foundation, took it upon itself to uncover 'threats to national security'. It identified nine 'anti-democratic states' ready for "rollback" – Afghanistan, Angola, Cambodia, Ethiopia, Iran, Laos, Libya, Vietnam, and Nicaragua.[99] In his 1985 State of Union Address, Reagan emulated Truman exhorting Congress to continue to finance anti-communist struggles abroad since "support for freedom fighters is self-defense."[100]

Throughout the 1980s the Pentagon worked with the relevant intelligence agencies (most notably the CIA under its hawkish Director, Committee on the Present Danger member, William Casey) adopted a wide range of strategies to topple such as undesirable regimes involving training and equipping domestic terrorist/opposition forces – e.g. the aforementioned *mujahideen* (Afghanistan), the *Contras* (Nicaragua), National Union for the Total Independence of Angola [UNITA] (Angola), the

Coalition Government of Democratic Kampuchea/Khmer People's National Liberation Front (Cambodia), the "death squads" (Columbia and El Salvador) – without ruling out financing proxy wars (Iran-Iraq War); direct military strikes (Libya); or full invasions (Grenada).[101]

Second, a new nuclear arms race, in accordance with the 'friend-foe' logic, would increase tensions with the USSR and help the US reassert its military hegemony over the Western capitalist alliance by dragging West Germany and Japan back into the fold. In truth, this process was underway even before Reagan came into power. The Carter administration announced plans to upgrade its nuclear strike force in Europe to close the 'Soviet military spending gap', the late-1970s version of the 'bomber gap' (1950s), and the 'missiles gap' (1960s). Despite mass demonstrations throughout Europe – most notably in the FRG – a total of 572 *Tomahawk Cruise* and *Pershing II Missiles* would be deployed in Britain, Italy, the Netherlands, Belgium, and West Germany (the latter being the recipient of all of the 108 Pershing II Missiles) to "restore the balance" following the Soviet establishment of 'theatre nuclear forces' (SS-20s, SS-5s, and SS-4s) in the region (East Germany and Czechoslovakia).[102]

Claiming Moscow was outlining plans for a new generation of missiles – which was later proved to be false[103] – the Pentagon launched a major rearmament programme, placing a mass order for expensive airplanes such as the B-1 and B-2 bombers and F-15 and F-16 fighters and rebuilding the navy commissioning Trident missile-carrying nuclear submarines, *Iowa*-class battleships, and *Nimitz*-class supercarriers. But Reagan's definitive Cold War statement came with the announcement of the *Strategic Defense Initiative* (or *Star Wars*) in 1983, earmarking $26 billion for research purposes over the next five years, and which threatened to make Soviet nuclear missiles redundant.[104]

While taking the arms race to outer space was universally denounced by friends and enemies alike in the UN General Assembly, the launching of a Second Cold War itself was warmly received in some quarters. Britain, for example, saw it as a way to reinforce the transatlantic (nuclear) 'special relationship' and retain some of her former glory by riding on the back of the hegemon,[105] to "punch above her weight", in the words of former Foreign Secretary, Douglas Hurd.[106] London dutifully authorised the deployment of more American nuclear missiles on national soil, granting permission for the Americans to use British Royal Air Force bases to bomb Libya in April 1986. And even NATO-sceptic France recognised the benefits of increased military tensions to discipline West Germany and forestall its possible reunification; François Mitterrand winning warm praise from Reagan by urging Bonn to take Pershing II missiles.[107]

The mission to bring the core country's back under its wing was accomplished. Yet the unintended consequence of *Star Wars*, together with a dramatic reduction in global oil prices, so pivotal to its economy, dealt a deadly blow to the USSR, who was forced to sue for peace. Unsurprisingly, Gorbachev's push for wide-scale nuclear disarmament, nuclear test-bans, and removal of American and Soviet fleets from the Mediterranean, in addition to public announcements of plans to dramatically reduce the size of the Red Army, was greeted with dismay by Western conservatives.[108] Notwithstanding official peace rhetoric, Washington was also loath to countenance an end to Cold War security arrangements and accompanying NSS given its centrality to US hegemony over the capitalist world.

The subsequent fall of the Berlin Wall did not provoke the kind of unadulterated enthusiasm amongst the Western political elite that one might have expected. There were, however, certain positive sides. On an ideological level, for example, the US could claim the moral high ground, claiming its socio-economic system had proved to be superior to its supposed Leninist-Marxist. Hegelians neocons such as Francis Fukuyama felt free to announce "the end of history"[109]: the definitive victory of Western liberal democracy and free-market capitalism over all other societal models.

Second, the eventual break-up of the Soviet Union and Russia's 'shock therapy' meltdown under Boris Yeltsin would present the US a golden opportunity to expand its influence over Europe in the form of NATO enlargement, first absorbing East Germany (contravening the terms and spirit of the 1990 Gorbachev-Bush administration agreement[110]), but later driving deep into Central and Eastern Europe during, and long after, the Yugoslavian Wars of the 1990s;[111] a strategy which was even criticised within US foreign policy circles.[112] Moreover, Clinton would take advantage of the conflict to completely rewrite NATO's constitution, converting it onto a pro-active (rather than defensive) alliance which no longer required prior Security Council authorisation to carrying out 'benevolent' humanitarian intervention against a regime threatening its own population or world peace.

The biggest problem for the US with the end of the Cold War, however, was perfectly summed up by Gorbachev's advisor Georgi Arbatov: "We are going to do the worst thing we can do to you. We are going to take your enemy away".[113] Washington needed to find another overarching ideological (*Grand Strategy*) to justify and legitimise its world hegemony and on a basic level, salvage the scaling down of the MIC. Even before the Berlin Wall came down, the incumbent president, ex-CIA chief, George H. W. Bush (Bush I) had resurrected Nixon/Reagan's *War on Drugs*[114] as a short-term focus to justify continuing intervention in Latin America.

Whether guilty of duplicity or not,[115] the Bush administration wasted no time in fully exploiting Iraqi's invasion of Kuwait on 2nd August 1990. Speaking to Congress on the 11th September 1990 the president declared "the crisis in the Persian Gulf, as grave as it is, also offers a rare opportunity to move toward an historic period of cooperation. Out of these troubled times, our fifth objective – a new world order – can emerge."[116]

Though the exact nature of this *new world order* (NWO) remained purposely vague,[117] the Bush administration followed the classic Rooseveltian idealist line, calling for more cooperation amongst the world powers, strengthening of the UN[118] and a greater respect for international law and humanitarian causes (e.g. launching *Operation Restore Hope* in Somalia).[119] Such was the White House's impatience to establish the NWO via a US-led multilateral military invasion that it refused to: (1) let the extremely harsh UN-imposed economic sanctions take their full effect (Security Council *Resolution 661*), supported by many Senators and experts appearing before US Congressional Committees; (2) accept Moscow's offer of mediation; or (3) negotiate with Baghdad following their offer to withdrawal.[120]

The Gulf War itself constituted a successful exercising of US politico-military hegemony, and with its intellectual and leadership, in a number of ways. First, there was almost universal support the UN Security Council for Resolution 678 authorising *Operation Desert Storm*; and second, the revival of the 'friend-foe' device helped to reassert hegemony over the capitalist core countries (especially Japan and Germany) – even France abandoned its traditional neo-Gaullist independence to participate in the 34-country coalition force. Indeed, over 90% of the bill for the war was picked up by Saudi, Arabia, Kuwait, UAE, Japan, and Germany.[121] Third, as an important military media event, it helped demonstrate US's unchallenged military supremacy. Thanks to the so-called *Revolution in Military Affairs* (RMA) – a combination of the latest satellite and computing technology – the Pentagon was now able to wage war from air, sea, or land with unparalleled rapidity, absolute precision, and selective destructiveness (e.g. the use of laser-guided "smart" bombs), carry out vital sophisticated surveillance, reconnaissance, early warning, and intelligence gathering systems (e.g. AWACs, RC-135 River Joint electronic intelligence-gathering aircraft, and JSTARS), while avoiding unnecessary loss of life (especially American).[122]

Another positive aspect of the war, Bush I's confirmed to US armed forces stationed in the Gulf on 2nd March 1991, was that it had helped to erase the 'Vietnam syndrome' from the collective American public memory.[123] The message was clear: the US remained the unchallenged guarantor of the global capitalist system – the world policeman. Washington possessed the military capabilities and political will to discipline any renegade regime that opposed the expansion of American sponsored financialized neoliberal market-place society (Open Door) or threatened to upset the established international balance of power. The memorandum was not just directed towards the core but to the *Second* World – an ever-increasingly fragmented Soviet Bloc and ex-socialist countries like Yugoslavia and China embarking on their economic and political transitions – and the supposed 'problematic' areas of the *Third* World.[124] The defeat of communism meant it was no time for the US to drop its guard, Defence Secretary Dick Cheney insisted, the world was full of new dangers such as "rogue states", "similar future regional threats", and "ethnic conflicts".[125]

Under new president, Bill Clinton, Cheney's predictions would ring true in Europe with regards to the aforementioned Yugoslavia Wars, where following press reports of Serbian ethnic-cleansing/massacres Washington armed, trained, and supported a Croat counter-attack in 1995, largely eradicating all Serbs in Krajina, before directing a NATO-endorsed aerial bombing of in Bosnia (August/September 1995). US 'intellectual and moral leadership' was further demonstrated in the brokering of the Dayton Accord the following December (putting an end to the Bosnian Wars), with its military primacy, later on, show during the subsequent Kosovo Wars (Operation Allied Force) beginning in March 1999. In the 78-day campaign, described in RMA terms as "the most precise application of air power in history", allied pilots flew around 37,000 sorties (including 14,000 strike missions) launching 400 Tomahawk cruise missiles and dropping 20,000 'smart' and 5,000 conventional bombs on Serb forces to protect the Albanian population in Kosovo and expel the Serbian military and security forces from Kosovo.[126]

Indeed, despite its largely peaceful image – sponsoring the 1993 Oslo Accords between the Israelis and the Palestinians, apologising for US campaigns of repression in Guatemala,[127] and reiterating the importance of the UN, at least during his first term of office – the Clinton administration entertained clear 'hawkish' elements. During the presidential election campaign, Clinton denounced Bush I for his 'dovish' foreign policy and failure to adopt a tougher position with regards to non-democratic regimes (e.g. China and Cuba) or other systemic abusers of human rights, and having his candidacy endorsed by power-politics realists such as Paul Nitze, Zbigniew Brzezinski, and Robert Kagan. Just six months after his arrival at the White House, for example, Clinton sent the United States Air Force to bomb Baghdad in response to a supposed plot to assassinate ex-President Bush. Similarly, client-states such as Israel, Egypt, Columbia, Turkey, Pakistan, and Indonesia continued on the payroll, receiving generous economic and military aid – much of which was used to suppress internal pro-democratic opposition forces and human rights campaigners – in return for executing Washington's will in their respective regions.

The 'hawks' within the Clinton administration were also bolstered by the Republican Party seizure of Congress in 1994, itself a reflection of the on-going restructuring of American industrial capitalism underway since the mid-1970s.[128] Conservative social forces, many with vested interests in the WDPDC, urged the 'anti-Vietnam President' to adopt more of an aggressive foreign policy position and increase the military budget.[129] This would be reflected in the tougher trade sanctions against three of the six 'rogue states'[130] – Cuba (Helm-Burton Act), Libya, and

Iran (D'Amato Act – refused to sign the 1997 Ottawa Treaty banning anti-personnel landmines, opposition to the Rome Statute of the International Criminal Court in 1998, and signing of the Iraq Liberation Act (October 1998) which overtly called for "regime change" in Baghdad before authorising a four-day Anglo-American bombing campaign (*Operation Desert Fox*).

Nonetheless, it is fair to say that the Clinton presidency acquired more of an enlightened 'consensual' Wilsonian idealist sheen than Bush I. For many mainstream IR scholars, the *Clinton Doctrine* is synonymous with greater reliance on 'consensual' 'low politics', setting up of multilateral organisations and regimes (Gramsci's *second moment*) to promote neoliberalism and financialization around the world (see below), and therein boost American wealth, power and influence, rather than a reliance on traditional security 'high politics' and the MIC (the *third moment*).[131] This greater emphasis on the *capitalist* rather than the *territorial* logic of power constituted a sophisticated instrument of hegemonic governance and leverage over countries in the periphery/semi-periphery as they embarked on their neoliberal 'passive revolutions' (see below).

That there was no concerted attempt by the Clinton administration to resort to familiar binary 'friend-foe' logic,[132] was a testimony to the fact that the mid-1990s represented the hiatus of post-Cold-War US hegemony. Globalization was at its height and Wall Street and even Main Street were sitting on the top of the world. According to mainstream academics and media pundits, the US was leading global capitalism to a new golden age embodied in the *New Economy*. Thanks to advances in the financial sector, telecommunications. and information technology (IT), symbolised in *dot.com* boom,[133] traditional business models no longer served. The 'New Economy' could bring about such improvements in productivity, distribution, efficiency, and above all in achieving perfect information, that business cycles, recession, and hence declining profit rates were a thing of the past. Profits on Wall Street soared, selling securities to the public to fund Silicon Valley investment in telecommunications and high-tech goods, while overseeing the 'new media' merger mania, linking up telecommunications companies with 'content' companies to deliver new online services.[134]

High corporate profits attracted attention around the world. Surplus capital from Japan, Germany, OPEC states, and especially East Asia, Russia, and Latin America following their respective financial crisis (see below), flooded into Wall Street reinforcing the centrality of American finance, which was granted even more opportunity to exploit economies of scale and scope following banking reforms announced under the 1999 Gramm-Leach-Bliley Act. More than ever, Washington felt vindicated in lecturing other countries' elites on suitable policy options. Transnational corporate elite and conservative think tanks used their connections in government, academia, and the media to openly criticise the 'rigidity' of European, Japanese, and East Asian (labour) markets and the counter-productive and unsustainable nature of their social welfare programmes.

Embedding Neoliberalism Globally

With international monetary governance increasingly in the hands of 'market forces' following the collapse of Bretton Woods, the DWSR – headed by the US and British Treasury departments and associated financial sectors – began lobbying other OECD states to open up domestic finance and banking systems from 1979 onwards. The aim was to gain access to their funds, link up with 'domestic' private operators, and ultimately mould financial systems in line with American business interests and practices. Highly influential elements of 'civil society' also engaged in nurturing society-wide 'common sense' with regards to the virtues of neoliberalism. Anglo-Saxon elite print media (Wall Street Journal, Time and Business Week Magazines, the Financial Times, the Economist) and the prestigious business schools and international management training programmes (Harvard, Yale, Stanford), all overtly endorsed the merits of financial deregulation.

These messages were not falling on stony ground. As neo-Gramscians observed, thanks to IOS and IOP processes there already was a degree of economic integration within the 'Lockean heartland'. The internationalisation of American finance intensified the IOP, facilitating the further global expansion of American MNCs in the finance, retail, insurance, and other service sectors. This, in turn, reinforced the process of cultural homogenisation and contributed to the socialisation of global economic and political leaders in the liberal values, lifestyles, language, and efficient business practices of American capitalism. The social forces generated would have a huge impact on the dynamic of core countries' internal social structures (HBs) and form of state (FOS). The more businesses were locked into transnational structures, the more capital pushed for open capital markets, deregulated finance and capital mobility (Open Door), and adjustment of domestic policies to the requisites of competitive hierarchically structured global economy. For many neo-Gramscians, as we have seen, this engendered genuine transnational class formation.

The adoption of neoliberalism/financialization thus was not an 'externally imposed' hegemonic project. All businesses were concerned about declining profits rates and the rightward shift promised to subordinate labour to capital and therefore permit greater exploitation and limit domestic policy options, not least with regards to welfare state expenditure. With Keynesianism in crisis, capital within across the core urged the liberalisation of capital markets. In Western Europe, Britain's decision to remove capital controls in 1979 was soon followed by the Netherlands and West Germany (1981), France (partially in 1984), Sweden (1985), and

Italy and Denmark (1988). This was institutionalised in the 1989 OECD Capital Movements Code, while the Anglo-American sponsored Basle Accord (1988) established regulatory guidelines for the international banking system, as well as giving banks the incentive to privilege the buying of government (especially US) bonds.

The adoption of neoliberalism around the world would prove a slow, complex, and uneven process. The social transformation was affected by the internal balance of class forces within a particular state – its HB – and the degree of its integration into/dependence on, circuits of global capital, notably Anglo-American finance. The greater the relative power, autonomy, and cohesion of capital to act as a class, the greater its success at pressurising state power to dismantle Keynesian and neo-mercantilist/developmentalist growth model.

For neo-Gramscians, as we have seen, the restructuring of SROP, HB, and FOS often took place under the guise of *disciplinary neoliberalism* and institutionalised via *new constitutionalism*, be it at the regional level (e.g. regional integration) or global level (e.g. the Bretton Woods institutions). The idea was to limit fiscal and monetary policy options by transferring competence over these areas to external institutions staffed by 'apolitical' experts and technocrats and therein embed both neoliberal practices and implicitly, the neoliberal FOS domestically.

These multilateral institutions did not just promote a new system of accumulation but, consistent with Gramsci *second moment*, to consolidate and legitimise class hegemony and neutralise or assimilate of opposition groups, often via a 'passive revolution' in its *trasformismo* version. A good example of this elite *trasformismo* was van Apeldoorn's account of the European integration process, cited in Chapter 1, and the eventual victory of the 'globalist' neoliberal faction over its hegemonic project rival. Maastricht constituted a clear example of new constitutionalism: laying out tight 'convergence criteria' for euro membership and provided, "a supranational anchor for the purpose of a politics of austerity".[135] Indeed, once a country joined the euro it not only had to abide by eurozone norms but also keep a tight rein on fiscal policy or face punitive action (e.g. the Stability and Growth Pact, the Euro-Plus Pact, and the European Fiscal Pact). Member states' governments were thus voluntarily 'ceding economic sovereignty' to Brussels and Frankfurt under self-imposed 'disciplinary neoliberalism'. As intended, this *embedded neoliberalism* process of integration has dramatically moulded SROP in line with the demands of neoliberal system of accumulation right across the EU, creating, as far van der Pijl is concerned: "a free space for capital, with separate state jurisdictions keeping political sovereignty and democracy away from the larger structure".[136]

Again, it is worth reiterating - contrary to the Coxian view - that this 'new constitutionalism' was not 'imposed from the outside' but actually championed by class interests at the domestic level engaging in a dialectic interaction with global social forces. The dismantling of the 'social market economy' in the FRG is a good example of how, against the backdrop of the on-going IOP process, substantial pressure from internal social forces, dialectically interrelated with external ones, conspired to use integration to break apart the close institutional ties between the banks, corporations, and labour. Simply put, German financial and manufacturing companies pressed the government to go ahead with integration as a way to expand market share, access cheaper credit, reduce labour costs, and increase competitivity, especially post-Plaza Accords.[137] Reunification and Maastricht's convergence criteria provided the perfect cover for Berlin to restructure German SROP. Similar motives led Sweden to join the EU in 1995, where a small potent capitalist class used 'disciplinary neoliberal' norms (without accepting the euro) to dismantle the social democratic model and associated rates of corporate tax and wealth distribution which no national government had proved able to do.

European integration, and its associated new constitutionalism arrangements, inspired a genuine explosion of Regional Trade Agreements (RTA) around the world, be they in North American (NAFTA), Latin American (MERCOSUR), Asia (ASEAN), Africa (ECOWAS), or the Middle East (PAFTA). Indeed, as of 1st May 2018 the World Trade Organisation (WTO) had received notification of 459 RTA with 287 actually in force.[138] Typically under these RTAs deserves investors' rights and capital accumulation are prioritised above formal national sovereignty concerns and the domestic population's well-being. Chapter 11 ("Investment") of NAFTA, for example, apart from insisting on non-discrimination and equal standards of protection for non-national firms, insists that any enterprise that "seeks to make, is making or has made an investment" in any of the member states can sue any of the latter for losses deemed to be incurred by an alleged breach of NAFTA norms.[139]

One core country that did not initially opt for the regionalist route to restructure neoliberalism/financialization was Japan, a testimony to both relative weakness of the unions within its HB and its regional hegemonic ambitions. As noted in Chapter 2, Japan's post-war growth strategy was to adhere to neo-mercantilist *developmental state*[140] model – the 'Asian developmental state' (ADS) – directed by its famous bureaucracies, the Ministry of International Trade and Industry (MITI), and the Ministry of Finance (MOF) in an economy dominated by its vertically and horizontally integrated business conglomerate networks – *keiretsu*.[141] Again, like Germany, internal and external social forces would interact to weaken the institutional relationship between large manufacturing forms and associated banks, which once capital controls were officially loosened in 1980, currency revaluation (1984–85), and opening up of capital markets. This led to a massive inflow of international capital a rising yen,[142] mounting inflation, dubious bank lending practices, and ultimately a real estate and equity market bubble[143] (which crashed in the early 1990s[144]).

It was in this context, and in order to circumvent external trade barriers – many resulting from the RTA explosion – Japanese FDI flooded abroad in the 1980s, notably to the US and Europe. The other main destination, and the basis of Tokyo's regionalisation strategy, was East Asia where it set up a new vertical division of labour with itself at the apex. Under this so-called 'flying geese' format, uncompetitive industries (e.g. consumer electronics, automobiles, chemicals, and textiles) or production processes would be relocated/outsourced sub-contracting the four 'newly industrialised economies' (NIE-4) of Taiwan, South Korea, Hong Kong, and Singapore, these 'Asian Tigers', who in turn would import lower valued-added/labour intensive goods and raw materials from poorer countries occupying the next level – Thailand, Indonesia, Malaysia, and the Philippines (ASEAN-4), with China, occupying the base.

It is important to emphasise that although many countries would undergo neoliberal restructuring via regionalism (or regionalisation) these arrangements always took place within, and had to be compatible with, an on-going *global* 'new constitutionalism' process under the revitalised Bretton Woods institutions. Again, returning to Cox's analysis, the function of these institutions was to help legitimise/facilitate 'passive revolutions': provide the necessary global regulatory and juridical framework to embed neoliberalism, limit, the scope of state intervention in the market guarantee access to foreign markets (Open Door), and standardise international business practices.

With regards to global trade this was within the new enlarged version of GATT, the WTO, whose 60 accords: extended free trade into agriculture (albeit with the maintenance of high US, European, and Japan subsidies), textiles, the service sector (under the General Agreement on Trade in Services); obliged states to adopt a 'favourable business climate' (including the removal of non-tariff barriers); guaranteed intellectual property (monopoly) rights with the establishment of Trade-Related Aspects of Intellectual Property Rights; and prohibited placing conditions on foreign investors with regards to 'local content requirements' under the Trade Related Aspects of Investment Measures. All in all, the members agreed to limit the scope of state intervention in the market and prioritise the interests of exporters and producers over those of consumers, public health, workers, or the environment.[145] Importantly, any trade disputes that might arise under the agreements were taken to a legally binding multilateral mechanism – the Dispute Settlement Understanding – whose decisions are taken behind closed door by a three-person panel, albeit with an option of recourse to an Appellate Body (instituted at the behest of the Europeans and Canadians).

Given their erroneous interpretation of hegemony, many neo-Gramscians such as Gill mistakenly interpreted the anti-globalization protests at the WTO's 1999 Ministerial Conference in Seattle as indicating the seeds of a genuine counter-hegemonic movement, reflected in the launching of the World Social Forum. This dramatically over-stated the strength/unity of opposition forces. Nonetheless, to offset such criticisms, the Geneva-based institution, cleverly repackaged itself through a process of *trasformismo*, assimilating 'common sense' anti-globalization language/discourse into its press releases and policy initiatives with constant references on the need to guarantee fair trade, social justice, institutional transparency, labour rights, health safeguards, and environment protection. The subsequent WTO round launched in November 2001 entitled the "Doha Development Agenda" was specifically sold as extending the benefits of the globalization to less developed countries.[146] Notwithstanding the rhetoric, however, the underlying constitution of the WTO would not undergo substantial change. Though north-south differences would hold up sectorial advancements in the Doha Development Round, the overall tendency was towards the Open-Door process, be it via the WTO or RTAs.

But for many developing and less developed countries the neoliberal restructuring process was carried out in a more aggressive form, guided by the other two revitalised Bretton Woods institutions, Washington-based IMF, and World Bank, who together with the US Treasury Department, drew up an identikit of policy reforms to restructure 'failing countries' SROP, HB, and FOS. Contrary to the argument forwarded by many neo-Gramscians (and all liberals), however, this new hegemonic discourse – the "Washington Consensus" – was not purely *ideological*, but underpinned by real *material* power, which Robert Wade and Frank Veneroso have termed the *Wall Street-Treasury-IMF* (WSTI) *Complex*.[147]

American hegemony, as observed, was underpinning a new regime of accumulation. The *WSTI Complex* constituted a vital part of this, promoting Open Door financialization and neoliberal orthodoxy throughout the 1980s and 1990s. The coercive character of the WSTI Complex with this would be most graphically demonstrated in their design and imposition (albeit with the acquiescence of the countries' elites) of Chicago School-inspired SAPs.

The key mechanism to unlocking the Open Door and triggering the associated 'accumulation by dispossession' process that followed was dollar-denominated sovereign debt, which had risen steadily post-OPEC crisis, but ballooned uncontrollably following the Volcker Shock.[148] When Mexico announced it was unable to service its $90 billion debt, fear of a precedent being set[149] threatening both Wall Street and the global financial system in general, the US Treasury Secretary resuscitated the moribund IMF (now purged of Keynesians) and charge it specifically with rescheduling Third World. The deal imposed on Mexico, approved by the US Federal Reserve and Treasury Department, would be the template for future SAPs, helping local elites restructure their internal SROP and hence FOSs,[150] integrating the region more fully into US-led financialization[151] while dealing a deadly blow for ISI strategies and NIEO aspirations.[152]

Given the considered universal applicability of neoliberal tenets the SAPs prescribed for debtor countries throughout Latin America, Central and Eastern Europe,[153] Asia, and Africa would be virtually identical. In a variant on Gramsci's *Caesarism*, a 'strong man' would lead a 'passive revolution' and restructure the SROP, HB, and FOS[154] supported by a powerful section of the economic and political elite who were well-placed to benefit from the stripping of national assets and other 'accumulation by dispossession' practices in collusion with foreign financial operators.[155] The process would involve implementing over a hundred neoliberal IMF "conditionalities", namely privatisation of state industries, austere fiscal and monetary policy, market liberalisation and removal of price controls, tariff reduction, devalued/fixed exchange rate, labour flexibility, the facilitating of foreign direct investment, currency convertibility, and the opening up of capital markets.[156]

The latter would enrich Anglo-Saxon finance even further. First, once countries opened up to global finance the instability of the post-Bretton Woods international monetary system forced more and more foreign businesses to buy 'insurance' against possible exchange rate and security fluctuations in the form of derivatives (e.g. credit defaults swaps), which again benefitted Wall Street and London. Second, the failure of debt rescheduling and neoliberal SAPs to kick-start the economies, together with the entrance of large-scale short-term financial capital (hot money) would often lead to a further crisis (in the form of a banking crisis[157]) and another wave of 'accumulation by dispossession' directed by the WSTI Complex, to the benefit of American capital, exemplified by Treasury *Brady Bond* debt-equity swaps arrangements with most Latin American governments in the late 1980s and 1990s, to disastrous regional effect.[158]

What also became evident in the 1990s with the experiences of Japan (1992), Mexico (1995), East Asia (1997), Russia (1998), and Brazil (1998), was that the more economies *financialized* (financial 'deregulation' and open capital markets included), the more they were: (1) at the whim of foreign exchange and interest rates fluctuations; and (2) likely to be engulfed in capital (as a result of the uneven development of capitalism) resulting in an asset-bubble and eventual crash,[159] resembling the models set out by economists Charles P. Kindleberger and Hyman Minsky.[160] Even Washington accepted this as a truism. Robert Rubin, US Treasury Secretary between 1995 and 1999, admitted that "financial crises of one sort or another are virtually inevitable;" but what mattered, he insisted was that the US State (encompassing the WSTI Complex) act as "chief of the fire department" and show itself to be able to manage domestic and international crises.[161]

And when it did act the WSTI Complex made sure that burden of debt repayment would fall squarely on the borrowing countries and not on the lenders (Western banks) and that any IMF directed bailout package involved the imposition of even stricter neoliberal SAPs since the diagnosis of the malady, inescapably, was an insufficiently open market economy. Indeed, with a special focus on the East Asian crisis, Peter Gowan, has even claimed the WSTI Complex (well-connected heavily leveraged, American hedge funds included) has consciously conspired to *provoke* financial crises as part of national economic statecraft, using panic in the markets not to make short-term profits on breaking currencies, but a part of Washington's broader political agenda in the region of restructuring countries' SROP, HB, and FOS.[162] Certainly once the crisis hit East Asia the IMF part of the WSTI Complex wasted no time imposing its Washington Consensus SAP on the region East, with the US Treasury under Robert Rubin and Larry Summers rejecting other alternatives systems of financial governance in the area such as Japan's suggested Asian Monetary Fund (favoured by all East Asian countries except China).[163]

Financialization had its 'blowback', however. Although the massive inflow of capital into Wall Street from the East Asia crisis would stimulated share prices and compensated for plunging internal saving rates[164] contagion led to Russia sovereign debt default which provoked a global financial panic.[165] Unfortunately, for the colossal speculative hedge fund Long-Term Capital Management Fund (LTCM), mobile global capital sought the safest harbour, US Treasury Bonds (TBs), which happened to be their core investment (along with derivatives), driving yields way down. LTCM's size, structure, and political contacts[166] made it 'too-big-too-fail' enabling it to engage in heavy leveraging.[167] When the Fund's equity in free-fall, the Federal Reserve organised a $3.6 billion bailout by 16 financial institutions to avoid the collapse of the financial system.

The LTCM crisis was important, not only because it indicated the interconnectedness and essential unstable nature of the neoliberal/financialization project, but it showed that even the 'heartland' was not immune, seen with more devastating effects in 2008.[168]

Notes

1 Quoted in Cunningham (2004), p. 557.
2 Quoted in McCrisken (2003), p. 11.
3 Quoted in Panitch & Ginden (2005a, 2005b), p. 87.
4 Amongst the regimes who enjoyed economic, political, and military support in return for their subservience to Washington included: South Korea (SyngmanRhee/Park Chung-hee); Iran (the Shah); Thailand (Plaek Phibunsongkhram/Sarit Thanarat/Thanom Kittikachorn); Taiwan (Chang Kai-shek); Indonesia (Suharto); Laos (the Royal Lao Government); Congo (Mobutu); Nicaragua (the Somoza family); Guatemala (various from

Castillo Armas onwards); Paraguay (Alfredo Stroessner); the Philippines (Ferdinand Marcos); and Brazil (Castelo Branco). See, for example, Leffler & Westad (eds.) (2010), Johnson (2002), Askin & Collins (1993). According to John Coatsworth, the US participated directly or indirectly in the overthrow of 24 Latin American governments during the Cold War; see Coatsworth (2010), pp. 220–1.

5 Over 58,000 Americans were killed and 300,000 wounded, with the total number of slain estimated to stand around 1.4 to 1.7 million. See The Vietnam Veterans Memorial: The Wall-USA (2018) and *The British Medical Journal* (2008).

6 For information on the human costs of the Vietnam War see Turse (2013), pp. 11–15, 79–80, 174–91.

7 Powaski (1998), p. 167.

8 By 1979 Japan was the USSR's largest 'Western bloc' trading partner (measured in terms of total volume of trade) after West Germany. Kimura (2000), p. 239.

9 Kissinger (1973).

10 Prebisch (1950).

11 UNCTAD (1974).

12 Armstrong *et al.* (1984), p. 15.

13 Quoted in Fouskas & Gökay (2012), p. 45.

14 See Brenner (1998).

15 The hourly manufacturing costs in the US were three times higher than Europe and ten times that of Japan Armstrong *et al.* (1984), p. 179. During the 1950s, for example, West German manufacturing output grew by an average of 10% p.a. and GDP 8%, the highest in Europe.

16 Brenner (1998).

17 Block (1977), p. 145. Block notes that from the late 1950s onwards the US became a massive importer of consumer goods; significantly by the late 1960s that even extended to the automobile sector.

18 Armstrong *et al.* (1984), p. 257. Significantly, the rate of profit in the American manufacturing sector in 1970 was a third below the average from the mid-1950s to mid-1960s. Panitch & Ginden (2012), p. 135.

19 Spero (1977), p. 92.

20 By 1971, the US was running a BOP deficit of $29 billion. Cherunilam (2010), p. 233.

21 The 1968 US budget deficit of $24.2 billion, David Painter, observed, coincided very closely with the amount spent on the Vietnam War that year. Painter (1999), p. 68.

22 These included the Civil Rights Act and Economic Opportunity Act, both 1964, and the Elementary and Secondary Education Act, the Voting Right Act, the Immigration and Nationalist Act and the Social Security Act (out of which came Medicare and Medicaid), all in 1965.

23 The US inflation rate rose from 1.3% in 1950, 5.7% in 1970, 6.2% in 1973, to 11% in 1974. US Inflation Calculator (2018).

24 Block (1977), p. 195.

25 Cherunilam (2010), p. 233.

26 Campbell (2005), p. 188.

27 Chernow (1990), p. 402.

28 Roberts (2002), p. 31.

29 According to Panitch and Gindin, the profit ratios of *finance* to *non-finance* firms were 18% to 11% (1945–52) and 7.5% to 4.5% (1953–69). Panitch & Ginden (2005a, 2005b), p. 53.

30 Tsoukalis (1985).

31 Once again it is worth remembering here the clash between Keynes and Dexter White over the future structure of the IMF at Bretton Woods, 1944. Keynes had alerted the latter of the danger of placing the responsibility of exchange rate adjustment solely on the deficit nation. It was with some irony, then, that when White's system prevailed it gave the US little room for manoeuvre when Japan and Germany refused to revalue their respective currencies the late 1960s.

32 Quoted in Eichengreen (2007), p. 244.

33 Rupert (1995), p. 179.

34 Rupert (2000), p. 28.

35 Jankowski (1998), p. 33.

36 Moody (1988), Chapter 4.

37 Aronowitz (2003), p. 8.

38 According to Paul Baran and Paul Sweezy, the world had entered a new age of "monopoly capitalism" by the mid-1960s, one in which the large corporations no longer tended to compete with each other on price, but on reducing costs, market/resource access, and product differentiation. Competition between 'workers' replaced competition between 'companies'. Baran & Sweezy (1966), pp. 57–9.

39 For data comparative data on falling profits, see Desai (2004), p. 233.

40 Cox claims levels of inflation are proportionate to the degree of class polarisation under the various corporatist frameworks, illustrating his point by contrasting the experiences of US, Britain, and Italy with that of Germany, Holland, Sweden, or Japan. See Cox (1987), p. 22. A similar argument is set out in: Hibbs (1978), pp. 153–75.

41 By the end of the 1960s, for example, 40% of the largest French and German firms had adopted this corporate form, See Djelic (2001), pp. 6–7, p. 271.

42 Marx & Engels (2010) "Chapter 14. Countervailing Influences".

43 See, for example, Clarke (1988), Chapter 11, pp. 287–341

44 Between 1970 and 1972 inflation averaged 5.3% annually, in 1973 8%, and from 1974 more than 10%; cited in Cox (1987), p. 274.

45 Unemployment in Western Europe, for example, rose from its average of 1.5% in the 1960s to 4.2% in the 1970s. van der Wee (1987), p. 77.

46 Inflation stood around 26% and unemployment above 1 million. Harvey (2007), p. 57.

47 Burk (1992).

48 Significantly, the proportion of total assets controlled by the richest 1% households in the US dropped from its peak of 35% in 1965, to 30% in 1970 and then plummeted to 22% in 1975. See Duménil & Lévy (2004a), pp. 138–9.

49 Gowan (1999), pp. 21–2.

50 Engdahl (2004), pp. 130–8.

51 Perkins (2006), Chapter 15; Blanchard (2009), p. 4.

52 Nitzan & Bichler (2002), pp. 198–247.

53 Cordesman (2003), pp. 86–9.

54 Nitzan & Bichler (2002), pp. 24–7, 198–273.

55 Indeed, as Perkins observes, the 'revolving door' between Bechtel and the Republic Party Perkins is particularly well-developed: Richard Helm (Nixon's Director of CIA under Reagan/Bechtel Consultant); William Simon (Nixon's Treasury Secretary/Bechtel Consultant); George Shultz (Reagan's Secretary of State/Bechtel Vice-President); Caspar Weinberger (Reagan's Secretary of Defense/Bechtel Vice-President); William Casey (Director of CIA under Reagan/Bechtel Consultant). See also Perkins (2006), Chapter 15.

56 Basel (2013).

57 Gowan (1999), pp. 24–5.
58 Helleiner (1995).
59 The assets of foreign banking offices in the US increased eight-fold in the 1970s, US assets abroad seven-fold and foreign portfolio investment (FPI) in the G7 11-fold. Panitch & Ginden (2005a, 2005b), p. 58.
60 Volcker brought inflation down from 13.5% in 1980 to 3.2% in 1983. Stiglitz (2004), p. 37.
61 Poor countries, conversely, viewed the Volcker Shock with great dismay. Suddenly a stream of cheap credit from private transnational financial markets came to an end. Debts, contracted in dollars, were now unpayable. The scene was set for the early 1980s debt crisis which began in Mexico in 1982 and spilled over to the rest of Latin America and Central and Eastern Europe.
62 Henwood (2003), p. 208.
63 Cox (1987), p. 390.
64 Hayek (2001).
65 Kinzer (2006), p. 4.
66 Central Intelligence Agency (1970); Subcommittee on Multinational Corporations (1973).
67 See, for example, Valdés (1995) and Frank (1976). The Chilean model for regime change and subsequent neoliberal 'shock therapy' was repeated in other countries in Latin America in the 1970s, notably Uruguay, Argentina, Bolivia, and Brazil, relying on similar brutality and producing similarly poor results. Klein (2008), pp. 75–97.
68 Friedman would later lobby Reagan to name Rumsfeld his Vice President instead of George H. Bush.
69 Interview with Milton Friedman conducted 1st October 2000. Commanding Heights (2000).
70 According to a Harris poll, conducted in 1975, only 15% of Americans had "a great deal of confidence" in corporate leaders, a drop of 40% from its mid-1960s level. Cited in Silk & Vogel (1976), p. 21.
71 Time Magazine (1975).
72 Gramsci (1971), pp. 365–6.
73 In 1974, for example, the United States Chamber of Commerce set up its "Economics for Young Americans" programme to teach the national youth the importance of "preserving and advancing the free enterprise system".
74 Testimony of the paradigm shift underway was the granting of the Nobel Prize for Economics to both Friedrich Hayek and Milton Friedman for their work on monetarist theories in 1974 and 1976, respectively.
75 Zinn (2005), p. 532.
76 Gill (1991). The stated objectives of the Trilateral Commission were improving US-European-Japanese business environment; acting as a forum for large industrial, financial and service-based corporations from the respective regions to debate; and helping facilitate greater transnational business.
77 See Chapter 3: "The United States", by Samuel P. Huntington in Crozier *et al.* (1975).
78 Huntington (1975).
79 Once sworn in as President, Carter dutifully named fellow Trilateral Commission members to the posts of Vice President (Walter Mondale), Secretary of State (Cyrus Vance), Treasury Secretary (W. Michael Blumenthal), Secretary of Defense (Harold Brown), National Security Adviser (Zbigniew Brzezinski), and Energy Secretary (James Schelinger).
80 The Carter Center (1979).

81 Capital, Gramsci insisted, was always eager to play one political group off against the other, without committing:

> The great industrialists utilise all the existing parties turn by turn, but they do not have their own party. This does not mean that they are in any way 'agnostic' or 'apolitical' Their interest is in a determinate balance of forces, which they obtain precisely by using their resources to reinforce one party or another in turn from the varied political checkerboard.
>
> Gramsci (1971), p. 155

82 Attributed to a 1620 sermon by English puritan preacher John Winthrop, and in whose phrase "the eyes of all people are upon us" has been interpreted, wrongly according to Godfrey Hodgson, as signifying that the new Christian colonies would serve as an example to the world: "a city upon a hill". Hodgson (2009), pp. 1–3.

83 "And we Americans are the peculiar, chosen people", Herman Melville declared in the 1850s, "the Israel of our time; we bear the ark of the liberties of the world". Quoted in Barry (2011), p. 304.

84 Reagan's exceptionalist stance is best captured in a speech he made to the first Conservative Political Action Conference, sponsored by the Conservative Political Union, in January 1974. See Hodgson (2009), p. 176.

85 Strauss (1999).

86 Brenner (2007), p. 47.

87 Reagan (1981).

88 Declaring the industrial action both illegal and a "peril to national security", Reagan demanded they return to work within 48 h or face immediate dismissal, resulting in the firing of 11,345 workers (of 13,000 total) who failed to meet the deadline. Early (2006).

89 Quoted in Taylor (1995), p. 778.

90 Greenspan (2003).

91 Citing the *Laffer curve* amending the tax code so as to be more favourable to the corporations and the wealthy – notably the Economic Recovery Tax Act (ERTA) and the Tax Reform Act (TRA), of 1981 and 1986, respectively – thereby continuing the process began under the Carter administration. Duménil & Lévy (2004b), pp. 105–33.

92 Brenner (2006), pp. 214–15.

93 Halliday (1983).

94 Powaski (1998), p. 233.

95 See Rothkopf (1998).

96 Such an example would include launching ill-fated SALT II talks, the Panama Canal Treaties, and the Camp David Accords.

97 Kaplan *et al.* (2003).

98 According to former CIA director, Robert Gates the US aid to the *mujahideen* guerrillas in Afghanistan began six months *before* the Soviet invasion and was specifically designed to provoke an attack from Moscow in order to bog down the Kremlin in its 'own Vietnam'; Gates (1996), pp. 146–7. This version of the story would be later confirmed by Carter's security adviser, Zbigniew Brzezinski, in an interview with a French magazine, *Nouvel Obervateur* in January 1998. Brzezinski (1998).

99 Butler (1984), p. 268.

100 Reagan (1985).

101 Bodenheimer & Gould (1989), Chapter 4.

102 Blacker & Duffy (eds.) (1984), p. 308.

103 In fact, according to the CIA's own figures, the Soviets, bogged down in Afghanistan, had actually reduced defence spending between 1976 and 1983 and strictly limited arms procurement. Holzman (1989).

104 US Congress, Office of Technology Assessment (1985).
105 This relationship conformed to the established pattern of post/present hegemons, according to world-system theory. See Chase-Dunn (1998), Chapter 9.
106 Hurd (1992).
107 Sutton (2007), pp. 197–201.
108 On hearing of Gorbachev's offer at Reykjavik to scrap *all* nuclear weapons, Thatcher took the first flight to Camp David to urge the President not to dismantle the Western defence system.
109 Fukuyama (1992).
110 Sarotte (2014).
111 Chollet & Goldgeier (2008).
112 A group of some 50 high-profile former senators, cabinet ministers, ambassadors, military officers, and foreign policy analysts signed an open letter to President Clinton warning him that such a policy was "ill-conceived" and likely to both destabilise the region and unnecessarily provoking Russia. Rauchhaus (ed.) (2001). pp. 203–6.
113 Quoted in Buchanan (1999), p. 4.
114 Considered in some quarters to be a smokescreen for demonisation of ethnic minorities. See, for example, Bucerius & Tonry (eds.). (2014).
115 According to the documents published in the *New York Times*, Washington expressed sympathy for Baghdad's demands and gave the impression it would turn a blind eye if an invasion of Kuwait were to take place. The New York Times (1990).
116 Quoted Krahmann (2005), p. 532.
117 Showing remorse for his "life of sin" in stoking Cold War antagonisms, the George Kennan publicly denounced Bush I's NWO strategy and urged the US to avoid searching for "a single grand strategy of foreign policy, to replace our fixation on the Soviet Union". The New York Times (1994).
118 Between 1984 and 1987, the Reagan administration was solely responsible for blocking 150 General Assembly Resolutions. Blum (2001), 185–97.
119 The US intervention in client-state Panama and bloody removal of hitherto CIA-bankrolled General Manuel Noriega in December 1989, represented, one can only assume, the last gasp of moribund 'old-thinking'. In fact, according to Zoltan Grossman, the US staged more military interventions between 1990 and 2001 (averaging 2.0 invasions a year) than during the Cold War (1.29) or between 1890 and 1945 (1.15). Cited in Sardar & Wyn Davies (2002), p. 68.
120 On 12th August 1990, for example, Saddam Hussein offered to withdraw from Kuwait as part of a settlement of "all issues of occupation", which would include Israel pulling out of the Gaza Strip and the West Bank and Syria from the Lebanon, respectively. Washington Post (1990).
121 Johnson (2004), p. 25, 307.
122 NATO (1998).
123 "The spectre of Vietnam", Bush affirmed, "has been buried forever in the desert sands of the Arabia peninsula". Bush (1991), p. 245.
124 Wallerstein (2003).
125 Cheney (1991).
126 Balabanova (2007), p. 45.
127 Broder (1999).
128 Thanks to its low wage, low tax, low social spending, anti-union line, and generous Pentagon military contracts the South – the Republican Right's traditional electoral heartland – had become as industrialised as the North by the 1990s. See Brenner (2007), p. 47. Consequently, the Republican Party became increasingly dominated by the southern-based evangelical

Christian Right and the Constitutional separation of church and state brought into question.

129 Gingrich (1994).

130 The Defense Department under Clinton identified six *rogue states*: Cuba, Libya, Iran, Syria, Sudan, and North Korea.

131 For Nitzan and Bichler Clinton's 'benign' foreign policy can be attributed to a switch on the basis of dominant capital within the US from the *weapondollar-petrodollar coalition* (defence contractors, construction firms, and big oil) to the *technodollar-mergerdollar coalition* (representing civilian high tech, global capital, and company mergers). Nitzan & Bichler (2002).

132 In fact, Clinton's Secretary of State, Madeleine Albright, even officially downgraded 'rogue states' to "states of concern", while the 'war on drugs' had limited application outside the Western Hemisphere.

133 The NASDAQ Composite Index, containing mostly technology shares, soared from 500 in April 1991, 1,000 in July 1995, 2,000 in July 1998, reaching its peak of 5,132 in March 2000 at which time market capitulation of US stock hit $1.7 trillion, or 1.7 times the value of US GDP. Stiglitz (2004), p. 5, p. 138.

134 According to Stiglitz, between 1992 and 2000, the telecommunications industry's share in the national economy doubled, providing two-thirds of the new jobs and a third of new investment. Stiglitz (2004), pp. 91–2.

135 Bonefeld (2002), pp. 117–42.

136 van der Pijl (2006), p. 266.

137 Goodman & Pauly (1993), pp. 60–4.

138 WTO (2018).

139 NAFTA (2018), Chapter 11: "Investment".

140 The term was first used by Chalmers Johnson in Johnson (1982).

141 Fingleton (2008), pp. 92–5.

142 By September 1987, two years after the Plaza Accord, the yen had risen 60% against the dollar.

143 In the ten years before its peak in 1989, stock and real-estate prices rose 500%. Tasker (2009).

144 Equivalent to a 70% drop in both stock market and urban real-estate prices. Lincoln (2009).

145 Under the *Agreement on Technical Barriers to Trade* and the *Agreement on Sanitary and Phytosanitary Measures*, for example, both built on the 'environmental charter' of GATT, Art. XX, governments have to ensure that any trade restrictions introduced to protect public health or the environment have to meet the 'necessity test' requiring them to adopt "least trade-restrictive' alternative measures rather than maintaining a 'discriminatory' import ban (Art. 5.6).

146 See Paterson (2009).

147 Wade & Veneroso (1998).

148 Less developing countries' external debt rose from $50 billion to $600 billion between 1968 and 1980, and up to over $2.5 trillion by 2003. See Millet & Toussaint (2004), p. 20; see Schwartz (2006), p. 60.

149 At least another 40 countries were seriously in arrears. Total Latin America external debt quadrupled from $75 billion in 1975 to $318 billion in 1983; while debt servicing rose (interest payments and payments of principal) from $12 billion in 1975 to $66 billion in 1982. Gruppen (1986), p. 69.

150 Mexican President, Miguel de la Madrid Hurtado wasted no time selling off the nation's most lucrative industries, utilities, and services at fire-sale prices to international investors and a small section of well-connected

domestic elites (witness the emergence of billionaires such as Carlos Slim onto Forbes' rich list), reducing state intervention on the economy, while opening up capital markets and locking the peso onto the dollar.

151 Within a year of Mexico's announcement, 27 countries had rescheduled their payments, with four countries in Latin America (Mexico, Brazil, Argentina, and Venezuela) holding 74% of the international debt. Duménil & Lévy (2005), p. 17.

152 Advocators countered that ISI had been very successful in pushing a high growth in the South, including Latin America, right up until the mid-1970s. See for example Roderick (1997).

153 The 'shock therapy' conditions imposed on Poland, Yugoslavia, and Russia to guide their transition from centrally planned to the market economy were particularly severe, having devastating long-term socio-economic and political/geopolitics effects for the countries concerned. For 'common sense' neoliberal recommendations for Poland, see 'organic intellectual' Jeffrey Sachs: Sachs (1990a, 1990b, 1993).

154 In a famous editorial in December 1990 the *Economist* urged Mikhail Gorbachev to adopt "strong-man rule", to drive through a "Pinochet approach to liberal economics" in the old Soviet Union, despite the "possible blood-letting". Their prayers would be answered in the form of Russian leader, Boris Yeltsin who, acting in the IMF's advice, named Chicago School disciple to the post of deputy prime minister to execute the "Sachs Plan". See The Economist (1990); Cox & Sinclair (1996).

155 Albo (2003), pp. 88–113.

156 See Stiglitz (2002), pp. 43–52.

157 Camdessus (1995).

158 It was due to the social unrest generated by national asset-stripping, industrial dislocation, unemployment, and rising inequality that local elites in Latin America opted to join RTAs (e.g. NATFA and MERCOSUR) seeking to insulate themselves from opposition groups while pushing ahead with further neoliberal reforms.

159 According to Barry Eichengreen and Michael Bordo between 1945 and 1971, there were 38 financial crises worldwide, but between 1973 and 1997 there were 139 (44 in high-income countries). Quoted in The Economist (2009).

160 Kindleberger (1979) and Minsky (1982).

161 Rubin & Weisberg (2003), 213–15.

162 Gowan (1999), pp. 95–100, p. 114.

163 Lipscy (2003).

164 Harvey (2007), p. 55.

165 Countries such as Argentina, Brazil, Estonia, Turkey, and even Australia and New Zealand were all teetering on the brink of default.

166 Run by a cartel of the biggest US investment banks (e.g. Merrill Lynch and Bears Stearns) and one European one (UBS) and advised by a couple of Nobel Prize winners (Myron Scholes and Robert C. Merton) and a former deputy chairman of the Fed (David W. Mullins Jr.). The LTCM enjoyed excellent access to government and ran a large PR management programme employing journalists and academics to preach the virtues of financialization.

167 With just $4.8 billion in capital it was able to borrow around $125 billion from banks and securities firms leverage of 25:1 to engage in 'highly aggressive' (i.e. speculative) derivate trading strategies involving an estimated $1.4 trillion (290 times their material base). Scalcione (2011), pp. 114–15.

168 See Lowenstein (2000); Doyran (2011), pp. 94–6; and Greenspan (2007), pp. 193–5.

Bibliography

Aglietta, M. (1985), "The Creation of International Liquidity", in Tsoukalis, L. (ed.)., *The Political Economy of International Money*, London: Sage.

Albo, G. (2003), "The Old and New Economics of Imperialism", in Panitch, L. and Leys, C. (eds.), *The Socialist Register 2004*, London: Merlin.

Armstrong, P., Glyn, A. & Harrison, J. (1984), *Capitalism since World War II: The Making and Break-Up of the Great Boom*, London: Fontana.

Aronowitz, S. (2003), *How Class Works. Power and Social Movement*, New Haven, CT: Yale University Press.

Askin, S. & Collins, C. (1993), "External Collusion with Kleptocracy: Can Zaire Recapture its Stolen Wealth?" *Review of African Political Economy*, 20, no. 57, 72–85.

Balabanova, E. (2007), *Media, Wars and Politics: Comparing the Incomparable in Western and Eastern Europe*, Aldershot: Ashgate Publishing Limited.

Baran, P.A. & Sweezy, P.M. (1966), *Monopoly Capitalism*, New York: Monthly Review Press.

Barry, J.C. (2011), "Empire as a Gated Community: Politics of an American Strategic Metaphor", *Global Society*, 25, no. 3, 287–309.

Basel. (2013), *Basel Committee on Banking Supervision*. "A brief history of the Basel Committee", July (available online at www.bis.org).

Blacker, C.D. & Duffy, G. (eds.) (1984), *International Arms Control: Issues and Agreements*, 2nd Edn., Stanford: Stanford University Press.

Blanchard, C.M. (2009), "Saudi Arabia: Background and U.S. Relations", *Congressional Research Service*, 16th December, Washington DC.

Block, F. L. (1977), *The Origins of International Economic Disorder. A Study of United States International Monetary Policy from World War II to the Present*, Berkeley, University of California Press.

Blum, W. (2001), *Rogue State*, London: Zed Books.

Bodenheimer, T. & Gould, R. (1989), *Rollback! Right-Wing Power in US Foreign Policy*, Boston, MA: South End Press.

Bonefeld, W. (2002), "European Integration: The market, the Political, and Class", *Capital and Class*, 77, 117–43.

Brenner, R. (1998), "The Economics of Global Turbulence: A Special Report on the World Economy, 1950–1998," *New Left Review*, 229, 1–265.

Brenner, R. (2006), *The Economics of Global Turbulence: The Advanced Capitalist Economies from Long Boom to Long Downturn, 1945–2005*, London: Verso.

Brenner, R. (2007), "Structure versus Conjuncture: The 2006 Elections and the Rightward Shift", *New Left Review*, 43, 33–43.

Broder, J.M. (1999), "Clinton Offers His Apologies to Guatemala", *New York Times*, 20th February.

Brzezinski, Z. (1998), Interview in *Nouvel Obervateur*, January 15th–21st 1998, University of Arizona (available at dgibbs.faculty.arizona.edu/ brzezinski_interview).

Bucerius, S. & Tonry, M. (eds.) (2014), *The Oxford Handbook of Ethnicity, Crime, and Immigration*, Oxford: Oxford University Press.

Buchanan, P.J. (1999), *A Republic Not an Empire: Reclaiming America's Destiny*, Lanham, MD: Regnery Publishing Inc.

Burk, K. (1992), *Goodbye to Great Britain: 1976 IMF Crisis*, New Haven, CT: Yale University Press.

Bush, G.H. (1991), "Radio Address to United States Armed Forces Stationed in the Persian Gulf Region", 2nd March 1991, *Weekly Compilation of Presidential Documents* 27, no. 10.

Butler, S. (1984), *Mandate for Leadership II*, Washington DC: The Heritage Foundation.

Camdessus, M. (1995), "Drawing Lessons from the Mexican Crisis: Preventing and Resolving Financial Crisis – the Role of the IMF", Address by Michael Camdessus, Managing Director of the IMF at the 25th Washington Conference of the Council of the Americas, *International Monetary Fund*, 22nd May (available online at www.imf.org).

Campbell, A. (2005), "The Birth of Neoliberalism in the United States: A Reorganisation of Capitalism", in Saad-Filho, A. and Johnston, D. (eds.), *Neoliberalism: A Critical Reader*, London: Pluto Press.

Central Intelligence Agency (1970), "CIA. Notes on Meeting with the President on Chile", September 15, 1970, declassified, *National Security Archive: The George Washington University* (available online at nsarchive2.gwu.edu/).

Chase-Dunn, C. (1998), *Global Formation: Structures of the World-Economy*, 2nd Edn., Lanham, MD: Rowman & Littlefield.

Cheney, R.B. (1991), *Statement to the Senate Armed Forces Committee*, 21st February (available online at history.defense.gov/).

Chernow, R. (1990), *The House of Morgan: An American Banking Dynasty and the Rise of Modern Finance*, New York: Simon and Schuster.

Cherunilam, F. (2010), *International Business: Text and Cases*, 5th Edn., New Delhi: PHI Learning.

Chollet, D. & Goldgeier, J. (2008), *America between the Wars: From 11/9 to 9/11*, New York: Public Affairs.

Clarke, S. (1988), *Keynesianism, Monetarism and the Crisis of the State*, Aldershot: Edward Elgar Publishing Company Limited.

Coatsworth, J.H. (2010), "The Cold War in Central America, 1975–1991", in Leffler, M.P. and Westad, O.A. (eds.), *Cambridge History of the Cold War*, Vols. I–III, Cambridge: Cambridge University Press.

Commanding Heights. (2000), *The Battle for the World Economy* (available online at www.pbs.org).

Cordesman, A.H. (2003), *Saudi Arabia Enters the Twenty-First Century: The Military and International Security Dimensions*, Westport, CT: Greenwood Publishing Group.

Cox, R.W. (1987), *Production, Power, and World Order: Social Forces in the Making of History*, New York: Columbia University Press.

Crozier M.J., Huntington, S.P. and Watanuki, J. (1975), *The Crisis of Democracy: Report on the Governability of Democracies to the Trilateral Commission*, New York: New York University Press (available online at www.trilateral.org).

Cunningham, K. (2004), "Permanent War? The Domestic Hegemony of the New American Militarism", *New Political Science*, 26, no. 4, 551–67.

Desai, M. (2004), *Marx's Revenge: The Resurgence of Capitalism and the Death of Statist Socialism*, London: Verso.

Djelic. M.L. (2001), *Exporting the American Model: The Postwar Transformation of the European Business*, Oxford: Oxford University Press.

Doyran, M.A. (2011), *Financial Crisis and the Pursuit of Power: American Pre-eminance and the Credit Crunch*, Farnham, Surrey: Ashgate Publishing Ltd.

Duménil, G. & Lévy, D. (2004a), *Capital Resurgent: Roots of the Neoliberal Revolution*, London: Harvard University Press.

Duménil, G. & Lévy, D. (2004b), "Neoliberal Income Trends: Wealth, Class and Ownership in the USA", *New Left Review*, 30, 105–33.

Duménil, G. & Lévy, D. (2005), "The Neoliberal (Counter-) Revolution", in Saad-Filho, A. and Johnston, D. (eds.), *Neoliberalism: A Critical Reader*, London: Pluto Press.

Early, S. (2006), "An Old Lesson Still Holds for Unions", Op-ed, *The Boston Globe*, 31st July (available online at www.boston.com).

Eichengreen, B. (2007), *The European Economy Since 1945: Coordinated Capitalism and Beyond*, Princeton: Princeton University Press.

Engdahl, F.W. (2004), *A Century of War: Anglo-American Politics and the New World Order*, London: Pluto Press.

Fingleton, E. (2008), *In the Jaws of the Dragon. America's Fate in the Coming Era of Chinese Hegemony*, New York: Thomas Dunne.

Fouskas, V.K. & Gökay, B. (2012), *The Fall of US Empire: Global Fault Lines and the Shifting Imperial Order*, London: Pluto Press.

Frank, A.G. (1976), *Economic Genocide in Chile: Monetarist Theory versus Humanity*, Nottingham: Spokesman Books.

Fukuyama, F. (1992), *The End of History and the Last Man*, London: Penguin.

Gates. R.M. (1996), *From the Shadows: The Ultimate Insider's Story of Five Presidents and How They Won the Cold War*, New York: Simon & Schuster.

Gill, S. (1991), *American Hegemony and the Trilateral Commission*, Cambridge: Cambridge University Press.

Gingrich, N. (1994), "The Republican 'Contract with America'", *Presidents and the American Presidency Resources*, Chapter 6, Oxford University Press (available online at global.oup.com/us/companion.websites/9780195385168/resources/).

Goodman, J.B. & Pauly, L.W. (1993), "The Obsolescence of Capital Controls? Economic Management in the Age of Global Markets", *World Politics*, 46, no. 1, 50–82.

Gowan, P. (1999), *The Global Gamble: Washington's Faustian Bid for World Dominance*, London: Verso.

Gramsci, A. (1971), *Selections from the Prison Notebooks of Antonio Gramsci*, Hoare, Q. and Nowell Smith, G. (eds. and trans.), London: Lawrence & Wishart.

Greenspan, A. (2003). "Remarks by Chairman Alan Greenspan: The Reagan Legacy", *The Federal Reserve Board*, Ronald Reagan Library, Simi Valley, California, 9th April (available online at www.federalreserve.gov).

Greenspan, A. (2007), *The Age of Turbulence: Adventures in a New World*, London: Penguin Press.

Gruppen, N. (1986), *The Debt Crisis in Latin America*, Stockholm: Institute of Latin American Studies.

Halliday, F. (1983), *The Making of the Second Cold War*, London: Verso.

Harvey, D. (2007), *A Brief History of Neoliberalism*, Oxford: Oxford University Press.

Hayek, F.A. (2001), *The Road to Serfdom*, London: Routledge Classics [orig. 1944].

Helleiner, E. (1995), "Explaining the Globalisation of Financial Markets: Bringing States Back In", *Review* of *International Political Economy*, 2, no. 2, 315–41.

Henwood, D. (2003), *After the New Economy*, New York: New Press.

Hibbs. D.A. Jr. (1978), "On the Political Economy of Long Run Trends in Strike Activity", *British Journal of Political Science*, 8, no. 2, 153–75.

Hodgson, G. (2009), *The Myth of American Exceptionalism*, New Haven, CT: Yale University Press.

Holzman, F.D. (1989), "Politics and Guesswork: CIA and DIA estimates of Soviet Military Spending", *International Security*, 14, no. 2, 101–31.

Huntington, S.P. (1975), "The Democratic Distemper", *National Affairs*, no. 42 (available online at www.nationalaffairs.com).

Hurd, D. (1992), "Making the World a Safer Place: Our Five Priorities", *The Daily Telegraph*, 1st January.

Jankowski, R. (1998), *Profit, Taxes and the State*, West Point, CT: Praeger Publishers.

Johnson, C. (1982), *MITI and the Japanese Miracle: The Growth of Industry Policy 1925–1975*, Stanford: Stanford University Press.

Johnson, C. (2002), *Blowback: The Costs and Consequences of American Empire*, London: Time Warner Paperbacks, Askin, S. & Collins.

Johnson, C. (2004), *The Sorrows of Empire: Militarism, Secrecy, and the End of the Republic*, New York: Metropolitan Books.

Kaplan, D.E., Ekman, M. & Latif, A. (2003), "The Saudi Connection: How Billions in Oil Money Spawned a Global Terror Network", *The U.S. News & World Report*, December 15th.

Kimura, H. (2000), *Japanese Russian Relations under Gorbachev and Yeltsin*, New York: M.E. Sharpe.

Kindleberger, C.P. (1979), *Manias, Panics and Crashes: A History of Financial Crises*, New York: Basic Books.

Kinzer, S. (2006), *Overthrow: America's Century of Regime Change from Hawaii to Iraq*, New York: Times Books.

Kissinger, H. (1973), *Address given by Henry A. Kissinger to Associated Press's Annual Dinner*, New York, 23rd 1973 (available online at www.cvce.eu/en).

Klein, N. (2008), *The Shock Doctrine: The Rise of Disaster Capitalism*, London: Penguin.

Krahmann, E. (2005), "American Hegemony or Global Governance? Competing visions of International Security", *International Studies Review*, 7, 531–45.

Leffler, M.P. & Westad, O.A. (eds.) (2010), *Cambridge History of the Cold War*, Vols. I–III, Cambridge: Cambridge University Press.

Lincoln, E.J. (2009), "What Japan Got Right", *Newsweek*, 16th February.

Lipscy, P.Y. (2003), "Japan's Asian Monetary Fund Proposal", *Stanford Journal of East Asian Affairs*, 3, no. 1 (available online at www.stanford.edu).

Llewellyn, D.T. (1985), "The Role of International Banking", in Tsoukalis, L. (ed.), *The Political Economy of International Money*, London: Sage.

Lowenstein, R. (2000), *When Genius Failed: The Rise and Fall of Long-Term Capital Management*, New York: Random House.

Marx, K. with Engels, F. (2010), *Capital: A Critique of Political Economy: Volume III* (available online at www.marxists.org) [orig. pub. 1894].

McCrisken, T.B. (2003), *American Exceptionalism and the Legacy of Vietnam: US Foreign Policy since 1974*, New York: Palgrave Macmillan.

Millet, D. & Toussaint, E. (2004), *Who Owes Who? 50 Questions about World Debt*, London: Zed Books.

Minsky, H.P. (1982), *Can "It" Happen Again? Essays on Instability and Finance*, Armonk, New York: M.E. Sharpe.

Moody, K. (1988), *An Injury to All: The Decline of American Unionism*, London: Verso.

NAFTA. (2018), NAFTA Secretariat: Texts of the Agreement: "North American Free Trade Agreement" (available online at www.nafta-sec-alena.org/Home/Legal-Texts).

NATO. (1998), *NATO Parliamentary Assembly: Committee Reports – Science & Technology*: "The Revolution in Military Affairs", November (available online at www.iwar.org.uk).

Nitzan, J. & Bichler, S. (2002), *The Global Political Economy of Israel*, London: Pluto Press.

Painter, D.S. (1999), *The Cold War: An International History*, Routledge, New York.

Panitch, L. & Ginden, S. (2005a), "Unconcealed Empire: 'The Awesome Thing America is Becoming'", in Bronner, S.E. (ed.), *Planetary Politics: Human Rights, Terror & Global Society*, Lanham, MD: Rowman & Littlefield.

Panitch, L. & Ginden, S. (2005b), "Finance and American Empire", *Socialist Register,* 41, 46–81.

Panitch, L. & Gindin, S. (2012), *The Making of Global Capitalism: The Political Economy of American Hegemony*, London: Verso.

Paterson, B. (2009), "Trasformismo at the World Trade Organization", in McNally, M. and Schwarzmantel, J. (eds.), *Gramsci and Global Politics: Hegemony and Resistance*, Oxford.

Perkins, J. (2006), *Confessions of an Economic Hit Man*, London: Ebury Press.

Powaski, R.E. (1998), *The Cold War: The United States and the Soviet Union 1917–1991*, Oxford: Oxford University Press.

Prebisch, R. (1950), *The Economic Development of Latin America and Its Principal Problems*, Lake Success, New York: Economic Commission for Latin America, United Nations Department of Economic Affairs, (available online at repositorio.cepal.org/?locale-attribute=en).

Rauchhaus, R.W. (ed.) (2001), "An Open Letter to President Clinton", *Explaining NATO Enlargement*, London: Frank Cass.

Reagan, R. (1981), *The American Presidency Project*: "Ronald Reagan, Inaugural Address, 20th January" (available online at www.presidency.ucsb.edu).

Reagan, R. (1985), *The American Presidency Project*: "Ronald Reagan: Address before a Joint Session of the Congress on the State of the Union", 6th February, (available online at www.presidency.ucsb.edu).

Roberts, R. (2002), *Wall Street*, London: Profile Books.

Roderick, D. (1997), "Globalization, Social Conflict and Economic Growth", at *Prebisch Lecture*, UNCTAD, Geneva, 24th October.

Rothkopf, D.J. (1998), "Beyond Manic Mercantilism", in James J. and Shinn, J.J. (eds.), *Study Group Report*: "Riding the Tigers: American Commercial Diplomacy in Asia", New York: Council on Foreign Relations, , 1st February.

Rubin, E.R. & Weisberg, J. (2003), *In An Uncertain World: Tough Choices from Wall Street to Washington*, New York: Random House.

Rupert, M. (1995), *Producing Hegemony: The Politics of Mass Production and American Power*, Cambridge: Cambridge University Press.

Rupert, M. (2000), *Ideologies of Globalization: Contending Visions of a New World* Order, Florence, Kentucky: Routledge.

Sachs, J.D. (1990a), "Creating a Market Economy in Eastern Europe: The Case of Poland", in Lipton, D. and Sachs, J.D. (eds.), *Brookings Institution: Brookings Papers on Economic Activity*, 1 (available online at www.brookings.edu).

Sachs, J.D. (1990b), "What Is to Be Done?" *The Economist*, 13th January (available online at www.economist.com).

Sachs, J.D. (1993), "The Lionel Robbins Lectures at the LSE", *Poland's Jump to the Market Economy*, Cambridge, MA: MIT Press.

Sardar, Z. & Wyn Davies, M. (2002), *Why Do People Hate America?* Cambridge: Icon Books.

Sarotte, M.E (2014), "A Broken Promise? The Real Story behind NATO expansion", *Foreign Affairs*, September/October.

Scalcione, R. (2011), *The Derivative Revolution: A Trapped Innovation and a Blueprint for Regulation Reform*, The Netherlands: Kluwer Law International.

Schwartz, H.M. (2006), "Globalization: The Long View", in Stubbs, R. and Underhill, G.R.D. (eds.), *Political Economy and the Changing Global Order*, Oxford: Oxford University Press.

Silk, L. & Vogel, D. (1976), *Ethics and Profits: The Crisis of Confidence in American Business*, New York: Simon & Schuster.

Spero, J.E. (1977), *The Politics of International Economic Relations*, New York; St. Martin's Press.

Stiglitz, J.E. (2002), *Globalisation and Its Discontents*, London: Penguin Books.

Stiglitz, J.E. (2004), *The Roaring Nineties: Why We're Paying the Price for the Greediest Decade in History*, London: Penguin Books.

Strauss, L. (1999), *The Natural Right and History*, Chicago: University of Chicago Press [orig. 1950].

Subcommittee on Multinational Corporations. (1973), "The International Telephone and Telegraph Company and Chile, 1970–71," *Report to the Committee on Foreign Relations United States Senate*, 21st June (available online at catalog. hathitrust.org/Record/003212627).

Sutton, M. (2007), *France and the Construction of Europe 1944–2007: The Geopolitical Imperative*, Oxford: Berghahn Books.

Tasker, P. (2009), "Bonuses Don't Create Bubbles", *Newsweek*, 6th April.

Taylor, J.B. (1995), "Changes in American Economic Policy in the 1980s: Watershed or Pendulum Swing?" *Journal of Economic Literature*, XXXIII,777–84.

The British Medical Journal. (2008), "Fifty Years of Violent War Deaths from Vietnam to Bosnia: Analysis of Data from World Health Survey Programme," June, 336, 1482 (available online at www.bmj.com/content/336/7659/1482).

The Carter Center. (1979), "Crisis of Confidence", 14th July (available online at www.cartercenter.org).

The Economist. (1990), "Order, Order: Can Mikhail Gorbachev Deliver the Soviet Union from Chaos without Restoring Centralised Autocracy", 12th December.

The Economist. (2009), "Greed and Fear", 22nd January.

The New York Times. (1990), "Confrontation in the Gulf; Excerpts from Iraq Document on Meeting with U.S. Envoy", 23rd September (available online at www.nytimes.com).

The New York Times. (1994), "Opinion: The Failure in Our Success", George F. Kennan, 14th March (available online at www.nytimes.com).

The Vietnam Veterans Memorial: The Wall-USA. (2018), "US Military Casualties in South East Asia" (available online at thewall-usa.com).

Time Magazine. (1975), "Can Capitalism Survive", July 14th 1975, Vol. 106, no. 2.

Turse, N. (2013), *Kill Anything that Moves: The Real American War in Vietnam*, New York: Metropolitan Books.

UNCTAD. (1974), "Declaration on the Establishment of a New International Economic Order", *United Nations General Assembly resolution 3201* (S-VI), 1st May (available online at unctad.org/en/Pages/Home.aspx).

US Congress, Office of Technology Assessment. (1985), "Ballistic Missile Defense Technologies", OTA-ISC-254, September (available online at www.fas. org).

US Inflation Calculator. (2018), *US Inflation Calculator: Historical Inflation Rates 1914–2018* (available online at www.usinflationcalculator.com).

Valdés, J.G. (1995), *Pinochet's Economists: The Chicago School in Chile*, Cambridge: Cambridge University Press.

van der Pijl, K. (2006), "A Lockean Europe?" *New Left Review*, 37, 9–36.

van der Wee, H. (1987), *Prosperity and Upheaval: The World Economy 1945–1980*, Harmondsworth: Middlesex.

Wade, R. & Veneroso, F. (1998), "The Asian Crisis: The High Debt Model versus the Wall Street-Treasury-IMF Complex", *New Left Review*, 228, 3–23.

Wallerstein, I. (2003), "US Weakness and the Struggle for Hegemony", *Monthly Review*,55, no. 3, 23–9.

Washington Post. (1990), "Saddam Firm on Demands", William Claiborne 13th August 1990.

WTO. (2018), *World Trade Organization*: "Regional Trade Agreements" (available online at www.wto.org) [accessed 26th May 2018].

Zinn, H. (2005), *A People's History of the United States*, New York: Harper Perennial Modern Classics.

4 Change & Continuity under Bush and Obama...and Beyond

As the US entered the 21st century the future of American hegemony was not looking so rosy. Having reached its post-1970s peak in 1997, the rate of profit in the US went into rapid decline manifested in a sharp reduction in investment.[1] The latest of the financialization asset-bubbles – the much-hyped dot.com New Economy – burst in March 2000 after investors finally realised that internet companies' share prices had little or no connection to profits generated, but more a result of financial manipulation, creative accounting, conflicts of interest, dubious compensation packages, and purposely 'slack' regulatory system.[2]

The new incoming president G.W. Bush (Bush II) was not just faced by looming recession, the grave realities of neoliberalism had started to hit home (e.g. rising inequality, social fragmentation, and household debt), the corporate sector was awash with scandal (e.g. Enron), and serious questions existed over the president's own political legitimacy and personal honesty.[3] The White House's reaction, consistent with its political programme was to blow another asset-bubble (see below) to adopt a more aggressive foreign policy.

With regard to the latter affirmation, a common view not just amongst mainstream academics, both also within neo-Gramscian circles, is that the take-over of the Republican Party by neocons under Bush II[4] indicated the end of American 'hegemony' (however they define it) in favour of 'dominance'[5] or 'empire'.[6] This is a complex but crucial debate, lying at the heart of the *Neo* Neo-Gramscian (NNG) perspective forwarded in this book. The first part of the present chapter, therefore, aims to shed some light on this question which inevitably involves assessing the significance of Bush II's *War on Terror* (WOT): a topic on which much has been written, but one which remains fundamental to understanding the dynamics and nuances of American hegemony in the 21st century.

Bush's 'New Imperialism'

The ideological touchstone for the Bushite neocons – a group of economic neoliberals, social conservatives, military-industrial-complex (MIC)

DOI: 10.4324/9780429459061-5

hawks and the Christian/Jewish Right – was the *Project for a New American Century* (PNAC) think tank, set up by Robert Kagan and William Kristol in 1997 "to make the case and rally support for American global leadership" on the basis of "a Reaganite policy of military strength and moral clarity".[7] Amongst its numbers were familiar names from the Bush I administration such as Dick Cheney, Paul Wolfowitz, I. Lewis 'Scooter' Libby, and Donald Rumsfeld along with 'fresh blood' additions including Francis Fukuyama, Eliot Cohen, and John Bolton.

In reality, the neocons had been imploring Washington to launch a new more assertive *Grand Strategy* position since the early 1990s, articulated in a doctrinal form in the first draft of the Pentagon's *Defense Planning Guidance 1992–94* (DPG 1992), urging the government to "prevent any hostile power from dominating regions whose resources would allow it to attain great power status". The interests of the core countries should be taken into account, the document continued but discouraged "from challenging our leadership" or "seeking to overturn the established political and economic order", including "the emergence of European-only security arrangements which would undermine NATO". The objective of the DPG, in short, was to "preclude the emergence of any potential future competitor", insisting Washington should not shy from adopting a more aggressive unilateralist foreign policy position (e.g. *pre-emption*) and making good use of the one area the US still reigned supreme, and which its European and Asian allies still remained as dependent as ever: *hard power* (i.e. militarism).[8] Unfortunately, for defence contractors and right-wing think tanks[9] a watered-down version of DPG 1992 ("Defense Strategy for the 1990s"), was effectively sidelined by the Clinton administration.

Throughout the 1990s, the neocons 'hegemonic project' drew on the work of 'organic intellectuals' such as Samuel Huntington[10] and Robert D. Kaplan[11] to paint a depressing picture of the new post-Cold War WO awash with civil wars, rogue/failed states and terrorist activities nurtured by the re-emergence of historical, ethnical, and cultural animosities. Washington had both the moral obligation and military capacity to pursue its imperial destiny and adopt a more proactive foreign policy, especially now the USSR was no more and Russian best by economic and political turmoil.

The Middle East remained a top priority for PNAC and associated right-wing think tanks,[12] all supporting a 'greater Israel' (and hence end to the Palestine Peace Process), the removal of Saddam Hussein's regime from power (considered a threat to Israel, Saudi Arabia, and Kuwait) and extending and strengthening US military capacity (and permanent role) in the Gulf.[13] It remains unclear to what extent Clinton's launching of Operation Desert Fox (carried out without support from the UN Security Council) can be attributed, at least in part, to heavy lobbying pressure from these groups, expressed in a series of 'open letters' to the

White House and Congress in early 1998.[14] Tellingly, ten of the 18 PNAC members that signed the aforementioned letters to Clinton/Congress in 1998 became members of Bush II's cabinet,[15] while the anti-Islamic military lobby Center for Security Policy could boast around two dozen of its former advisory board members within the ministration.[16]

Drawing up plans to attack Iraq and remove Saddam Hussein dominated the Bush II's very first National Security Council meeting on 30th January 2001;[17] the main problem facing the White House was how to legitimise such intervention.[18] The 9/11 attacks provided the justification, it was just a matter of getting the security services to trace them back to Baghdad.[19] Much to the chagrin of Defense Secretary Donald Rumsfeld the Al Qaeda link 'demanded' the WOT began in Afghanistan,[20] but he would not have to wait long.

Just a month after the UN-authorised[21] *Operation Enduring Freedom* began (on 7th October 2001), retired General Wesley Clark was told during a visit to the Pentagon that said the strike against Kabul would be the first shot of a "five-year campaign plan" to restructure a total of seven Middle Eastern and targeted African states, "beginning with Iraq, the Syria, Lebanon, Libya, Iran, Somalia, and Sudan".[22] Such a view was perpetuated by prominent PNAC member Eliot Cohen who interpreted the forthcoming invasion of Iraq as the opening volley of a broader World War IV (World War III being the Cold War); an argument which was later popularised by fellow neocon Norman Podhoretz.[23] Meanwhile, Bush's speak-writers set about preparing the terrain, conflating terrorism, Iraq, and weapons of mass destruction (WMD).[24]

As part of this new 'hegemonic project', the *empire* began to permeate the US 'hegemonic apparatus', entering mainstream political and popular discourse for the first time in 50 years. 'Organic intellectuals' from academia (e.g. Niall Ferguson, Michael Ignatieff, and Jean Bethke Elshtain) and the written press (e.g. Robert D. Kaplan, Charles Krauthammer Thomas Friedman, and Max Boot), drew on familiar American exceptionalism myths to encourage/legitimise 'common sense' foreign intervention and expansionism in order to guarantee global stability, guard against global threats, and promote liberal democracy and respect for human rights.

The insinuation, expressed in a more explicit form by Max Boot, Senior Fellow at the US State Department's conduit, the Council on Foreign Relations, was that the 9/11 attacks could have been avoided had Washington been far more globally assertive beforehand.[25] Most neocons had little problem in acknowledging their imperial aspirations. Speaking following the Iraqi invasion, William Kristol affirmed: "We err on the side of being strong. And if the people want to say we're an imperialist power, fine".[26] This amounted to little more than a progressive twist on European 19th-century colonial theory about the need to 'civilise barbarians', Boot actually citing Rudyard Kipling's blatantly racist

"White Man's Burden" metaphor, when ruing over the often thankless but necessary task of imperial rule.[27]

Similarly, Ferguson doubted whether national independence constituted a "universally viable model" posing the question as to whether "for some countries some form of imperial governance, meaning a partial or complete suspension of their national sovereignty, might be better than full independence",[28] while Ignatieff held there was no intrinsic contradiction between self-determination and imperialism: by submitting themselves to imperial rule, poor countries would access skills, knowledge and technology, etc. which will help them to be free in the long-term.[29] "[B]efore the names of just and unjust can have meaning" Kaplan remarked in 1994, "some coercive power must exist",[30] and it just so happened, he later commented following the launching of the 2003 Iraq invasion, that "it is American power, and American power only, that can serve as an organizing principle for the worldwide expansion of a liberal civil society".[31]

To mark the first anniversary of 9/11, Bush set out his administration's imperial mission statement in an interview in the *New York Times*:

> We will use our position of unparalleled strength and influence to build an atmosphere of international order and openness in which progress and liberty can flourish in many nations. A peaceful world of growing freedom serves American long-term interests, reflects enduring American ideals and unites American allies.[32]

The White House fleshed out these objectives in clearer policy format in the official White House's *National Security Strategy 2002* (NSS-2002) document which was, in effect, a re-write of the aforementioned DPG 1992 report with Rumsfeld's signature replacing that of Cheney.

Like DPG 1992 the NSS-2002 sought to guarantee American primacy, reiterating the idea that the US enjoyed "unprecedented – and unequalled – strength and influence in the world" sustained "by principles of liberty, and the value of a free society", but such liberties and societal model (and global free trade system itself) were under threat from 'rogue states', global terrorists, and WMD. "It is time", the NSS-2002 stressed,

> to reaffirm the essential role of American military strength. We must build and maintain our defenses beyond challenge …The US must and will maintain the capability to defeat any attempt by an enemy to impose its will on the US, our allies, or our friends…Our forces will be strong enough to dissuade potential adversaries from pursuing a military build-up in hopes of surpassing, or equalling, the power of the United States.[33]

Regarding *rogue states*,[34] the NSS-2002 made it clear that it retained the option of carrying out "preemptive" strikes (including nuclear weapons) "to counter a sufficient threat to our national security".[35] But while a 'preemptive war' – carrying out the first strike when an attack is imminent – was considered a legitimate act of self-defence under international law, the *Bush Doctrine*[36] actually appeared to sanction 'preventative war' – granting countries the right to strike a potentially belligerent rogue state or terrorist group even *before* the latter posed a threat, let alone had drawn up concrete plans for attack, which had no base in international law.[37] When the 'international community' showed itself less than convinced by the proof of Iraqi WMD offered before the UN Security Council on 5th February 2003,[38] Washington made it clear it would go ahead regardless.

For most mainstream American international relations (IR) academics, the Bush II administration seemed to be abandoning the classic *Pax Americana* model of hegemonic governance and risked being counter-productive, destabilising the entire international system to the detriment of its greatest beneficiary: the US itself.

Leading the pack, perhaps surprisingly, were realist IR thinkers. Cold War warrior Zbigniew Brzezinski denounced as "meaningless" the declaration of a war against a "technique of warfare" (terrorism) rather than against an enemy (concrete political group) or ideology (communism).[39] John Mearsheimer criticised the Iraqi War from a more pragmatic position, considering it unnecessary and potentially disastrous, both in terms of the military and civilian casualties, and with regards to the stability of the Middle East and American long-term interests there.[40] What worried Henry Kissinger, meanwhile, was the doctrine of 'pre-emption'. "It cannot be either in American national interest or the world's interest", he argued, "to develop principles that grant every nation an unfettered pre-emption against its own definition of threats to its security."[41]

For liberal institutionalists IR scholars, on the other hand, they feared for the future of the whole *liberal, rule-based international order* (LRBIO). From the outset, the Bush II had made it clear that the White House's room for manoeuvre would not be restricted by multilateralism or by the "illusory international community", as National Security Adviser, Condoleezza Rice referred to the UN during the presidential 2000 campaign.[42] Most international organisations, the administration complained, lacked democratic accountability (despite the fact that many were set up under American hegemony). The solution proposed, somewhat incongruently, was for the US to act unilaterally outside existing norms of international practice and law, exempting the country from a whole array of international treaties/initiatives over the following years, be it with regards environment (the Kyoto Protocol), international finance (OECD's initiatives to regulate tax havens), defence (the Anti-Ballistic Missile Treaty, the Ottawa Land Mine Convention) or, perhaps the most symbolic of all, its military operations (the Rome Statute of the International Criminal Court [ICC]).

This contempt for the LRBIO and resorting to military solutions (*hard power*) would do untold damage to the US's prestige, legitimacy, and hence of *soft power*,[43] Joseph Nye insisted: the very basis of its hegemony. The crisis of authority engendered at the international level, G. John Ikenberry lamented, could send the system into a period of Hobbesian anarchy.[44] This "new imperial grand strategy", Ikenberry noted, reduced the US to "a revisionist state seeking to parlay its momentary power advantage into a world order in which it runs the show".[45] There were also the unforeseen unintentional consequences of promoting freedom and democracy to consider. Michael Mann likened American action to "a disturbed, misshapen monster stumbling clumsily across the world. It means well. It intends to spread order and benevolence, but instead, it creates disorder and violence".[46]

The US's loss of 'intellectual and moral leadership' was clearly not just limited to academic circles. As an exercise in mobilising core countries' elites under American hegemony the contrast between support for the Gulf War and Iraq War could not have been more pronounced. The UK aside, no other Security Council Permanent Member endorsed invasion.[47] The so-called "Coalition of the Willing" was top-heavy with small countries contributing little, if anything to the cause,[48] while Rumsfeld's "Old Europe" core (Germany, France, and Belgium) publicly denounced what they considered Washington's unjustifiable aggressive unilateralism. *The Wall Street Journal* referred to the "ugly" mood present at the annual *World Economic Forum* (entitled "Building Trust") held on 23rd–28th January 2003 in Davos, Switzerland, and how "a chorus of international complaints about the American march towards war with Iraq was reaching a crescendo at this gathering of some 2,000 corporate executives, politicians, and academics".[49] And at the other end of the spectrum, the formation of the "Coalition of the Willing" and imminent planned attack mobilised the world's first and largest ever coordinated mass protests. Reminiscent of, but easily surpassing, the anti-Vietnam mobilisations, angry public demonstrations took place in over 600 cities from the 15th February 2003 onwards, some a million-strong, significantly in those countries whose governments supported the war (witness a record-breaking 3 million in Rome).

Once the horrors of war and the effects of Bush II's radical overhaul of the CIA came to light, US 'intellectual and moral leadership' plummeted still further.[50] It was not just the scale of the death and destruction wrought which shocked the world, but the cruelty of state-sponsored 'extraordinary rendition' (government-sponsored abduction and extrajudicial transfer to third countries) and use of so-called 'black sites' (foreign detention centres outside national jurisdiction, e.g. Guantánamo, Abu Ghraib, Basra) where 'unlawful enemy combats' could be subjected to all manner of 'enhanced interrogation techniques' (i.e. torture). These violated the Geneva Conventions, the

UN Convention Against Torture, and the very liberal values Washington was supposed to be defending.[51]

And even when the wars were declared 'over' attempts at state-building were nothing short of disastrous, proving far costlier in economic and human terms than envisaged. Indeed, thanks to the power vacuums meant the countries would soon be engulfed in sectorial wars and beset by the of radical political Islam and terrorist activities (e.g. Al Qaeda and later the Islamic State).

Bush's 'Old Imperialism'

So, did the Bush Doctrine, Iraq War, and WOT constitute a complete break from the traditional US form of hegemonic governance and therein signal the end of US hegemony?

Understood as a dynamic *social process* (as opposed to a 'static position') it appears clear that US hegemony under Bush II did undergo a qualitative change, arising out of a complex interplay of contingent domestic and international social forces, manifested in the neocon shift within GOP favouring weapondollar-petrodollar coalition (WDPDC) elements. Thirty-two major appointees in the first Bush II administration were either "former executives with, consultants for, or significant shareholders of top defense contractors",[52] reflected in more an overtly militarist/belligerent foreign policy.

Chapter 1 argued that domination is *implicit* in exercising of hegemony; indeed, politico-military coercion constituted Gramsci's *third moment* of hegemony. We have also seen how the national security state (NSS) and launching of the NSC-68 under Truman underpinned Pax Americana, helping reproduce capital relations both on a domestic and global level, and used to discipline enemies and friends alike. Nonetheless, as Gramsci also insisted, the use of military power had to have a consensual element: to appear proportionate and legitimate; as working to further the 'common good' (e.g. protecting the capitalist core countries from external threats). Where Bush II did digress somewhat from the hegemonic template was not so much in the recourse to militarism, but the fact that the threat posed by the 'foe' in its 'friend-foe' ('self-radical Other') within the Grand Strategy was not sufficiently credible, at least with regards to Iraq. Charles Tilly differentiated between *legitimate protection* (against a real external threat) and *racketeering* (protection being offered at a price against an imagery threat or danger created by the state itself).[53]

The problem for Washington, as we saw in Chapter 3, that none of the 'foes' identified by Bush I, and to a lesser extent Clinton, proved sufficiently plausible replacements for the Warsaw Pact.[54] As Bush II entered the White House, the Grand Strategy was at crisis point, Joint Chief of Staff, Colin Powell lamenting: "I'm running out of demons, I'm running out of villains...I'm down to Castro and Kim II Sung".[55] The future of

US's huge MIC, 'empire of bases' and actually military hegemony *per se*. There was a real risk of American security arrangements appearing unnecessary, granting core countries a greater degree of foreign policy independence Deputy Defence Secretary, Paul Wolfowitz, summed up the mood in the Pentagon, thus: "What we were afraid of" were people who would say, 'Let's bring all the troops home, and let's abandon our position in Europe'.[56]

While the post-9/11 attack on Afghanistan and even the broader war WOT garnered international support the eagerness to remove Saddam Hussein on less than convincing proof smacked of a *protection racket*, especially following the financing of the Gulf War.[57] This was reflected in the embarrassing low sums raised at the Madrid International Donors' Conference for Iraqi Reconstruction, on 23–24th October 2003.[58]

On the other hand, the launching of the WOT *per se* represented a logical political extension of economic tendencies. Understood in *emergentist materialist* terms (Chapter 1), power-politics, empire, and militarism (driven by a *territorial* logic of power) were emergent from economic globalization (driven by the *capitalist* logic of power). That an efficient globalized market-driven society had to be backed up by militarism was openly admitted by celebrated globalization enthusiast, Thomas L. Friedman: "The hidden hand of the market will never work without the hidden fist – MacDonald's cannot flourish without McDonnell Douglas, the builder of the F-15. And the hidden fist that keeps the world safe for Silicon Valley's technologies to flourish is called the US Army, Air Force, Navy, and Marine Corps"; "ideas and technology don't just win and spread on their own", he declared, quoting Robert Kagan, but required "a strong power that promotes those ideas by example and protects those ideas by winning on the battlefield".[59] For Niall Ferguson, there was little difference between the 19th-century imperialism promoting the Open Door and present-day "Anglobalisation"[60] in their recourse to coercion. Situated on opposite ends of the political spectrum, Friedman and Ferguson had reached similar conclusions on the connection between capital accumulation and militarism as Rosa Luxemburg.[61]

Extending Arendt's assertion that endless capital accumulation requires an endless accumulation of power, it was only logical that the hegemon periodically had recourse to its huge military capacities to reproduce capital on a global scale. Washington was merely drawing on the *territorial* logic of power to expand markets and guarantee on-going capital accumulation via the creation of a new *spatial fix* and associated restructuring of social relations of production (SROP) and form of state (FOS) abroad. This is summed up neatly in Kaplan's above affirmation ("it is American power, and American power only, that can serve as an organising principle for the worldwide expansion of a liberal civil society"[62]) if "liberal civil society" is replaced with "capital accumulation".

The implication, coinciding with Arrighi's characterisation of world hegemony, was that the US was claiming that the expansion of its military power was in the interests of all in its role as the *Global Leviathan*.

From here to envisioning a Hobbesian/Orwellian world of *perpetual war* did not involve a huge quantitative leap. On the 14th September 2001, Bush II claimed the US had a "responsibility to history" to "rid the world of evil",[63] with Cheney confirming the forthcoming global war on terror ('terror' permitting even wider scope for action than 'terrorism') "in a sense it may never end. At least not in my lifetime",[64] making such event more likely with the announcement of the so-called "one percent doctrine".[65] Even such a low threshold of proof appeared too high for Rumsfeld who insisted the US had to have the necessary military capacity to defend the nation "against the unknown, the uncertain, the unseen and the unexpected" and prepare its forces "to deter and defeat adversaries that have not yet emerged to challenge us",[66] the "unknown unknowns".[67]

The Bush Doctrine, at the end of the day, bore a striking resemblance similar to the Truman Doctrine, both in its open-endedness and drive to remake the world 'after its own image'. In his second inaugural speech (20th January 2005), Bush II insisted his administration was committed to the "ultimate goal of ending tyranny in our world" since "[t]he survival of liberty in our land increasingly depends on the success of liberty in other lands" and, indeed, that "[a]dvancing these ideals is the mission that created our Nation".[68] Almost 60 years earlier, in a speech delivered at Baylor University Truman declared; "the American system can survive in America only it becomes a world system".[69] And for all the talk of "political globalization" remained, for Ferguson, "just a fancy word for imperialism, imposing your values and institutions on other".[70]

While the Bush II's discourse might have been more overt than most recent presidents, empire, as underscored in Chapter 3, has been omnipresent in the US history: American exceptionalism myths dominating social discourse during periods of maximum power projection. The father of liberal idealism and the League of Nations, Woodrow Wilson, for example, classified himself as "American exceptionalism personified",[71] claiming the nation's unique cultural heritage had bestowed on it "the infinite privilege of fulfilling her destiny and saving the world",[72] and making it "safe for democracy",[73] effectively repeating Thomas Jefferson and John Quincy Adams' earlier rallying calls. Yet driving this *democratic* or *benign imperialism* and celebrated cosmopolitanism of the "Fourteen Points", as observed, lay the very mundane exigencies of establishing the Open Door. "If America is not to have free enterprise", Wilson insisted, "then she can have freedom of no sort whatsoever".[74] And where the 'capitalist logic' did not suffice the President had no qualms in resorting to more coercive forms – sending more troops into more Caribbean and Central American states (e.g. Nicaragua, Haiti, Dominican Republic, Honduras) than any of his predecessors.[75]

In reality, neocon calls for a 'New American Century' and Henry Luce's "first great American Century",[76] which it sought to update were merely extensions on Wilson's 'benign imperialism'. "Freedom is the Almighty's gift to every man and woman in this world", Bush announced in 2004, and "as the greatest power on earth we have an obligation to help the spread of freedom".[77] The world could rest assured there would be no abuse of power, given the country's commitment to egalitarianism, universal liberal values,[78] free market capitalism and "unusually high degree of morality"[79]; any conflict it *did* get involved in would be, by definition, a *just war* against evil-doers[80] and not in any way driven by imperial ambitions,[81] despite its ever-expanding 'empire of bases'.[82]

Furthermore, despite the clear ideological incompatibility between Hobbes ('might') and the US's traditional liberal or Lockean ('right') allegiance[83] there was a point of coincidence. At his most Hobbesian, Locke acknowledged as legitimate the temporary suspension of the rule of law when public security was threatened (albeit sparingly, and in a very particular set of circumstances) and prioritising executive over legislative power.[84] Since Teddy Roosevelt, there has been a frequent usage of this *executive prerogative* to sidestep Congress.[85]

In accordance with its neocon authoritarianism, the Bush II administration would make frequent recourse to the executive prerogative not just at home (see below), but also abroad. In its capacity as the world's moral guardian and possessor of quasi-monopoly of the legitimate use of violence, the Global Leviathan could choose, as and when to opt-out of international law itself, while punishing those it considered to err into illegality, acting as "the bully on the block", in the words of US Chairman of the Joint Chiefs of Staff, Colin Powell.[86] In a peculiar twist on Immanuel Kant's 'Perpetual Peace', Washington claimed Hobbesian means (unaccountable coercive power and unending war) could lead to Lockean ends (democracy, liberty, market expansion, and world peace).

Using military means to extend neoliberalism into one of the few remaining areas of the semi-periphery had resisted it, the Middle East, might not have been the most orthodox but the process of 'accumulation by dispossession' began almost immediately and proved enormously profitable. The perks of hegemony meant politically well-connected American engineering, construction, and servicing corporations within the MIC were the best situated to take advantage of the occupation, organisation, and reconstruction of Iraq,[87] but Washington promised there would be an Open Door to all global capitalists. In this sense for neo-Gramscians, US militarism was serving the interests of the *transnational capitalist class*.[88]

The chosen instruments to achieve this were the so-called *Bremer's Orders*, a hundred binding/irrevocable instructions and directives presented on 19th September 2003 by Paul Bremer, "Director of the Office for Reconstruction and Humanitarian Assistance for Iraq" (retitled the *Coalition Provisional Authority*). These 'Washington Consensus' edicts – drawn up before the invasion by the US Agency of International Development – were based upon US Treasury Departments plans for market deregulation and the restructuring and subsequent privatisation of around 200 state-owned enterprises,[89] which Joseph Stiglitz denounced as an "even more radical form of shock therapy than pursued in the former Soviet world"[90] and imposed illegally under international law (e.g. the Fourth Geneva Convention of 1949 and the Hague Convention of 1907).

Pointedly, two sectors were omitted from market deregulation: one was the labour market, where strikes in some industries were prohibited and rights to unionise curtailed; the other was petroleum. Oil seizure was widely cited as the main reason for the invasion. Again, this is a complex (and well-trodden) issue, but worthy of clarification as it is illustrative of the limits of neoliberalism when it clashes with US hegemony.

The arguments supporting the 'appropriation thesis' appeared quite compelling. First, as argued, control of the Middle East and its oil flow has been vital for American hegemony underpinning the Dollar-Wall Street Regime (DWSR) and at the time Iraqi boasted the second largest proven reserves (and both inexpensive to produce and of high quality). Second, the 'Big Oil' component of WDPDC had long been a huge political and economic sponsor of the Republican Party,[91] enjoying particular close relations with both the Bush family and members of his cabinet such as Dick Cheney, Donald Evans, and Condoleeza Rice. Indeed, Chevron CEO Kenneth T. Derr, in a Commonwealth Club speech in San Francisco, in November 1998, had urged the US to heighten sanctions against Iraq, famously declaring the country possessed "huge reserves of oil and gas-reserves I'd love Chevron to gain access to".[92] Third, against the backdrop of Hubbert's "peak oil" thesis[93] about global demand outstripping supply, Western energy corporations were becoming increasingly concerned about access to global oil reserves, with Anglo-American firms suffering the largest drop in market share,[94] and neither the American nor the British energy companies were very happy when TotalFinaElf, Russia's Lukoil, and China's National Petroleum Corporation holding talks with Baghdad to develop Iraqi fields once sanctions were lifted.

In March 2001, the National Energy Policy Development Group, created by Executive Order on 29th January 2001, chaired by Dick Cheney's (known as Cheney Energy Task Force), and made up of executives from America's largest energy companies, recommended that Washington support initiatives by Middle Eastern countries "to open up areas of their energy sectors to foreign investment".[95] Questioned at the Asian Security Summit in Singapore, June 2003, on why the US had invaded Iraq and not North Korea Wolfowitz responded that economically speaking it had no choice since "the country swims on a sea of oil".[96] The Bush administration for its part vehemently denied oil was the motivation,[97]

Rumsfeld, speaking in 2002, dismissed such allegations as "Nonsense... It has nothing to do with oil, literally nothing to do with oil".[98]

This was clearly a disingenuous statement. But the reality was that while Big Oil may have been enthusiastic about regime change in Baghdad, it vehemently opposed to Wolfowitz's plan to privatise Iraq oil fields, fearing the increased competition would drive down prices as well as undermining the OPEC quota system, and potentially leading to the cartel's dismantling which had served it so well. Through its links to the dollar (i.e. the DWSR) OPEC was also structural to American hegemony, so Big Oil's position was backed both by the Treasury Department and Wall Street. The State Department was also concerned that the privatisation of Iraqi oil would not only unleash a revolt amongst its workers, but seriously jeopardise the future economic stability of the Iraqi state.[99]

As a result, neocon neoliberals found themselves increasingly isolated within the WDPDC (Paul Wolfowitz, for example, would soon be shifted to the World Bank and John Bolton to the UN). Bush II appointed former CEO of Shell, Philip Carroll, as chief of the Iraqi Oil Ministry advisory board who immediately made it crystal clear to Paul Brenner that there would be *no* privatisation of oil resources or installations under his watch.[100] Former Secretary of State, James A. Baker III – whose legal firm Baker Botts was the legal representative of the Saudi Arabian government, Exxon Mobil, ConocoPhillips, and Halliburton – was then delegated the task of drawing up plans for a pro-OPEC state-owned company to oversee Iraqi oil. Over 35 years after losing their oil concessions under Saddam Hussein's nationalisation programme, the original partners in the *Iraqi Petroleum Company* (Exxon-Mobil, Shell, BP, and Total) resumed drilling there, accompanied by a long list of international operators – in keeping with the US's Open-Door pledge – but all, to this day, under licenses granted by the Ministry of Oil in Baghdad.

In short, it is reasonable to assume that oil was one contributory factor to the invasion of Iraq, but the over-ruling of the doctrinaire neoliberals indicated the objective was more about gaining *control* over rather than straight *ownership*. The Chairman of PFC Energy, one of the main advisory companies to the industry observed, "The main reason was to consolidate our position as a superpower".[101] Indeed, oil from Iraq and Kuwait constituted a very small percentage of energy imports to the US, but significantly, it was absolutely crucial for the US's competitors Japan and Germany. David Harvey places the Iraq War in its broader geopolitical context, as "an attempt to control the global oil spigot and hence the global economy through the domination of the Middle East", and constituting a "powerful military bridgehead on the Eurasian landmass".[102] For Michael Klare, the Bush Doctrine was merely extending the so-called *Carter Doctrine* (which considered the defence of Gulf region oil as a primary national interest) to the Caspian Sea, the Andean region of Latin

America, and West Coast of Africa, which as such, have been identified as future US military bases.[103] Iraq War apologist Michael Ignatieff held Washington's real motives for the various post-Cold War interventions, spanning from the Balkans to Afghanistan had been "to maintain imperial order in zones essential to the interests of the United States",[104] which included trying to prise Russia away from both the Middle East and the Central Asian 'stans' (Uzbekistan, Kazakhstan, etc.).

Under the cover of the WOT, the Bush administration authorised counter-terrorist military interventions (often of a covert, nature) in dozens of countries throughout Africa, the Middle East, West and Central Asia, and on to the Pacific Ocean.[105] The result was the most comprehensive restructuring of US military bases since 1953 US, with the Pentagon able to open new facilities in hitherto inaccessible countries such as Uzbekistan, Pakistan, Qatar, Djibouti, and of course Iraq. These new military installations were called *lily pads*: strategic points from which the US could launch its 'preventative war'. Having military bases in 130 of the 193 UN member states – including Saudi Arabia – placed the US in a major power position.

The Iraq War also sought to reassert politico-military hegemony over an advanced capitalist core, while sending out a clear political message to potential rivals (China and Russia) and 'rogue states' threats (Iran and North Korea) that the US was, and sought to remain, the *indispensable nation* (NSS-2002). The conflict, like the Gulf War before it, was to be a televised media event. Friends and foe alike could witness the risks of falling foul to the full technologic strategic and military supremacy of the US (the RMA), exemplified in Rumsfeld's *shock and awe* doctrine. The "new powers of technology", Bush II explained allowed the America "to strike an enemy force with speed and incredible precision...a combination of creative strategies and advanced technologies", he continued, "redefining war in our terms".[106] Furthermore, in the same way, social forces released under economic globalization had helped restructure other countries SROP and FOS along neoliberal lines, social forces emitted out of American politico-military hegemony would push all states to restructure their coercive apparatus to fit its strategic concerns.

A constant theme in this monograph, in line with Madison's earlier affirmation, and illustrated with the launching of the Cold War and Reagan's Second Cold War, is that military projection abroad goes hand-in-hand with militarisation at home. For Karl Polanyi's authoritarianism was a natural political reaction to the social fragmentation proclivities of market capitalism,[107] a perspective shared by Hannah Arendt who added that the capitalist state was as "a vacillating structure", constantly having to "provide itself with new props from outside; otherwise it would collapse overnight into the aimless, senseless chaos of the private interests from which it springs".[108] In the case of the US, with its hyper-individualistic capitalist model there was an even greater risk of societal fragmentation, hence the more frequent recourse to the politics of fear and the 'friend-foe' mechanism.

We saw in Chapter 3 that the neocon 'movement' actually appeared in the 1970s – forming the hardcore of Reagan's 'hegemonic project' – and was very much driven by the need to reverse what it considered as the increasingly 'ungovernability' of the population. Although, as Chapter 1 indicated, 'surface' hegemony and 'structural' hegemony do not necessarily coincide, emerging as they do at different ontological levels, there appeared a natural 'fit' between neoconservativism (surface) and the neoliberal regime of accumulation (structure), the former providing the 'political arm' to help reproduce underlying SROP and guarantee profits. Like Reagan's hegemonic project, Bush II neocon 'movement' was consolidated by drawing on American exceptionalist myths, non-class-based identity politics[109] and an aggressive foreign policy (swapping the WOT for the Second Cold War).

One can identify two principal differences between the two administrations. First, Bush II's HB was even more reliant on the Religious Right and the Southern/Mid-Western subaltern classes than Reagan, explaining Bush's campaign strategist, Karl Rove's labours to emphasise the leader's born-again credentials, the divine nature of his mission,[110] and his unpretentious down-to-earth Southern values.[111] Second, by the turn of the millennium neoliberal policies of deregulation, privatisation, welfare-state reduction, tax reductions for the wealthy, etc. unleashed such market volatility, hyper-individualism, nihilism, job instability, poverty, and unprecedented inequality, as to seriously threaten the stability of society, and which the Bush II administration would only exasperate,[112] explaining it's more authoritarianism and militarist version and permanent recourse to security threats, be they domestic or international, genuine or fictional.

As Thomas Hobbes observed, security threats greatly augmented the state's legitimacy and authority: a frightened citizen, like a small child, had little choice but to swear obedience to their protector when their lives are at risk.[113] For the eighteen months following 9/11 the White House skilfully exploited the climate of hate and fear and "paranoid style in American politics"[114] exercising its executive prerogative to issue colour-coded "strategic communications" on the possibility of imminent attack, employing an army of Pentagon-approved 'message multipliers', to present the homeland as a nation under siege from 'evil-doers'.[115] The further militarisation of American society was underway.

Ad hoc restrictions aside, the institutionalised curtailment of American civil liberties and freedoms began in earnest with the USA PATRIOT Act and Homeland Security Act, signed into law on 26th October 2001 and 25th November 2002, which took the US back to the Truman era with the *Red Scare* with a new enlarged NSS. New counter-terrorism laws greatly expanding police investigative powers and ability to arrest, tighter immigration controls, limits on press freedom, and the setting up of a massive nationwide surveillance/intelligence/security bureaucracy involving thousands of government organisations and private compa- nies. The security agencies, with the National Security Agency (NSA) at the helm, were given an effective *carte blanche* to carry out the same kind of warrantless wire-tapping and control of private communications (now including mobile phone conversations, e-mails, and instant mes- sages) access to personal records (be they medical, financial, criminal, or consumer) and surveillance methods (in this case CCTV, biometrics, web tracking, data mining) which the aforementioned *Church Committee* had denounced in 1975. Indeed, the definition of 'enemy' was left purposely vague to encompass an infinite list of potential 'opponents' including critics of neoliberalism, the same way the CIA used anti-communism to target counter-hegemonic forces in the late 1960s. Keeping the public in a permanent state of hysteria would even drive Brzezinski to denounce Bush II's "fear-mongering".[116]

That such rhetoric and tactics were successful in garnering support for the Iraq War was not a surprise[117]: national security had long constituted what Gramsci recognised as a *hegemonic discourse* in American public life, effectively trumping all others since the launching of the NSS in 1947. There were, of course, material reasons for this too. The MIC had converted into colossal bureaucratic security apparatus whose tentacles penetrated virtually all areas of American life, be it via lucrative indus- trial contracts, academia (the Department of Defence being the single largest funder of university research), the media, or the entertainment industry (e.g. television, films, video games, etc.).[118] As a consequence, the 'permanent war economy' did enjoy legitimacy amongst large sectors of the American public who held that belief that war, or at least its prepa- ration, brought prosperity.

Indeed, one of the important domestic corollaries of the WOT, again repeating the Reagan template, was to justify 'pump priming' the ailing national economy via military Keynesianism and stimulate the MIC. Af- ter the dip in the 1990s, the WOT finally returned the Pentagon budget to (and even surpassing) Korean and Vietnam War levels, military spending doubled in Bush II's first year in office alone, representing 50% of all fed- eral discretional spending.[119] Rumsfeld's "capacity-based approach" and need to defend the country from a limitless list of "unknown unknowns" meant a boom for the high-tech capital-intensive military contractors (e.g. Boeing, General Dynamics, and United Technologies) and asso- ciated suppliers of cyber, laser, robotics, biotechnology, and advanced electronic technologies. And all paid for by US taxpayer (or treasury bonds (TB) purchasers).[120]

Nor did the corporate-welfare scheme end there. Milton Friedman's protégé Rumsfeld announced it was time to "liberate" the military establishment from its bloated Soviet-style bureaucracy and subject it neoliberal logic.[121] Greatly extending Reagan's Logistics Civil Augmentation Program (LOGCAP)[122] the Pentagon would be turned into a modern corporation: retaining control over key responsibilities such as providing soldiers and arms and 'fighting wars', while outsourcing non-essential production, 'logistical support' and high-risk duties to 'more efficient' private contractors who, it was claimed, could supply the latest, more advanced military and satellite technology at a lower cost. A new defence paradigm was established: the state no longer *provided* security itself; it merely *guaranteed* it via private sector subcontracting. Well-connected companies such as Brown & Root (Halliburton) and Lockheed Martin won highly lucrative contracts to supply the US military with a whole series of services, including constructing/running domestic and overseas bases and extending into data management, surveillance tax-collecting, air traffic controller, etc.[123] Similarly, the aforementioned PATRIOT and Homeland Security Acts meant a boon for the private sector spying organisations such as Booz Allen Hamilton (employer of whistle-blower Edward Snowden), forming part of what we can term a *security-industrial complex* (SIC), broader in scope than the MIC. Indeed, as Naomi Klein notes, many of the modern surveillance technologies were originally developed by private companies, many prior to 9/11, as a way to better monitor, collect, and process data on consumer patterns but now were developed for sale to the government at a high cost: a fusion she described as "a bizarre merger of security and shopping cultures" or "shopping mall and secret prison".[124]

This chapter has sought to contextualise the commonly held view that the Bush II's so-called 'new imperialism' digressed substantially from the established pattern of hegemonic governance. One further way this debate can be breached is by analysing to what extent the subsequent occupant in the White House sought to reverse his predecessor's policies.

"Yes We Can?..."

Barak Obama's entire presidential campaign was based on a promise of wide-reaching change, epitomised by the electoral slogan ("Yes we can") and personified in the Afro-American candidate himself. Internationally, his mandate was clear: rectify the damage done by the previous Bush administration and reassert American 'intellectual and moral leadership', and thus hegemony. This was to be done by returning to the traditional form of hegemonic governance: US-led multilateral institutions ('moderate multilateralism'). Under Obama, the message went out, Washington would seek a more moral, transparent, benign, and cooperative foreign policy – a 'new diplomacy' – based upon a respect for international law, regard for allies and out-stretching the hand of peace to hitherto enemies. In June 2009, Obama spoke in Cairo of his desire for a new beginning between US and Muslim world. In September, Obama told the UN General Assembly the US was seeking, "in word and deed, a new era of engagement with the world".[125]

True to his word, in the first year of office, Obama put an end to WOT discourse, ordered the withdrawal of all 50,000 remaining combat troops from Iraq by August 2010 and all remaining troops by December 2011, warned Israel to stop building settlements in Palestine, and signed two presidential directives: Executive Order 13491, forbidding state-sponsored torture[126] and Executive Order 13492, to close down Guantánamo within the year.

The international reaction to Obama's *détente*[127] charm initiative belied the claim that US 'intellectual and moral leadership' was finished. In his first year in the White House, and much to the embarrassment of the winner himself, Obama was granted the 2009 Nobel Peace Prize. Without citing any concrete accomplishments, the prize committee praised "his extraordinary efforts to strengthen international diplomacy and cooperation between peoples", creating "a new climate in international politics", giving the world "hope for a better future" with his diplomacy "founded in the concept that those who are to lead the world must do so on the basis of values and attitudes that are shared by the majority of the world's population".[128]

With regard to Russia, Obama promised to press the "reset" button following mutual accusations of meddling in Georgia and Ukraine, tensions over anti-ballistic missile installation in Poland, and the Iraq War. Washington announced plans to replace the long-range missile defence system began under Bush with shorter range intercepts. In return, Moscow would sign a new START treaty; facilitate the transportation of materials through Central Asia to Afghanistan; and support or abstain with regards to the passing of two US-sponsored Regulations through the Security Council in 2010–11, with regards to the imposition of economic sanctions on Iran[129] and a "no-fly zone" (subsequently used to justify the invasion) of Libya.[130]

The official, multilateralist, *Obama Doctrine*, set out in the *National Security Strategy 2010* (NSS-2010)[131], appeared a far cry from Bush II's NSS-2002, emphasizing that Washington "will continue to underwrite global security through our commitments to allies, partners, and institutions", pursue national interests, but as part of an international society where all countries share responsibilities and duties. Distancing itself from the previous administration Obama asserted that US engagement must take place within the confines of a LRBIO considered vital to "a just and sustainable international order".

The NSS-2010 also recognised the existence of "other centres of power". Consequently, Washington would pay greater attention to regional problems (understood as referring to the political rise of the People's Republic of China [PRC] in South East Asia, to which it would "pivot") and to seek to use diplomatic (rather than military) means to try to achieve its goals (so-called 'smart power'), in which the State Department would take on a greater responsibility at the expense of the Defense Department. Indeed, the Budget Control Act of 2011 announced a $487 billion cut in defence spending over the following 10 years, much to the chagrin of the Pentagon.[132]

But when it came to foreign policy, change of emphasis and style aside, no radical overhaul was forthcoming. Troops were removed from Iraq – which was by now feeling the real costs of the invasion[133] – but their numbers effectively doubled in Afghanistan, which would become the longest war in the US history. Israel was able to keep on constructing settlements in occupied Palestinian territories unmolested. Obama did outlaw 'enhanced terrorist techniques' and close down 'black sites' (although the latter were largely emptied by 2007 under Bush II anyway) but Guantánamo remained 'open for business', while the CIA armed, funded, and trained anti-Assad rebel groups in Syria.

Indeed, the WOT would continue in all but name. As Obama declared in *Foreign Affairs* article in 2007 he asserted: "Iraq was a diversion from the fight against the terrorists who struck us on 9/11", urging the need to "refocus our efforts on Afghanistan and Pakistan – the central front in our war against Al Qaeda".[134] Instead of the global WOT, the Grand Strategy focused on 'countering violent extremism'; the principal target being transnational Salafi jihadi groups such as Al Qaeda and later the Islamic State of Iraq and Syria (ISIS). The latter arose in the power-vacuum in Iraq in 2011 post-US withdrawal, and according to Secretary of Defense Chuck Hagel, posed a threat "beyond anything we have seen".[135]

Granted, military tactics did evolve under Obama. Increasingly, the Pentagon resorted to the extra-juridical assassination of suspected 'enemy combats', often by the crack elite U.S. Special Operation Command (SOCOM), whose number were greatly augmented. According to Nick Turse, since 2001, SOCOM has been involved in "plethora of forever war fronts" either as reconnaissance or "direct action" combat raids against insurgents in a long list of countries including Afghanistan, Iraq, Libya, Syria, Yemen, Somalia, Niger, Tunisia, Cameroon, Kenya, Mauritania, Mali, and the Philippines, resulting in hundreds of civilian deaths.[136] The 'enemy combats' were also eliminated by remotely-controlled Hellfire-equipped drones whose use was augmented *tenfold* under the Obama administration,[137] many of which, following Rumsfeld's Pentagon reforms, were carried out by private contractors based on information passed to them by SIC.[138] It is estimated that Pakistan and Yemen were subjected to some 450 attacks by 2015 alone.[139]

Just how successful these *perpetual* or *forever wars* are, and the damage they do to US 'intellectual and moral leadership' and politico-military hegemony, is quite another question. In 2017 *The Wall Street Journal* estimated the total costs of the wars in Afghanistan, Iraq, Pakistan, and

Syria since 2001 as standing around $5.6 trillion which, if interest payments are added could reach $8 trillion.[140] The shadow of Paul Kennedy's "imperial overstretch" paradigm looms large.[141]

Despite promising greater democratic accountability and claiming to be "the most transparent administration in history", the Obama administration was at least as secretive and Hobbesian as its predecessor, exercising the executive prerogative to oppress the freedom of information while sanctioning a massive increase in extra-judicial activities by its intelligence and security services. The SIC, for example, was transformed into a multibillion-dollar global surveillance and intelligence network,[142] used not only to spy on potential 'anti-systemic' elements but also to shadow and collect huge amounts of data on world political leaders (especially from core competitors such as Angela Merkel), corporations, and the public at large.[143]

Immigrants came in for special surveillance attention. Obama dramatically stepped up monitoring and deportation processes, taking a small programme created by Bush II in 2003 and expanded it by 3,600% by the end of his first term, leaving Donald Trump with "the most sophisticated and well-funded human-expulsion machine in the history of the country". Indeed, despite soaring rates of expulsion under Trump in 2017, these number still palled in comparison to the peak years under the 'deporter-in-chief' (Obama), estimated to have ejected a record 3 million immigrant workers and families, and possessing the fingerprints of 32 million people (three times the undocumented population).[144]

Furthermore, and while establishing a National Declassification Center to facilitate the declassification of documents, Obama used the 1917 Espionage Act to pursue and prosecute more whistle-blowers and 'leakers' (e.g. Shamai Leibowitz, Chelsea Manning, Thomas Drake, Jeffrey Sterling, and Edward Snowden) than all previous governments, and severely curtailed the scope for investigative journalism.[145]

As reiterated throughout this work, hegemony cannot be understood as a static *position*, but a dynamic *process*, in which domination and coercion are omnipresent, as they are within capitalism itself (structural hegemony), with the term *authoritarian neoliberalism* increasingly used to describe the present conjuncture.[146] Thus, the recourse to militarism *per se* does not denote the end hegemony (Gramsci's *third moment*) as some neo-Gramscian and liberal institutionalist scholars have implied. Testimony to that was palpable international enthusiasm which greeted Obama's election and initial multilateralist discourse (Nobel Peace Prize included), being largely able to reassert American leadership, at least during the first term.

While it may be true that Bush II's neocon hegemonic project placed more emphasis on militarist means to revolve certain domestic/international structural problems than Obama – a reflection of its particular HB – it is important, as we have seen, not to overstate these differences, which were more about style than substance. As Jack Goldsmith, head of the Office of Legal Counsel in Department of Justice under Bush II commented: "The new administration has copied most of the Bush programmes, expanded some of it, and has narrowed only a bit. Almost all the Obama changes have been at the level of packaging, argumentation, symbol, and rhetoric", classifying the strategy as "an attempt to make the core Bush approach to terrorism politically and legally more palatable, and thus more sustainable".[147]

The reality was of course that there was partisan agreement up on Capitol Hill on the desirability of Bush II's class agenda. Domestically, for example, while Obama might have had partial victories in social policy (raising the minimum wage and workplace benefits for federal contract workers, lesbian, and gay rights) and environment (introducing the Clear Power Plan and joining the Paris Accord), Republicans and conservative Democrats made sure the mildly progressive American Jobs Act (autumn 2011) never went ahead, 'Obamacare' was watered, while tax cuts for the rich, business deregulation, and weak environment/consumer protection laws remained in place. Democrats, after all, are equally beholden to Corporate America for campaign financing as GOP.[148]

The same broad bi-party agreement also existed with regards to the absolute necessity of maintaining *American primacy*. Rhetoric aside, neither Bush II nor Obama questioned this elite 'common sense', long embedded in the nation's HB. Clear continuity existed between US Secretary of State, Dean Acheson's testimony during 1963 ASIL Proceedings on the quarantine of Cuba in 1963,[149] the DPG 1992, the NSS-2002, and Obama's calling for "another American century",[150] reiterating in his 2010 State of the Union address, "I do not accept second place for the United States".[151]

Belief in exceptionalism and the US's divine right to engage in 'benign imperialism' remained unquestioned amongst the Washington foreign policy establishment, regardless of party affiliation. As US Secretary of State, Madeleine Albright observed in February 1998 when seeking to justify the Clinton administration's intervention in Iraq: "if we are to use force, it is because we are America; we are the indispensable nation. We stand tall and we see further into the future"[152] American mainstream IR scholars may criticise Bush II's aggressive unilateralism but all shared Brzezinski's affirmation that: "There is no realistic alternative to the prevailing American hegemony and the role of U.S. power as the indispensable component of global security".[153]

All US presidents, especially from Wilson onwards, have acknowledged that the survival of 'the American way of life' necessarily depended on the on-going capacity of Washington to defend the model of global capitalism on which it was based. As President-elect, Obama announced during a press conference in December 2008, that: "To ensure prosperity here and peace abroad, we all share the belief we have to maintain the strongest military on the planet".[154]

In the *National Security Strategy 2015* (NSS-2015), the last one published during Obama's term of office, the White House set out its plan for future military hegemony. "We embrace our responsibilities for underwriting international security because it serves our interests, uphold our commitments to our allies and partners, and addresses threats that are truly global". Since "[t]here is no substitute for American leadership", and "American leadership is a global force for good", Washington promised to lead "with purpose...with strength...by example...with capable partners...with all the instruments of US power...[and] with a long-term perspective". The US sought "full-spectrum dominance" reserving itself the right to project its massive military power virtually anywhere in the world – and military dominance over sea, air, land, information, space – and sent out a direct warning to China not to challenge the status quo in East Asia (see Chapter 5).[155]

The US, in short, aimed to continue its Global Leviathan status as "system shaper" – to help reconstruct SROP and FOS for geostrategic or on-going capital accumulation needs – albeit in a responsible manner and act accordance with its position as a benign exceptionalist hegemonic power. But whether it could do so, ultimately would depend on its material base and the strength of the American-led accumulation regime, which appeared to be on its last legs.

Crisis in the 'Heartland'

As we saw in Chapter 3, the creation and subsequent bursting of asset-bubbles was considered not just an inevitable consequence of financialization by the US Treasury, Federal Reserve, and Wall Street,[156] but also as necessary to meet the demands of the liquidity-driven American economy. The more volatile the international financial system the more international operators would seek a safe harbour ('flight-to-quality') in Wall Street, which apart from boosting share prices kept interest rates low in turn benefits businesses/house-owners.[157] Indeed, as the Chapter 3 underscored, the Wall Street-Treasury-IMF (WSTI) Complex played a pivotal role in managing and manipulating crises to further 'accumulation by dispossession'. According to Harvey, they "were orchestrated, managed, and controlled both to rationalise the system and to redistribute assets", noting that between 1980 and 2007 $4.6 trillion (i.e. around 50 Marshall Plans) had been sent to the core creditors from the Global South.[158] Given their pervasiveness/desirability, it was vital that when these financial bubbles did occur, a system of 'crisis management' was in place. This depended upon international organisations and inter-state cooperation but at the very core of global regulation was the American state – Treasury and the Federal Reserve – Ruben's 'chief of the fire department' analogy.

Thanks to the on-going financialization process (the commodification of pensions included), by the late 1990s the whole of American society was dependent directly/indirectly on Wall Street and confidence in the dollar. Capital flowed into the US from around the world, not just as an 'imperial tithe' (e.g. Saudi Arabia), to stabilise exchange rates (e.g. the PRC), or during as part of a 'flight-to-quality', but for reasons of profitability. American financial markets were *deep* (offering comparative safety, liquidity, and high returns) and thanks to the New Economy, based on a strong productive economy, or so it seemed. For all these reasons, thus, when the dot.com speculative bubble finally burst in March 2000, it was an essential blow to another asset-bubble.

Real estate had always part of financialization (finance, insurance, and real estate [FI*RE*]) but it was not until the Federal Reserve lowered interest rates to almost zero following 9/11 and therein, cutting the cost of borrowing, lowering mortgage rates, and reducing yields on TBs – not to mention the lack of alternative profitable investments – that the debt-driven housing bubble really took off. With access to abundant cheap domestic credit, pension funds money[159] and trillions from overseas (notably China, Japan, and the OPEC[160]) – and 'bolstered' by an expanded derivative market (e.g. credit default swaps), dubious credit rating, and creative accounting practices (use of off-balance sheet) – the largest investment banks[161] and hedge funds were free to engage in risky, highly leveraged trading in securitised debt (often in the form of 'collateralised debt obligations'),[162] whose real value became obscured or simply unknown.[163]

Regulators turned a blind eye to such highly speculative and opaque trading practices, not just because both main political parties were heavily dependent on Wall Street campaign finance and the heads of the key financial institutions – the Treasury and the Federal Reserve – were usually recruited from the big investment bank,[164] but because of the positive effects it had on the economy. On the supply side, it helped to generate investment in the 'productive' economy, especially in those well-connected Pentagon-subsidised areas – IT, telecommunications, aerospace, electronics, automobiles, and pharmaceuticals – and the construction industry.[165] On the demand side, it greatly stimulated the consumption of goods and non-financial services which would have otherwise have been impossible given neoliberalism's success in driving down salaries for working people. Thus, thanks to these asset-price bubbles, the US could enjoy a virtuous circle of high asset price, consumer spending, high corporate profits, job creation, and lower default rates hence easy credit, ad infinitum. Significantly, in 2006, around 40% of American corporate profits derived from the financial sector.[166]

As reiterated throughout this book, one of the central requirements of world hegemony is that it acts as a motor for growth. Pax Americana was ultimately based upon the US's ability to serve as a 'container of power' for capitalism: a *global consumer of last resort* for surplus capital. The problem was that the very accumulation regime the US used to re-float its hegemony – financialization/neoliberalism – was undermined the ability to fulfil that responsibility.

The dismantling of the Keynesian-welfare state, privatisation of the public sector (and loss of social welfare provisions), attacks on organised labour/workers, and subsequent de-industrialisation, had led to the loss of high-paying, stable jobs, and stagnating, using declining incomes for American working and middle classes. Not only had cheap imports lowered the costs of the reproduction of labour, but also transnational capital mobility and the perennial threat of 'capital flight' and job loss successfully disciplined labour, keeping wage demands to a minimum while raising the rates of exploitation. Real wages in the US, which had been more-or-less constantly declining since 1973 started to nose-dive in the late 1990s, while wealth-holdings of the upper-middle classes, benefitting from pro-rich tax reform, tax havens, rising corporate profits/stock market prices/executive pay, soared.[167] Between 1977 and 2007, 60% of the increase in national income had been appropriated by just 1% of the population, while the rate of income growth amongst the 'bottom' 90% during this period stood around 0.5% GDP; little surprise that the US was witnessing levels of inequality not seen since the 1920.[168]

Concomitant with underlying logic, the US was merely witnessing the same massive wealth redistribution away from the lower-middle and working classes towards rich that had occurred wherever neoliberalism had been implemented, be it China, Russia, Latin America, or Europe. Neoclassical economics' emphasis on capital accumulation by export-led growth assumed that demand was unlimited. Short term, the only way a mass consumption-based society could reproduce itself was by asset-price inflation (based on a mortgage). At the end of 2008, householder and consumer debt accounting for around $6 trillion.[169] And yet, the housing bubble was just *one* part of a much wider debt problem. According to Gérard Duménil and Dominque Levy, US aggregate debt as a percentage of GDP between 1980 and 2008 was more than doubled (155% to 353%), reflected in household debts (from 48% to 96%), while financial sector debt increased almost sixfold (20% to 119%).[170] It was, in short, getting increasingly hard for the US to fulfil its hegemonic 'global consumer' responsibility.

In Marxist terms, the capital was facing a systemic *realisation crisis* due to the uneven development of capitalism. Perennial overproduction (and overexploitation) in the PRC, Germany, Japan, etc. was now reinforced by underconsumption in the US. The blowing of an asset-price bubble, no matter how large, and how 'sophisticated' the financial instruments used, could not ultimately resolve global overcapacity, imbalance, and inequality. And given the scale and depth of global financial integration, inter-bank lending and the centrality of Wall Street, when the Global Financial Crisis of 2008 (GFC) hit the US – shrinking credit by an estimated $24 trillion[171] – the whole world entered into a recession for the first time since the 1970s. Those countries which had followed the US's credit-financed growth strategy of attracting foreign capital to blow their own debt-financed speculative bubbles, despite declining average real incomes, were doubly hit. In the case of the EU, the resultant sovereign debt crisis would drive the eurozone to the brink of dissolution in 2011, which would only be avoided by the mobilisation of massive bail-outs ultimately paid for by the public via heightened austerity programmes, the burden of which fell disproportionately on those of lower income.

Once the crisis hit, ironically, US 'intellectual and moral leadership' was temporarily restored via the Federal Reserve-Treasury axis. Overnight, the Fed assumed the mantle of *World Central Bank*: the international lender and spender of last resort, using quantitative easing (i.e. printing money and increasing money supply), pumping billions of dollars via foreign central banks into the inter-bank markets abroad to provide liquidity to their banking system (and therefore indirectly to Wall Street too) and avert a systemic collapse. Meanwhile, at home, the Fed-Treasury axis worked tirelessly to stabilise the 'heartland', guaranteeing take-overs (e.g. JPMorgan's acquisition of Bear Stearns), carrying out nationalisations (Fannie Mae and Freddie Mac), granting credit facilities (AIG), seizing/re-selling companies (Washington Mutual), underwriting mutual funds deposits ($3.4 trillion), announcing plans the purchase of toxic securities ('troubled asset relief program' – TARP), and issuing emergency regulatory measures (ban on 'shorting').

In November 2008, Bush II held court in Washington for the heads of states of the world's wealthiest states to present a picture of class harmony and confidence against the backdrop of global melt-down. The formal aim of this new international forum – the G20 – representing around 90% of the world's GDP, was to debate institutional failures and reconfigure a new institutional framework. Yet few concrete measures were forthcoming, short of launching a *voluntary* regulatory framework regarding capital adequacy under the Bank of International Settlement's *Basel III* accord.

There was to be no radical reform of the American financial sector, despite the much-heralded passing of Obama's 2,300-page Wall Street Reform and Consumer Protection Act of 2010 – commonly known as the Dodd-Frank Act. It promised to 're-regulate' the banks and prevent the possibility of a financial crisis occurring again and at least on paper looked impressive: setting up a new regulatory umbrella group under the Treasury –the Financial Stability Oversight Council – to oversee the financial system and prevent banks from becoming 'too-big-to-fail', who were made to produce reports on how they would fail without bail-outs ('living wills'); tightening up over-the-counter-trading, most derivatives to be traded through a central exchange; banning proprietary trading (the "Volcker rule"); while credit rating agencies had to be more transparent, accountable, and conflicts of interests prevented.

But thanks to legal challenges, the creation and exploitation of loopholes, Wall Street lobbying, fragmentary institutional oversight, and intentional underfunding of regulatory bodies, many of the original reform provisions were diluted or simply side-stepped, actually resulting in the large American banks getting *even bigger.* Yet even that was too strict for Trump's administration who signed a bipartisan bill in May 2018 to "rollback" the "Dodd-Frank disaster", raising $50 billion the too-big-to-fail asset threshold, requiring Fed oversight and Volcker Rule restrictions to $250 billion with the promise of further financial de-regulation.[172] Given the underlying contradictions and inbuilt systemic failings of the capital accumulation model, the likelihood of a future GFC appears likely.

Indeed, and compatible with the *emergentist materialist* philosophy of science set out in Chapter 1, the appearance and consolidation of Trump's hegemonic project (surface hegemony) is best understood as emerging out of a deeper structural crisis afflicting the neoliberal regime of accumulation (structural hegemony) and manifested in the crisis of US world hegemony. Economic inequality, stagnant real incomes, and loss of well-paid jobs rose even quicker under Obama, aggravated by the GFC, the maintenance of Bush II regressive tax reforms, and the signing of a "comprehensive free trade agreement" with Panama in 2011 (allowing corporation/the wealthy to further evade fiscal obligations. Burdened down by "debt peonage", and increasingly angry, and alienated from society (work, consumer lifestyle, political process, etc.),[173] a sizeable proportion of disillusioned white middle and rural-based working classes[174] found solace in Trump's right-wing popularist hegemonic project: an indictment on successive Democrat administrations effectively forsaking the working class.[175]

In accordance once again with Gramsci's observation that political problems are often best solved by cultural means, Trump's campaign strategist Breitbart News CEO, Steve Bannon, exploited the insecurities and prejudices of a section of the electorate, expounding a neo-Reaganite identity politics agenda, based on ultra-nationalism, anti-immigrant/Islamism (replacing anti-communism), and social/religious conservativism. Like Reagan, Trump preached anti-declinist rhetoric ("make American great, again"), although more Jacksonian in orientation, blaming globalization, 'outsiders', 'crony capitalism', and Washington 'elites' for the societal decline and loss of national sovereignty.

It was time to promote the interests of 'working families' and the 'common man' by focus on national economic growth ("America First"), to generate more and better jobs by encouraging American multinational corporations (MNCs) to reverse their 'go global' strategy, while promising to increase infrastructure investment, social security protection, and lower drug prices. Just how the Trump administration will manage to square the circle of economic nationalism with neoliberalism/financialization (Open Door) and world hegemony remains to be seen. But those hoping that the multi-billionaire real estate mogul might abandon the neoliberal class agenda, are likely to be disappointed, at least judging by the aforementioned Dodd-Frank reform, the Tax Cuts and Jobs Act of 2017, and proposed cuts to welfare programmes, such as Supplemental Nutrition Assistance Program.

An inward-looking tone reverberates throughout the *National Security Strategy 2017* (NSS-2017),[176] constantly referring to threats posed, 'competitors' and 'rival powers', which while understandable for a document of this nature, and complicit with Trump's overall "America First" political agenda, transmits more of an image of a nation 'under siege' (back to Rumsfeld's house metaphor) than one confident about its future, manifested in the launching of trade wars and questioning long-standing US-founded multilateral institutions (see Chapter 5). But while Trump's foreign policy hitherto has proven erratic – a testimony to his formal independence from the national security establishment – the essence of NSS-2017 remains the same as NSS-2015. The White House is committed to US primacy: "to be strong and ready to lead abroad", to "advance American influence" and "reassert American advantages on the world stage".[177]

The problem was that the WO was changing. China, for one, interpreted the GFC and its aftermath as definitive proof that the US-led accumulation regime was unstainable, and began to investigate other options.

Notes

1 Moseley (2003), p. 221.
2 See Stiglitz (2004). Stiglitz notes that between 1998 and 2000 accounting companies donated $15 million in 'campaign contributions' to 50% of the House and 94% of the Senate. Stiglitz (2004), p. 90.
3 Apart from questions over the licit nature of his electoral victory over John Kerry, Bush II was accused of engaging in 'opaque' business practices prior to entering the White House, involving insider information, share-price manipulation, tax dodging, and questionable friendships (disgraced Enron boss Kenneth Lay). See for example Green (2002).
4 Lang (2004).
5 See for example Arrighi (2008).
6 See for example Golub (2004).
7 Project for the New American Century (1997).
8 Leaked to *The New York Times*, see The New York Times (1992).
9 Amongst the most politically active conservative think tanks are the American Enterprise Institute, Ohlin Foundation, National Institute for Public Policy, the Rand Corporation, the Smith Richardson Foundation, and Center for Security Policy. See van der Pijl (2008), p. 150.
10 According to Johnson, the publication of the *Clash of Civilization* was financed by the Ohlin Foundation. Johnson (2004), p. 310.

11 See Kaplan (1994).
12 Especially active here were those of a militant Zionist orientation: American Israel Public Affairs Committee, the Jewish Institute for National Security Affairs, the Washington Institute for Near East Policy, the Middle East Media Research Institute, the National Institute for Public Policy, the Institute for Advanced Strategic and Political Studies, and the Middle East Forum.
13 See for example Project for the New American Century (2000), p. 63.
14 See for example Project for the New American Century (1998).
15 Project for the New American Century (1998).
16 Center for Security Policy (2002).
17 Suskind (2004), p. 72.
18 Interview with Bush's Treasury Secretary, Paul O'Neill in *Time Magazine*, 10th January 2004. O'Neill's affirmation is collaborated by many authors, amongst them Clarke (2004) and Woodward (2004).
19 On the 12th September, Bush instructed counter-terrorism chief, Richard A. Clarke, "See if Saddam did this. See if he's linked in any way". Clarke (2004), p. 32. Assistant Secretary of Defense for Global Strategic Affairs, Richard Perle stressed to CIA Director, George Tenet that "Iraq has to pay a price for what happened yesterday. They bear responsibility". Tenet (2007), p. xix.
20 Of the 19 terrorists, none were Afghans (15 of which were actually Saudis) nor residents there. Rumsfeld famously lamented that there were "no decent targets" in Afghanistan. Clarke (2004), pp. 30–1.
21 UN Security Council *Resolution 1368 (2001)* authorised "all necessary steps" to respond to the previous day's attacks, while NATO invoked article 5 for the first time in its history, therein obliging members to come to the defence of the US. UN Security Council (2001).
22 Clarke (2004), p. 130.
23 Cohen (2001) and Podhoretz (2004).
24 Of the 13 speeches Bush gave between 12th September 2001 and May 2003, 12 referenced terror and Iraq in the same paragraph, and ten placed them within the same sentence. Gershkoff & Kushner (2005), p. 527.
25 Boot (2001).
26 The New York Times (2003a).
27 Boot (2002), p. 344.
28 Ferguson (2003), p. 170.
29 Ignatieff (2003), p. 61.
30 Kaplan (1994).
31 Kaplan (2003).
32 Bush (2002c).
33 National Security Strategy (2002).
34 In his "State of the Union Address" on 29th January 2002, Bush identified Iraq, Iran, and North Korea as constituting the "Axis of Evil" in helping to spread terrorism and seek weapons of mass destruction. Bush (2002a).
35 National Security Strategy (2002).
36 For the *Bush Doctrine*, see for example Jervis (2003), pp. 365–88.
37 According to Noam Chomsky the target of "preventive war" had to have the following characteristics, all of which Iraq bore: (1) be virtually defenceless; (2) be important enough to be worth the trouble; and (3) there must be a way to portray it as the ultimate evil and immanent threat to the US survival. Chomsky (2004), p. 17.
38 United Nations (2003).
39 Brzezinski (2007).
40 Mearsheimer & Walt (2003).

41 Quoted in Council on Foreign Relations (2002). Other realist critics included Andrew Bacevich, Kenneth Waltz, and Stanley Hoffman. See for example: Hoffman (2006), pp. 1–2.
42 Rice (2000).
43 See Nye (2004).
44 Ikenberry (2004), p. 615.
45 Ikenberry (2002), p. 60.
46 Mann (2003), p. 13.
47 Though China and Russia were sympathetic over 9/11 and originally enthusiastic supporters of the WOT – legitimating as it did state repression of domestic groups or separatists, e.g. the Uyghurs and Chechnya – they quickly realised it involved the US's increasing expansion into the Middle East, Central Asia, and Eastern Europe. Russia particularly concerned about NATO's expansion eastward (Rumania, Bulgaria, Slovenia, and Slovakia incorporated in 2002).
48 In March 2003, the list was made up of 49 states although only four – the UK, Australia, Poland, and Denmark – actually contributed troops to the invasion force.
49 Quoted in Chomsky (2004), p. 40.
50 The day before the changes were announced, Cheney explained in a television interview the need to let American security services pass over to the "dark side" and "use any means at our disposal, basically, to achieve our objective". Cheney (2001)
51 When news of these activities began to filter out the Bush administration announced a reform of the intelligence services, replacing CIA Director, George Tenet with Porter Goss, in July 2004, while 'hawks' John Negroponte and former CIA director, Robert Gates, were brought in as Director of National Intelligences as ("intelligence czar") and Defense Secretary, in May 2005 and December 2006, respectively.
52 Hartung & Ciarrocca (2003).
53 Tilly (1985), pp. 170–1.
54 The US's military capacity, for example, was 26 times greater than the combined collective force of the so-called *rogue states*. Klare (1995).
55 Quoted in Peschek (2006), p. 47.
56 Quoted in The Washington Post (2004).
57 In fact, one could argue the Gulf War itself was an example of *racketeering*: the US was getting the rest of the world to pay to remove a threat – Saddam Hussein's regime – that it had helped to create.
58 According to the Council on Foreign Relations, the sum amounted to $33 billion in grants and loans, well short of the then estimated $55 billion required. Of the $33 billion, $18 billion came from the US, $3–5 billion from the World Bank and $2.5–4.25 billion from the IMF. The European Union pledged a measly $812 million, China $24.2 million and France, Russia, and Germany nothing. Council on Foreign Relations (2003).
59 Friedman (1999). See also Friedman (2000), pp. 443–4.
60 Cited in Mabee (2004), p. 1365.
61 Militarism, according to Luxembourg, had "a specific function in the history of capital" and "accompanies every historical phase of accumulation". Luxemburg (2003), Chapter 32, "Militarism, Fields of Action for Capital".
62 Kaplan (2003).
63 Quoted in The Washington Post (2001) and The New York Times (2001).
64 Woodward (2001).
65 Cheney ordered the intelligence services to treat a 1% possibility of a terrorist group threatening the security of the US as if it were a certainty. See Suskind (2006).
66 Rumsfeld (2002b).

67 Rumsfeld (2002a).
68 Bush (2005).
69 Cited in Pietese (2004), p. 131.
70 Quoted in Callinicos (2004), p. 99.
71 Cited in Hughes (2015), p. 541.
72 Wilson (1990), p. 469.
73 Hughes (2015), p. 541.
74 Barry (2011), p. 304.
75 Speaking in the mid-1930s, self-defined "gangster for capitalism", US Marine Corps Major General Smedley Butler voiced remorse after 30 years of leading military coups throughout Central America and the Caribbean for the benefit of American business interests (e.g. Brown Brothers Banking House, National City Bank, Standard Oil, sugar and fruits companies). See Butler (1933, 1935).
76 Luce (1941) pp. 61–5. See Hartz (1955).
77 Bush (2004).
78 According to the NSS-2002, this *universal liberalism* was based upon on "non-negotiable demands of human dignity, the rule of law, limits on the power of the state, respect for women and private property and free speech and equal justice and religious tolerance". National Security Strategy (2002).
79 Kagan & Kristol (2000), p. 22.
80 See for example Elshtain (2003), p. 168.
81 Bush (2002b).
82 American foreign mobilisation of troops has often been followed by the establishment of permanent military bases, be it the Spanish-American War (Puerto Rico, Guam, Cuba), Panama War of Independence (Panama), the Second World War (Japan and Germany), the Cold War (Western Europe), the Korean War (South Korea), the Second Cold War (Egypt, Omar, Saudi Arabia), the Gulf War (Kuwait, Qatar), the Balkan Wars (Central and Eastern Europe, the largest base being at Kosovo), Post-9/11 (Iraq, Afghanistan).
83 Hartz (1955).
84 Locke (1980), pp. 83–8.
85 The American Presidency Project (2018).
86 Quoted in Prestowitz (2003), p. 23.
87 Those corporations that did particularly well, often via no-bid contracts, included the omnipresent Bechtel, Brown & Root (Halliburton), Lockheed Martin, Kellogg, Blackwater, Carlyle, Northrop Grumman, AT&T and General Electric.
88 See for example Robinson (2005) and van der Pijl (2006).
89 The orders required, amongst other things: a flat tax rate of 15% and dramatic reduction of corporate tax (Order 37); privatisation of state companies, including full ownership and lease rights (up to 40 years) by foreign firms and their rights to repatriation profits (Order 39); the opening of Iraq's banks to foreign control (Order 40); the elimination of nearly all trade barriers, and stricter laws on intellectual property rights. See The Coalition Provisional Authority (2018).
90 Quoted in Stone & Kuznick (2013), p. 530.
91 According to the data reported to the *Federal Election Committee*, cited in OpenSecrets.org (2018), the oil and gas industries together contributed a total of around $182 m to the Republican Party (1990–2010) with $59 million going to the Democrats.
92 Arnove (ed.) (2003), pp. 95–6.
93 Simmons (2005).
94 At the time, six major vertically integrated oil companies dominated the oil market, three of which are from the US (Exxon-Mobil, Chevron-Texaco, and

ConocoPhillips); two from the UK/UK-Netherlands (BP and Royal Dutch Shell); and one from France (TotalFinaElf). Nevertheless, since the 1960s, the percentage of known reserves fully open to international companies has dropped dramatically from 85% to 16%, the rest being under state control. Furthermore, in 1979, the US and British companies accounted for 27.8% of world gas and oil production, but by 2004 this was just 14%. See Businessweek (2006).

95 Quoted in The New York Times (2007).

96 Originally quoted in *The Guardian*, "Wolfowitz: Iraq was about oil", George Wright, 4th June 2003. The newspaper subsequently removed it from its web-page issuing an apology in its "Correction and clarifications" section, claiming that it had misconstrued and misrepresented Wolfowitz's declaration, who had actually remarked that the huge wealth of Iraq meant applying economic sanctions would be less effective (than North Korea). See The Guardian (2003).

97 The White House originally inadvertently terming the campaign for regime change in Baghdad as *Operation Iraqi Liberation* (which is spelt out as OIL) before changing it to *Operation Iraqi Freedom*.

98 Gardner (2008), p. 223.

99 With an estimated outstanding debt of $100 billion, with a further $100 billion to come in reparations, it was clear that without a constant flow of revenue from drilling concessions, the state would be bankrupt. The New York Times (2003b).

100 BBC Newsnight (2005). According to Carroll: "Many neo-conservatives are people who have certain ideological beliefs about markets, about democracy, about this, that and the other. International oil companies, without exception, are very pragmatic commercial organisation. They don't have a theology".

101 Quoted in Hopkins (2007), p. 103.

102 Harvey (2003), p. 85.

103 Klare (2004), pp. 17–21.

104 Ignatieff (2003), p. 63.

105 Golub (2004), pp. 763–4.

106 Quoted in Bacevich (2008), p. 127.

107 Polanyi (1954).

108 Arendt (1966), p. 142.

109 Such as individualism, the traditional family, religious orthodoxy, ethnocentrism, hyper-nationalism, and militarism, which extended into patriarchy, macho bravado, and vigilantism.

110 In typical Old Testament rhetoric, Bush would later describe the period between the Cold War and the start of the WOT as "years of repose, years of sabbatical – and then there came a day of fire". Bush (2005).

111 So ingrained were these values in the South states that Harold Meyerson quipped, "[T]he American President – though not of the United States – who George Bush most nearly represents is the Confederacy's Jefferson Davis." Meyerson (2003), pp. 25–8.

112 For statistics on US inequality and poverty under Bush II, see Stone & Kuznick (2013), pp. 545–6.

113 Hobbes (1985), p. 254.

114 Hofstadter (1964).

115 Rumsfeld, for example, was fond of the 'besieged house' metaphor: drawing a parallel with the US and a house in a tough neighbourhood which is susceptible to attack from burglars. See for example Rumsfeld (2002b).

116 Writing in the spring 2007, Brzezinski denounced the "culture of fear" created by the WOT, noting that the number of sites identified as potential terrorist

targets by the Congress increased from the original 160 to 28,360 by the end of 2004, 77,679 in 2005, and 300,000 by March 2007. Brzezinski (2007).

117 Polls taken just before/after the launching of Operation Iraqi Freedom reported that between 66% and 76% of the American population supported the invasion, with Bush's job approval rate up to 71%. Gallup (2003).

118 Gibson (1994).

119 Cunningham (2004), p. 557.

120 In 2008, Joseph Stiglitz and Linda Bilmes estimated the Iraq War stood around $3 trillion. Stiglitz & Bilmes (2008).

121 Rumsfeld (2001).

122 LOGCAP was set up in 1985 with the responsibility of providing 'logistical support' for the US military, contracting private companies to supply a whole range of services connected to 'operations' (e.g. ammunition, petroleum, medicine), 'field services' (e.g. alimentation, sanitation, laundry), or 'other services' (e.g. transportation, power, construction).

123 See Klein (2008), pp. 291–3.

124 Klein (2008), pp. 301–3. According to Klein, between 201 and 2006 the Department of Homeland Security handed out $130 billion to private contractors.

125 Obama (2009b).

126 In April 2009, CIA Director Leon Panetta announced that the CIA no longer employed "enhanced interrogation techniques" authorised by the Justice Department for 2002–09, that the US had ceased to operate "detention facilities or black sites". Central Intelligence Agency (2009).

127 Indeed certain parallels can be drawn between the first administration and that of Richard Nixon in the late 1960s, both: (1) came into power during a period of hegemonic crisis; bogged down in a dubious foreign war; suffering serious economic problems in the form of BOP deficits and structural crises (e.g. the demise of Bretton Woods/Keynesianism and 2008 credit crunch); (2) promoted arms reductions and no proliferation (SALT and START); and (3) prioritised developing better relations in Asia-Pacific, noticeable with China (though for different motives).

128 Nobel Prize Organization (2009).

129 UN Security Council (2010).

130 UN Security Council (2011).

131 National Security Strategy (2010).

132 US Department of Defense (2014).

133 By the time Obama entered office over a million Iraqis had died, three million refugees on the move and five million orphans created, according to government statistics. Quoted in Ali (2010), p. 103.

134 Obama (2007), pp. 4–9.

135 Quoted in The New Yorker (2014).

136 Turse (2018).

137 The Bureau of Investigative Journalism (2017).

138 The Guardian (2015).

139 Stern (2015), p. 63.

140 The Wall Street Journal (2017).

141 Kennedy (1987).

142 In 2011, this encompassed 1,271 government organizations and 1,931 private companies, intercepting around 1.7 billion e-mails, phone calls, and other communications each day. See Barry (2011), p. 302.

143 The Guardian (2013).

144 Franco & Garcia (2016).

145 Freedom of the Press Foundation (2017).

146 See Tansel (ed.) (2017).
147 Goldsmith (2009).
148 The Democrats received about the same amount of money as the Republicans from the FIRE sectors (finance, insurance, and real estate), and even more from the telecommunications, high tech, and entertainment sectors. The Republicans, for their part, raised more money from big oil, big pharma, and the agribusiness. See Brenner (2007), p. 57.
149 During his appearance, Acheson insisted that Washington's fundamental priority in the post-war world order had to be taking the necessary measures to prevent any country from challenging its "power, position, and prestige". Acheson (1963).
150 Obama (2009a).
151 Obama (2010).
152 Albright (1998).
153 Barry (2011), p. 299.
154 Barry (2011), p. 304.
155 National Security Strategy (2015).
156 Greenspan (2008).
157 Gowan (1999), p. 124.
158 Harvey (2007), p. 162.
159 An estimated $2 trillion sloshed around in 401K pension plans looking for profitable investment – Augar (2006) p. 12.
160 *The Economist* estimates that between 2000 and 2008 the US received $5.7 trillion from foreign investors. The Economist (2009).
161 Philip Augar noted that by 2005 Wall Street was essentially dominated by just five investment banks holding over $4 trillion of assets and able to call on trillions more from commercial banks, the money-market funds, pension funds, etc. Augar (2006), pp. 29–48.
162 Duménil & Levy (2011), p. 39.
163 Stiglitz (2008).
164 High profile examples would include Treasury Secretaries Robert Rubin (Goldman Sachs), Hank Paulson (Goldman Sachs), and Tim Geithner (Citigroup) and Fed chiefs Paul Volcker (Chase Manhattan), Alan Greenspan (J.P. Morgan).
165 According to *The Economist*, the financial-services industry share of total corporate profits stood rose from 10% in the early 1980s to its 40% peak in 2007 while its share of the stock market grew from 6% to 23% and accounting for 14% of American GDP. The Economist (2009).
166 Gowan (2009), p. 7.
167 See Harvey (2007), pp. 17–18.
168 Piketty (2014), pp. 292–7.
169 The Economist (2009). Between 1983 and 2006 US GDP had been rising at a rate of 5.9% p.a. yet private debt was running at 8.0% p.a. during the same period.
170 Duménil & Levy (2011), p. 104.
171 Gowan (2009), p. 5.
172 Bloomberg (2017).
173 Harvey (2017).
174 At the same time, one should not overstate the scale of Trump's electoral victory. First, the overall voting turnout was down from the previous two presidential elections. Second, despite the electoral college, Trump actually lost the popular vote to Hillary Clinton by 2.8 million votes – the biggest margin by any president in US history. Third, Trump's voting figures remained very similar to that of defeated Republican presidential candidate,

Mitt Romney in 2012. Fourth, victory depended on winning tiny majorities in key marginal wards, totalling less than under 78,000. See Anderson (2017), pp. 41–3.
175 Davis (2017), pp. 5–8.
176 National Security Strategy (2017).
177 National Security Strategy (2017).

Bibliography

Acheson, D. (1963), "Remarks by Hon. Dean Acheson on 'The Cuban Quarantine: Implications for the Future', Before the American Society of International Law Panel (25th April 1963)", *Proceedings of the American Society of International Law*, 57, 13–5.

Albright, M.K. (1998), "Interview on NBC-TV 'The Today Show'", *U.S. Department of State Archive*, 19th February 1998 (available online at 1997-2001.state. gov/www/statements/1998/980219a.html).

Ali, T. (2010), "President of Cant", *New Left Review*, 61, 99–116.

Anderson, P. (2017), "Passing the Baton", *New Left Review*, 103, 41–64.

Arendt, H. (1966), *The Origins of Totalitarianism*, New York: Harcourt, Brace and World.

Arnove, A. (ed.) (2003), *Iraq under Siege: The Deadly Impact of Sanctions and War*, London: Pluto Press.

Arrighi, G. (2008), *Adam Smith in Beijing: Lineages of the Twenty-First Century*, London: Verso.

Augar, P. (2006), *The Greed Merchants: How the Investment Banks Played the Free Market Game*, London: Penguin.

Bacevich, A.J. (2008), *The Limits of Power: The End of American Exceptionalism*, New York: Metropolitan Books.

Barry, J.C. (2011), "Empire as a Gated Community: Politics of an American Strategic Metaphor", *Global Society*, 25, no. 3, 287–309.

BBC Newsnight. (2005), "Secret US Plans for Iraq Oil", *Greg Palast*, 17th March 2005 (available online at news.bbc.co.uk/2/hi/4354269.stm).

Bloomberg. (2017), "Trump Signs Biggest Rollback of Bank Rules since Dodd-Frank Act", *Elizabeth Dexheimer*, 24th May (available online www.bloomberg. com/).

Boot, M. (2001), "The Case for American Empire", *Weekly Standard*, 15th October 2001 (available online at www.weeklystandard.com/Content/Public/ Articles/000/000/000/318qpvmc.asp).

Boot, M. (2002), *The Savage Wars of Peace*, New York: Basic Books.

Brenner, R. (2007), "Structure versus Conjuncture: The 2006 Elections and the Rightward Shift", *New Left Review*, 43, 33–59.

Brzezinski, Z. (2007), "Terrorized by War on Terror", *The Washington Post*, 25th March (available online at www.washingtonpost.com).

Bush, G.W. (2002a), "State of the Union Address", 29th January (available online at www.presidency.ucsb.edu).

Bush, G.W. (2002b), "President Bush Delivers Graduation Speech at West Point", United States Military Academy, West Point, New York, *The White House: President George W. Bush*, 1st June 2002 (available online at georgewbush-whitehouse.archives.gov).

Bush, G.W. (2002c), "Securing Freedom's Triumph", *New York Times*, 11th September (available online at www.nytimes.com).

Bush, G.W. (2004), "President Addresses the Nation in Prime Time Press Conference", 13th April (available online at www.whitehouse.gov/).

Bush, G.W. (2005), "Inaugural Address", President G.W. Bush, *The American Presidency Project*, 20th January (available online at www.presidency.ucsb.edu).

Businessweek. (2006), "Why We Should Worry About Big Oil", 15th March 2006.

Butler, S.D. (1933), *On Interventionism: War Is a Racket* speech on Veterans and War, delivered in 1933 (available online at www.fas.org/man/smedley.htm).

Butler, S.D. (1935), "American Armed Forces in Times of Peace", *Common Sense*, 4, no. 11 (available online at msuweb.montclair.edu/~furrg/Vietnam/butler.pdf).

Callinicos, A. (2004), *The New Mandarins of American Power: The Bush Administration's Plan for the World*, Cambridge: Polity Press.

Center for Security Policy. (2002), "Precision-Guided Ideas, 2002 Annual Report" (available online at www.centerforsecuritypolicy.org/).

Central Intelligence Agency. (2009), "Statement to employees by Director of the Central Intelligence Agency Leo E. Panetta on the CIA's Interrogation Policy and Contracts", 9th April 2009 (available online at www.cia.gov/news-information).

Cheney, D. (2001), "Vice President Dick Cheney Discusses the Attack on America and Response to Terrorism", NBC News Transcript, *Meet the Press*, 16th September 2001.

Chomsky, N. (2004), *Hegemony or Survival*, London: Penguin.

Clarke, R.A. (2004), *Against All Enemies: Inside America's War on Terror*, London: The Free Press.

Clarke, W.C. (2004), *Winning Modern Wars: Iraq, Terrorism and the American Empire*, New York: Public Affairs.

Cohen, E. (2001), "World War IV", *The Wall Street Journal*, 29th November.

Council on Foreign Relations. (2002), "Policy Implication of the Bush Doctrine on Preemption", Ivo Dalder, 16th November 2002 (available online at www.cfr.org/).

Council on Foreign Relations. (2003), "Iraq: Madrid Conference", Esther Pan, October 23rd 2003 (available online at www.cfr.org/).

Cunningham, K. (2004), "Permanent War? The Domestic Hegemony of the New American Militarism", *New Political Science*, 26, no. 4, 551–67.

Davis, M. (2017), "Elections 2016", *New Left Review*, 103, 5–8.

Duménil, G. & Levy, D. (2011), *The Crisis of Neoliberalism*, Cambridge: Harvard University Press.

Elshtain, J.B. (2003), *Just War Against Terror: The Burden of American Power*, New York: Basic Books.

Ferguson, N. (2003), *Empire*, London: Allen Lane.

Franco, M. & Garcia, C. (2016), "The Deportation Machine Obama Built for President Trump", *The Nation*, 27th June 2016 (available online at www.thenation.com).

Freedom of the Press Foundation. (2017), "Obama used the Espionage Act to Put a Record Number of Reporters' Sources in Jail, and Trump Could be Even Worse", *Peter Sterne*, 21st June 2017 (available online at freedom.press/).

Friedman, L.T. (1999), "A Manifest for a Fast World", *The New York Times Magazine*, 28th March 1999 (available online at www.nytimes.com/books/99/04/25/reviews/friedman-mag.html).

Friedman, L.T. (2000), *The Lexus and the Olive Tree*, New York: Farrar, Straus & Giroux (Revised Edition).

Gallup. (2003), "Seventy-Two Percent of Americans Support War against Iraq", *Frank Newport*, 24th March 2003 (available at news.gallup.com/poll/8038/seventytwo-percent-americans-support-war-against-iraq.aspx).

Gardner, L.C. (2008), *The Long Road to Baghdad: A History of U.S. Foreign Policy from the 1970s to the Present*, New York: New Press.

Gershkoff, A. & Kushner, S. (2005), "Shaping Public Opinion: The 9/11-Iraq Connection in the Bush Administration's Rhetoric", *Perspectives on Politics*, 3, 525–37.

Gibson, J. (1994), *Warrior Dreams*, New York: Hill and Wang.

Goldsmith, J. (2009), "The Cheney Fallacy", *New Republic*, 18th May (available online at newrepublic.com/).

Golub, P.S. (2004), "Imperial Politics, Imperial Will and the Crisis of US Hegemony", *Review of International Political Economy*, 11, no. 4, 763–86.

Gowan, P. (1999), *The Global Gamble: Washington's Faustian Bid for World Dominance*, London: Verso.

Gowan, P. (2009), "Crisis in the Heartland: Consequences of the New Wall Street System", *New Left Review*, 55, 5–29.

Green, D. (2002), "Bush-Connected Company Set Up Offshore Subsidiary", *Baltimore Sun*, 1st August 2002.

Greenspan, A. (2008), "We Will Never Have a Perfect Model of Risk", *Financial Times*, 17th March.

Hartung, W. & Ciarrocca, M. (2003), "The Military Industrial Think-Tank Complex: Corporate Think Tanks and The Doctrine of Aggressive Militarism", *Multinational Monitor*, 24, no. 1–2 (available online at multinationalmonitor.org).

Hartz, L. (1955), *The Liberal Tradition in America: An Interpretation of American Political Thought Since the Revolution*, New York: Harcourt, Brace & World.

Harvey, D. (2003), *The New Imperialism,* Oxford: Oxford University Press.

Harvey, D. (2007), *A Brief History of Neoliberalism*, Oxford: Oxford University Press.

Harvey, D. (2017), *Marx, Capital, and the Madness of Economic Reason*, Oxford: Oxford University Press.

Hobbes, T. (1985), *Leviathan*, London: Penguin Classics.

Hoffman, S. (2006), "The Foreign Policy the U.S. Needs", *The New York Review of Books*, 53, no. 13, 60–4.

Hofstadter, R. (1964), "The Paranoid Style in American Politics", *Harper's Magazine*, November (available online at harpers.org/archive/1964/11/the-paranoid-style-in-american-politics/).

Hopkins, A.G. (2007), "Capitalism, Nationalism and the New American Empire", *Journal of Imperial and Commonwealth History*, 35, no. 1, 95–117.

Hughes, D. (2015), "Unmaking and Exception: A Critical Genealogy of US Exceptionalism", *Review of International Studies*, 41, no. 3, 527–51.

Ignatieff, M. (2003), "The Challenges of American Imperial Power", *Naval War College Review*, 56, no. 2, 6.

Ikenberry, G.J. (2002), "American Imperial Ambitions", *Foreign Affairs*, 81, no. 5, 44–60.

Ikenberry, G.J. (2004), "Liberalism and Empire: Logics of Order in the American Unipolar Age", *Review of International Studies*, 30, no. 4, 609–30.

Jervis, R. (2003), "Understanding the Bush Doctrine", *Political Science Quarterly* 18.

Johnson, C. (2004), *The Sorrows of Empire*, New York: Metropolitan Book.

Kagan, R. & Kristol, W. (2000), *Present Dangers: Crisis and Opportunity in American Foreign and Defense Policy*, San Francisco, CA: Encounter Books.

Kaplan, R.D. (1994), "The Coming Anarchy", *The Atlantic*, February (available online at www.theatlantic.com/magazine).

Kaplan, R.D. (2003), "Supremacy by Stealth", *The Atlantic*, July 2003 (available online at www.theatlantic.com/magazine/archive/2003/07/supremacy-by-stealth/302760/).

Kennedy, P. (1987), *The Rise and Fall of the Great Powers: Economic Change and Military Conflict from 1500 to 2000*, New York: Random House.

Klare, M.T. (1995), *Rogue States and Nuclear Outlaws,* New York: Hill and Wang.

Klare, M.T. (2004), "The Carter Doctrine Goes Global", *The Progressive*, 68, 17–21.

Klein, N. (2008), *The Shock Doctrine: The Rise of Disaster Capitalism*, London: Penguin.

Lang, W.P. (2004), "Drinking the Kool-Aid", *Middle East Policy*, 11, no. 2, 39–60.

Locke, J. (1980), *Second Treatise of Civil Government*, Indianapolis, IN: Hackett Publishing Company.

Luce, H.R. (1941), "The American Century", *Life Magazine*, 17th February.

Luxemburg, R. (2003), *The Accumulation of Capital*, London: Routledge.

Mabee, B. (2004), "Discourse of Empire: The US Empire, Globalisation and International Relations", *Third World Quarterly*, 25, no. 8, 1359–78.

Mann, M. (2003), *Incoherent Empire*, New York: Verso.

Mearsheimer, J.J. & Walt, S.M. (2003), "An Unnecessary War", *Foreign Policy* (available online at mearsheimer.uchicago.edu/pdfs/A0032.pdf).

Meyerson, H. (2003), "The Most Dangerous President Ever", *The American Prospect*, 14, no. 5, 25.

Moseley, F. (2003), "Marxian Crisis Theory and the Postwar US Economy", in Saad-Filho, A. (ed.), *Anti-Capitalism: A Marxist Introduction*, London: Pluto Press.

National Security Strategy. (2002), *The National Security Strategy of the United States of America*, September 2002 (available online at www.state.gov/documents/organization/63562.pdf).

National Security Strategy. (2010), *The National Security Strategy of the United States of America*, Washington, DC, May 2010 (available online at nssarchive.us/NSSR/2010.pdf).

National Security Strategy. (2015), *The National Security Strategy of the United States of America*, February 2015 (available online at nssarchive.us/wp-content/uploads/2015/02/2015.pdf).

National Security Strategy. (2017), *National Security Strategy of the United States of America*, December 2017 (available online at nssarchive.us/wp-content/uploads/2017/12/2017.pdf).

Nobel Prize Organization. (2009), "Nobel Peace Prize 2009 – Press Release" (available online at www.nobelprize.org).

Nye, J.S. (2004), *Soft Power: The Means to Success in World Politics*, New York: Public Affairs Books.

Obama, B. (2007), "Renewing American leadership", *Foreign Affairs*, 86, no. 4, 2–16.

Obama, B. (2009a), "Remarks of President Barack Obama – As Prepared for Delivery Address to Joint Session of Congress Tuesday, 24th February 2009" (available online at www.whitehouse.gov/).

Obama, B. (2009b), "Remarks by the President to the United Nations General Assembly", New York, 23rd September 2009 (available online www.white house.gov/).

Obama, B. (2010), "Remarks by the President in State of Union Address", 27th January 2010 (available online at www.whitehouse.gov/).

OpenSecrets.org. (2018), "Oil & Gas" (available online at www.opensecrets.org).

Peschek, J.G. (2006), *The Politics of Empire: War, Terror and Hegemony*, Oxford: Routledge.

Pietese, J.D. (2004), *Globalization or Empire?* London: Routledge.

Piketty, T. (2014), *Capital in the Twenty-First Century*, Goldhammer, A. (trans.), Cambridge: Harvard University Press,

Podhoretz, N. (2004), "World War IV: How It Started, What It Means, and Why We Have to Win," *Commentary*, 118, no. 2, 17–54.

Polanyi, K. (1954), *The Great Transformation*, Boston: Beacon Press.

Prestowitz, C. (2003), *Rogue Nation: American Unilateralism and the Failure of Good Intentions*, New York: Basic Books.

Project for the New American Century. (1997), "Statement of Principles", 3rd June 1997 (web.archive.org/web/20070810113753/www.newamericancentury. org/statementofprinciples.htm).

Project for the New American Century. (1998), "Letter to President Clinton on Iraq", January 26 1998 (available online at www.newamericancentury.org/ iraqclintonletter.htm).

Project for the New American Century. (2000), "Rebuilding America's Defenses: Strategy, Forces, and Resources for a New Century", September 2000 (available online at www.informationclearinghouse.info/pdf/RebuildingAmericas Defenses.pdf).

Rice, C. (2000), "Promoting the National Interest", *Foreign Affairs*, 79, no. 1, 45–62.

Robinson, W.I. (2005), "Gramsci and Globalization: From Nation-State to Transnational Hegemony", *Critical Review of International Social and Political Philosophy*, 8, no. 4, 1–16.

Rumsfeld, D.H. (2001), "Rumsfeld Attacks Pentagon Bureaucracy, Vows Changes", *Department of Defense News* (available online at archive.defense. gov/news/newsarticle.aspx?id=44916).

Rumsfeld, D.H. (2002a), *Department of Defense New Briefing*: "Secretary Rumsfeld and Gen. Myers", 12th February (available online at archive.defense.gov/ Transcripts/Transcript.aspx?TranscriptID=2636).

Rumsfeld, D.H. (2002b), "Transforming the Military", *Foreign Affairs*, May/June (available online at www.foreignaffairs.com/).

Simmons, M.R. (2005), *Twilight in the Desert: the Coming Oil Shock and the World Economy*, Hoboken, NJ: Wiley.

Stern, J. (2015), "Obama and Terrorism: Like It or Not the War Goes On", *Foreign Affairs*, 94, no. 5, 62–70.

Stiglitz, J.E. (2004), *The Roaring Nineties: Why We're Paying the Price for the Greediest Decade in History*, London: Penguin Books.

Stiglitz, J.E. (2008), "The Fruits of Hypocrisy", *The Guardian*, 16th September 2008.

Stiglitz, J.E. & Bilmes, L.J. (2008), *The Three Trillion Dollar War: The True Cost of the Iraq Conflict*, New York: W.W. Norton & Co.

Stone, O. & Kuznick, P. (2013), *The Untold Story of the United States*, London: Elbury Press.

Suskind, R. (2004), *The Price of Loyalty: George Bush, the White House, and the Education of Paul O'Neill*, New York: Simon & Schuster.

Suskind, R. (2006), *The One Percent Doctrine: Deep Inside America's Pursuit of Its Enemies Since 9/11*, London: Simon & Schuster UK Ltd.

Tansel, C.B. (ed.) (2017), *States of Discipline: Authoritarian Neoliberalism and the Contested Reproduction of Capitalist Order*, London: Rowman & Littlefield International.

Tenet, G. (2007), *At the Center of the Storm: My Years at the CIA*, New York: HarperCollins.

The American Presidency Project. (2018), "Executive Orders: Washington-Trump" (available online at www.presidency.ucsb.edu/data/orders.php).

The Bureau of Investigative Journalism. (2017), "Obama's Covert Drone War in Numbers: Ten Times More Strikes than Bush", Jessica Purkiss and Jack Searle, 17th July 2017 (available online at www.thebureauinvestigates.com).

The Coalition Provisional Authority. (2018), "CPA Official Documents" (available online at www.iraqcoalition.org/regulations/#Regulations).

The Economist. (2009), "Fixing Finance", 22nd January 2009.

The Guardian. (2003), "Corrections and Clarifications", 6th June 2003 (available online at www.guardian.com/uk).

The Guardian. (2013), "The NSA File Decoded" (available online at www.theguardian.com/us-news/the-nsa-files).

The Guardian. (2015), "Revealed: Private Forms at Heart of US Drone Warfare", Abigail Fielding-Smith, Crofton Black, Alice Ross and James Ball, Thursday 30th June 2015 (available online at www.theguardian.com/us-news).

The New York Times. (1992), "US Strategy Plan Calls for Ensuring No Rivals Develop", Patrick E. Tyler, 8th March 1992 (available online at www.nytimes.com/).

The New York Times. (2001), "A Day of Mourning", Robert D. McFadden, 15th September 2001.

The New York Times. (2003a) "American Empire, Not 'If' But 'What Kind'", in Daalder, I.H., and Lindsay, J.M., 10th May 2003 (available online at www.nytimes.com/).

The New York Times. (2003b), "Cutting James Baker's Ties", 12th December 2003 (available online at www.nytimes.com/).

The New York Times. (2007), "Whose Oil Is It, Anyway?" Antonia Juhasz, 13th March 2007.

The New Yorker. (2014), "In Search of a Strategy", Steve Coll, 8th September 2014.

The Wall Street Journal. (2017), "U.S. Spent $5.6 Trillion on Wars in Middle East and Asia: Study", Gordon Lubold, 8th November 2017.

The Washington Post. (2001), "Bush: US Must 'Rid the World of Evil'", Charles Babington, 14th September 2001.

The Washington Post. (2004), "The True Rationale? It's a Decade Old", James Mann, 7th March 2004.

Tilly, C. (1985), "War Making and State Making as Organized Crime," in Evans, P.B., Rueschemeyer, D. and Skocpol, T. (eds.), *Bringing the State Back In*, Cambridge: Cambridge University Press.

Turse, N. (2018), "Commandos Sans Frontières: The Global Growth of U.S. Special Operations", 17th July 2018, *TomDispatch.com* (available online at www.tomdispatch.com).

United Nations. (2003), "Briefing Security Council, US Secretary of State Powell Presents Evidence of Iraq's Failure to Disarm", 5th February (available online at www.un.org/press/en/2003/sc7658.doc.htm).

UN Security Council. (2001), *Resolution 1368* (available online at www.un.org/Docs/scres/2001/sc2001.htm).

UN Security Council. (2010), *Resolution 1929*, 9th June 2010 (available online at www.un.org/en/sc/documents/resolutions/).

UN Security Council. (2011), *Resolution 1973*, 17th March 2011 (available online at www.un.org/en/sc/documents/resolutions/).

US Department of Defense. (2014), "Quadrennial Defense Review 2014" (available at archive.defense.gov/pubs/2014_Quadrennial_Defense_Review.pdf).

van der Pijl, K. (2006), *From the Cold War to Iraq*, London: Pluto Press.

van der Pijl, K. (2008), "Atlantic Ideologies", *New Left Review*, 50, 147.

Wilson, W. (1990), *Papers of Woodrow Wilson*, "Address in the Princess Theatre in Cheyenne", 24th September 1919, Vol. 63, Princeton.

Woodward, B. (2001), "CIA Told to Do 'Whatever Necessary' To Kill Bin Laden", *The Washington Post*, 21st October.

Woodward, B. (2004), *The Plan of Attack*, London: Simon & Schuster UK Ltd.

5   The China 'Challenge'

The Geopolitics of Chinese Economic Statecraft

China's socio-economic transformation has been nothing short of spectacular. According to the World Bank, it constitutes "the fastest sustained expansion by a major economy in history",[1] thanks to a real gross domestic product (GDP) average growth rate of 9.5% for almost 40 years (1979–2017), albeit one which is slowing down as of late (down from 7.8% in 2012 to an expected 6.6% in 2018).[2] The People's Republic of China's (PRC) GDP, measured in purchasing power parity, went from being amongst the poorest countries to the world's richest, overtaking the US in 2014. In so doing it lifted 800 million people out of poverty – improving life-expectancy and slashing maternal and child mortality rates into the bargain – qualifying it as the greatest poverty-reduction programme again in history.[3]

The effects on the global economy have been enormous and multifaceted, simultaneously driving down the international price of manufacturing goods and driving up the price of raw materials (to the benefit of many developing countries including its fellow BRICS [Brazil, Russia, India, China and South Africa] members). By the end of 2009, China assumed Germany's crown as a top global exporter,[4] replacing the US as the 'workshop of the world' in 2010 – producing, or at least being the final assembly point for, around half of the worlds' goods (including around 80% of its air-conditioners, 70% of its mobile phones, 60% of its shoes, 45% of its clothing).[5]

In order to feed this production dragon, the PRC has had to access raw materials on a massive scale. In the decade prior to the Global Financial Crisis (GFC), China's consumption of crude oil doubled, copper and iron ore tripled, and aluminium quadrupled. By 2010, it was the world's largest buyer of copper, iron ore, nickel, cement, and cotton, and the world's largest producer/consumer of steel, aluminium, lead, and zinc. According to the International Energy Agency (IEA), the OECD's energy watchdog, China overtook the US in 2009 to become the world's biggest energy user, consuming 2,252 million tonnes of oil equivalent energy from resources including coal, oil, nuclear power, natural gas, and hydropower,

DOI: 10.4324/9780429459061-6

about 4% more than the US (a 100% increase since 2000) though far less per capita (about a third of the West).[6]

Given the extreme resource-intensity of its growth model, the breakneck speed of urbanisation, and relatively poor endowment of raw materials, China has had little option but to enmesh itself deeper into global trade networks. Furthermore, concurring with Harvey's imperialist paradigm, the *territorial* and *capitalist logics of power* would increasingly drive Chinese businesses abroad to seek out new markets and investment opportunities – an ever-larger geographical *spatial fix* – in which to bury its domestic surplus and counter chronic overproduction/capacity at home. Replicating Washington's example in the 1950s, the Chinese state encouraged its companies, both public and private, to 'go global', setting up a $200 billion sovereign wealth fund, Chinese Investment Corporation in September 2007, to facilitate the process.[7] After the GFC, this process became even more accentuated. Far better to invest some of the huge trade surplus,[8] large national savings, not to mention estimated $3.1 trillion in foreign exchange reserves[9] in opening new markets, acquiring tangible assets, guaranteeing long-term commodity supplies, or acquiring foreign companies than to see it suffer devaluation or eaten up by inflation.[10]

Evidently, one sector the PRC has been particularly active in is *energy*. Around 61% of China's energy is derived from coal.[11] Despite being the world's largest producer – three times larger than the second country, the US – the PRC is also the world's largest importer (the bulk of which comes from Australia, Indonesia. Mongolia, North Korea, and Russia), consuming about 45% of all global coal[12] with the grave environmental and health problems that provokes, both local and global.[13]

But it is perhaps its reliance on oil and gas – overtaking the US as the world's biggest importer of crude in 2017[14] – which has most concerned Beijing, aware that any disruption of supply will leave the country highly vulnerable. With energy demands expected to grow, securing stable long-term energy supplies has become one of the greatest economic/political challenge facing the Communist Party of China (CPC) leadership. *State-owned enterprises* (SOEs) such as China National Petroleum Corporation (CNPC), Sinopec, China National Offshore Corp (CNOOC), and Sinochem, hence, have been encouraged to gain control over foreign sources of energy, especially following the 2007–08 oil price hike (reaching $150 a barrel). As the GFC hit, some of the announced $586 billion stimulus package was loaned out to companies via the Chinese Development Bank (CDB) and other government agencies, to encourage them to expand abroad, to guarantee access to oil, gas, and mining interests and invest in associated delivery systems (e.g. pipelines and refineries). This has had major geopolitical repercussions, not least for North-South relations, as seen with China's reforging of its relationship with Africa.

Washington had specifically targeted expanding American commercial presence on the continent (at the expense of the Europeans) under the Clinton administration,[15] as expressed in the "African Growth and Opportunity Act" of 2000. But while the US's international prestige was at its lowest ebb in January 2006, bogged down in the Iraq fiasco, the PRC's Ministry of Foreign Affairs published an *African Policy Paper* setting out the country's objectives on the continent, offering Africa the chance to break away from the traditional North-South dominance-subservience dynamic, and to "establish and develop a new type of strategic partnership" based upon "political equality and mutual trust" for "mutual benefit, reciprocity, and common prosperity", cooperating in a wide range of political, diplomatic, economic, social, and cultural areas.[16] The details of this long-term Sino-Africa partnership began to take shape that November during the Forum on China-Africa Cooperation summit, with then president, Hu Jintao promising the 48 African country delegations to provide $5 billion worth of preferential loans/buyers credit, set up a China-Africa Development Fund to encourage investment in Africa, double assistance aid by 2009, cancel debt, and open up the Chinese market to tariff-free African exports.[17] Since then Sino-African bilateral trade has grown at an astounding rate: increasing tenfold in the first decade of the 21st century,[18] reaching $170 billion in 2017 (up 14.1% year-on-year) which is triple that of the continent's next largest trading partner, the vast majority signing bilateral trade deals with Beijing.[19]

Recording the fastest rate of foreign direct investment (FDI) growth (though fourth in accumulated stock after the US, the UK, and France),[20] Chinese investment in Africa has been traditionally centred on three sectors: fossil fuels, mineral extraction, and construction/infrastructure. Nonetheless, and supported by state banks such as the CDB and the China Export-Import Bank (EximBank), investment has also poured into other sectors such as manufacturing, telecommunications, tourism, and agriculture (e.g. sale of land for food production and exportation to the PRC). And it is not just SOEs that have set up business in China; hundreds of thousands of Chinese entrepreneurs have also arrived, noticeably in the service sector, manufacturing, retail, and food. Indeed, a recent study held 90% of the estimated 10,000 Chinese companies in Africa are privately owned.[21] With a population of around a billion people, Africa is considered one of the world's largest untapped markets, a good base for Chinese companies to learning the ropes where competition is weak (e.g. mobile phone market).

Calculating the exact level of Chinese FDI is complicated by the use of the so-called 'Angola Mode' arrangements, named after the landmark intergovernmental 'infrastructure for resources' agreement Beijing signed with Luanda 2004. Here, in return for its SOE's gaining rights to access oil, gas, and minerals in a particular country, Chinese state banks pay their construction and engineering SOEs to carry out vital infrastructure projects which, for a variety of economic or political reasons, foreign private investors, and institutions – notable the International Monetary Fund (IMF) and the World Bank – have been reluctant to finance.[22] Thanks to these projects and the technology transfer it involves, China has arguably had a far greater effect on Africa's development than both the US and the European Union (EU).

Beijing repeated this template in Latin America, signed hundreds of commercial agreements with the region, with China-Latin American trade increasing from $12 billion in 2001 to $260 billion in 2017 (an 18% increase year-on-year).[23] With the US and the EU hit by the GFC, Latin American exporters (headed by Brazil, Chile, and Venezuela) were happy to find an alternative market for their raw materials, while others sought to nurture new markets for its manufacturing goods (notably in Brazil, Mexico, Chile, and Argentina). Mexico, for example, saw its trade with the PRC increase sevenfold in the decade following the "Strategic Partnership" signed in 2003, a relationship consolidated with the signing of a dozen energy, mining, trade, banking, and construction agreements by the respective Presidents in June 2013.[24] Brazil's trade with China, meanwhile, increased 13 times between 2001 and 2013, reaching $83.3 billion in 2014 and crowned with the announcement that Beijing planned to invest a further $53 billion in the former's crumbling infrastructure (e.g. roads, railways, airports, ports, and electric power lines) over the next ten years and ahead of the 2016 Rio Olympic Games.[25]

As with Africa, Chinese investment strategy in Latin America was dominated by Angola Mode-type resource for infrastructure deals (e.g. the multibillion-dollar Sopladora and Coca Codo Sinclair hydro-electric power plants in Ecuador) to gain access to energy sector, mining/mineral industries, and the agribusiness. Energy giants Sinopec, CNPC, CNOOC entered into numerous joint ventures with state-owned companies such as Petroecuador and Petróleos de Venezuela S.A. or bought buy assets in private companies such as Repsol, Bridas Corp. or Pan American Energy LLC, to develop oil and gas fields in Brazil, Ecuador, Venezuela, and Argentina, respectively. Beijing also extended credit to foreign state-owned companies credit loans for them to expand production (e.g. granting $10 billion to Brazil's Petroleo Braseliero SA for deep sea oil exploration) or lending directly to governments themselves (e.g. giving the Bolivian government $15 billion to develop the *El Mutun* mine).[26] At the First Ministerial meeting of the Forum for China and the Community of Latina American and Caribbean States (China-CELAC) held in Beijing in January 2015, President Xi Jinping made very clear his government's intentions announced to the 33 countries that China pledged to invest investment $250 billion in the region over the next ten years and hoped that in those years the bilateral relationship would generate $500 billion of trade.[27]

Predictably, Chinese increasing business (and hence political presence) in Africa, Latin America, and other developing countries have ruffled many feathers in Washington, Brussels, and Tokyo.[28] The Angola Mode has been continually criticised by the West for its 'opacity' (conceding mineral rights at the inter-governmental level and behind closed doors, instead of via 'open auctions') and non-competitive nature (resulting in Chinese construction and engineering SOEs able to carry out shoddy work). Li Ruogu, president of EximBank, responded: "Western countries should set an example by making public the resources they have grabbed in Africa in the past 400 years. Only after that can we come to the issue of China's transparency".[29] Such *renminbi diplomacy* in Latin America, of course, constituted a direct challenge to the long-established *Monroe Doctrine* and perennial dominance of US-based multinational corporations (MNCs) there. Worse still, Beijing heavy investments bolstered left-leaning/nationalist political regimes in the cone such as Brazil, Bolivia, Ecuador, Argentina, and Venezuela, who remained critical of the Washington Consensus.[30]

But perhaps most worrying of all for American hegemony, such arrangements allowed developing countries to by-pass established control mechanisms. After decades of disastrous neoliberal structural adjustment programmes (SAP)[31] many welcomed alternative routes to growth other than those sanctioned by the IMF and the World Bank.[32] African states, US Embassy cables (via *Wikileaks*) revealed, were "uncomfortable" with Western states' "interference" and suspicious of their underlying motives, preferring China's fast, efficient, "no strings attached" bilateral approach to development, which involves setting out tangible projects (e.g. infrastructure) rather than the traditional Western "tied aid" development cooperation model and vague references to "capacity building".[33] By the end of 2010, the PRC was lending more money to the developing world, and increasingly in renminbi,[34] than the World Bank, contributing to macroeconomic growth.[35]

Yet the 'Chinese challenge' went further than ad hoc bilateral lending arrangements. Following the template set out by Washington in the 1940s, and compatible with Coxian analysis and Gramsci's *second moment* of hegemony conceptualisation, Beijing increasingly sought to assert is economic and political hegemony over developing countries by embedding them in alternative China-led *multilateral organisations*, offering more stable long-term bank lending arrangements than their highly liquid financialized Anglo-Saxon counterparts. This was most clearly visible with the setting up of the Brazil, Russia, India, China, South Africa (BRICS) association and system of summits in 2001 and its initiatives to promote developing countries' interests. Of these, perhaps, the most significant are the launching of two $100 billion multilateral funds in July 2015, both underwritten by China, and clearly designed to complete with the World Bank and IMF, respectively. The *New Development Bank* (NDB) is geared towards financing infrastructure projects in developing countries; the *Contingent Reserve Arrangements* (CRA), on the other hand, provides liquidity for counties suffering short-term balance of payment (BOP) problems.

China crowned this process the following December with the launching of the $100 billion *Asian Infrastructure Investment Bank* (AIIB). Based in Beijing, the AIIB has the same objectives as the NDB – to support the building of infrastructure – but this time right across the Asia-Pacific region, with the host laying out 30% of the capital. Two aspects make the AIIB institution-building particularly 'revolutionary'. First, amongst its 64 current members (another 22 approved), categorised as 'regional' (Asia-Pacific) and 'non-regional' (elsewhere) are found staunch allies of Washington (amongst them Canada, South Korea, Saudi Arabia, Israel, Australia, and Britain), but not the US itself. Second, in a clear attempt to mimic the US's privileges in the IMF and World Bank, Beijing enjoys the right of veto, major decisions requiring 75% of the votes while it possesses 31% of the vote.[36]

One other geopolitical challenge to US hegemony has been China's incursion into that most sensitive of regions: the Middle East. While Obama was announcing a 'pivot to Asia', seemingly at the expense of the Gulf States, the PRC's was consolidating its economic presence, increasing trade by around 600% in the decade up to 2014 (amounting to $230 billion in trade),[37] supplanting the US as the region's most important energy client. As with Africa and Latin America, Chinese trade with the Middle East was not limited to oil/gas exploration, production, exploitation, and importation. Beijing has signed a whole plethora of deals with governments across the region to construct roads, metros, rail links, bridges, and harbours, while its private sector supplies a whole range of goods and services (e.g. machinery, automobiles, steel, plastics, agriculture, and retail).

The world's largest oil exporter and unofficial American military protectorate since 1945, Saudi Arabia, now sells over half its oil to Asia following the launching of King Abdullah's "Look East" trade policy in 2005. For Khalid A. al-Falih, the Energy Minister and the head of Saudi Aramco, the state-owned oil giant, this shift represented "a long-term transition" to shift supply towards Asia. "Demographic and economic trends are making it clear – the writing is on the wall", he continued, "China is the growth market for petroleum".[38] While Saudi Arabia Oil and Saudi Basic Industries have been given the green light to invest in Chinese refinery and petrochemical projects, the PRC has acquired a growing stake in Saudi industry and infrastructure (e.g. a $1.8 billion contract to build a high-speed train from Mecca to Medina) and allowed better market access for its exports (e.g. manufactures, textiles, toys, plastics, and food).

The PRC is quick to stress these are straight commercial transactions and deny that this closer bilateral trading relationship carries any great geopolitical significance. Some voices in Riyadh, on the other hand, have welcomed the opportunity to lessen political dependence on Washington. There was, as Prince Turki al-Faisal, a former Saudi ambassador to the US and brother of the Foreign Minister, Prince Saudi al-Faisal observed, "less baggage" and "easier routes to mutual benefit" with Beijing than Washington, whose pro-Israeli stance stirs up such large opposition at home.[39]

Much to the chagrin of Washington Beijing has maintained close economic and political ties with its bête noir, 'rogue state' Iran, despite the UN/US-imposed sanctions.[40] Not only is the Islamic Republic one of the PRC's top oil suppliers, but it has also been the recipient of enormous FDI from Chinese SOEs eager to tie up exclusive deals for the supply of natural gas and access to minerals (notably chrome, iron ore, and celestine). Beijing has been converted into Tehran's largest trading partner (overtaking the EU in 2009) and Iran into China's "main trading partner" in the region.[41] Once sanctions were lifted in 2015, the PRC pumped billions of dollars (directly or via the Angola Mode) into major infrastructure projects for water supply systems, dams, roads, etc. (which European banks refused to finance), and most strikingly the electrification of a 926 km railroad connecting Tehran to Mashad, a strand of the 3,200 km *New Silk Route* (see below).[42] This bilateral trade has not only helped to stabilise its economy, bringing in vital machinery, technology, and investment, but it has also helped to bolster the Islamic Republic, again clashing with the US's regional geopolitical objectives.

China's 'low key' strategic economic (as opposed to American militaristic) policy to access foreign markets also paid dividends next door in Iraq. In October 2009, for example, a CNPC and BP-led a consortium simply outbid its competitors to win the contract to develop the Iraqi Rumaila oilfield, tipped by many to be the world's biggest oil reservoir. Celebrating the first visit by an Iraqi head of government for 50 years, then Prime Minister Wen Jiabao told his counterpart, Nuri Al-Maliki, that "The Chinese government will encourage companies to establish long-term stable relationship on oil and natural gas supply and demand with the Iraqi side and expand cooperation in oil exploration, refinery, and equipment trade". Nuri Al-Maliki, added he hoped Chinese companies would invest not just on oil and gas but also on electricity, transportation, housing, telecommunications, and agriculture.[43]

A 2012 IEA study claimed that by 2035 almost 90% of all Middle Eastern oil would flow to Asia.[44] While it is impossible to predict the geopolitical effects, at a minimum it would constitute a serious challenge to the primacy of the dollar (and of course the aforementioned weapondollar-petrodollar coalition [WDPDC]) and thus American hegemony, especially if as the *Iran Daily* reports, talks are currently underway to carry out transactions in local currencies (i.e. yuan) rather than dollars (see below).[45]

As China's resource supply chains take global proportions so necessarily do the security threats it faces, especially around Eurasia. Significantly, 80% of its oil import passed through the Strait of Malacca, an 800 km-long shipping channel between the Indian and Pacific Oceans with Singapore to the North and Indonesia to the South. At just 2.8 km wide at its narrowest point this stretch of water makes it extremely vulnerable to piracy, terrorism, and worst of all foreign (i.e. American) naval blockade. In its quest to establish alternative safer routes, and again spurned on by the GFC, the PRC began financing the construction of a network deep-water ports in 'friendly' countries across the Indian Ocean periphery – such as Gwadar (Pakistan), Kyauk Pyu (Myanmar),[46] Chittagong (Bangladesh), Hambantota (Sri Lanka)[47] – with the idea of transferring the resources overland (via specially designed pipelines, roads, or rail links) to landlocked western provinces such as Xinjiang.

Another strategic option for energy supply has been for the PRC to augment its overland trade with Eurasia, notably with its hitherto estranged neighbour, though fellow BRIC, member Russia, and other ex-Soviet Central Asian countries, who shared a common scepticism about the continual eastward expansion of US influence in Europe, the Middle East, and right up to Chinese frontier: be it via NATO enlargement or as part of a war on terror (WOT). Diversifying from its usual European market, from January 2011, Russia began to export crude oil eastwards via the joint-financed/constructed Eastern Siberia-Pacific Ocean pipeline which ran from Russia's Amur region to the northeastern industrial Chinese city of Daqing. For the head of PetroChina pipeline, the opening of the conduit heralded "the start of a new phase in China-Russia energy cooperation"[48]: the world's largest oil producer now directly supplying the world's biggest energy consumer. Further south, the PRC negotiated similar energy supply deals with Central Asian producers such as Turkmenistan, Uzbekistan, and Kazakhstan, guaranteed gas and oil supplies via a specially constructed 7,000 km-long gas and oil pipeline stretching from the Caspian Sea to the Chinese western province of Xinjiang much to the chagrin of the West.[49] Indeed, the PRC would go even farther by launching the Shanghai Cooperation Organisation (SCO) in 2003, bringing together of Asian, Central Asian, and European countries[50] in a common multilateral organisation largely concerned with common security challenges (terrorism, extremism, and separatism) with the potential– though far from realisation at the time of writing – to 'counterbalance' NATO.

One other key geopolitical effect of China's meteoric economic rise worthy of note was the refashioning of East Asia division of labour. In spite of serious on-going territorial disputes (see below), regional development has seen a shift away from the classic Japan-centred 'flying geese' model towards a *Sinocentric* production network, with the PRC emerging as the final assembler and exporter to the Global North. While hitherto this has involved China importing machinery and semi-finished goods from South Korea, Taiwan, Hong Kong, and Japan, one of *the* biggest challenges facing East Asia, and the capitalist world in general, is how to cope with the PRC once it moves up the value-added chain to produce a whole range of high-quality goods and services.

Considered an integral part 'One-China', quasi-US protectorate Taiwan, for example, is finding it hard to resist the economic magnetism of mainland giant, where 44% of its FDI[51] and 45% of its exports end up.[52] Fearing possible regional isolation unless it followed suit, Kuomintang (KMT) president, Ma Ying-jeou, signed more than 20 deals with Beijing on trade, FDI, shipping, direct fights and tourism, culminating in the landmark Economic Co-operation Framework Agreement (ECFA) in June 2010, arguably the most significant cross-strait initiative since the civil war. True to its hegemonic role, under the terms of the ECFA agreement China would make immediate concessions, cutting import tariffs across 539 products and the opening up 11 service areas and 18 farming and fisheries categories (with no reciprocal liberalisation in Taiwan) worth $13.8 billion in trade. Taipei for its part agreed committed to cut tariffs on 267 Chinese goods and offer wider access in seven service areas together worth $3 billion.[53]

Unsurprisingly, the ever-closer economic relationship between Beijing and Taipei was not popular in all quarters. The bridge too far came when the KMT government signed the Cross-Strait Service Trade Agreement (CSSTA) in June 2013, aiming to liberalise bilateral trade/investment flows in a wide range of sectors including construction, banking, insurance, telecommunications, transport, tourism, and cultural industries, not to mention renewal residential visas for business chiefs. Opposition forces, led by the Democratic Progressive Party, academia and the mobilisation of the 500,000 strong Sunflower Student Movement, have thus far prevented the CSSTA's ratification, arguing it would provoke the effective absorption of the country into China's economy and hence Beijing's political control *en route* to unification. With large capital on both sides of the strait eager for the CSSTA's completion, and the PRC able at any time to engage in punitive economic statecraft against a 'region' it considers part of its 'unnegotiable sovereignty', the gravitational pull may be hard to avoid.

To the north, economic integration with the Korean peninsula has also sped ahead. In the two decades following the re-establishing of regular high-level diplomatic contacts (1992), for example, bilateral between the PRC and South Korea increased 35 times from $6.37 billion to $220.63 billion,[54] converting Beijing converted into Seoul's most important trading partner by a long way (larger than the US and Japan combined) in 2016,[55] expediated by the coming into force of the China-South Korean

Free Trade Agreement in December 2015. The "Strategic Cooperative Partnership" signed in 2008 extends the relationship way beyond trade into legislative and juridical cooperation, scientific and technological projects, cultural/tourist exchanges (eight million Chinese visited South Korea in 2016) and the twinning of over 130 towns/cities. South Korea's dependency on the PRC was revealed following Seoul's decision to deploy an American missile-defence system in 2016. In response, the Chinese state-run media ran a campaign to boycott South Korean goods (e.g. cars, cosmetics, confectionery), while Beijing closed down selected Korean businesses (e.g. the Lotte supermarket) on questionable grounds, banned tour groups from visiting the peninsula (affecting the retail trade), and even cancelled *Hallyu* cultural events. The South Korean economy was badly hit, already under increasing market pressure from China in key sectors (ship-building, automobiles, chemicals, and home appliances).

Needless to say, the dependence of North Korea on its northern neighbour is even more pronounced, representing over 80% of its imports of (oil, machinery, vehicles, and arms) and exports (e.g. minerals, textiles, and food) despite US attempts to enforce a trade embargo. Under Angola Mode arrangements, Chinese companies have been granted the right to extract coal and minerals in return for the building of infrastructure, notably road and rail links connecting the country with China's booming North Eastern provinces, and developing the Rason port over which they secured a ten-year lease, thereby gaining its first foothold in the South China Sea for over a century, and easier access to the South Korean and Japanese markets.

The promise of cheap labour and market access also proved too lucrative for China's old regional adversary, Japan. Occupying the rear guard in Japan's 'flying geese' arrangement, China's meteoric rise in no small measure benefitted from capital and technology generated by the vertically structured division of labour 'pyramid', especially once its own internal reforms (see below) and East Asia crisis broke it apart. From 2006, economic interdependence has increased considerably, with Japanese companies, especially small and medium-sized, eager to target China's growing urban middle class for their high-value goods and services exports. Tellingly, the very same year, the PRC surpassed Japan as the world's second-largest economy (2010), it also replaced the US as Japan's biggest export market. Despite the fact that Sino-Nippons relation hit a period of political turbulence between 2009 and 2015 (see below), by 2016, 32,313 Japanese companies operated in China, 50% of all operating abroad – dwarfing the 2nd favourite destination, the US (with 8,422) – while value of Chinese e-commerce purchases from Japan rose by 30.3% in the previous year, and estimated to grow a further 84% by 2020.[56] In 2017, Tokyo even backtracked on its original opposition to the "Belt & Road Initiative" (BRI) (see below), agreeing to cooperate and provide capital for the multibillion-dollar infrastructure development projects.

The more Chinese capital expands, the more an enthusiastic promoter of free trade and participant in regional institutional arrangements it becomes. By the summer of 2018, the PRC had signed 16 free trade areas (e.g. with ASEAN,[57] South Korea, Iceland, Australia, Peru, etc.) with a further eight under construction. Amongst the latter include negotiations with the Cooperation Council of the Arab States of the Gulf (including Saudi Arabia, Kuwait, UAE, Qatar, Bahrain), the Regional Comprehensive Economic Partnership (including with ASEAN, Japan, India, South Korea, Australia, and New Zealand) and a trilateral deal with Japan and South Korea.[58] In November 2014, during the APEC summit in Beijing Xi called for a renewed effort to achieve a Free Trade Area of the Asia-Pacific (FTAAP), first proposed by the US over a decade ago. Between 2009 and 2012, the Chiang Mai Initiative – a region-wide currency swap scheme amongst ASEAN Plus Three countries[59] opposed by the IMF and set up *post-East Asia crisis* – was reformed and relaunched (*post-GF*) as the more powerful Chiang Mai Initiative Mulilateralized (CMIM), doubling its foreign exchange to $240 billion, and including mechanisms to help countries facing short-term liquidity problems.

One ironic side-effect of Donald Trump's aggressive 'American First' trade position (see below) is that it may well bring China, Japan, and Korea closer together, clashing with Washington's traditional strategy of driving a wedge between (see below). In May 2018, the first high-level trilateral summit since 2015, China's Li Keqiang impressed with his Japanese and South Korean counterparts (Prime Minister Shinzo Abe and President Moon Jae-in, respectively) the need for the three countries to "stand even more firmly together, uphold the rule-based multilateral trading system, and proudly oppose protectionism and unilateral actions". There was a need, Li insisted, Li called for the need "to raise the level of regional integration, accelerate talks on China-Japan-Korean free trade area, and push forward early completion of a Regional Comprehensive Economic Partnership"[60] (which also includes India, the ASEAN countries, Australia, and New Zealand).

With so many infrastructure, free trade, and investment projects – not to mention corporations acquired and land leased – throughout Eurasia, Latin America, and Africa, the fact that the CPC leadership Beijing might seek to establish some sort of overall framework for their coordination (and expansion) would, on its own, not carry particular significance. The launching of the "Belt & Road Initiative" (BRI) by Xi in September 2013, however, is being billed as a 'game-changer'. Originally called "One Belt, One Road Initiative" – encompassing the Silk Road Economic Belt (SREB) the Maritime Silk Road Initiative (MSRI) – the BRI, according to Foreign Minister Wang Li in 2014, represents Xi's most important foreign policy. Yet it is arguably much more than that: constituting a springboard for the establishment of Chinese regional, if not world, hegemony.

Beijing, we have seen, has long played a pivotal supporting role in Chinese capital's geographical expansion abroad in accordance with Harvey's *spatial fix* template. This became imperative once the post-GFC domestic investment-led boom – centred on infrastructure and real estate – reached bubble proportions in 2011 reflected chronic overproduction in sectors such as steel, aluminium, energy, petrochemicals and cement, and decreasing capital return rate. Driven by the *territorial logic of power*, the CPC leadership began to elaborate plans to redraw formal spatial boundaries, reacting to capital's demands for a far larger 'container of power' to bury its surplus. Fittingly, 2014 was the year the PRC became a net capital exporting country.[61]

China finds itself in a similar to the 'over-heated' US in the late 1940s and there exist certain parallels between the BRI and the Marshall Plan. Not only could it potentially help its industries recover profitability and mitigate chronic overcapacity –the domestic 'investment boom' on a downward slide since 2012[62] – put its huge quantities of foreign exchange reserves to good use and open up foreign markets (e.g. ultra-high-voltage electricity transmission and high-speed rail) it would enable Beijing, like Washington in the late 1950s, to reshape social relations of production (SROP) and form of state (FOS) in line with the Chinese model which, inevitably will help strengthen the country's political and cultural hegemony ('intellectual and moral leadership'). The main objective of the BRI, in short, was to reorganise global capitalism – or at least Eurasia – around a *Sino-centric* accumulation model and restore profit rates.

The strategic importance for China of the BRI is indicated by the fact that the "action plan" was jointly released in March 2015 by the National Development and Reform Commission, the Ministry of Foreign Affairs and the Ministry of Commerce gives an indication of the importance Beijing gave this initiative.[63] The BRI was converted into Xi Jinping's principal foreign policy objective, constituting the over-arching framework for all other international projects, financed by Beijing itself (to the tune of around $150 billion p.a.[64]) through the Asian Infrastructure Investment Bank (AIIB) and a specially created Silk Road fund.

Set out in its 2015 "Vision and Actions" document[65] the Beijing appeared to be reading from Adam Smith's *Wealth of Nations*, extolling the huge benefits of the free flow of trade, capital and ideas across the BRI's the three land (SREB) and two (MSRI) maritime routes spanning Asia, the Persian Gulf, Africa, and Europe. This was to be done by prioritising five so-called "connectivities": (1) policy coordination, (2) facilities connectivity (infrastructure, logistics, communications, and energy infrastructure), (3) unimpeded trade (free trade areas, customs cooperation, balancing trade flows, and protecting the rights of investors), (4) financial integration (including the internationalisation of the Renminbi (RMB) and the establishment of new development banks; and

(5) a "people-to-people bond" (to be forged through tourism and students exchange).

To those not possessing rose-coloured glasses, it was evident that the "connectivity" Beijing speaks so enthusiastically about was *its own*, connecting the country to Europe. The three land routes of the SREB would construct a network of roads, bridges, railways, ports, oil and natural gas pipelines, and power grids running from China, passing through Central Asia (Kazakhstan, Kyrgyzstan, Uzbekistan, and Turkmenistan), Russia, Turkey and taking in the Indian Ocean shore, the Persian Gulf, and Europe. The MSRI maritime routes would connect the Chinese coast with Europe (and Africa and the Persian Gulf) through a series of ports – the famous 'string of pearls' – spanning the Indian Ocean and on to the South China Sea/South Pacific, and the Indian Ocean. Port construction/ acquisition which had begun as an ad hoc initiative was now greatly expanded,[66] converted into a central pillar of the PRC's foreign policy, a maritime version of Spyman's Rimland strategy first forwarded by Alfred Thayer Mahan.

Meanwhile, in a classic 'hub-and-spoke' arrangement, the SREB would position the PRC at the centre of six international corridors, linking a network of metropolitan nodes and international transport routes and pipelines with the MSRI ports. Furthermore, by large infrastructural projects along the domestic sections of these corridors, it was hoped, would help reduce the PRC's chronic internal uneven development, stimulating growth in, and helping to stabilise the West and South/South West of the country (e.g. Xinjiang and Tibet) and neighbouring Central Asia. Wealth creation would also have its geopolitical importance in the South China Sea, bolster the PRC's legitimacy and land claims there and deter others from intervening in its 'internal affairs' (see below).

Featuring in the 13th Five-Year Plan (setting out key priorities for 2016–20), the BRI was formally launched at the World Economic Forum in Davos in January 2017. The first Chinese leader to attend the forum, Xi was entreated with the keynote speech, insisted on its commitment to global free trade and investment, market liberalisation/facilitation, and open multilateral trade (Open Door).[67] Underscoring the country's world hegemonic credentials, Xi drew a clear parallel with the US post-WWII, emphasising how China's dramatic rise had served the common good, acting as the prime engine for sustained and stable economic growth in the global economy, with the BRI the natural heir to the Marshall Plan. A few months later, the BRI was launched in Beijing in May 2017, in a summit attended by 28 heads of state/government.

To support the BRI social forces across the Chinese 'state-society complex' exploited the hegemonic apparatus (e.g. the education system, the press, television, film, books, museum exhibition, etc.) to promote an idealised vision of the ancient silk routes. The new versions, foreign governments, and businesses were assured, would be based upon similar values and principles: an open, peaceful, inclusive, reciprocal, and advantageous integration project based upon mutual respect and state equality.

Whilst stressing that the BRI, unlike the Marshall Plan, was open to the rest of the world, at least as far as investment went, its focus evidently was on Eurasia – primarily on Asia and then by extension Europe and Africa – which constituted a historic shift away from the classic US-centred transatlantic developmental model. The on-going crisis of US hegemony, manifested in the entrance of Trump into the White House, has only served to strengthen Beijing's credentials as would-be leading capitalist state and guardian of the liberal rule-based international order (LRBIO) and Open Door. Trump's inward-looking 'American First' policy, tariff war (see below) and preference for a bilateral deal over multilateral trading arrangements (e.g. withdrawing from the Trans-Pacific Partnership (TPP), renegotiating North American Free Trade Agreement (NAFTA) and criticism of the World Trade Organisation (WTO)) undermines US leadership in favour of the PRC. In a speech, in May 2015, Obama declared: "if we don't write the rules for trade around the world – guess what – China will. And they'll write those rules in a way that gives Chinese workers and Chinese businesses the upper hand, and locks American-made goods out".[68]

The BRI is also important for the way it has situated a bold China centre stage, breaking with the traditional Dengist maxim: 'hide our capabilities, bide our time; never try to take the lead'. Whether it proves to be successful in stimulating growth and bolstering Chinese economic and political hegemony remains to be seen. Certainly, it is a very ambitious project in its scope: 71 countries participating with over $900 billion worth of loans underwritten by China as of spring 2018,[69] but whose total investments are estimated to reach anything between $4 trillion and $8 trillion.[70]

At the same time, it is important to acknowledge that the BRI is very much in its infancy and a number of questions still remain to be answered, including the following:

1   How Beijing is going to manage the internal competition between the different ministries (commerce, foreign affairs), planning commission, and provincial governments?
2   The BRI envisages the free movement of capital, goods, ideas, and communications but not labour; is that feasible over the medium term, and if rules were amended would it lead to large-scale migration from China, and how would that be received and affect SROP abroad?
3   What measures will non-participating regional powers (noticeably India and Australia) take and how will the US and EU react?
4   Though the success of the BRI is fundamental to national economic stability and hence the stability of the CPC, how will Beijing square

the circle of unlimited/unrestrained commercial and ideational with the exigencies of guaranteeing state control?

5 Most importantly of all, will the project actually prove profitable, generating real long-term returns on capital or will it just turn into another asset-bubble? Especially, in the West, concerns have been expressed with regards to the creditworthiness of the countries in Central Asia and their abilities to pay back such colossal loan.

Sino-American Relations

The transition of the PRC from a socialist centrally planned economy to hybrid state-directed market economy, of course, took place within a US-directed, competitive liberal economy. Deng Xiaoping's 'reform and opening up' (*gaige kaifang*) programme depended upon gaining access to foreign investment, technology, know-how, and markets, which only went ahead once Washington granted the PRC full diplomatic recognition (1979), 'most-favoured-nation' treatment (1980) – later 'observer status' to General Agreement on Tariffs and Trade

(GATT) (1982) – and allowed to join the IMF and World Bank (1980). Although the *passive revolution* it embarked upon was complex (see below), China's transformation was based upon it adopting a variation of the classic neo-mercantilist Asian Developmental State (ADS) template (see Chapter 3): setting itself up as a producer of low-end labour-intensive manufacturing products for export to the West from purposely built experimental *Special Economic Zones* (SEZ) originally set up along the southern seaboard.

The rise of China served US hegemony in many ways. First, those Western corporation that did outsource operations there were able to tap into the world's cheapest, most abundant, and productive labour force. Second, cheap imported goods and raw materials lowered the costs of reproducing labour in the US, therefore, helping capital to recue salaries even further. Third, the huge dollar surpluses Chinese businesses accumulated were either hoarded by the state banking system or recycled back through the purchase of treasury bonds (TBs) or assets on Wall Street, keeping interest rates low and the stock market booming. The down-side was a huge structural BOP deficit with China and rising debt.

The GFC exposed the unsustainability of this global imbalance. In 2010, China still owned around 30% of world foreign reserves, equivalent to $2.5 trillion, of which $1.5 trillion was US debt. The *Financial Times'* assistant editor and chief economics correspondent, Martin Wolf, commented: "Never in history can the government of one superpower have lent so much to that of another".[71] Bucking the classic Braudel/Arrighi model of hegemonic transitions – Italy City State to Holland; Holland to Britain; Britain to the US – it was the rising power that was lending to the incumbent hegemon, not the other way around.

Though the Fed/Treasury under Bush II bailed-out/nationalised Fannie Mae and Freddie Mac predominantly to safeguard Chinese investments, the huge quantity of dollar-denominated assets owned made Beijing more and more concerned about further greenback devaluation. In a news conference in March 2009, Prime Minister Wen Jiabao implored the US "to honour its words, stay a credible nation and ensure the safety of Chinese assets".[72] When Standard & Poor's downgraded US government debt from risk-free AAA to AA+ on the 5th August 2011 – the first time for 70 years – Beijing was livid. The PRC issued no formal response but the CPC's official news agency – *Xinhua* – blasted the US's "addiction to debt" and called on Washington to "live within its means" notably by cutting its "gigantic military expenditure" and "bloated social welfare programmes". State newspapers fell in line denouncing the US decadence and announcing that the good old days were over.[73]

The GFC marked a turning point in Chinese economic statecraft. For the short/immediate term Beijing was not prepared to take the 'nuclear option' of dumping part of its dollar assets ($1.2 trillion of which are in US TBs[74]), aware that any major sudden diversification would cause the greenback to nosedive thereby devaluing its remaining dollar assets and therein hurt slash its US-bound exports. But since 2008, however, CPC elites have sought to restructure its domestic economic growth model (see below) and lessen its dependency on the dollar predominantly by gradually internationalising the RMB/yuan.[75] The benefits of the latter include: (1) reduce the volatility and costs that its exporters face when they are paid in foreign currency; (2) avoid accumulating potentially devaluing pieces of paper; (3) enabling Beijing to borrow cheaply; and (4) permit the RMB to form part of the IMF's *Special Drawing Rights* (SDR) basket (see below). No great power, as CPC elite know full well, as has ever established global or even regional hegemony without internationalising their currency.

As a result, Beijing began tentatively to permit a degree of currency convertibility (on its current account) first between the mainland and Hong Kong, Macau, and later ASEAN countries. Selected countries, including Russia, Japan, and Canada are now allowed to finance their trade with yuan, while swap lines have been established between China's central bank and over 30 foreign counterparts. By December 2013, the yuan had overtaken the euro as the world's second most-used currency in global trade, and the following year, in what is considered a significant move, the UK signed a deal with Beijing to permit London to sell RMB denominated Chinese governmental debt.[76] As part of this internationalisation process, *Reuters* reported in March 2018 that Beijing was contemplating taking the first steps to pay for imported crude oil exclusively in yuan from the latter part of the year, with Russia and Angola tipped to be the testing grounds.[77]

Inclusion in the SDR basket, the expansion of the BRI and oil purchases are likely to greatly augment the use of yuan abroad. If this internationalisation is successful over the medium/long-term, the RMB could directly challenge the dollar's supremacy as the world's reserve currency, which the US has enjoyed unbroken since WWII, and with a deal direct blow to financialization and American hegemony itself.

Such a strategy incurs great risks, however. In order to promote global use of the yuan, Beijing would have to remove capital controls and permit the influx/outflux of funds, therein loosening its tight grip over the domestic bond market and banking systems. China's carefully state-directed 'passive revolution' (see below) could find itself seriously undermined by the whims of global finance led by the Wall Street-Treasury-IMF (WSTI) Complex. Any reckless opening of the capital account could lead to a massive inflow of 'hot money' which not only would hike up the price of the yuan and hence damage the export industry but could also inflate an already over-capitalised banking sector, blowing an asset bubble of enormous proportions and eventual crash and capital flight á la East Asia crisis. The Shanghai stock market crash in the summer of 2015 reminded Beijing of the unpredictability of finance while reinforcing Western economists' arguments of the need for a *fully* liberalised capital market. Investors will only want to hold yuan long-term, mainstream economists emphasise, if they have to have access to a wide range of safe, stable, and easily sold financial instruments (using the depth of Wall Street as a reference).

Obviously, the rise of China has provoked much debate amongst the guardians of US hegemony. A good key guide to understanding American elite thinking and political strategy is the *Princeton Project on National Security*, entitled "Forging a World of Liberty Under Law: US National Security in the 21st Century", written by G. John Ikenberry and Anne-Marie Slaughter. The report stresses the need to "foster and strengthen a regional order that is trans-Pacific, rather than pan-Asian – that is, one in which the United States plays a full part". This would require "developing a combined political and economic strategy" to "engage China" and "look for opportunities to strike strategic bargains", offering Beijing "greater status and position within the regional and global systems", while in return expecting the "to accept and accommodate our core strategic interests, which include remaining a dominant security provider within East Asia". The paper advised US policy-makers to maintain "a strong military capability" to dissuade China "from regional hegemonic ambitions", while at the same time forming a closer alliance with other democratic states, most notably the EU, India, and Japan, the US-Japan alliance considered the "bedrock of American strategy in East Asia".[78]

What the Ikenberry-Slaughter paper recommends is classic hegemonic statecraft: combining consensus and coercion to 'delimit' Beijing policy options. This was most clearly demonstrated under Obama's so-called 'pivot to Asia' – a rather inappropriate slogan, since the US had never abandoned the most easterly point of its Eurasia Rimland strategy.

On the consensual side, the 'pivot' involved conducting a concerted diplomatic campaign. One of the first foreign leaders Obama called after his inauguration was President Hu Jintao[79] while Secretary of State, Hilary Clinton's first official trip abroad was to Asia and specifically, the PRC. A new *G-2* relationship started to find institutional form with the announcing of the *US-China Strategic and Economic Dialogue* in April 2009. During his Asian tour later that year, Obama billed himself as 'America's first Pacific president', the first occupant of the White House to place Asia-Pacific at the top of his geopolitical agenda (as NSS-2006 recommended). During the Obama-Hu summit in November 2009, each pledged to respect each other's core interests – which for Beijing boiled down to acknowledging the CPC's legitimacy and respecting the country's sovereignty and territorial integrity (Tibet, Taiwan, the Diaoyu Islands, and other South East Asia islands). To side-step problems, Obama had refused to meet Dalai Lama in the run-up to the tour and rarely publicly criticised China for its human rights record.

Similarly, President Hu Jintao's state visit to the White House on 18th January 2011 was "full of pomp and pageantry that American presidents seldom lay on even for their closest friends",[80] with the leaders holding lengthy talks extending to bilateral trade, market liberalisation, currency reform, and intellectual property. "China's peaceful rise is good for the world and it's good for America", Obama announced in a joint press conference on 19th January, adding "We want to sell you all kinds of stuff. We want to sell you planes, we want to sell you software", such enticements being dependent on Beijing to push ahead with liberalisation reforms, reminding Hu that the PRC's rapid growth was partly due to US hegemony underwriting a global trading system and guaranteeing "decades of stability in Asia" by its "forward presence in the region",[81] a wink to the Sino-American maritime clashes in the Asia Pacific (see below).

What Washington was doing in accordance with the Ikenberry-Slaughter's hegemonic strategy, was to offer China the possibility of becoming what then Deputy Secretary of State (and future World Bank chief), Robert Zoellick called a "responsible state-holder" (i.e. privileged junior partner) in the US-led liberal international system. As such the PRC would be granted a far higher profile in global forums such as the newly created G20, the WTO, and the IMF. In the latter, for example, Washington finally agreed to reform voting shares, raising China's from 3.8% to 6.0%, while reducing its own from 16.7% to 16.5%, still woefully short of reflecting the PRC's economic might or challenging the US's effective veto.[82] The US also gave the green light for the RMB's inclusion within the IMF SDR basket of currencies in October 2016, worth 11% of total above the yen and sterling, both 8%, but well below the euro 31% and dollar 42%.

Although the Obama administration clashed with their Chinese counterparts on market access, intellectual property protection, alleged cyber-attack on its corporations (e.g. Google), growing trade deficits and dumping (slapping a 35% import tariff on tyres), it refused to endorse Congressional bills calling for the PRC to be designated a 'currency manipulator' and therefore force the Department of Trade to apply countervailing measures on the Asian power's imports. Aware of the structural role China played in bolstering American finance, Obama opposed the initiative, fearing it would also: (1) be illegal under WTO rules; (2) provoke a trade war and worsen Sino-American relations; (3) raise costs for American businesses and consumer at home and US corporations based in China; (4) cause inflation and hence lead to an increase in interest rates; and (5) have a very little effect on the US's BOP deficit, which was more about the country's declining productivity, lack of investment, higher labour costs, and demand for imported goods.

The Trump administration adopted a more aggressive trade position on the PRC than Obama: "American First" a clear response to the "Made in China 2025" initiative (see below). Critical of the way Chinese SOEs have been using their leverage to acquire American know-how (guilty of 'intellectual property theft'), the White House has promised to tighten technology and investment flows in key sectors such as IT, communication, aerospace, and machinery, while slapping punitive tariffs on $50 billion worth of selected Chinese goods in an attempt to slash $200 billion off the country's $337 billion trade deficit with its "strategic competitor" by 2020. Considering trade wars "easy to win", Trump has to date, however, avoided the 'nuclear option' of designating the PRC a 'currency manipulator', which would affect *all* goods and services. The irony is that the application of the tariffs, China's reciprocal actions (affecting 128 imported American goods), and subsequent talk of an all-out trade war (no doubt with the blessing from Beijing), has caused the yuan to drop even more against the dollar.[83]

Thus far, as we have seen, the PRC has been careful not to rock the boat too much, content for the present to work within, and take full advantage of, the US-led liberal system. Multilateral institution-building such as the AIIB, NDB, CRA, and CMIM, important as they are at projecting Chinse power, have yet to be pitched directly against the Bretton Woods organs, preferring to 'shadow' their Anglo-Saxon counterparts, offering developing countries alternative forms of financing. Similarly in foreign policy, the PRC has shown displayed its 'responsible shareholder' characteristics by: (1) tacitly approving the US's WOT campaign aimed at Muslim extremism in Central Asia (claimed to fan the flames of radical elements within its own Uyghurs minority population); (2) increasing participating in UN peace-keeping operations from 2008 onwards (e.g. anti-piracy in the Gulf of Aden); (3) consenting to a UN Security Council resolution referring Libyan leader Muammar Gadaffi to the International Criminal Court (ICC) for brutal repression of Arab Spring in 2011;[84] (4) ceding to US pressure to reduce dealings with Iran in

2012–13 (though rapidly restored/augmented following US-Iran thaw in late 2013); (5) agreeing on a bilateral deal with Washington in November 2014 to reduce greenhouse gas emissions; and (6) signing the UN Paris Agreement on climate change in 2016. Furthermore, Beijing has voiced support for nuclear-free zones, treaties to ban the first use of nuclear weapons and prohibiting an arms race in outer space, all of which the US has shunned.

But as Eikenberry-Slaughter paper indicated Washington's response to China's rise could not rely solely on improvement bilateral cooperation. In what realists/neorealists would recognise as *balance of power* arrangements Washington has been engaging in busy diplomatic activity with the PRC's neighbours. In the area of trade, for example, this has manifested itself in the signing a Treaty of Amity and Cooperation in Southeast Asia (2009) with ASEAN countries, joining the East Asia Summit forum (2010), ratifying a free trade deal with South Korea (2011), opening up trade and investment dialogue with Myanmar (2013), and joining the ill-fated TPP in February 2016, from which China was excluded.

But where Washington's most significant regional 'balance of power' construction has taken place has been in the area where the Global Leviathan still remains the "indispensable nation" – and one traditionally ignored by neo-Gramscians – Gramsci's *third moment* of hegemony, "the relation of military forces", which we are reminded, "from time to time is directly decisive".[85]

As we have seen, the larger the Chinese economy becomes, the more it becomes reliant on access to foreign markets, and the more the *territorial* logic of power finds greater expression within capitalist imperialism. Just as Washington pushed back the 'internal frontier' all the way to the Pacific in the 19th century, and then into Central and South America, before declaring its dominion over the entire Western Hemisphere under the *Monroe Doctrine*, so Washington interprets the PRC's more assertive position around its coastal seas – the East China Sea, the South China Sea, the Yellow Sea, and even onto the East Indian Ocean, classified as "core" regions of "national interest", and reinforced over time with the launching of Xi's "China Dream" – as part of a fledgling *Asian* Monroe Doctrine,[86] which he himself has constantly denied ("No matter how much stronger it may become, it will never seek hegemony or expansion. It will never inflict its past suffering on past suffering on other nations").[87]

Necessarily a national security state (NSS) from its inception, the PRC has become increasingly militarised over the last two decades. According to the *Stockholm International Peace Research Institute*, China's expenditure for 2017 stood at around $228 billion, up 110% increase on 2007. It spends over three times more than the third place (Russia), and represents approximately 13% of global total. Beijing counters that this fall well short of the US's $610 billion, constituting 35% of global total, and that it only spends 1.9% of its GDP on military compared to the US's 3.1%,[88] while constantly stressing such expenditure was to safeguard its national sovereignty and territorial integrity. And while it is true that the PRC could soon become the world's second most important aircraft-carrier nation, with at least one, possibly two type 001 presently under construction, adding to their ex-Soviet refitted *Liaoning* (first engaged in live-drills in April 2018),[89] the People's Liberation Army (PLA) would respond that the Pentagon possesses *20* aircraft carriers (almost half of the world's total), ten of which are *Nimitz*-class supercarriers.

Washington has repeatedly warned that Beijing had been expanding and upgrading its nuclear arsenal. Cruise missiles apart, the PLA is said to have introduced a new generation of medium, intercontinental, and submarine launched ballistic missiles and anti-ship ballistic missiles, which includes the satellite-directed *Dongfeng* 21 D (DF-21D). The Pentagon considers DF-21D a "game changer" in the Western Pacific due to its ability to sink an aircraft carrier from a distance of 2,900 km and able to change course in mid-flight to evade US Aegis anti-missiles interceptor. It forms a central pillar, they claim, of China's "A2/AD" (anti-access/area denial) strategy, using aircraft, vessels, and missiles – backed by enhanced cyber capabilities (see below) – aimed to prevent US military forces to operating freely in the seas and skies around the PRC and its "security environment". Nonetheless, in quantitative terms, its estimated 270 warheads pale into comparison to Russia (7,010) and the US (6,550), who together make 90% of the global total.[90]

What concerns the Pentagon insists is the pace of PLA's military modernisation programme: the recent launching of a new generation of stealth jet fighters, the J-20 and J-31 (potentially with similar capabilities to the US J-35 Joint Strike Fighter), the build-up of a large number of relatively inexpensive, but highly accurate non-nuclear ballistic missiles, and sea/air-launched missiles in the region, updating its submarine fleet, and the development of *anti-satellite weapon* systems, capable of destroying enemy satellites (contradicting its asserted opposition to the militarisation of space). In addition, Washington warns that Beijing is compensating for its relative military inferiority by developing *asymmetric warfare* techniques concentrating on so-called C4ISR (i.e. Command, Control, Communications, Computers, Intelligence, Surveillance, and Reconnaissance) defence system, aimed at gaining the upper hand in space, cyberspace, and information operations and thus to paralyse – to "blind and disrupt" – the US's military operations at source.

Tensions over cyber-security dramatically increased under Obama, the White House accusing Beijing of hacking and engaging in cyber-espionage targeting both American commercial and military interests,[91] including the theft of 5.6 million fingerprints of federal government officials in September 2015, while the PRC countered by citing National Security Agency's whistle-blower, Edward Snowden's revelation of American cyber-spying activities (e.g. against Huawei, the telecommunications giant). Though a Sino-American agreement was reached in 2015 prohibiting hacking private companies for commercial gain, distrust remains, exemplified in the Trump administration fining and temporary banning of ZTE Corporation for dealing with Iran and North Korea. Both prioritise cybersecurity as a national defence priority: the US set this out in the NSS-2017, deeming China a "revisionist power" determined to gather/exploit data and use cyber capabilities to undermine democracy and sovereignty worldwide,[92] while Beijing set up a new power state body, the Cyberspace Administration of China, to protect its "critical information infrastructure" (prioritising finance, energy, telecommunications, and transportation sectors) and regain "cyberspace sovereignty" seize control over its data/communications from western internet companies[93] and implicitly bolster its A2/AD military strategy.

As previously noted, bipartisan agreement existed amongst American political elite on NSS-2002's affirmation that "no state will be allowed to challenge the military supremacy of the United States in the 21st century" and the PRC's dramatic rise threatened the Washington-sanctioned East Asian 'balance of power' security arrangements and hence Rimland geostrategic imperatives (see Chapter 2). According to a 2015 RAND Corporation report, there was a "receding frontier of US military dominance" in the region, and even though China had not yet caught up, the speed of change had been "striking".[94] RAND's East Asian security expert, Roger Cliff went even further, claiming that American military dominance will be so eroded by the 2020s that China will feel confident to make a bid for regional hegemony.[95]

Ultimately, if the hegemonic transition were to be settled by military means, as world-systems theorists indicate,[96] the most likely 'theatre' seems the Asia-Pacific maritime part of the Rimland. Suffice to say that the Global Leviathan would take every measure to combat any challenge to the US Navy's exclusive right to monitor all commercial and military activities throughout the Western Pacific and into the Indian Ocean: a privilege enjoyed since the WWII. Earlier, in an article entitled "How we would fight China", published in the *Atlantic Monthly*, June 2005, American hegemony 'organic intellectual', Robert D. Kaplan insisted: "[t]he American military contest in the Pacific will define the 21st century. And China will be a more formidable adversary than Russia ever was".[97] Similarly, Princeton's Woodrow Wilson School scholar, Aaron L. Friedberg, implored Washington not to scale down its military presence in the West Pacific given the threat the PRC's growing authoritarianism posed to Western liberal values, national economic interests, and US hegemony, quoting former Singapore Prime Minister, Lee Kuan Yew: "If you do not hold your ground in the Pacific, you cannot be a world leader".[98]

He need not worry, Obama was committed to the "strategic rebalancing" of the Asia-Pacific region, the "safe passage" across which Secretary of State, Hillary Clinton described as a pivotal "national interest", the NSS-2015 insisting Washington was determined to exercise its capacity as a "system shaper"; leading with "purpose", "strength", and "all the instruments of US power".[99] 'Freedom of navigation operations' was also non-negotiable for the Trump administration. China, according to NSS-2017, was "determined to erode American security and prosperity", and although actions in the South China Sea "endanger the free flow of trade, threaten the sovereignty of other nations, and undermine regional stability", the US would stand firm, committed to maintaining "a forward military presence capable of deterring, and if necessary, defeating any adversary".[100]

Undoubtedly, China's Asian neighbours had genuine cause for concern about the latter's meteoric rise, expansive foreign policy, and heightened militarism, not to mention insecurity over their increasing economic dependency on Beijing, as we have seen. This has permitted the US to reinforce its politico-military hegemony over the region, offering 'legitimate protection' (in contrast to much of the WOT) to those countries who have felt most threatened. Reverting to the classic Cold War template, Washington has sought to weave a web of 'balance of power' containment arrangements across East Asia/West Pacific in line with Ikenberry-Slaughter prescriptions.

Unsurprisingly, and a political clear reaction/counter-reaction to the material restructuring underway, military tensions in East Asia greatly augmented in the wake of the GFC (especially 2009–11), with Washington magnifying the severity of the situation somewhat, in order to drive a wedge between the PRC and its neighbours and maintain its military hegemony in the Asia-Pacific region.

Hostilities kicked off in the East China Sea in January 2010 when Washington announced its intention to conclude a $6.4 billion arms deal with Taiwan[101] – long considered a non-negotiable "core area" of "one China" national. While refusing to supply Taiwan with the eight submarines and 66 latest F-16 C/D fighters it requested – due to their 'offensive' character – the US offered to 'retro-fit' 150 F-16 A/B fighters addition to the 114 patriot anti-missile missiles, 12 harpoon anti-ship missiles, and 60 Black Hawk helicopters, as part of the $6.4 billion deal.[102] Beijing denounced the proposed arms deal as highly provocative, a threat to a peaceful resolution strait relations and an illegal intervention into its "domestic affairs", declaring it was severing military-to-military relations with Washington (restored 12 months later) and threatened economic sanctions on American companies implicated in the arms deal. Countering the "arrogant" and "disrespectful" Congressmen's initiative in August 2011, the CPC's newspaper *People's Daily* urged "to use its 'financial weapon'" (e.g. stop buying TBs) to "teach the United States a lesson" for violating the joint communiqué.[103] Washington cited China's claim over the Taiwan Strait as yet another example (see the South

China Sea below) of Beijing trying to extend its territorial claims beyond the 12-nautical-mile limit accepted through customary international and codified by the UN Convention on the Law of the Sea (UNCLOS) (see below).

The entrance of Trump into the White House has further intensified Sino-American disagreements over Taiwan, indeed even prior to his swearing-in, the president-elect broke with standard protocol by phoning independent advocator Tsai Ing-wen to congratulate him on his presidential electoral victory. Trump followed this by strengthening the bilateral defence partnership (under the National Defense Authorisation Act for the Fiscal Year 2018), re-establishing port of call between Taiwanese and American navies, and inviting Taipei to participate in military exercises,[104] before signing the Taiwan Travel Act in January 2018, allowing high-level diplomats to travel between the countries after decades. On 7th April 2018, Trump granted a licence to US manufacturers to sell technology to Taipei enabling them to build their own submarines, topping this two days later with the appointment of Bush II apparatchik, John Bolton, to the post of National Security Adviser. Self-defined 'Goldwater conservative' Bolton is known to favour closer relations with Taiwan, ranging from inviting Tsai to the White House, upgrading diplomatic relations – even to the point of recognising Taipei – and augmenting defence links and arms sales. These initiatives have greatly angered Beijing, claiming they jeopardise the US-Chinese relationship and warning any military exercises in Taiwan waters (recently approved in the US Senate in June 2018) will be responded to.

Nowhere has the unpredictability of the Trump administration been more clearly demonstrated than his summit with Kim Jong-un summit in Singapore, June 2018. For over 60 years one of the central pillars of US hegemony over South Korea, following the classic hegemonic template, had been to safeguard its security against North Korean or Chinese incursion, reflected in its heavy military presence there.[105] Enjoying wartime operational control over Seoul's military, Washington led annual joint annual war-simulation naval exercises in and around the highly contested maritime demarcation line that separated the two Koreas: the Northern Line Limit (NLL).[106] Traditionally, any steps towards unification short of North Korean capitulation were rejected, South Korean president's Kim Dae-jung's "Sunshine Policy" (1998–2007)[107] never accepted in Washington, who breathed a sigh of relief when he was replaced by neocon hawk, former Hyundai CEO, Lee Myung-bak in 2008, determined to reverse all the peace initiative.

For the next two years, again coinciding with the GFC, inter-Korean relations entered a dangerous dynamic manifested in a series of tit-for-tat actions. On the side of Pyongyang, this involved engaging in underground nuclear testing,[108] torpedoing the South Korean warship, *Cheonan*, and unveiling its 'ultramodern' uranium enriching faculty at

Yongbyon. Seoul and Washington reacted by hitting Pyongyang with tough economic and political sanctions[109] and engaging in joint military and war simulation exercises in the Sea of Japan and Yellow Sea (near the NLL), some headed by the colossal nuclear-powered aircraft carrier *USS George Washington*, and involving live fire and anti-submarine missiles and backed up by F-15K fighter-bombers.[110]

Although multifaceted, the 2010 Korean 'crisis' can be considered as a successful piece of geopolitical statecraft by Washington, exploiting regional rivalries to assert its political-military hegemony and with it undermine the CPC leadership. Three aspects of which are worth noting. First, it increased security concerns, justifying aircraft carrier-led fleets patrolling its seas and regular military manoeuvres, within China's geographic sphere of influence.[111] Second, Washington made it clear *who* the regional 'peace-maker' was, refusing Beijing's repeated calls for emergency multilateral talks as part of a Six-Party peace forum (China, US, North Korea, South Korea, Japan, and Russia), preferring instead an exclusive tripartite deal with Tokyo and Seoul, scolding Beijing for not bringing Pyongyang into line.[112] And third, the US cleverly boxing the PRC state elite into a corner regarding North Korea. On the one hand, for domestic and international prestige reasons, Beijing could not be seen to cave in to Washington's politico-military pressure, fearful of destabilising Pyongyang (risking a civil/peninsula war, a flood of refugees, the acquisition of the nuclear arms by political adversaries, and possible assimilation into a US-directed South Korea). On the other hand, and as *Wikileaks* divulgations revealed, the CPC elite were growing increasingly tired of North Korea's nuclear testing/brinkmanship, poor communication, and secrecy.

Time will tell if the Trump-Kim Jong-un summit will actually produce concrete advances or will remain more as a public relations exercise. It may well be that the initiative came from North Korea, under pressure from the PRC, who along with South Korea and Japan all support its denuclearisation. What has taken analysis by surprise is the rapidity with which the Trump administration went from the imposition of tough economic sanctions and threatening "fire and fury" on the "rocket man" – following the latter's testing of its intercontinental missile (Hwasong-15) in November 2017 – to holding a "fantastic" bilateral summit with the "very talented" Mr. Kim, and the promise to end the US's "very provocative" "war games" on the Korean peninsula,[113] long considered central to American balance of power arrangements in East Asia.

Officially, North Korean denuclearisation has always been Washington's objective, reiterated by American Secretary of State, Hillary Clinton in 2010.[114] The reality, however, is that Washington has repeatedly shunned Pyongyang's offer, on the table from since 1994, to abandon its nuclear programme, let in UN inspectors and put itself at the disposal of the International Atomic Energy Agency, in return for a negotiated peace to the Korean War and settlement of border issues.[115] Adhering to the classic 'friend-foe' template, on-going tension in the region (the tit-for-tat "wargames"/nuclear testing) help maintain US politico-military hegemony over Seoul. The threat of North Korean nuclear threat, for example, served as a pretext for the installation of the US's Terminal High Altitude Area Defense (THAAD) anti-ballistic missile system along the South Korean border in 2016, paralysing tripartite peace talks between the latter, China and Japan (ceased in 2012, resumed in 2015), which Washington took a dim view of.

If North Korea is sincere in its June 2018 commitments, the question remains as to whether the US security establishment, which as we have seen extends deeply into, and enjoys huge influence right across, the American *state-society complex* (and associated 'hegemonic apparatus'), will actively work to derail such a process. And even if the denuclearisation of North Korea and its peaceful unification with South Korea were to take place over the medium to long-term, one might expect certain resistance in Washington to withdraw troops and forgo its military primacy on the peninsula.

Sino-Nippon rivalry and distrust clearly predate US presence in the region, the latter's heavy militarisation on its status as the US's primary and longest-serving client-state in East Asia, drives a further wedge between them. When the progressive Democratic Party of Japan (DPJ) finally swept the incumbent conservative Liberal Democratic Party (LDP) from power in August 2009, after almost 55 years of continuous 'democratic' rule, it did so on a campaign promising to improve diplomatic relations with China, re-examine its long-standing subservience to Washington, and adopt a more independent foreign policy (including the launching of an East Asian Community with the PRC). Top of the wish list was the removal of the US Futenma airbase from Okinawa, which remained highly unpopular with the Japanese population (a situation replicated in South Korea) and the commitment to make public any secret agreement which allowed the US to bring nuclear weapons to the island.

Once in power, however, the DPJ was told point-blank by Washington that such a policy shift was unacceptable. Forced to backtrack, the DPJ alienated its Social Democrat coalition partners and own voters, Prime Minister Yukio Hatoyama's popularity plummeting below 20% in the polls. He dutifully resigned in shame in June 2010 while his fellow 'foreign policy radicals' found themselves marginalised. Asked about the significance of the political change Pentagon press secretary, Geoff Morrell, expressed confidence that "whoever is in power will respect the agreements that have been forged by previous administrations".[116] The new pro-American DPJ prime minister, Naoto Kan, who wasted no time in shelving the Okinawa request and ending tradition post-war pacifist stance, ceding to Washington pressure to adopt a more assertive military stance and expand its defence budget (e.g. increasing its submarine fleet and buying US F-35s) to 'send a signal to the Chinese' in the light of the latter's rising power in the Yellow Sea (see below). In September 2010 at the APEC Summit, Kan committed Japan to the TPP aimed at killing the East Asian Community idea, while Tokyo agreed to collaborate more closely with Washington on military affairs. The latter reciprocated, ordering its ambassador to Japan, John Roos, to attend the Hiroshima memorial service on the 6th of August, the first representative of the US government to do so in 65 years. The same month a joint US-Japan military exercise took place on Okinawa.

Sino-Nippon diplomatic relations now took a turn for the worse, flaring up over the disputed maritime border in the East China Sea, focused on around the Senkaku islands – the Diaoyo Islands to the Chinese – off the East coast of Taiwan. Annexed by Tokyo following the Sino-Japanese War (1895), claimed by the PRC, Taiwan, and Japan these islands not only occupy key geostrategic positions but span rich oil and gas deposit, as well as fishing grounds. The tacit Sino-Nippon agreement in place since Deng Xiaoping to avoid over the Senkaku Islands ended in September 2010 following the arrest and jailing of a Chinese fishing boat captain by the Japanese Coast Guards and for allegedly ramming two Japanese boats attempting to drive him out of disputed waters. After expressing surprise that Tokyo would risk worsening bilateral relations over such an issue,[117] Beijing took the incident very seriously, introducing a series of diplomatic, political, and economic sanctions,[118] while demanding the captain's release, a full apology, and economic compensation. Kan responded by naming pro-US 'China hawk' Seiji Maehara as new Foreign Minister while calling on Beijing to act as a "responsible member of the international community" and denounced the latter's military build-up and "increasingly ambitious maritime activities in the area stretching from the Indian Ocean to the East China Sea".[119]

As with the above 'Korean conflict', the US has played a double game with regards the Senkaku islands. On the one hand, in its capacity as neutral peacemaker Washington declared it had 'no position' on the territorial dispute, calling on both sides to seek an amicable solution, proposing to chair a three-way summit. On the other hand, it insisted that it will not tolerate any sovereignty claim that jeopardised the "safe passage" through the waters; that all parties had to respect the US Navy's unreserved right to patrol and monitor maritime traffic in the region; maintaining the islands were protected under the terms of the US-Japanese *Treaty of Mutual Cooperation and Security* of 1960 (officially approved by the US Senate in November 2012); and, as with Korea, carrying out provocative joint military operations with Japan near the Senkaku Islands. The Sino-Nippon tensions reached boiling point following Tokyo's purchase three of the disputed islands in September 2012. New LDP Prime Minister Shinzo Abe (since December 2012) adopted an even more hawkish foreign policy, including announcing changes to article 9 of its constitution in July 2014 which now permits sending national troops to fight to oversee for the first time since the WWII; talk about deploying US's THAAD (or Aegis Ashore) anti-ballistic missile system to defend itself from Pyongyang; and relocating the Futenma base to Henoko. As expected, this policy shift provoked an angry reaction in Beijing (and Seoul) and not a little internal opposition.

But perhaps where the clash between US hegemony and PRC's geopolitical ambitions is most starkly revealed in the South China Sea over the Paracel and Spratly islands, which Beijing maintains were illegally annexed by French-Indochina in the 1930s. Claimed by Taiwan, Malaysia, Brunei, and the Philippines, these islands are located on one of the world's chief shipping lanes – through which $1.5 trillion of China's trade passes – and, like their Senkaku counterparts, are thought to sit atop vast reserves of hydrocarbon energy resources and minerals and surrounded by abundant fishing grounds (especially the much-prized bluefin tuna).

Once more with the GFC as a backdrop, regional hostilities intensified there in 2010, especially with Vietnam, who accused the Chinese navy of carrying out "unprecedented" aggressive military exercises in the South China Sea, harassing both its fishermen (confiscating their boats and imposing a unilateral fishing ban to restore deteriorating fish stocks[120]) and legitimate oil exploration activities (cutting seismic survey cables, demanding such exploration cease, etc.). Furthermore, according to Hanoi, Beijing put pressure on a number of foreign energy companies which has exploration and production joint ventures in the region, such as Exxon Mobil, Chevron, Shell, and BP, not to do deals with other countries at the risk of having their business opportunities in China curtailed.[121]

Against this background, the US was quick to extend the hand of friendship to its hitherto estranged partner, Vietnam, and its neighbours. At the annual ASEAN Regional Forum (Asian security forum) in Hanoi in July 2010, then Secretary of State, Hillary Clinton vocalised traditional post-war US geopolitical position that "freedom of navigation and unimpeded lawful commerce" in the South China Sea was part of her country's "national interest" and "pivotal to regional stability".[122] At the same time, Washington claimed to have *no* position on the territorial dispute, again offering itself as neutral peace-broker before ordering in the *USNS Impeccable* to patrol the waters. Beijing condemned the intervention as both provocative and illegal, meanwhile, the Pentagon faced numerous "aggressive actions" by Chinese vessels (e.g. fishing trawlers, merchant ships, and government frigates).

The US then launched what Douglas Paal of the Washington think-tank, Carnegie Endowment described as "the most comprehensive burst of diplomatic and military activity in Asia, particularly South-East Asia in decades",[123] provoking an angry reaction by China's Secretary of State, Yang Jiechi, accusing the US of plotting against it and warned Washington of the risks it was running by 'internationalising' what

Beijing considered bilateral matters.[124] Beijing was even more livid when 12 of the 27 countries (including Indonesia, Malaysia, Taiwan, Vietnam, Brunei, and the Philippines) openly expressed their support for US intervention, while Hanoi and Washington increased two-way trade and investment and embarked on what Robert Gates, US Defense Secretary described as "real bilateral defense relationship" in order to "confront the most important security challenges in the region".[125]

Beijing denied it threatened free navigation and open trade in the South China Sea, citing the fact that over 40,000 vessels passed through one of the world's busiest shipping lanes each year. Liu Feitao at the Chinese Institute of International Studies, countered that Washington had been carrying out military surveillance activities in the South China Sea for years, and that the "freedom of navigation" referred to was merely the "freedom of the U.S. military to threaten our country".[126] More diplomatically, Liang Guanglie, the PRC's Defence Minister, reiterated that "China pursues a defense policy that is defensive in nature" and that its recent military build-up "was not aimed at challenging or threatening anyone but to ensure its security and promote international and regional peace and security".[127]

Significantly, Obama's trip to India was the first stop of his ten-day, unsubtly titled, "tour of Asian *democracies*", taking in Japan, South Korea, and Indonesia. "The primary purpose" of this journey, according to the White House was to gain access to "some of the fastest growing markets in the world" which was "an important part of the President's National Export Initiative" to double US exports over the next five years.[128] Yet this explanation deliberately obscured the essential geopolitical objectives of the trip. The "underlying focus of the grand tour", this "celebration of Asia's liberal bastion", *Time* magazine noted, was the "dragon in the room".[129] The tenser the situation in the Asia-Pacific region, the more the US could exercise intellectual moral leadership and reassert itself. "The most common thing that Asian leaders have said to me in my travels over the last 20 months", claimed Hillary Clinton, on the verge of embarking on her own two-week seven-country tour of the Asia-Pacific Rimland," was "Thank you, we're so glad that you're playing an active role in Asia again".[130]

To try and resolve the South China Sea territorial dispute, the UN Commission on the Limits of the Continental Shelf's requested in 2013 that all nations file formal claims to extend continental shelves beyond those established by the UNCLOS, that is 200 nautical miles, by the end of the year,[131] Beijing declared the bulk of the South China Sea as constituting its Exclusive Economic Zone (EEZ) – considered a "core interest" (on a par with Taiwan, Tibet, and Xinjiang). When the UN's International Tribunal for the Law of the Sea (under UNCLOS) ruled in July 2016 that there was no legal basis for 85% of China's claim over the South China Sea, Beijing refused to accept the ruling, pressing ahead with land reclamation (constructing artificial islets) and building civilian and military infrastructure on and around the disputed territory.

As the NSS-2017 indicates, the Trump administration remains just as opposed to China's A2/AD (and in favour of a "free and open Indo-Pacific"), engaging in regular fly-overs and sending vessels close to the disputed islands and insisting there can be no construction on Scarborough Shoal. When it came to light in May 2018 that China had: (1) installed anti-ship and surface-to-air missiles on three islands on the Spratly archipelago; (2) engaged in its largest-ever naval review in the region; and (3) landed several bombers on the Paracels, Washington reacted angrily, Defense Secretary James Mattias warning of "larger consequences" if Beijing continued with its maritime militarisation programme.[132] As a reaction to the rising tensions in the South China Sea, there was even talk in 2017 about reviving the Quadrilateral Security Dialogue between the US, Japan, Australia, and India[133] to discuss the 'Indo-Pacific security (and even the establishment of joint regional infrastructural projects to rival the BRI). Indeed, the US's Asian 'empire of bases' runs from Japan, South Korea to India, taking in Singapore, Guam, Indonesia, Thailand, Vietnam, Australia, and has talked about installing an Asian Missile System.

Beijing, evidently, is deeply unhappy about present security arrangements across the Asia Pacific, based upon hub-and-spokes bilateral deals with the US, with Xi calling for more 'Asia-for-Asia' agreements. In a January 2017 White Paper on China's policy on Asian-Pacific security, for example, it made it very clear that greater regional integration demanded parallel regional security arrangements,[134] a new 'Asia security architecture', such as the SCO: a natural security umbrella for the BRI.

To date, the PRC has avoided direct military conflict as a means to resolve the various islands disputes in the East China and South China Sea – exemplified by its reaction following Japan's nationalisation of the Senkakus – preferring to either use its coastguards or 'maritime militias' to harangue intruders (rather than mobilising the PLA Navy) or chose economic and political sanction. For the medium term this makes sense. Despite increased defence expenditure, the 'string of pearls' strategy, and the ongoing terraforming efforts in, and militarisation of, the South China Sea, the PRC is a long way from challenging to US naval supremacy in Asia-Pacific. Furthermore, the CPC elite are well aware that the more volatile the political/military situation in East Asia, the greater the threat to its economy growth model and any aspirations it might have of exercising 'intellectual and moral leadership' (*en route* to hegemony) in the region. Reacting too forcefully to Japan, for example, would risk driving them further into the US camp and possibly to seek nuclear weapons.

But the problem for the US is that while it may maintain its politico-military dominance over Asian powers for the foreseeable future, China, as we have seen, is increasingly exercising regional hegemony corresponding to Gramsci's the *first* and *second moments* as countries get sucked into the PRC's regime of accumulation, becoming their principal trading partner, export destination and source of FDI (tantamount to 'renminbi diplomacy'). Over the long-term, it is reasonable to assume that political allegiances too will shift.

Indicative of this is Philippines' recent *volte-face* under the premiership of Rodrigo Duterte. Having being the country that denounced China's maritime border policy under the UNCLOS, Manila subsequently decided not to apply the UN's International Tribunal for the Law of the Sea's favourable decision, finding the carrots (market access, possible joint gas exploration, and BRI-connected infrastructure projects) and sticks (trade restrictions) offered by Beijing either too succulent or too dangerous to ignore. Malaysia too has decided not to ignore the tribunal's decision, coincidently being the site of massive Chinese infrastructural development (e.g. rail links and Malacca deep sea port) as part of the BRI. Right across the Asia Pacific region, Chinas' economic magnet is similarly shaping bourgeois opinion and reshaping the state policy. Symptomatic of this, at the 31st ASEAN conference in Manila in November 2017, members agreed to negotiate what appears to be a non-binding Code of Conduct with the PRC in regard to the South China Sea controversy, which suits Beijing fine.

Military hegemony ultimately must be underwritten by economic hegemony. For 110 years, the US has been the no.1 manufacturing nation by output; replaced by China in 2010. And although production in the US tends to be more capital/technology-rich and of higher value-added content, the PRC's state-led "Made in China 2025" aims to reduce this difference (and therein avoiding the 'middle country trap'), innovating and upgrading manufacturing in ten key sectors,[135] and converting the country into leading manufacturer of telecommunication, railways, and electric power – and ranking second or third in robotics, high-end automation, and new energy vehicles industries – by the date indicated.[136]

Historically, military dominance not backed up with productive superiority has proven unsustainable: Paul Kennedy's 'imperial overstretch' paradigm. For the medium-term, the US may well continue to dominate the financial, service, and cultural sectors. But it is reasonable to assume that as competition rises and Wall Street's dominance diminishes so too will the attractiveness of US TBs for foreign investors, who in July 2018 held $6.2 trillion, $1.2 trillion of which corresponded to mainland China.[137] This would complicate considerably Washington's financing of its 'empire of bases' (estimated to stand at over 800 military installations worldwide). As Sino-US hegemonic rivalry intensifies and Chinese corporations become less dependent on the American market, Beijing may be less likely to payroll its jailer.

But while the struggle for world hegemony 'status' may manifest itself in inter-state/bourgeois competition, as Gramsci remind us it is ultimately always material-based, driven by social forces emerging out of the HB, embedded in a particular 'state-society complex' (albeit always dialectically interacting with global social forces). Whether China is able to 'challenge' the US for world hegemony, will depend upon it being able to 'create a world in its own image': exercising not just economic, political, and militarily, but also cultural hegemony. In order to assess that likelihood and how it affects American hegemony in the 21st century (see Conclusion), it is fitting to end this chapter with a brief analysis of the dynamics of the PRC's on-going 'passive revolution'.

Dynamics of China's Passive Revolution

We have argued throughout this book that capitalism is necessarily expansive, seeking to break down all limitations to accumulation, but develops unevenly, reflected in and reproduced by, a competitive hierarchically structured inter-state system. Countries must assimilate new production systems and techniques or face the consequences. In most advanced countries, this process of social restructuring is driven by the private sector, with a supporting role by the state. But where the domestic bourgeois class is too weak to execute such changes (i.e. does not enjoy hegemony), Gramsci tells us, it is left to the 'state class' to direct proceedings in the form of a top-down, 'passive revolution'.[138] This has been the case with PRC. Driven on by the need to 'catch up' with its Asian neighbours, but lacking a capitalist class to carry it out it has been the task of the CPC elites to restructure underlying SROP and shape the new economic growth model from the late 1970s onwards.[139]

The first stage of Deng's 'opening up' (1978–92), as alluded to, involved setting up purposely-built *Special Economic Zones* (SEZ) along the southern seaboard (initially in the Guangdong and Fujian provinces) where foreign investors were invited to establish low-end labour-intensive manufacturing operations for export to the West. China received foreign capital, new technology, the latest production/management and critically, access to global markets, in return foreign corporations would enjoy a range of tax and profit-repatriation benefits, suffer little direct political interference in their affairs and, most importantly of all, be free to tap into the world's cheapest, most abundant, and productive labour force. Significantly, the bulk of this 'foreign' investment (and remaining true to this day) came overseas Chinese in Hong Kong, Macau, and Taiwan[140] (and to a lesser extent Singapore and Malaysia), the so-called *bamboo network*. Indeed, Guangdong and Fujian were chosen, not only because they were on the coast and far from political life (Beijing), they just happened to be adjacent to said 'overseas territories', respectively.

Apart from access to foreign markets and strict control over the monetary and financial system – notably a competitive fixed exchange against the dollar – this neo-mercantilist ADS model required a constant supply

of cheap labour which was only made possible by a deep structural reform of SROP right across the country. Rural areas were amongst the
first to experience the discipline of the market. Under the new *household
responsibility system*, control of the land and associated surplus passed
from Maoist era communes towards families. Peasant households were
given long-term leases on communal land and encouraged to make their
own produce and sell their surpluses at free market prices. Though initiated amongst the peasantry by 1983 more than 93% of producers were
involved.[141] Rural areas also witnessed the rise of *town and village enterprises* (TVE): public, market-orientated manufacturing enterprises.
The Constitution of December 1982 allowed newly created township and
village governments to take the communes' industrial assets and turn
them into TVEs. These were then expected to operate for the benefit of
village life: supporting agriculture, providing infrastructure, and generating employment.

Political decentralisation played/plays a crucial role in embedding
capitalist social relations. From the outset, the central state would retain overall political and economic direction – including control over the
SOEs – but an important degree of fiscal and political autonomy (not
to mention competence over property rights), would be delegated to the
provincial, county, and local governments. With the slashing of central
government revenue/spending[142] local governments' revenue became
almost entirely dependent on local taxes, especially business taxes and
rents, leases, and transaction fees on a landed property (see below). Since
cadres would be evaluated on the basis of their localities' economic performance, this greatly increased inter- and intra-provincial competition
for capital, both domestic and foreign, and the expansion of TVEs.[143] As
a result, and thanks to later state bank loans, large foreign capital injec-
tions, and a symbiotic relationship with SOEs, TVEs which constituted
the most dynamic sector of the Chinese economy from the mid-1980s
to the mid-1990s, creating millions of non-agricultural jobs for rural
workers.

Market exchange also began to creep into the central planning system.
The SOEs continued to be owned by the state and run according to broad
socialist production relations but since managers were legally liable for
the companies' profits and losses, they were given greater autonomy on
how to run their firms and allowed to retain a certain proportion of the
profits generated and sell any surplus they produced over their planned
targets at free market prices, without enjoying property rights.

In general, however, during this first stage of its transition, the Chinese
economy would retain much of its non-capitalist nature, a testimony to
the relative weakness of the bourgeois class. In both state-owned and collective enterprises, the Maoist 'work units', or *danwei*,[144] were retained,
although Beijing did introduce new labour laws in the 1980s which introduced new flexibility into the proto-labour market (e.g. allowing the

easier hiring and firing of workers, removing wage controls, and reducing state benefits). Public-sector enterprises, for their part, remained 'social enterprises'; private TVEs had to be owned collectively; de-collectivised land still belonged to the village, and associated use rights enjoyed by peasant families.

China's definitive step towards a full (albeit nuanced) capitalist economy and began in spring 1992, with the aim of 'catch up' with the 'four little dragons of Asia' in 20 years. There was nothing wrong in the rich getting richer, Deng explained, as long as higher taxes were paid and redistribution to poorer areas took place. "One of my one biggest mistakes", he lamented, "was leaving out Shanghai when we launched our special economic zones.[145] That would be soon rectified, extending SEZs to the north and eastward most crucially to Shanghai, the Yangtze River Delta, the Pearl River Delta, and Pudong New Area. At the XIV Congress of the CPC in October 1992, the PRC was officially proclaimed as a "socialist market economy". With the confirmation of Zemin as Secretary General of the Communist Party, China embarked on its second and most profoundly neoliberal stage of transition,[146] marked by a deeper integration into the international value chain and division of labour. To support its export industry, Beijing devalued the yuan by 33% in January 1994, before fixing it at a rate of 8.28 to the dollar the following April.[147]

As already mentioned, China's ADS model differed from previous models – notably Japan, South Korea, and Taiwan – adopting a more welcoming attitude towards FDI: by 2000 almost 30% of Chinese manufacturing was carried out by joint ventures.[148] This tendency was enhanced still further when, after 15 years of negotiations, the PRC was accepted as a member of that very symbol of neoliberal orthodoxy, the WTO, surpassing the US as the world's largest FDI recipient in 2003,[149] although increasingly these figures were being inflated by Chinese SOEs on the mainland 'round tripping' to take advantage of tax rebates offered to foreign investors.[150]

But while FDI was vital for modernisation and exports, it is important to emphasise that it actually accounted for *less than 10%* of total capital formation during the reform era; as Clyde Prestowitz notes, "if the foreigners were investing it was only because the Chinese were investing more",[151] not least on the construction of roads, railway networks, ports, and dams. This fact is often overlooked due to the biases within liberal theory, which typically overstates the importance of international *trade* while underplaying the significance of domestic *production*.

China's fabulously successful export-driven growth model was only the tip of an exploitative iceberg which had its origins in the *primitive accumulation* first initiated by Deng aforementioned land and fiscal reforms.[152] Indeed, despite their differing spatio-temporal, socio-economic, and politico-cultural contexts there do appear some striking similarities between the process of primitive accumulation initiated in 1978, and the transition to capitalism in Western Europe, North America, Latin America, and Asia: all involving, to a greater or lesser extent, the *commodification* of land and labour (not to mention the natural world in general), together with growing urbanisation.

The commodification of *land* in China began in the 1980s connected to spectacular urban growth around the SEZs in the South in Shenzhen, Guangzhou, and Dongguan and medium-sized TVEs in the Yangtze River and Pearl River Deltas. Beijing consciously promoted urban development in large cities/metropolises as a key vehicle of economic transition at the expense of the countryside, introducing a whole range of policy initiatives and fiscal and monetary measures to transfer resources from the agricultural to the industrial sector.[153]

Urban development, other advanced capitalist countries had demonstrated, not only created employment and dramatically increased GDP, but a thriving real estate market, specifically private housing, helped to generate a genuine *mass* consumer society. This commodification of urban land greatly augmented following further fiscal reforms (1994), allowing urban residents to purchase their own homes (1995), and the privatising of *danwei* housing (1999). Once a mortgage market was created, home ownership rose sharply, creating a huge property boom in the big northern and central coast cities as the upper-middle classes moved into exclusively gated suburbs and the transient poor into rented older houses or subleased from established tenants.[154] Beijing, Shanghai, Chongqing, and Tianjin, particularly were granted considerable autonomy regarding urban development, permitted to annex nearby territory (including small cities), and clearing large sectors of their cities for development.

But where this urban development process was most acutely felt was at the local level which resembled the Wild West. Thanks to the 'land fiscal policies' local governments (be it at the municipal, provincial, or county level) were given every incentive to convert themselves into profit-orientated real estate dealers, seizing nominally public terrain, often for little compensation, and leasing/selling to the highest bidders, or using it as collateral bank loans to finance a multitude of public projects. And as vast areas of land were forcibly vacated to make way for industrial parks, factories, infrastructure projects, transport networks, property development, etc., millions of people were displaced.[155] Although this real estate bonanza did benefit some peasant farmers, needless to say the main beneficiaries were very wealthy: a new powerful class of property developers, construction companies, large agribusinesses, banks and government administrators, and CPC officials.[156] The size of the market was further greatly expanded in the autumn of 2008 when the CPC Central Committee authorised the sale of land by individual households.

Much of the initial commodification of *labour* occurred following the large-scale privatisation of the smaller/inefficient SOEs from the early 1990s onwards, intensified with further market reform, deregulation, and the second wave of privatisations coinciding with China's WTO bid. The PRC, unlike the Asian Tigers before it, was undergoing its economic transition during the post-Cold War *globalization* age. Domestic firms now faced fierce competition from their larger and more advanced Western and Japanese counterparts, complicating the nurturing of infant industries. Unprofitable SOEs could face the axe. Others, in the name of efficiency, were allowed to merge, downsize, or rescind their obligations of providing workers required their social welfare benefits.[157] By the early 2000s, restructuring had reduced the number of people working for the SOEs by some 30–40 million people, many of which were left jobless, without redundancy payment, or health and welfare coverage.[158] The industrial damage did not end there, however. The fate of the TVEs was intrinsically linked to that of the SOEs to whom they became subcontractors. So, when the SOEs hit a rough patch so did the TVEs, making millions more rural workers unemployed.[159] Added to that an estimated 80 million peasants and 50 million farmers who had their property commandeered, often with little, compensation during the aforementioned 'land grab'.[160]

Driven by unemployment or the desire to improve their quality of life, millions of workers left their *danwei* and hence *hukou* (official place of residence), travelling hundreds of kilometres to the expanding urban industrial centres around the Pearl River Delta (Guangdong), the Yangtze River Delta (Shanghai region), and the Yellow River Valley (Beijing-Tianjin). Still legally bound to their *hukou*, where their social and political rights are guaranteed (access to health care, pension scheme, and education system, right to vote, etc.) these people are disenfranchised and treated as illegal immigrants. At the end of 2017, there were an estimated 287 million rural migrant workers living in the cities;[161] a mobile 'reserve army' of labour prepared to the toughest, lowest-paid jobs while being denied the formal work contracts, education, and basic health services enjoyed by their urban counterparts.

The basis of the 'Chinese miracle' and status as 'workshop of the world' outlined earlier ultimately would depend on a highly efficient system of extracting surplus-value from a seemingly limitless inexpensive domestic labour force who, separated from their means of production – and service-providing *danwei* – had no choice but to spend a substantial part of their wages on consumer goods and services, augmenting domestic demand.

Despite this major social upheaval, the state class made sure that the 'passive revolution' would avoid the mistakes made by other 'transition economies' throughout Latin America, Eastern Europe, and East Asia. The route to neoliberalism would be gradual. There would be no foolhardy Washington Consensus-sanctioned cut-price sell off of the nation's assets to foreigners, or other such 'shock therapy' recommendations such as capital account liberalisation. Rather Beijing insisted on retaining a controlling interest over the largest SOEs and most strategic sectors – the 'commanding heights' of Chinese capital accumulation – notably in telecommunications, banking and financial services, infrastructure construction, steel, energy and raw materials, and armament industries. Nonetheless, and although the directors were hand-picked by the Politburo to ensure political consistency, these SOEs were restructured to conform to a 'corporate' model: the executives answerable to a board of directors and their assets listed on public stock exchanges (albeit with non-residents subjected to certain trading). As profitability remained the primary goal, more and more of SOE business was outsourced to the private sector. A similar arrangement occurred at the regional level where public-sector assets (belonging to the state or to the local/provincial governments) were invested in otherwise privatised corporate-run enterprises.

Thanks to these processes by the late 1990s Chinese society was beset by growing wealth disparity with a *nouveau riche* occupying the pinnacle of the pyramid. Made up of the upper echelons of the CPC, their families/friends and well-connected private individuals, these were the best situated to take advantage of national and international contacts to take advantage of the land seizures, property development, privatisations, technology parks, export industries, or expanding domestic consumer market.[162]

As a result of the party elites' growing involvement in private businesses/corporatised SOEs ("embourgeoisement of cadres") and role a guardian/backer of particular private businesses ("patronisation of capitalists"), it was becoming appropriate, according to Alvin Y So, to talk of a "hybrid cadre-capitalist class". A cadre-capitalist class, So claims, which began, in Marxist terms, to consciously act as a 'class-for-itself', calling for constitutional reform and greater political representation to expand their class interests.[163] That some of the most vehement supporters of the continuance of a communist regime would be the richest of capitalists remained one of modern China's enduring paradoxes.

The problem was that while many capitalists had joined the CPC and participated in various governing councils, their *formal* integration into the ruling HB lacked both legal and ideological justification for many years, endangering both their private property and on-going business activities. Although the 3rd amendment to the Chinese constitution in 1999 upgraded the private sector from a "complement to the socialist public sector of the economy" to "an important component" of the country's "socialist market economy" (Article 16),[164] the re-writing of official state policy did not occur till the launching of Premier Jiang Zemin's *Three Represents.*

According to Zemin, the CPC still enjoyed a pivotal role in the modernisation of the PRC because it represented three key constituencies: "the fundamental interests of the greatest majority of people" (the general public); "the direction of advanced culture" (intellectuals and technical experts); and pointedly, "the development of advanced social production forces" (referring to the new capitalists/entrepreneurs), whose membership of the Party was formally sanctioned.[165]

In this Orwellian "Doublethink" world, the restoration of capitalism found its justification in Marxist theory. References to class and class struggle were removed from official CPC doctrine, 'capitalism' was no longer analogous to 'exploitation', while entrepreneurs were classified as "workers who have changed their jobs" or "special type of risk-taking worker". 'Organic intellectuals' at Chinese universities such as Renmin University of China, Peking University, Fudan University, Nankai University, and Nanjing University, explained that turning SOEs into 'efficient' joint-stock corporations, was in keeping with Marx and Engel's insistence on the need to 'socialise ownership of production'. It was not the 'nature of ownership' (e.g. public or private) that determined whether a country was capitalist or socialist, the CPC intellectuals argued. As if to reiterate the point, senior cadre followed their Western counterparts in being converted into board members of companies they had just privatised.

Seemingly counter-intuitively, the constitutional recognition of capitalism gave a huge boost to the *Communist* Party of China. But on the other hand, it made perfect sense given the omnipresence of the state party; entrepreneurs needed to nurturing connections inside the political establishment, finding a 'patron' at the national or local party level to help them navigate through the complex bureaucracy, win contracts and gain access to state-controlled credit, resources and markets, and importantly whether or not to enforce existing legislation, since "relationships are the law".[166] And the more capitalist incentives were institutionalised into the internal workings of the CPC – officials' promotion and salaries depending on meeting productivity, profit, investment, or employment targets – the tighter the cadre-capitalist class relationship, with senior public-sector managers and technicians abandoning their modest apartments in the *hukou* to join their capitalist class counterparts in the suburban gated communities and luxury high-rises that mushroomed in China's major cities.

It was only a question of time before China's super-wealthy began to appear on the *Forbes* rich list. The magazine maintained that by 2018 mainland PRC (i.e. not including Hong Kong) had 373 dollar-billionaires, the second highest number in the world, after the US with 578 (of a global total of 2,208).[167] The *Hurun Rich List* went even further, inverting the relationship, albeit looking at Greater China. It estimated the actual number of billionaires in the PRC in 2018 closer to 819 (32% of the total of 2,694), adding four new ones every week, and more than 40% greater than the US's 571.[168] Moreover, even a conservative estimate would indicate there are at least another 1.13 million individuals on the mainland with $1 million assets (measured at market value).[169] New professions began to spring up to defend the wealthy, exemplified with the dramatic expansion of law firms and private security companies, while a new Private Property Law was adopted in a huge margin by the National People's Congress (NPC) on 16th March 2007; 99.1% of the country's 2,889 legislators voting in favour of authorising the creation, transfer and ownership of property (state, collective, and private) on the PRC mainland.[170]

Below this ultra-wealthy is a burgeoning middle class of small businessmen (employing less than ten people), middle and high-level civil servants, managers, lawyers, consultants, technicians, etc. many of which provide services to the very wealthy or corporate sector and have links to the CPC.[171] Since the turn of the millennium, this group has been engaging in 'conspicuous consumption' for the first time, acquiring televisions, mobile phones, domestic electrical appliances, computers, and even cars. Apart from the aforementioned universities and educational institutions, the cultural *bourgeoisification* of Chinese society was reflected and reproduced the official media,[172] publishers,[173] private clubs, and societies (e.g. chambers of commerce, leisure clubs, property-owners committees, NGOs, etc.)

Evidently, not everyone had benefitted from the reforms to the same extent. While the scale of its poverty reduction programme is extremely impressive (reaching the UN Millennium Development Goals by 2015) neoliberal reform, predictably, has also manifested itself in a dramatic rise in inequality. In 1980, China's Gini coefficient (income inequality measurement) stood at 0.28, one of the lowest in the world, but hitting 0.50 in 2013 (0.4 considered 'severe') according to the IMF,[174] with the PRC's *National Bureau of Statistics* putting it around 0.465 for 2016 (on a par with the US's 0.479), with the poorest 25% of mainland households holding just 1% of the aggregate wealth, compared to the 1% who owned a third.[175] Nor did that tell the whole story.

The statistics leave out an important large part of the Chinese economy – the undeclared black economy – thought to stand around at 30% of the country's GDP and of which the main beneficiaries (via bribery and corruption) are the richest 10% of the population.[176] Nor did they record the loss of goods and services (e.g. subsidised housing, utilities, foodstuffs, household necessities, healthcare, pensions, and education), peasants and workers used to enjoy free of charge from their *danwei* (as part of the *hukou* system) before rural reform, collapse of TVEs, the privatisation of SOEs, or voluntary migration.

Added to that hospitals were privatised in the 1990s, for example, it meant basic healthcare was beyond the reach of the lower classes, resulting in widespread public unrest at the exorbitant costs of treatment costs. In 2000, the World Health Organisation ranked countries according to the effectiveness and equity of their respective health systems (the last time it would do so) placing the PRC in position 144 out of 191 (below Kenya, Haiti, and Sudan),[177] leaving around 40% of sick people to go untreated and with only 10% with health insurance cover.[178] No doubt things have improved considerably since then, but according to the UN Development Programme's "Human Development Report 2016" China ranked at position 90 (out of 188 countries) – medium developed country – on the Human Development Index, measuring life expectancy, literacy, education, and standards of living.[179]

Herein lay the CPS's Achilles' heel, of course. The *People's* Republic of China claimed to be Maoist/Marxist-inspired workers' state and led by a *communist* party in the interests of the workers and peasants who supposedly controlled the *means of production*. While 40 years of reforms had managed to largely eradicate Maoist ideals of the commune, revolution, collectivism, solidarity, egalitarianism, and social justice amongst all but the elderly and most politicised, *liberal hegemony* had yet to be imposed.

Capital accumulation was seen in less idealistic and more coercive terms in China than in the West, where euphemisms such as the 'market' constituted 'common sense'. Indeed, American myths such as the 'self-made-man', the 'American Dream', and the virtues of 'trickle-down' economics, had no equivalent in the PRC. The *nouveau-riche* were commonly judged to have amassed their wealth through exploitation, the illicit appropriation of public assets, political connections (*guanxi*) or corruption, rather than talent or hard work. Widespread *fen fu* ('resentment towards the rich') amongst the population[180] fed into subaltern anger over increasing inequality, low wages/poor working conditions, loss of entitlements, disenfranchisement, and their own personal circumstances (e.g. forced eviction and land seizures, loss of entitlement, disenfranchisement) and expressed itself in class conflict.

As neoliberal have deepened Beijing has become more concerned that hitherto sporadic, spontaneous, and uncoordinated protests from the subaltern classes could consolidate into a genuine popular movement, in possession of a 'collective will'. While commonly resorting to coercive means to deal with political protests and social unrest, including resorting to detainment without trial, brutal *laojiao* ("re-education through labour") and even the death penalty, the CPC leadership learnt from the demise of the USSR that even long-serving one-party regimes still needed to enjoy a degree of legitimacy amongst the public.

Beijing has adhered to classic *trasformismo* techniques to nurture subaltern consent, granting them minimal concessions, while seeking to assimilate them into their neoliberal hegemonic project. Increasingly the State Council would manage internal political by wrapping up reforms in liberal democratic rhetoric.

This was most clearly demonstrated by the 'institutionalising' labour relations which appeared to assimilate workers' demands for greater legal transparency over workers' rights ('rule of law') but in effect reinforced the CPC's regulating capacity ('rule *by* law'), a type of "authoritarian legality,"[181] behind an impersonal legalistic bureaucratic smokescreen based on abstract legal norms. Such codification aimed to *depoliticise* industrial relations and avert political opposition away from Beijing since the implementation of this law was cleverly delegated to the local level.[182]

The process began with the 1993 "Regulation of the Handling of Labour Disputes" (regarding the legal procedures for local level arbitration and civil court litigation) and then more broadly with the introduction of the PRC's first "Labour Law" in 1995, covering areas such as labour contracts and dispute resolution. The Constitution was amended in 1999 referring specifically to "ruling the country by law" (*yifazhiguo*) in its Article 5. In principle, there now existed a legal basis for the mediation of labour-capital relations. Over time, further Labour Laws were introduced, while adhering to the established template: shunning any reference to exploitation, class struggle or indeed class *per se*, while codifying abstract workers' rights as individuals, rather than collectively. In addition, workers were also now free to joining unions but only those within the officially sanctioned vertical trade-union group – the *All-China Federation of Trade Unions* (ACFTU) – whose task as a 'business union' was to enforce the new capitalist regime: collude with company managers and local government against workers' interests; guarantee that the latter's demands always remained within the parameters set by the CPC; and prevent a genuine independent trade union movement developing 'from below'.[183]

However weak, the new laws did constitute some form of institutional basis for the defence of labour rights vis-à-vis capital, leading to a dramatic increase in the number of cases brought before municipal courts. But since local judges were drawn from the cadre-capitalist class their interpretation of the law was usually favourable to business, which was a contributory factor in the dramatic rise in subaltern class militancy.[184] Between 1990 and 2008, the PRC witnessed some of the world's largest mass demonstrations. Though reliable statistics are difficult to come by, the number of these denominated 'mass incidents' are thought to have risen from 8,700 a year in 1993, 74,000 in 2004, 90,000 in 2006, to around 127,000 in 2008.[185]

Rising class conflict caused a reshaping of the 'passive revolution'. According to Cheng Li, this coincided with shift of power within the seven-member Politburo Standing Committee away from Jiang Zemin and Zeng Qinghong – the so-called *Shanghai gang* 'elitists'– towards the *Tuanpai* 'popularists' – enjoying greater support amongst rank-and-fine CPC members and the Communist Youth League, represented by leaders Hu Jintao and Wen Jiabao (elected the new President/CPC Secretary and Prime Minister, respectively, in November 2002).[186]

CPC official discourse adopted a more conciliatory position towards labour, talking of the need to mitigate the social consequences of rapid marketisation, and building a "harmonious society". Continuing the *trasformismo* process, emphasis was now placed on the *third* of Jiang Zemin's "Represents", the general public (i.e. the workers), and not just the *first* (the new bourgeoisie), insisting on modifying the economic growth model to redistribute the wealth more fairly from the rich to the poor, from coastal to inland regions and critically, from urban to rural areas, where communities had seen their both their livelihoods/rights disappear and populations heading for the cities. At the annual NPC meeting in March 2006, Wen Jiabao inaugurated "a new socialist coun-tryside", promising new investments for rural areas and cultivated areas and changes in the tax system to favour rural farmers and peasants.[187] Advancements in industrial relations were also announced. Despite 18 months of vociferous lobbying from domestic and foreign companies and business organisations (with the American Chamber of Commerce at the forefront), the NPC's Standing Committee of the NPC launched a new *Labour Contract Law* (LCL) in January 2008, standardising the estab-lishment, performance, variation, and termination of labour contracts.

Under the new Labour Laws employers had to (with a few exceptions) offer their workers written contracts (LCL, article 10); pay their work-ers in full and on time (LCL, article 30); and refrain from forcing work-ers to do overtime (LCL, article 31) or perform dangerous operations (LCL, article 31). The parts that particularly angered employer groups were articles 4 (LCL), which made the employers consult with employee representation with regards to variations in working conditions, and ar-ticles 37–47 (LCL), regarding the discharge and termination of labour contracts.[188]

Certainly, the LCL left many loop-holes enabling employers to deny their employees said benefits. Many of the rights recognised, notably those regarding redundancy payments, for example, depended on the type of contracts offered, be they 'fixed', 'continuing', or 'project' (arti-cles 13–15). Nor was it made clear just what the correlative remedial or penalty provisions were in the case of non-fulfilment of obligations. And crucially, there was no recognition of the right to strike. But once again, whether employers, local/state officials or the ACFTU actually took the new LCL seriously or not, workers did. As the GFC hit many sought to exercise their newly codified rights. In 2008, there was a massive increase in the number of labour disputes going to mediation – nearly 700,000, almost double that of 2007 – while the number of labour cases in civil courts (where workers can appeal arbitration committees' decisions) stood at 280,000, a rise of 94% on the previous year.[189]

Nor were workers actions confined to legal conduits, frustrated as they were by the gulf between formally protected rights and the reality. As a result, the next two years saw a huge upsurge in the number of labour mobilisations, with 2010 being especially active. In the spring of that year, a number of high-profile strikes hit the international headlines. The most significant of these took place at the 400,000-strong live-in Longhua

Science and Technology Park plant of the Taiwan-owned Foxconn Electronics, the world's largest contractor of electronics manufacturers[190] where, sparked by the fourth suicide in two weeks, workers protested against declining real wages, and the slave-like working and living conditions. The Foxconn case not only alerted the world's public to the true scale of scientific labour exploitation in China and how integral said exploitation was to rich countries' technology and consumer requirements, it produced a domino effect of 'non-official' strikes at other foreign-owned MNCs first at Honda and then a plethora of other auto supply and electronics factories throughout the Pearl River Delta, the most high profile perhaps being the Toyota-related components factory in Tianjin.[191]

Beijing's relative *laissez-faire* approach to the unrest at the foreign MNCs in 2010, together with atypically benevolent coverage by state-run media (e.g. *Xinhua*) seemed to suggest that the CPC elite harboured certain sympathy for the workers' cause.[192] Two years earlier it also denounced the virtual slave labour conditions endured by many workers (many of them children) in the brick kilns and coal mines of the Shanxi and Henan provinces and uncovered a child labour ring in Dongguan City (Guangdong). From Li's perspective, as noted, this could be attributable to the ascendency of the *Tuanpai* faction within the Politburo Standing Committee: institutionalising collective wage consultation and protecting workers legal rights was conducive to Hu Jintao's 'harmonious society' objective.

But apart from attempting to assimilate subaltern class demands within an on-going process of *trasformismo,* improved higher wages – though opposed by capital – would help serve a longer-term objective recognised as vital by many CPC elites: the nurturing of the domestic market following the GFC.

Beijing's immediate response to the US subprime crisis was to resort to old-style Keynesian deficit spending, ordering state banks to loan out 4 trillion yuan (then $586 billion) to finance massive infrastructure and transportation projects and diverse social programmes, amounting to a 50% expansion of money supply (M2) in two years. In effect, the State Council was attempting to compensate the loss of exports by expanding investment-led growth at home. As we have seen, local governments had already started to nurture a property market since the mid-1990s. Now, with easier access to state-bank credit, this boom reached epic proportions as dozens of cities competed amongst themselves to complete massive infrastructure, real estate and transportation projects (establishing the world's longest high-speed network), subways, and luxurious government complexes.[193] In 2011, *Barclay's Capital* estimated that over 40% of the world's skyscrapers due for completion in the following six years would be in China.[194]

Yet although blowing an infrastructure and real estate bubble proved highly profitable for corporations, even surpassing foreign trade as the single biggest contributor to the PRC's GDP, Western media began to express concern over the economic sustainability of the growth model, not least the debt situation.[195] Although state media dismissed such claims as exaggerations,[196] the investment bubble was beginning to concern CPC elites.[197] Not only was it inflationary, harming the country's export industries and devaluing the population's wages and savings, speculation left housing unaffordable for the subaltern classes – especially in the first-tier cities such as Beijing, Guangzhou, Shenzhen, and Shanghai[198] – while encouraging a wave of enforced evictions for urban development. Public anger was expressed in tens of thousands of protests and riots, which added more fuel to the fire of the above labour mobilisations.[199] From January 2010 onwards, the State Council introduced a series of policy initiatives to deflate the real estate bubble,[200] announcing stricter laws to protect homeowners from eviction and promising to launch a subsidised housing programme while.[201] The price of property did start to fall from the summer of 2013.

The underlying problem for China was perennial over-production/capacity. We have seen throughout this chapter the role Beijing has played in encouraged SOEs to 'go global' from the GFC onwards, both to guarantee supplies of vital resources but also to crucially find new markets to dump their surplus value in. This would find its ultimate expression in the BRI projects. But the flip side of this overproduction, reflected in the reliance on foreign customers, the accumulation of billions of dollars worth of foreign reserves and real estate/infrastructure over-investment/speculation itself, was domestic *under-consumption* or *over-exploitation* (see Chapter 1).[202] Not only could capital extract surplus value from the labour process, but also thanks to job insecurity and limited welfare services – especially for those workers outside their *hukou* – was able to gain access to cheap credit, taking advantage of the population's unparalleled propensity to save.[203] Workers, meanwhile, saw their share of GDP/corporate profits, and savings steadily decline.

The CPC elite were aware that any ambitions it had of being a regional, let alone world hegemonic power would depend, first, on it moving up the international division of labour, and second, on the development of a powerful internal market, to become, Arrighi's model outlined in Chapter 1, a 'container of power' for capital. Indeed, it was in the concern for the need to stimulate global demand during the GFC world that Chinese workers' struggle found support in unusual quarters. Not traditionally renown as champions of labour rights and industrial action, the *Financial Times* defended "alienated Chinese workers" and their right "to fight back".[204] Similarly, *The Economist* celebrated that "pay and protest are on the rise", insisting that what the world needed now were consumers, not short-term corporate profits and over-investment, that just a 20% rise in Chinese consumption would translate into an extra $25 billion worth of American exports.[205] The need for China to consume more, the *New York Times* reported, was one of the key issues reiterated by US Vice-President Joe Biden Jr. when he met with Vice-President Xi Jinping in August 2011.[206]

At the annual NPC conference in March 2011, the Twelfth Five-Year Plan (2011–15) was approved, setting as a key objective to the abandonment of 'labour intensive' production towards a serviced-based, technologically intensive 'knowledge economy', and stressing the need to "enhance national creativity", and "arouse innovative spirit".[207] Simultaneously, it acknowledged that the present national economy was "unbalanced, uncoordinated, and unsustainable", recognising that development based upon domestic demand (rather than foreign consumers) not only made economic sense, but was the best way to achieve Hu's "harmonious society". The CPC prioritised increasing the Chinese population's "happiness".[208] Apart from strengthening the welfare state, guaranteeing affordable housing and tackling environmental degradation, the main focus was on sanctioning a fairer redistribution of wealth and empowering the consumer. The aim was to increase the disposable income of urban and rural residents by at least 7% – in line with the GDP growth target – and minimum wage rate by at least 13% over the following five years.[209]

Most autonomous coastal regions, such as Shanghai, Shenzhen, Guangdong, Zhejiang, Fujian, and Shandong, announced further 20%-plus minimum wage increases in the spring of 2011 (in addition to those announced in 2010); in 2013, a total of 27 regions raised their minimum wage by an average of 17%, seven provinces (amongst them Shanghai, Shenzhen, Tianjin, and Beijing, announced a further 12.5% increase in 2014.[210] It was not just 'bottom-up' pressure from labour militancy and 'top-down' pressure from domestic and international elites that was driving salaries up, demography also appeared to be playing a role. Incredulous as it may seem, given the country's population size, but more and more sources claimed an important factor behind the annual wage rises was a shortage of labour (especially skilled in urban areas). Thirty years of low birth rates (thanks to 'one-child policy'), a largely unreformed *hukou* household registration[211] (hindering labour mobility), and rural immigrants returning to their inland villages in Wuhan, Chengdu, Zhengzhou, Jincheng, and Taiyuan, it was argued, had led to labour shortages and hence wage rises along the East Coast and Pearl River Delta. Alarming both national and foreign companies alike have attempted to counter rising labour costs/militancy on the coast by moving their factories to inland provinces such as Ningxia Hui and Shanxi but even there wages have remained high, forced to steadily increase minimum wages to guarantee labour supplies. By the end of 2016, monthly wages had increased fourfold relative to 2005 reaching $834 compared to $384 in Mexico and $210 in Vietnam[212] while average factory wages had risen 64% in the five years.[213]

Apart from labour rights, two other key initiatives constituted part of the *trasformismo* strategy: low-level democracy and the 'war on corruption'.

Cosmetic steps taken to improve democratic accountability at the grassroots began in the 1980s, bestowing on citizens the right to vote, and a certain say in choosing candidates in village elections. The 1998 Organic Law on Villager's Committees asserted that elections had to be 'competitive' (i.e. more candidates than positions available) and, importantly, candidates could be 'independent' (i.e. did not have to belong to the CPC, but neither could they belong to any other another party). Multi-candidate elections were then extended to the county level, while an amendment to the Election Law in March 2010 granted equal representation in legislative bodies to rural and urban residents, thereby rectifying a long-established bias in favour of the latter.

These changes have largely been a smokescreen. At the village level, for example, there has been a sharp increase in independent candidates putting themselves forward since the late 1990s but they seldom manage to get voted in, often subject to insuperable official impediments and numerous personal attacks. The *real* purpose of these village elections, according to Landry, Davis, and Wang was to give Beijing a way to control local leaders and, if need be, wash their hands of inadequate/corrupt officials: more a clever way to perpetuate top-down authoritarian rule than anything else.[214]

Countering criticism the official line promoted by the state media is that 'socialism with Chinese characteristics' pays more attention to "substantial democracy" where all areas, ethnic groups, and classes were represented together, unlike Western-style elections/separation of powers or similar multi-party revolving door system, it claimed, which were little more than "game[s] for the rich".[215] Evidently, those rights recognised in the Chinese Constitution, including freedom of speech, association, and demonstration, etc. will never be honoured where they challenge the regime. Democracy, where it did exist, was strictly limited to spaces *within* the CPC.

Wen Jiabao spoke in Shenzhen in August 2010 (significantly from where Deng Xiaoping launched his reforms) acknowledging that the CPC had to protect rights, address corruption, and make the government more accountable in order to build a fairer, democratic, law-abiding society where even the most vulnerable citizens were protected. "If we don't push forward with reform", Wen Jiabao insisted in October of the same year, "the only road ahead is perdition" quoting Deng Xiaoping's words to conservatives in 1992. Similarly, in a CNN interview, the Prime Minister proclaimed, "freedom of speech is indispensable for any country" and "the people's wishes and needs for democracy and freedom are irresistible".[216]

Few issues have angered the public more than *guanxi*, the realisation that getting on in life – be it guaranteeing a decent education, job, business deals, or just getting rich – all depends on or 'political connections'. Bribery and corruption have grown in direct proportion to the accumulation of capital, and inherent to the PRC business model. But what particularly has incensed the public is watching crooked state officials, party members, and wealthy businessmen remain immune to prosecution. To show that no one is above the law, and reinforce its legitimacy as 'neutral arbiter', Beijing (supported by state media) has organised periodic high-profile blood-letting show-trials to eradicate the 'isolated' cases of graft such as the railway minister czar, Liu Zhijun, and multibillionaire owner of retail electronic giant Gome, Huang Guangyu. Such cases were also important to distract from the government's often incompetence with regard to the handling of, or even complicity in, a series of national disasters.[217] Inevitable, this led to a lack of public trust in Beijing.[218]

Yet for all these 'consensual' gestures, policy initiatives and talk of 'harmonious society' a 'passive revolution' has always had to rely on *coercion* to suppress opposition elements. Two months after the arrest of Charter 08 activist, future Nobel Peace Prize winner, Liu Xiaobo (later sentenced to an 11-year sentence), for example, the Fourth Plenary Session of the 17th Central Committee in September 2009 dramatically extended the NSS to maintain better surveillance over potential dissident political groups and 'terrorists'. Along with the military and the regular police force (both uniformed and plain-clothed), Beijing also greatly expanded the resources of the paramilitary People's Armed Police (PAP), setting up 36 units across the country. In addition, the CPC mobilised an unarmed civilian militia (identified by their red-arm bands) to help 'keep order' in the cities.

The CPC had long controlled the flow of information through state-run media outlets (be it television, press, or radio), but in 1998 the Ministry of Public Security set up the Public Information and Internet Security Supervision Bureau to monitor the use of the internet. Over the following years the famous 'Great Firewall of China' was established giving state authorities a free rein to censor content, block websites, close down any publication, and fire/prosecute any journalists spreading 'dangerous' news or ideas. Access to most foreign news networks and social networks is prohibited. *Twitter*, for example, has been blocked since 2009 (along with all *Google* services, *Facebook*, *Instagram*, *YouTube*, *Dropbox,* etc.), benefitting the heavily monitored national versions (e.g. the microblog site, *Sina Weibo*, the search engine, *Baidu*, and instant-messaging app, *We-Chat*). According to *Reporters without Borders* "2018 World Press Freedom Index" China occupied position 176 out of 180.[219]

The CPC is still haunted by the social-media-fuelled pro-democracy movements that spread through North Africa and the Middle East during the Arab Spring of 2010, when it introduced draconian measures to censor information and suppress freedom of expression right across the old and new media platforms,[220] fearful that anti-authority images and messages emanating out of the "jasmine revolution" could spark what NPC chairman, Wu Bagguo, described as a possible "abyss of internal disorder" unless it stuck to its "correct political orientation".[221] The new annual budget announced by the NPC the following March (2011) increased internal security expenditure by 13.8% to stem what Wen Jiabao considered "an abundance of threats within": for the first time, the PRC would be spending more on police and domestic surveillance than it would on defence.[222]

Despite employing over two million 'internet public opinion analysts' to monitor/censor content, the Ministry of Public Security clearly has its work cut out to try and block 'dangerous' news/ideas circulating amongst the country's 730 million internet users.[223] Nonetheless, steps have been taken since the introduction of a ten-clause judicial interpretation in 2013, converting into Criminal Law in 2015, which established strict penalties (up to seven-year imprisonment) for people spreading 'false information' and 'slanderous rumours' about politicians or celebrities online.[224]

Until recently, for example, the well-connected and techno-savvy Chinese found a way to access a virtual private network (VPN) and skirt around the 'great firewall'. Stricter laws are now in place. Under state pressure, Apple agreed in July 2017 to remove VPN products from its Chinese app store with Android following suit, while national telecommunications companies must use government sanction VPN. That December Beijing sent out a clear signal to the public, sentencing small trader Wu Xiangyang to five and a half years in prison for 'illegal business' practices – selling software to access VPN.

Internet companies have always exercised self-censorship, but given the huge surveillance task facing the CPC, any firm operating social-media platforms, private chat groups, or sharing content are now obliged to employ in-house censors to police sites and remove any offensive material, be it of a political, sexual, or violent nature, since *they* are legally responsible for the content. Thanks to Beijing's increasingly conservative authoritarianism, concerns for national morality, family values and good taste, mean this self-censorship must now extend beyond politics into blogs and apps dedicated to 'low brow' popular culture such as entertainment, fashion, hip-hop, celebrity-gossip, and even joke-sharing.[225]

This internet crack-down has coincided with the naming of 'Shanghai Gang' member Xi Jinping as the president in November 2012, marking the beginning of a new, even more, authoritarian stage in the development of the Chinese 'passive revolution'. Chiming somewhat with Gramsci's definition of *Caesarism*, the 'strong man' Xi would be granted extended perpetual executive powers to drive through important structural changes and overcome splits within elite factions.

Launched at the conclusion of the Third Plenary Session of the 18th CPC's Central Committee on 12th November 2013, the package of reforms entitled "The Decisions on Major Issues Concerning Comprehensively Deepening Reforms"[226] promised to be the biggest single major overhaul of the Chinese FOS since Deng Xiaoping. Building up the aforementioned 12th Five -Year Plan, the so-called "deepening reforms" aimed "to develop socialism with Chinese characteristics, to advance modernisation in the State governance system, and governance capability". According to Xi Jinping, the PRC had reached a critical moment. Citing Deng Xiaoping, he declared: "only socialism can save China, and only reform and opening-up can save China, socialism and Marxism". "Reform and opening-up will decide the destiny of China".[227]

The saving of socialism, as we have seen, paradoxically depended upon globalization (e.g. the BRI), see previous sections: the SOEs were encouraged to 'go global' to move up the value-added chain by acquiring foreign technology, know-how, intellectual property rights (which has so incensed the Trump administration), and generally move up the value-added chain as part of the 'Made in China' indicative. Domestically, the market was to play a *decisive* role in resource allocation, reducing government intervention in the economy, relaxing *hukou* rules, granting more freedom to private capital within the market including within SOEs, reducing 'red tape', creating a single land market (unify both rural and urban areas), and respecting intellectual property rights.

In keeping with Wen's 'harmonious society' objectives, the 'deepening reforms' promised a fairer redistribution of wealth both between urban and rural areas, and capital and workers, and to improve access to social services and dramatically step up poverty elimination spending. Other progressive social and political measures announced included reforming the 'one-child' policy, strengthening grassroots democracy, tackling corruption, ensuring greater transparency in, and effectiveness of, the judicial system, abolishing the "re-education through labour" (*laojiao*) system (i.e. detainment without trial), reducing the use of capital punishment "step-by-step", launching a 'war on pollution' – air quality/ ozone levels in cities frequently 'off the scale' with 90% of groundwater contaminated[228] – and investing in renewable energy power (announcing in January 2017 that $361 billion would be to spent by 2020).

But there were limits to this 'opening up' under Xi. The "deepening reforms" made it clear that "political reform must evolve around the leadership of the Communist Party of China", which was greatly strengthened (reactivating 77,000 small CPC branches) and loyalty demanded. The NSS was augmented, the PLA reformed, and all components of national security centralised under a new National Security Commission (NSC) which was answerable to the CPC General Secretary (Xi). Clashing clearly with the BRI objective to encourage the free flow of ideas, Beijing announced stricter controls of 'civil society' in order to ensure adherence to the party line.[229] Under the newly-reinforced Central Commission for Discipline Inspection, the anti-corruption drive was stepped up considerably, disciplining over a million officials, indicating tens of thousands, including high-profile military (e.g. Xu Caihou and Guo Boxiong) and political figures (e.g. Ling Jihua and Zhou Yongkang) – not to mention billionaire businessmen (e.g. Xiao Jianhua and Wu Xiaohui) – something which had not been seen since the Cultural Revolution and commonly thought to be have been used by Xi as a way to eradicate powerful enemies.[230]

As we have seen from Bush II onwards, and in line with Polanyi and Arendt's analysis, neoliberalism, and authoritarianism are perfectly compatible. In China, under Xi, this has manifested itself in nurturing the 'leadership cult' not witnessed since Mao Zedong or at least Deng Xiaoping. During the 19th National Congress of the CPC in October 2017, the so-called "Xi Jinping Thought on Socialism with Chinese Characteristics for a New Era", a 14-point guideline for a future, modern CPC-directed socialist China was incorporated into the CPC's Constitution. Symptomatic of this hero-worship was the release in March 2018 of the state-financed "Amazing China", extolling Xi's many economic, political, and cultural accomplishments in defence of the nation and socialism which, thanks to CPC elites' block-booking cinema screenings has become the highest-ever grossing documentary.

The domestic challenges facing China in the 21st century are multiple and complex. Just how will a nominally socialist country manage to integrate more deeply into the global economy, making the transition towards a knowledge-rich service-based economy, and reliant on domestic consumption, remains to be seen. Certainly, nationwide rising wages or a general redistribution of wealth from coastal cities towards the rural hinterland are clearly not popular with sections of capital, least of all those national and foreign exporters based along the southern seaboard.

Despite Li Cheng's differentiations between factions, it is certainly too premature to envisage the possibility of the PRC developing anything approaching a bourgeois multiparty system or that the CPC is about to disintegrate or in any way voluntarily relinquishing its stranglehold over contemporary Chinese society. It may be, as Alvin Y. So suggests, that as the Chinese economy becomes more integrated into the global economy that the "influence of the market segment (which has little linkages to the party state) in the capitalist class is bound to increase", and that in the future "this will want to complete the 'unfinished business' of the neoliberal capitalism", including freer markets and greater legal accountability and intellectual property protection.[231]

This appears the thrust of Xi's 'deepening reforms'. The replacement of Hu's 'harmonious society' with Xi's 'Chinese Dream' vision, an obvious nod to its American counterpart and the lauding of the self-made man myth and entrepreneurial endeavour reinforces such an impression. That this will transpose into a coherent class agenda and seek to cut loose from the CPC, at least in the short term, seems unlikely, therein disproving classical liberal teleology which holds that demands for greater economic freedoms (capitalism) automatically transposes into political freedom (democracy).

Undoubtedly, there are issues of great concern amongst the middle classes, who frequently have expressed their unhappiness about a wide range of issues such as the lack of professional opportunities, pollution, housing, corruption, and civil and political rights (e.g. democratic accountability, freedom of speech/expression). Hitherto, Beijing has managed to deflect much of this anger by political decentralisation (let local politicians carry the can) and *transformismo*, assimilating many of these demands (however paradoxically) into its official programme/discourse. The growing middle class owes its newly acquired status and consumption opportunities to the PRC's incredible economic development, which few wish to see reversed. Added to that fear of working-class insurgence has meant the middle classes are amongst the most enthusiastic supporters of the CPC.

Any genuine counter-hegemony must come from the subaltern class. In absolute terms, few would deny China's success in reducing poverty levels over the last 40 years, with Xi promising in October 2017 to end rural poverty by 2020, through the development of local industries, education, and healthcare. Wealth distribution, as we have seen, along with forced land acquisitions, corruption, and pollution remain key sources of anger. Frustrated by their lack of real legal rights under China's idiosyncratic 'rule-of-law' system (arbitration committees included) not to mention independent unions, workers, and peasants often taken matters into their own hands. The *China Labour Bulletin* indicates that strikes and other forms of 'mass incidents' (involving 100+) are commonplace right across the country and in every industry.[232] But despite the increasing frequency over recent decades, these labour protests, to date, have tended to be small-scale (an exception being Yue Yuen shoe factory strike in 2014), short-lived, and predominantly economistic in scope (e.g. concerned with higher wages), which can within reason be bought off. Genuine systemic transformation, as Gramsci observed, required organisation and the elaboration of a *hegemonic project* which, ultimately depended on developing working class consciousness (Marx's class 'for itself'). At least thus far, this has proven elusive in the PRC, thanks to the interplay of domestic and international social forces manifested in the coercive and consensual measures of a 40-year 'passive revolution'. Nonetheless, with a working class estimated to stand around 750 million it would only require a fraction of these to get organised to seriously challenge power relations within China, the repercussions of which for global capitalism would be enormous.

Notes

1 The World Bank (2018a).
2 International Monetary Fund (2018).
3 The World Bank (2018a, 2018b).
4 BBC News (2010a).

5 The Economist (2015a).

6 International Energy Agency (2010).

7 In August 2018, the Chinese Investment Corporation's total assets surpassed $900 billion. China Daily (2017).

8 China's trade surplus for 2017 stood at $442 billion. Xinhuanet (2018a).

9 Reuters (2018c).

10 The perennial problem of export-driven countries is that the trade surpluses they generate eventually cause inflation unless the currency is revaluated and/or capital is exported abroad.

11 China Dialogue (2018).

12 International Energy Agency (2017).

13 According to a recent ExxonMobil report, China contributed 60% of the growth in global CO_2 emissions from 2000 to 2016. ExxonMobil (2018).

14 U.S. Energy Information Administration (2018).

15 U.S. State Department (2009).

16 Ministry of Foreign Affairs of the People's Republic of China (2006).

17 Forum on China-Africa Cooperation (2006).

18 The State Council of the People's Republic of China (2010).

19 Ministry of Commerce of People's Republic of China (2018).

20 McKinsey & Company (2017), p. 20.

21 McKinsey & Company (2017), p. 26.

22 The Angola Mode has been used to building electricity generators/transmission lines (Zambia), oil refineries (Niger), petroleum infrastructure and railway systems (Nigeria), natural gas infrastructure and airports (Chad), hydro-electric plants/dams (Guinea), roads and bridges (Ethiopia), telecommunication networks (Sudan), hospitals (Kenya), and water supplies (e.g. Mozambique).

23 Xinhuanet (2018b).

24 China Daily (2013a).

25 South China Morning Post (2015). Indeed, China would invest $20.9 billion in Brazil in 2017 alone. See CNBC (2018).

26 Beijing also lent Caracas $20 billion in return for supplying 400,000 barrels of crude a day. The Wall Street Journal (2010a).

27 BBC News (2015).

28 As early as 2006, German Chancellor Angela Merkel insisted "[w]e must take a stand in Africa" and that "[w]e Europeans should not leave the continent of Africa to the People's Republic of China". Quoted in Asian Times (2006).

29 Quoted in Financial Times (2010a).

30 Indeed, bilateral trade between China and Venezuela increased 50 times in a decade – from $200 in 1999 to $10 billion at the end of 2010 – transforming the Asian country into the latter's second largest trading partner (after the US). Agencia Nacional de Venezuela (2011).

31 Between 1980 and 2006, Africa had paid $675 billion in servicing its debt alone. Nakatina & Herrera (2007).

32 The IMF and World Bank complained that Chinese unrestrained lending had "undermined years of painstaking efforts to arrange conditional debt relief". The New York Times (2006).

33 *WikiLeaks cables* cited in The Guardian (2010b).

34 China Daily (2011d).

35 Financial Times (2011). According to the World Bank's "African Development Indicators 2011", between 2000 and 2009 Saharan Africa (excluding South Africa) experienced an average GDP growth of almost 6% p.a. (measured in constant prices) – reflected in an average 3% p.a. increase in GDP

per capita – a rate not witnessed since the 1960s, and far superior to its traditional 1% figure. The World Bank (2011), pp. 9, 11.

36 Asian Investment Infrastructure Bank (2018).
37 The Economist (2015b).
38 The New York Times (2010a).
39 The New York Times (2010b).
40 Speaking in 2011, marking 40 years of uninterrupted bilateral diplomatic relations, Chinese Foreign Ministry spokesman, Hong Lei, underscored the "normal and transparent business transactions with Iran, which have benefited the people of both countries". Chinese Government's Official Web Portal (2011).
41 Iran Daily (2018a).
42 Iran Daily (2018b).
43 Xinhuanet (2011b).
44 International Energy Agency (2012), p. 6.
45 Iran Daily (2018a).
46 Work began in October 2009 on the oil pipeline running 771 km from Kyauk Pyu to Ruili in the south-western Chinese province of Yunnan. Though completed in 2014, political and environmental concerns delayed its opening till April 2017. The China Post (2017).
47 Financing for this port, along with financing/building of a new airport, railway network and power plants, have turned the PRC into Sri Lanka's largest foreign lender. In December 2017, after accumulating $8 billion in debt to China, it handed control over the port to Beijing on a 99-year lease.
48 China.org.cn (2011a).
49 The Central Asian 'stans' decision to commit most of their gas and oil exports to China and Russia has undermined somewhat American and European plans to set up a trans-Caspian Sea pipeline, stretching from Turkmenistan, Azerbaijan, Georgia, Turkey, and onto Europe.
50 The SCO has eight full members (China, Russia, Kazakhstan, Kyrgyzstan, Tajikistan, Uzbekistan, India, and Pakistan), four observers (Mongolia, Afghanistan, Belarus, and Iran) and six dialogue partners (including Turkey).
51 Taiwan Insight (2018).
52 Xinhuanet (2018d).
53 The Economist (2010a).
54 Council on Foreign Relations (2012).
55 World Trade Organisation (2017).
56 East Asia Forum (2017).
57 Members of the Association of South East Asian Nations are Thailand, Indonesia, Malaysia, Singapore, Vietnam, Laos, Myanmar, Brunei, Cambodia, and the Philippines.
58 China FTA Network (2018).
59 The Plus Three are China (and Hong Kong), Japan, and South Korea.
60 Financial Times (2018).
61 China Daily (2015).
62 Financial Times (2012).
63 The State Council of the People's Republic of China (2015).
64 The Economist (2017).
65 National Development and Reform Commission (2015).
66 Ports Chinese SOEs have acquired a major stake include Antwerp-Zeebrugge (Belgium), Piraeus (Greece), Kumport (Turkey), Suez (Egypt), Lamu (Kenya), Bagamoyo (Tanzania), Obock (Djibouti), Port Victoria (Seychelles), and Melaka Gateway (Malacca, Malaysia).
67 World Economic Forum (2017).

68 The White House (2015).
69 The Economist (2018b).
70 South China Morning Post (2017b).
71 Financial Times (2010b).
72 The Guardian (2010a).
73 The New York Times (2011b).
74 Reuters (2018b).
75 Renminbi (RMB) and *yuan* will be used interchangeably throughout this chapter.
76 The Financial Times (2015).
77 Reuters (2018a).
78 The Princeton Project on National Security (2006).
79 The White House (2009).
80 The Economist (2011a).
81 Reuters (2011a).
82 The BRICS Post (2018).
83 South China Morning Post (2018).
84 One of the aims here was to avoid alienating African Union and Arab League supporters. Beijing would later react angrily when UN resolution 1973 in March 2011 to establish a 'No-Fly Zone' over Libya, which it abstained on, was stretched to authorise a NATO-led military intervention against Tripoli.
85 Gramsci (1971), p. 80f.
86 U.S. Department of Defense (2009).
87 Xi (2015).
88 Stockholm International Peace Research Institute (2018).
89 The People's Liberation Army Air Force chose to test its new generation of stealth jet fighter, the J-20, the very day (11th January 2011) that the then US Defence Secretary Robert Gates was in Beijing to meet Premier Hu Jintao.
90 Arms Control Association (2018).
91 Nathan (2012).
92 National Security Strategy (2017).
93 The Diplomat (2018).
94 Hegenbotham & Nixon (eds.) (2015), p. 321–3.
95 Cliff (2015), pp. 24–6.
96 See for example Chase-Dunn (1998).
97 Kaplan (2005).
98 Friedberg (2011).
99 National Security Strategy (2015).
100 National Security Strategy (2017).
101 Though the 1979 *US Taiwan Relations Act* required any US administration "to provide Taipei with arms of a defensive character", a subsequent "Sino-American joint communiqué", committed Washington to "reduce gradually the sale of arms to Taiwan", and to look for a "final resolution". See Taiwan Documents Project (1979) and Nuclear Threat Initiative (1982).
102 BBC News (2010b). The compromised deal failed to please anyone, least of all the pro-Taiwanese/MIC lobby in US Congress, 181 House Representatives and 47 Senators signing a joint letter to Obama in August 2011 pleading with him to sell the Taiwanese the new jets.
103 People's Daily (2011).
104 Taipei Times (2017).
105 It has an estimated the US has 23,468 troops stationed at its 83 military installations in South Korea. The Guardian (2017).
106 Pyongyang has never accepted the US-imposed NLL, claiming it in no way represents a maritime extension of the Military Demarcation Line dividing

the two Koreas on the mainland, clinging as it does to the North Korean coastline and separating the country from vital fishing grounds.

107 For which he won a Nobel Peace Prize.

108 Announced by North Korea's KCNAP news agency, supposedly to "to bolster up its deterrent for self-defence". The Korean Central News Agency (2009).

109 The US-sponsored UNSC Resolution 1874 (12th June 2009) not only imposed economic sanctions but gave other countries both the right and responsibility, to board North Korean ships and planes that landed at ports around the world and inspect them for the weapon.

110 US Permanent Representative to the UN Susan E. Rice described these manoeuvres as "exclusively defensive in nature". Embassy of the United States, Seoul, Korea (2010).

111 Even *The Economist* considered this "more subtly" as "a shot across China's bows". The Economist (2010b).

112 Joint statement by South Korean Chief of Staff Han and US Chief of Staff Admiral Mike Mullen on the 7th December quoted in The New York Times (2010e).

113 The Telegraph (2018).

114 BBC News (2010c).

115 This was confirmed by US President, Jimmy Carter, who with Bill Clinton's approval held bilateral talks with Kim Jong-il in 1994. See The Washington Post (2010).

116 The Telegraph (2010).

117 Even the *Wall Street Journal* agreed with Beijing. The Wall Street Journal (2010b).

118 These included suspending senior-level government contact; halting discussion on new flights between the new countries; arresting four Japanese businessmen on spying charges; ordering the 32 official exporters of rare earth metals to withhold shipments to Japan; suspending the May agreement to allow joint exploration of gas reserves in the East China Sea and cooperation in the coal industry; cancelling student exchanges; and encouraging anti-Japanese demonstrators to take to the streets.

119 The Financial Times (2010a).

120 Pedrozo (2010) and The New York Times (2010c).

121 World Oil (2011).

122 The Economist (2010d).

123 The Economist (2010d).

124 The Economist (2010b).

125 The U.S. Department of Defense (2010). In a show of good faith, Vietnamese officials were invited on board the *USS George Washington* aircraft carrier to observe naval manoeuvres in August 2011 and the US finally gave Hanoi permission to enrich their own uranium.

126 Global Times (2015).

127 Chinese Government's Official Web Portal (2010).

128 The White House (2010).

129 Time (2010).

130 The New York Times (2010d).

131 The US remains one of the few major countries not to ratify the UNCLOS.

132 The Economist (2018c).

133 Despite forming part of BRICs forum India adopted a more hawkish line with regards to China under BJP Prime Minister Narendra Modi, increasing military spending and doubling the number of troops and building railways/new airports in the disputed state of Arunachal Pradesh. Growing

concerned over the economic/geopolitical effects of PRC's BRI project and naval incursions in the Indian Ocean, not least how these have bolstered its bête noir, Pakistan, have further aligned its foreign policy with Washington.

134 The State Council Information Office of the People's Republic of China (2017).
135 Xinhuanet (2015).
136 China Daily (2018).
137 The U.S. Department of the Treasury (2018).
138 Gramsci (1971), p. 195.
139 Gray (2010), pp. 449–67.
140 Attracted by the lower costs on the mainland, these investors were less daunted by Chinese bureaucracy (often enjoying privileged access to local officials), culture, or language than their Western counterparts as well as already possessing knowledge of, and access to, global trade and marketing networks for the consumer good.
141 China.org.cn (2009).
142 Central government revenue plummeted from around 34% of GDP in 1978 to just 6% in 1995, with its expenditure similarly dropping from 31% to 11% of GDP in the same period. Beijing did reverse the fiscal decentralisation process somewhat in the 1990s, fearing it was putting at risk the territorial integrity of the country. By 2006, state revenue was back up to 17% of GDP and state expenditure around 22%. Jacques (2009), pp. 166–7.
143 Li & Zhou (2005), pp. 1743–62.
144 Under Mao the population was divided up and registered in 'work units', which organised production and provided employment. Though workers would be paid wages (so wage labour *did* exist), labour was not a freely traded commodity, so no one could be fired.
145 People's Daily (1992).
146 In 1993, for example, China received more FDI than the accumulated total for 1978–92. Breslin (2006), p. 466.
147 Reuters (2012).
148 Watkins (2008), p. 130.
149 Breslin (2006), p. 465.
150 High FDI arriving from tax havens such as the Cayman Islands, Bermuda, and the British Virgin Islands is also thought to originate in Hong Kong and Taiwan.
151 Prestowitz (2005), p. 61.
152 Sung (2005), p. 36.
153 Jikun, Rozelle & Honglin (2006), pp. 1–26.
154 Lin (2002), pp. 98–116.
155 By the end of 2004, local authorities in Beijing and Shanghai had authorised the demolition of around 4.2 million square metres and 22.5 million square metres of buildings in their respective centres, displacing a total of 2.5 million people. He & Wu (2005), pp. 1–23.
156 According to China's State Development Research Center, from 1996 to 2006 government officials and their business cronies illegally seized more than 4,000 square miles of land per year. Quoted in Gilboy & Heginbotham (2010).
157 Harvey (2007), p. 128.
158 Yusuf, Nabeshima & Perkins (2005). Between 1991 and 2005, the proportion of the urban work-force employed in the public sector fell from about 82% to about 27%. Watkins (2008), p. 130.
159 Chen & Wu (2006).

160 Quoted in Gilboy & Heginbotham (2010). From 2003 to spring 2006, for example, the sale of farmland for industrial residential purposes raised $600 billion, yet only 10% went to farmers with the vast majority (around $500 billion) being acquired by local governments and connected officials and their cronies.
161 Xinhuanet (2018c).
162 Hui (2003).
163 So (2013), p. 173.
164 China.org.cn (2011b).
165 China.org.cn (2002).
166 Osburg (2013).
167 Forbes.com (2018).
168 Hurun Report (2018).
169 Capgemini (2017), p. 9. The Boston Consulting Group report put the figure around 2.1 million, quoted in CNBC (2017b).
170 See BBC News (2017).
171 Ekman (2015).
172 Notably *Xinhua, People's Daily* and *CCTV.*
173 On the average city street, it became far easier to find articles, magazines, and books promoting the free market, privatisation, and Western democracy than on the ideas of Marx or Mao, who were strictly preserved for a cult of personality.
174 International Monetary Fund (2017), p. 70.
175 Quoted in South China Morning Post (2017a).
176 Save the Children (2013).
177 World Health Organization (2000).
178 The New York Times (2011c).
179 United Nations Development Programme (2016).
180 In a poll carried out by the Zhejiang Academy of Social Sciences in 2009, 96% of the public interviewed confessed to harbour such feelings. China Daily (2009).
181 Gallagher (2017).
182 Lee (2002), pp. 189–228; Lee (2008).
183 The ACFTU has not, for example, accepted the international labour standards of the International Labour Organisation (e.g. right to association).
184 Chen (2003).
185 Dong, Kriesi & Kübler (eds.) (2015), p. 3.
186 Cheng Li claims the *Shanghai gang* 'coalition' consists of high CPC members and their children (the "princelings"), capitalists, foreign-educated Chinese, the emerging middle classes and even the Shanghai Mafia; it has a powerful political base around the urban-industrial coastal regions and is the most integrated into the global economy (i.e. export industry). The *Tuanpai*, on the other hand, represent the reformists and generally place more emphasis on national cohesion and sustainability and domestic consumption, with its main power base is in the hinterland among rank-and-file CPC members, rural leaders, left wing academics, workers, and the peasantry. Li (2009, 2013).
187 Chinese Government's Official Web Portal (2006).
188 China Cultural Industries (2008).
189 Journal of Advances on Humanities (2014).
190 Making smartphones, tablets, game consoles, computers, etc for companies such as Apple, Dell, HP, Nintendo, Sony, and Nokia.
191 Bieler & Lee (2017) note the higher incidence of industrial conflict in the Pearl River Delta (focused on low-value -added electronic sectors) compared to the Yangtse River Delta (geared towards high-value-added IT sector) which employees more skilled workers on better pay and more stable contracts.

192 Chan & Hui (2014).

193 Wuhan, China's 9th largest city, for example, built a 140-mile long urban railway system, two new airports, a new financial district, a cultural district, a riverside promenade in addition to the massive office tower.

194 Quoted in The Economist (2011b).

195 Total local government debt in 2010 amounted to $2.2 trillion, around one-third of the PRC's GDP. The New York Times (2011a).

196 See for example China.org.cn (2011d).

197 This high systemic inflation was reflected in the rising costs of labour, raw materials, food prices, and consumer goods in general – the Consumer Price Index hit 6.5% in July 2011 which marked a 37-month high. China.org.cn (2011e).

198 The official CPC portal quoted a survey carried out by *Xiaokang Magazine* which claimed 24.8% of China's urban youth were postponing marriage and 21% postponing children due to housing pressure while 70% of respondents said they would not like to get married if they lived in rented accommodation. China.org.cn (2011c).

199 Sum & Jessop (2013), p. 463.

200 These included placing tighter restrictions on overseas speculative investment, second mortgages, bank reserve requirements, as well as raising interest rates.

201 First, any evictions now had to be carried out 'peacefully' by the local governments themselves (i.e. not contracted-out to private enforcers); second, said evictions were only permitted to further the 'public interest' (e.g. for defence, transport, diplomacy, education, healthcare, or housing for the poor) rather than for commercial ventures; and third, any family whose property was seized had to be paid 'fair' compensation.

202 According to The Economist Intelligence Unit, private consumption as a share of GDP in 2016 stood at 38.7% for China, way below that of the US (68.7%), the UK (65.2%), Japan (55.8%), France (55.1%), and Germany (53.5%). Quoted in Morrison (2018), p. 37.

203 The CIA estimated China's gross national savings rate as the percentage of its GDP in 2017 as standing at 45.2% compared to the UK (13.4%), US (17.5%), France (21.9%), Japan (27%), and Germany (27.6%). Central Intelligence Agency (2018).

204 The Financial Times (2010b).

205 The Economist (2010c).

206 The New York Times (2011d).

207 Xinhaunet (2011a).

208 Two days before the conference began official state media surprised the world by reproducing a recent survey which claimed only expressed by 6% of the citizens felt "happy".

209 Xinhaunet (2011a).

210 The US-China Business Council (2014).

211 From the mid-1990s onwards there has been a certain relaxing of labour laws. This has allowed rural migrants to acquire *hukou* citizenship in some small and medium-sized cities (with a population of less than 500,000), but in the large/super-large cities such as Beijing, Shanghai, and Guangzhou – which is just where the bulk of manufacturing and low-end service jobs are – strict rules over granting permanent residence remained.

212 Morrison (2018), p. 12.

213 CNBC (2017a).

214 Landry, Davis & Wang (2010).

215 See for example China Daily (2011a, 2011b).

216 The Financial Times (2010c).

217 In July 2011, for example, Beijing came in for criticism even from the normally complicit national media over its handling and, especially, its suspected cover up of the real causes of the Wenzhou train collision which claimed 39 lives.
218 Witnessed in comic fashion in February 2011 with the panic buying of salt following the Fukushima nuclear disaster in Japan.
219 Reporters without Borders (2018).
220 Apart from requiring that anyone seeking to download material from the internet supply ID and a mobile phone number, the Propaganda Department instructed the official media to only use the dispatches sent by the news agency, Xinhua, while private news portals, search engines and microblogs had to limit their coverage de-stabilising effects for the countries and Chinese residents there. On Sundays, throughout February and March, non-official peaceful rallies ("strolls") pushing for greater political freedom took place right across the country before they were broken up by uniformed/plainclothes policemen and civilian militias.
221 China Daily (2011a).
222 Reuters (2011b).
223 China Internet Network Information Center (2017), p. 1.
224 People could face defamation charges if their rumours were seen by over 5,000 netizens or retweeted more than 500 times. Global Times (2015).
225 The Economist (2018a).
226 For a good, albeit abridged, overview of the reforms, see China Daily (2013b).
227 Xinhuanet (2013).
228 Greenpeace claims 72,000 premature deaths occurred in 2015 due to ozone exposure. See Greenpeace Report (2018).
229 In ensuring educational material adheres to party conformity the Central Propaganda Department has even put pressure on foreign-owned peer review scientific journals to remove 'offensive' articles from their Chinese websites.
230 See Yuen (2014).
231 So (2013), pp. 177–8.
232 China Labour Bulletin (2018).

Bibliography

Agencia Nacional de Venezuela (2011), "China-Venezuela trade has been multiplied [sic] by 50 times in the last decade", 16th June (available online at www.avn.info.ve/node/63021).

Arrighi, G. (2008), *Adam Smith in Beijing: Lineages of the Twenty-First Century*, London: Verso.

Arms Control Association. (2018), "*Nuclear Weapons: Who Has What at a glance*", March (available online at www.armscontrol.org).

Asian Investment Infrastructure Bank. (2018), "AIIB Presentation", updated July 2018 (available online at www.aiib.org/en/about-aiib/basic-documents/_download/AIIB-presentation.pdf).

Asian Times. (2006), "China Swaggers into Europe's 'backyard'", Julio Godoy, 17th November (available online at www.atimes.com).

BBC News. (2010a), "China 'Overtakes Germany as World's Largest Exporter'", 10th January (available online at news.bbc.co.uk/2/hi/8450434.stm).

BBC News. (2010b), "China Hits Back at US Over Taiwan Weapon Sales", 30th January (available online atnews.bbc.co.uk/2/hi/asia-pacific/8488765.stm).

BBC News. (2010c), "US Renews Demand on North Korea to Change Behaviour", 7th December (available online at www.bbc.co.uk/news/world-asia-pacific-11929499).

BBC News. (2015), "What Will China's Investment do for Latin America?" Katy Watson, July (available online at www.bbc.com/news/world-33424532).

BBC News. (2017), "China Passes New Law on Property", 16th March (available online at news.bbc.co.uk/2/hi/asia-pacific/6456959.stm).

Bieler, A. & Lee, C.Y. (2017), "Exploitation and Resistance: A Comparative Analysis of Chinese Cheap Labour Electronics and High-Value Added IT Sectors", *Globalizations*, 14, no. 2, 202–15.

Breslin, S. (2006), "China and the Political Economy of Global Engagement", in Stubbs, R. and Underhill, G.R.D. (eds.), *Political Economy and the Changing Global Order*, 3rd Edn., Oxford: Oxford University Press.

Capgemini. (2017), "World Wealth Report 2017" (www.capgemini.com/wp-content/uploads/2017/09/worldwealthreport_2017_final.pdf).

Central Intelligence Agency. (2018), *The World Factbook* "Country Comparisons: Gross National Savings" (available online at www.cia.gov/library) [accessed on 4th August 2018].

Chase-Dunn, C. (1998), *Global Formation: Structures of the World-Economy*, 2nd Edn., Lanham, MD: Rowman & Littlefield.

Chan, K.C.C. & Hui, S.I.E. (2014), "The Development of Collective Bargaining in China: From 'Collective Bargaining by Riot' to 'Party State-led Wage Bargaining'", *China Quarterly*, 217, 221–42.

Chen, F. (2003), "Between the State and Labour: The Conflict of Chinese Trade Unions' Double Identity in Market Reform", *The China Quarterly*, 176, 1006–28.

Chen, G. & Wu, C. (2006), *Will the Boat Sink the Water? The Life of China's Peasants*, New York: Public Affairs.

China Cultural Industries. (2008), "Labour Contract Law of the People's Republic of China" (www.ilo.org/dyn/natlex/natlex4.detail?p_lang=en&p_isn=76384).

China Daily. (2009) "Rich Getting Richer, But Poor Becoming Resentful", Wu Yiyao, 10th December (available online at www.chinadaily.com.cn/).

China Daily. (2011a), "Top Legislator Warns of Chaos Unless Correct Path is Taken", 3rd March (available online at www.chinadaily.com.cn/).

China Daily. (2011b), "China's Election Won't be Western-style", Zhu Zhu, 20th March (available online at www.chinadaily.com.cn/).

China Daily. (2011c), "Poor Inland Region to Hike Minimum Wage by 25%", 31st March (available online at www.chinadaily.com.cn/).

China Daily. (2011d), "RMB Fund Planned to Aid Latin America", Wang Xiaotian and Chen Jia, 29th April (available online at www.chinadaily.com.cn/).

China Daily. (2013a), "China, Mexico Boosts Relations", Zhu Zhe, 5th June (available online at www.chinadaily.com.cn/).

China Daily. (2013b), "The Decision on Major Issues Concerning Comprehensively Deepening Reforms in brief", 16th November (available online at www.chinadaily.com.cn/).

China Daily. (2015), "China Now a Net Capital Exporter", 21st January 2015 (available online at www.chinadaily.com.cn/).

China Daily. (2017), "China's Sovereign Wealth Fund Hits 900bln USD", 7th October 2017 (available online at www.chinadaily.com.cn/).

China Daily. (2018), "'Made in China 2025' roadmap updated", 27th January (available online at www.chinadaily.com.cn/).

China Dialogue. (2018), "China's Coal Consumption Growth Slightly", Feng Hao, Lili Pike and Yao Zhe, 28th February (available online at www.china dialogue.net/).

China FTA Network. (2018), accessed 25th July (available online at fta.mofcom. gov.cn/english/).

China Internet Network Information Center. (2017), "The 39th Survey Report: Statistical Report on Internet Development in China", January (available online at cnnic.com.cn/).

China Labour Bulletin. (2018), "Labour Relations in China: Some Frequently asked Questions" (available online at www.clb.org.hk).

China.org.cn (2002), "Full Text of Jiang Zemin's Report at the 16th Party Congress" (available online at www.china.org.cn/).

China.org.cn (2009), "1983: Household Responsibility System" (available online at www.china.org.cn/).

China.org.cn (2011a), "China, Russia Oil Pipeline Starts to Operation", 1st January (available online at www.china.org.cn/).

China.org.cn (2011b), "Amendment to the Constitution of the People's Republic of China" (1999), adopted at the 2nd Session of the 9th National People's Congress, 12th February (available online at www.china.org.cn/).

China.org.cn (2011c), "Young Chinese Postpone Marriage due to Pressure", 4th June (available online at www.china.org.cn/).

China.org.cn (2011d), "Exaggerating China's Local Government Debt", 25th July (available online at www.china.org.cn/).

China.org.cn (2011e), "China's July CPI hits 37-month High of 6.5%", 10th August (available online at www.china.org.cn/).

Chinese Government's Official Web Portal. (2006), "Facts and Figures: China's Drive to Build New Socialist Countryside", 3rd March (available online at www.gov.cn/english/2006-03/05/content_218920.htm).

Chinese Government's Official Web Portal. (2010), "Chinese Minister: Non-traditional Security Issues Pose Grave Challenge, China No Threat to Anyone", 12th October (available online at www.gov.cn/misc/2010-10/12/ content_1720124.htm).

Chinese Government's Official Web Portal. (2011), "China Calls Its Business Ties with Iran 'Normal and Transparent'", 11th November (available online at www.gov.cn/misc/2011-11/11/content_1991129.htm).

Cliff, R. (2015), *China's Military Power*, Cambridge: Cambridge University Press.

CNBC. (2017a), "Made in China Isn't So Cheap Anymore and Could Spell Headache for Beijing", 27th February (available online at www.cnbc.com/).

CNBC. (2017b), "Inside Wealth: Millionaires Owns a Record 45% of the World's Wealth – And their Share is Growing", Robert Frank, 17th June 2017 (available online at www.cnbc.com/).

CNBC. (2018), "China Investment in Brazil hits 7-year High in 2017", Jake Spring, 18th January (available online at www.cnbc.com/).

Council on Foreign Relations. (2012), "South Korea Seeks to Balance Trade with China and the United States", Han-Suk-hee, November (available online at www.cfr.org/).

Dong, L., Kriesi, H. & Kübler, D. (eds.) (2015), *Urban Mobilizations and New Media in Contemporary China*, Farnham: Ashgate Publishing Ltd.

East Asia Forum. (2017), "Getting Down to Business on Japan-China Relations", R. Aoyama, 21st August (available online at www.eastasiaforum. org/2017/08/21/getting-down-to-business-on-japan-china-relations/).

Ekman, A. (2015), "China's Emerging Middle Class: What Political Impact?" *IFRI Center for Asian Studies*, June.

Embassy of the United States, Seoul, Korea. (2010), "Remarks by Ambassador Susan E. Rice, U.S. Permanent Representative to the United Nations, at a Security Council Meeting on the Situation on the Korean Peninsula", 19th December 2010 (available online at seoul.usembassy.gov/p_rok_121910.html).

ExxonMobil. (2018), "2018 Outlook for Energy: A View to 2040" (available online at cdn.exxonmobil.com/~/media/).

Financial Times. (2010a), Africa-China Trade Special Report: "Continent Drives a Hard Bargain", William Wallis and Tom Burgis, 14th June.

Financial Times. (2010b), "Currency Wars in an Era of Chronically Weak Demand", Martin Wolf, 29th September.

Financial Times. (2011), "China's Lending Hits New Heights", Geoff Dyer, Jamil Anderlini and Henry Sander, 17th January.

Financial Times. (2012), "Investment Boom Starts to Unravel", Jamil Anderlini, 14th May.

Financial Times. (2018), "China, Japan and South Korea Draw Closer on Trade", Robert Harding, Gabriel Wildau and Song Jung-a, 9th May.

Forbes.com (2018), "The Billionaires 2018: Meet the Members of the Three-Comma Club", Luis Kroll and Kerry Dolan, March 6th (available online at www.forbes.com/) [accessed 13th June 2018].

Forum on China-Africa Cooperation. (2006), "Address by Hu Jintao President of the People's Republic of China at the Opening Ceremony of the Beijing Summit of the Forum on China-Africa Cooperation", 4th November (available online at www.focac.org/eng/ltda/dscbzjhy/SP32009/t606840.htm).

Friedberg, A.L. (2011), *A Contest for Supremacy: China, America and the Struggle for Mastery in Asia*, New York: W.W. Norton and Co.

Gallagher, M.E. (2017), *Authoritarian Legality in China: Law, Workers and the State*, Cambridge: Cambridge University Press.

Gilboy, G.J. & Heginbotham, J. (2010), "China's Dilemma: Social Change and Political Reform", *Foreign Affairs*, 14th October.

Global Times. (2010), "US Making Waves in the South China Sea", Liu Feitao, 8th November (available online at opinion.globaltimes.cn/).

Global Times. (2015), "7-year Penalty for Spreading Rumors on Net", Xinhua Source, 28th October (available online at www.globaltimes.cn/).

Gramsci, A. (1971), *Selections from the Prison Notebooks of Antonio Gramsci*, Hoare, Q. and Nowell Smith, G. (eds. and trans.), London: Lawrence & Wishart.

Gray, K. (2010), "Labour and the State in China's Passive Revolution", *Capital & Class*, 34, no. 3, 449–67.

Greenpeace Report. (2018), "Analysis of air quality trends in 2017", *East Asia-China* (available online at secured-static.greenpeace.org/eastasia/).

Hart-Landsberg, M. & Burkett, P. (2005), *China and Socialism: Market Reforms and Class Struggle*, New York: Monthly Review.

Harvey, D. (2007), *A Brief History of Neoliberalism*, Oxford: Oxford University Press.

He, S. & Wu, F. (2005), "Property-Led Development in Post-Reform China: A Case of Xintiandi Redevelopment Project in Shanghai", *Journal of Urban Affairs*, 27, no. 1, 1–23.

Hegenbotham, E. & Nixon, M. (eds.) (2015), *The US-China Military Scorecard: Forces, Geography, and the Evolving Balance of Power, 1996–2017*, Santa Monica, CA; RAND Corporation.

Hui, W. (2003), *China's New Order: Society, Politics and Economy in Transition*, Cambridge, MA: Harvard University Press.

Hurun Report. (2018), "Hururn Global Rich List 2018", 28th February (available online at www.hurun.net/EN/Article) [accessed 13th June 2018].

International Energy Agency. (2010), "China Overtakes the United States to Become World's Biggest Energy Consumer" (available online at www.iea.org) [accessed 9th March 2015].

International Energy Agency. (2012), "World Energy Outlook 2012" (www.iea.org).

International Energy Agency. (2017), "Key World Energy Statistics 2017" (available online at www.iea.org/publications/freepublications/publication/).

International Monetary Fund. (2017), "People's Republic of China: Country Report No. 17/248" (www.imf.org/~/media/Files/Publications/.../cr17248.ashx).

International Monetary Fund. (2018), *World Economic Outlook, April 2018* (available online at www.imf.org/en/Countries/CHN) [accessed 20th April 2018].

Iran Daily. (2018a), "Iran, China's Main Trading Partner in the Middle East: Official", 8th April (available online at www.iran-daily.com/).

Iran Daily. (2018b), "China Still Iran's Top Business Partner", 15th April (available online at www.iran-daily.com/).

Jacques, M. (2009), *When China Rules the World: The End of the Western World and the Birth of a New Global Order*, New York: The Penguin Press.

Jikun, H., Rozelle, S. & Honglin, W. (2006), "Fostering or Stripping Rural China: Modernizing Agriculture and Rural to Urban Capital Flows", *The Developing Economies*, 44, no. 1, 1–26.

Journal of Advances on Humanities. (2014), "A Study on the Importance of the Trade Union in Organisation", Selvaraju Arun Prasath, S.A., vol. 1, no. 1, May (available online at cirworld.org/journals/index.php/JAH/article/view/2366/pdf_4).

Kang, D.C. (2008), *China Rising: Peace, Power and Order in East Asia*, New York: Columbia University Press.

Kaplan, R.B. (2005), "How We Would Fight China", *Atlantic Magazine*, June (available online at www.theatlantic.com/).

Landry, P.F., Davis, D. & Wang, S. (2010) "Elections in Rural China: Competition without Parties", *Comparative Political Studies*, 43, no. 6, 763–90.

Lee, C.K. (2002), "From the Spectre of Mao to the Spirit of the Law: Labour Insurgency in China", *Theory & Society*, 31, no. 2, 189–228.

Lee, C.K. (2008), *Against the Law: Labour Protests in China's Rustbelt and Sunbelt*, Berkeley: University of California Press.

Li, C. (2009), "One Party, Two Coalitions in China's Politics", *Brookings Institute*, 16th August (available online at www.brookings.edu/research/opinions/2009/08/16-china-li).

Li, C. (2013), "Rule of the Princelings", *Brookings Institute*, 10th February (available online at www.brookings.edu/articles/rule-of-the-princelings/).

Li, H. & Zhou, L.A. (2005), "Political Turnover and Economic Performance. The Incentive Role of Personnel Control in China", *Journal of Public Economics*, 89, 9–10, 1743–62.

Lin, G. (2002), "The Growth and Structural Change of Chinese Cities", *Cities*, 19, no. 5, 299–316.

Ma, L.J.C. & Wu, F. (eds.) (2005), *Restructuring the Chinese City: Changing Society, Economy and Space*, Abington: Routledge.

McKinsey & Company. (2017), "Dance of the Lions and the Dragons: How are Africa and China Engaging, and How will the Partnership Evolve?" Irene Yuan Sun, Kartik Jayaram and Omid Kasiri, June.

Ministry of Commerce of People's Republic of China. (2018), "Statistics on China-Africa Bilateral Trade in 2017" (available online at english.mofcom.gov.cn/) [accessed 24th February 2018].

Ministry of Foreign Affairs of the People's Republic of China. (2006), "China's African Policy", January (available online at www.fmprc.gov.cn/eng/zxxx/t230615.htm).

Morrison, W.M. (2018), "China's Economic Rise: History, Trends, Challenges, and Implications for the United States", *Congressional Research Service – CRS Report*, 15th February.

Nakatina, P. & Herrera, R. (2007), "The South has Already Repaid Its External Debt to the North, but the North Denies Its Debt to the South", *Monthly Review*, 59, no. 2, 31.

Nathan, A.J. (2012), "Cyber Security and U.S.-China Relations", *Foreign Affairs*, September/October.

National Development and Reform Commission. (2015), "Vision and Actions on Jointly Building Silk Road Economic Belt and 21st-Century Maritime Silk Road, People's Republic of China, 28th March (available online at en.ndrc.gov.cn/newsrelease/201503/t20150330_669367.html).

National Security Strategy. (2015), *The National Security Strategy of the United States of America*, February (available online at nssarchive.us/wp-content/uploads/2015/02/2015.pdf).

National Security Strategy. (2017), *National Security Strategy of the United States of America*, December (available online at nssarchive.us/wp-content/uploads/2017/12/2017.pdf).

Nuclear Threat Initiative. (1982): "Sino-American Joint Communiqué", 17th August (available online at www.nti.org/db/china/engdocs/commk82.htm).

Osburg, J. (2013), *Anxious Wealth: Money & Morality among China's New Rich*, Stanford: Stanford University Press.

Pedrozo, R. (2010), "Snapshot: Beijing's Coastal Real Estate", *Foreign Affairs*, 15th November.

People's Daily. (1992), "Excerpts from Talks given in Wuchang, Shenzhen, Zhuhai and Shanghai" (available online at en.people.cn/).

People's Daily. (2011), "China Must Punish US for Taiwan Arms Sales with 'Financial Weapon'", Ding Gang, 8th August (available online at en.people.cn/).

Prestowitz, C. (2005), *Three Billion New Capitalists: The Great Shift of Wealth and Power to the East*, New York: Basic Books.

Reporters without Borders. (2018), "2018 World Press Freedom Index" (available online at rsf.org/en/ranking_table).

Reuters. (2011a), "Remarks by Obama and Hu at Washington News Conference", 19th January (available online at www.reuters.com).

Reuters. (2011b), "China Internal Spending Jumps Past Army Budget", 5th March (available online at www.reuters.com).

Reuters. (2012), "Timeline: China's Reform of Yuan Exchange Rate", 14th April (available online at www.reuters.com) [accessed 20th May 2014].

Reuters. (2018a), "Exclusive: China Taking First Steps to Pay for Oil in Yuan this Year – Sources", Sumeet Chatterjee and Meng Meng, 29th March (available online at www.reuters.com).

Reuters. (2018b), "China, Holding Treasuries, Keeps 'Nuclear Option' in U.S. Trade War", Trevor Hunnicutt and Kate Duguid, 4th April (available online at www.reuters.com) [last updated 24th April 2018].

Reuters. (2018c), "China's Forex Reserves Rise Slightly as U.S. Dollar Weakness Continues", 8th April (available online at www.reuters.com) [last accessed 20th April 2018].

Save the Children. (2013), "Income Inequality in China: A Case Study", Dr. Sen Gong and Li Bingqin, January 2013 (available online at resourcecentre. savethechildren.net/sites/default/files/documents/inequality_in_china.pdf).

So, A.Y. (2013), *Class and Class Conflict in Post-Socialist China*, Hong Kong: World Scientific Publishing Company.

South China Morning Post. (2015), "China to Invest $50 bn in Brazilian Infrastructure Projects", 15th May (available online at www.scmp.com/news).

South China Morning Post. (2017a), "China's Dirty Little Secret: It's Growing Wealth Gap", Sidney Leng, 13th July (available online at www.scmp.com/news).

South China Morning Post. (2017b), "Cost of Funding Belt and Road Initiative is Daunting Task", David Ho, 27th September (available online at www.scmp.com/news).

South China Morning Post. (2018), "Is China a Currency Manipulator or is Donald Trump to Blame for the Yuan's Weakness", Neal Kimberley, 24th July (available online at www.scmp.com/comment).

Stockholm International Peace Research Institute. (2018), "SIPRI Fact Sheet: Trends in World Military Expenditure, 2017", May (available online at www.sipri.org/).

Sum, N.L. & Jessop, B. (2013), *Towards a Cultural Political Economy: Putting Culture in Its Place in Political Economy*, Cheltenham: Edward Elgar.

Sung, Y. (2005), *The Emergence of Greater China: The Economic Integration of Mainland China, Taiwan and Hong Kong*, Basingstoke: Palgrave Macmillan.

Taipei Times. (2017), "Taiwan Thanks US over Defense Act", Chin, J. and Yu, L., 14th December (available online at www.taipeitimes.com/News).

Taiwan Documents Project. (1979), "The Taiwan Relations Act: United States Code Title 22 Chapter 48 Sections 3301" (available online at www.taiwandocuments.org/tra01.htm#3302).

Taiwan Insight. (2018), "Taiwan FDI: Why Outflows are Greater than Inflows", Anthony Kuo and Ming-Sun Kao (available online at taiwaninsight.org/).

The BRICS Post. (2018), "IMF Reforms: China, India, Brazil get Greater Say", 28th January (available online at thebricspost.com/).

The China Post. (2017), "Oil Starts Flowing China-Myanmar Pipeline", 13th April (available online at chinapost.nownews.com/20170413-5738).

The Diplomat. (2018), "Scoping Critical Information Infrastructure in China", Xiaomeng Ju, 22nd May (available online at thediplomat.com/).

The Economist. (2010a), "China and Taiwan: The Ties that Bind?", 1st July.

The Economist. (2010b), "Testing the Water: Strategic Jousting between China & America", 29th July.

The Economist. (2010c), "The Rising Power of the Chinese Worker", 29th July.

The Economist. (2010d), "They have Returned", 12th August.

The Economist. (2011a), "Wary Détente between China and America: Another Go at Being Friends", 13th January.

The Economist. (2011b), "Building Excitement: Can China Avoid a Bubble?" 3rd March.

The Economist. (2015a), "Global Manufacturing: Made in China", 12th March.

The Economist. (2015b), "The Great Well of China", 20th June.

The Economist. (2015c), "Special Report: World Economy", 3rd October.

The Economist. (2017), "The Economist Explains: What is China's Belt and Road Initiative?" 15th May.

The Economist. (2018a), "No Laughing Matter: China Wages War on Apps Offering News and Jokes", 18th April.

The Economist. (2018b), "What's in it for the Belt-and-Road Countries", 19th April.

The Economist. (2018c), "China has Militarised the South China Sea and Got Away with it", 23rd June.

The Financial Times. (2010a), "Kan Urges China to be Responsible", 2nd—3rd October.

The Financial Times. (2010b), "Chinese Workers Swap Anger for Angst", Tom Mitchell, 1st June.

The Financial Times. (2010c), "Political Stasis is China's Achilles Heel", Jonathan Fenby, 14th October.

The Financial Times. (2015), "RMB Bond to Put UK at Forefront", Sam Fleming, 12th September.

The Guardian. (2010a), "China 'Worried' about Safety of US Assets", Tania Branigan and Simon Tidal, 14th March.

The Guardian. (2010b), "African Countries prefer Chinese aid to US-China development cooperation, *The Guardian: The US Embassy Cables*, 4th December (available online at www.guardian.co.uk/).

The Guardian. (2017), "What is the Military Presence Near North Korea?" Oliver Holmes, 19th August.

The Korean Central News Agency. (2009), "Report on One More Successful Underground Nuclear Test", 25th May (available online at www.kcna.co.jp/item/2009/200905/news25/20090525-12ee.html).

The New York Times. (2006), "China Courts Africa, Angling for Strategic Gains", Joseph Kahn, 3rd November (available online at www.nytimes.com/).

The New York Times. (2010a), "China's Growth Shifts the Geopolitics of Oil", Jad Mouwad, 19th March (available online at www.nytimes.com/).

The New York Times. (2010b), "China and Saudi Arabia Form Stronger Trade Ties", Henry Meyer, 20th April (available online at www.nytimes.com/).

The New York Times. (2010c), "US and Vietnam Build Ties with an Eye on China", Seth Mydans, 12th October (available online at www.nytimes.com/).

The New York Times. (2010d), "China's Fast Rise Leads Neighbors to Join Forces", Mark Landler, Jim Yardley and Michael Wines, 30th October (available online at www.nytimes.com/).

The New York Times. (2010e), "Mullen Criticizes China Over North Korea", Mark MacDonald, 8th December (available online at www.nytimes.com/).

The New York Times. (2011a), "China Is Poised to Raise Rates Again, Bankers Say", Keith Bradsher, 1st February (available online at www.nytimes.com/).

The New York Times. (2011b), "China Tells U.S. It Must 'Cure Its Addiction to Debt'", David Barboza, 6th August (available online at www.nytimes.com/).

The New York Times. (2011c), "Chinese Hospitals are Battlegrounds of Discontent", Sharon LaFraniere, 11th August (available online at www.nytimes.com/).

The New York Times. (2011d), "China Faces Obstacles in Bid to Rebalance Its Economy", Wong, E., 24th August (available online at www.nytimes.com/).

The Princeton Project on National Security. (2006), "Forging a World of Liberty under Law: US National Security in the 21st Century", September (available online at www.princeton.edu).

The State Council Information Office of the People's Republic of China. (2017), "Full Text: China's Policy on Asia-Pacific Security Cooperation", 11th January (available online at www.scio.gov.cn/).

The State Council of the People's Republic of China. (2010), "China-Africa Economic and Trade Cooperation" (available online at english.gov.cn).

The State Council of the People's Republic of China. (2015), "From Initiative to Reality: Moments in Developing the Belt and Road Initiative", 23rd April (available online at english.gov.cn).

The Telegraph. (2010), "Pentagon Expects Okinawa Military Base to Stay Even If Japanese Prime Minister Quits", Danielle Demetriou, 2nd June.

The Telegraph. (2018), "Trump-Kim Summit: Donald Trump Vows to 'End War Games' in 'New History' with Korea", Ben Riley-Smith et al, 13th June.

The US-China Business Council. (2014), "China Raises Monthly Minimum Wages in Shanghai, Shenzhen, Beijing", Wenham Shen (available online at www.uschina.org/china-raises-monthly-minimum-wages-shanghai-shenzhen-beijing).

The Wall Street Journal. (2010a), "China's $20 bn Loan Bolsters Chávez", Dan Molinski and John Lyons, 18th April (available online at www.wsj.com/).

The Wall Street Journal. (2010b), "The Other China Sea Flashpoint", 12th September (available online at www.wsj.com/).

The Washington Post. (2010), "North Korea's Consistent Message to the US", Jimmy Carter, 24th November (available online at www.washingtonpost.com/).

The White House. (2009), "Press Briefing by Press Secretary Robert Gibbs", January 30th (available online at www.c-span.org/video/?283757-1/white-house-daily-briefing).

The White House. (2010), "The President's Trip to Asia 2010", *President Barack Obama* (available online at www.whitehouse.gov/).

The White House. (2015), "Remarks by the President on Trade", 8th May (available online at obamawhitehouse.archives.gov/).

The World Bank. (2011), "Africa Development Indicators 2011" (available online on data.worldbank.org/).

The World Bank. (2018a) "China Overview" (available online at www.world bank.org/en) [last updated 20th April 2018].

The World Bank. (2018b) "Healthy China: Deepening Health Reform by Building High Quality and Value-based Service Delivery", 16th April (available online at www.worldbank.org/en)).

Time. (2010), "China: The Dragon in the Room on Obama's Asian Trip", Hannah Beech, 10th November (available online at content.time.com/).

United Nations Development Programme. (2016), "Human Development Report 2016: Human Development for Everyone" (available online at hdr.undp.org/en).

U.S. Department of Defense. (2009), "Military Power of the People's Republic of China", *Annual Report to Congress* (available online at www.defense.gov/).

U.S. Department of Defense. (2010), "Speech: As Delivered by Secretary of Defense Robert M. Gates, Hanoi, Vietnam, October 11, 2010" (available online at www.defense.gov/).

U.S. Department of the Treasury. (2018), "Major Foreign Holders of U.S. Securities (MFH Table)" (available online at ticdata.treasury.gov/Publish/mfh.txt).

U.S. Energy Information Administration. (2018), "China Surpassed the United States as the world's largest crude oil importer in 2017", 5th February (available online at www.eia.gov/) [accessed 27th February 2018].

U.S. State Department. (2009), "History of the Department of the State during the Clinton Presidency (1993–2001)" (available online at 2001-2009.state.gov/r/pa/ho/pubs/c6059.htm).

Watkins, S. (2008), "The Nuclear Non-Protestation Treaty", *New Left Review*, 54, 5–26.

World Economic Forum. (2017), "President Xi's Speech to Davos in Full", 17th January (available online at www.weforum.org/agenda/).

World Health Organization. (2000), "World Health Report 2000" (available online at www.who.int/whr/).

World Oil. (2011), "Regional Report: China 2011", vol. 232, no. 12, Nell Lukosavich (available online at www.worldoil.com/December-2011-Regional-Report-China.html).

World Trade Organisation. (2017) "Country Profiles: Republic of Korea" (available online at stat.wto.org/CountryProfile/).

World Trade Organization Press Releases. (2001), "WTO Successfully Concludes Negotiations of China's Entry", 17th September (available online at www.wto.org/english/news_e/pres01_e/pr243_e.htm).

Xi, J. (2015), "China will Never Seek Hegemony, Expansion: Xi Says", *Xinhua*, 3rd September (available online at www.xinhuanet.com/english).

Xinhaunet. (2011a), "China Unveils Five-year Development Blueprint as Parliament Starts Annual Session", 5th March (available online at www.xinhuanet.com/english).

Xinhuanet. (2011b), "China, Iran Pledge Further Reciprocal Cooperation as PM Visits", 18th July (available online at www.xinhuanet.com/english).

Xinhuanet. (2013), "Xi Explains China's Reform Plan," 15th November (available online at www.xinhuanet.com/english).

Xinhuanet. (2015), "Made in China 2025" Plan Unveiled, 19th May (available online at www.xinhuanet.com/english).

Xinhuanet. (2018a), "China's Trade Surplus Continues to Narrow in 2017", 12th January (available online at www.xinhuanet.com/english).

Xinhuanet. (2018b), "Economic Watch: Is China's development threatening Latin America", Liangyu, 12th February (available online at www.xinhuanet.com/english).

Xinhuanet. (2018c), "China Woos Migrant Workers Home for Rural Development", 24th February (available online at www.xinhuanet.com/english).

Xinhuanet. (2018d), "Taiwan Exports to Chinese Mainland Hit Record High in March", 9th April (available online at www.xinhuanet.com/english).

Yuen, S. (2014), "Disciplining the Party: Xi Jinping's Anti-Corruption Campaign and Its Limits, *China Perspectives*, 2014, no. 3, 41–7.

Yusuf, S., Nabeshima, K. & Perkins, D. (2005), *Under New Ownership: Privatising China's State-Owned Entreprises*, Stanford: Stanford University Press.

Conclusion

The objective of this book has not been to 'prophesise' on the future of US hegemony in the 21st century – precluded by the complex, dialectical, open, and ontologically stratified nature of the social sphere – but rather to shed some light on dominant global tendencies underway. To that end, it was first considered necessary to develop a Gramsci-inspired, historical materialist theory of hegemony: one that draws on, but differentiates itself from, neo-Gramscian perspectives, which despite their invaluable insights display certain ontological inconsistencies, notably failing to grant *structure* the primacy it merits. The *Neo* neo-Gramscian (NNG) theoretical framework forwarded in Chapter 1 seeks to rectify this shortcoming, rooting its conceptualisation of hegemony in an *emergentist materialist* philosophy of science. Drawing on the work of thinkers such as Giovanni Arrighi, David Harvey, Hannah Arendt, and Peter Gowan, the NNG theory then underscored some of the key characteristics of the world hegemon within a crisis-prone global capitalist system (beset by both "conjunctural" and "organic movements"[1]) using the systemic cycle of accumulation (SCOA) meta-narrative as a reference point.

Since world hegemony originates in the outward expansion of social forces emanating from the social relations of production (SROP) within a particular national historical bloc (HB) (albeit always dialectic inter-relation with 'international' social forces), any understanding of the dynamics of contemporary US hegemony must involve the 'historicising' of the present: study the historical evolution of the American *state-society complex* within a single capitalist world economy, special attention being paid to the 'hegemonic apparatus' (encompassing ideas, organic intellectuals, discourse, and myth) within 'hegemonic projects' (surface hegemony).

Accordingly, Chapter 2 analysed how, against the backdrop of uneven and combined development, manifested in a huge post-WWII wealth/power disparity between states, dominant social forces emergent from American capitalism mobilised behind a hegemonic project designed to expand global markets (and avoid over-production at home). This would involve restructuring domestic/core countries' SROP (Fordism) and form of state (FOS) (Keynesian), compatible with the needs of a mass

DOI: 10.4324/9780429459061-7

consumption/mass production economy orientated towards the Open Door. The aim was to create 'a world in our own image' (or at least one consistent with it) and involved the setting up of multilateral institutions organisations (e.g. the UN, Bretton Woods, the OEEC/OECD, etc.), the third of Cox's "categories of forces"[2] and consistent with Gramsci's *second moment* of hegemony.

True to Gramsci's understanding, the American bourgeoisie's exercising of hegemony over core elites and subaltern classes (both at home and abroad) involved an intricate interplay of consensual and coercive measures right across 'state-society complexes'. Though it would have many important cultural expressions, American *intellectual and moral leadership* (again incorporated both 'consensual' and 'coercive' aspects) was founded upon the US carrying two essential tasks. First, in its ability to act as a global motor for economic growth, to underwrite a new stable and expansive regime of accumulation and profitability; facilitated through military Keynesianism, foreign direct investment (FDI), technological transfer, and crucially permitting core country exporters access to its enormous internal market (in its capacity as a 'container of power'). Second, in its role as politico-military custodian, guaranteeing the political stability of the 'free world' for capital, protecting it from leftist/communist insurgency, be it from 'within' or 'without'.

The advent of the Cold War linked both of these together, launching a 'permanent war economy' and the establishment of the NSS at home, and with military expenditure and the setting up of security umbrellas abroad (e.g. NATO) around Spykman's Rimland. Military instruments to defend the realm from external attack, as James Madison noted, are usually used against the national population. The Cold War anti-communist campaign (NSC-68) required "just repression" within civil society and had clear domestic class objectives: discipline the subaltern classes, curtail leftist political parties, and eradicate radical elements within the union movement as part of the restructuring of SROP, and the integration of industrial labour within the Fordist/Keynesian HB.

Although the spoils were unevenly divided amongst social classes and ethnic groups, under *Pax Americana* and riding on the back of the postwar boom, core countries enjoyed almost 25 years of unprecedented economic growth, full employment, rising real standards of living, access to hitherto inaccessible consumer goods, and political stability. American 'intellectual and moral leadership' (including cultural hegemony) was at its height.

But just as capital accumulation is uneven, never-ending, and perpetually relocating (seeking a new *spatio-temporal fix*[3]), so hegemony itself is a dynamic and continually contested relationship. By the late 1960s, the very exercising of American hegemony and the social processes it unleashed (e.g. the IOS and the IOP) began to undermine US dominance itself, symbolised in, and magnified by, the Vietnam War, and expressed in *détente*. We noted in Chapter 3 how underlying class contradictions, which beset the post-war regime system of accumulation (Fordist SROP, Keynesian FOS, Bretton Woods, and embedded liberalism, included), would prove unsustainable exacerbated by dollar printing and systemic inter-capitalist competition, reflected in falling rates of profits.

With American hegemony apparently in decline, Western Europe, Japan, and even the 'Third World' sought to exercise greater independence, the latter even demanding a fundamental restructuring of the international economy. While this 'conjunctural' crisis and associated economic, political, and ideological malaise of the 1970s formed part of a long-term restructuring process, we have argued, contrary to neo-Gramscian assertions, that it did not signal the end of US hegemony (or its replacement by a transnational capitalist class version), but rather its reconstitution and relaunching via a new regime of accumulation: a Dollar-Wall Street-based *financialized* neoliberal growth model, consistent with the M-M' stage of Arrighi's SCOA and facilitated by financial sector reform (abandoning Bretton Woods petrodollarisation, the Volcker Shock, and 'deregulation') and crucially social class transformation.

Ultimately, the neoliberal hegemonic project (consolidated in the mid-1970s) was a class programme. Equipped with its own particular hegemonic apparatus, the aim was to restore profit rates, liberate capital from any 'social compromise', curb the populations' 'excessive' democratic demands, but above all discipline organised labour with which it engaged in an exemplary public showdown. Neoliberalism required the restructuring of countries' SROP and the FOS, not just in the capitalist core, but in the periphery and semi-periphery. At the global level, the hegemonic project found its ideological expression in 'common sense' Washington Consensus recommendations, but each 'state-society complex' underwent its own social restructuring programme depending on its particular class dynamics within an increasingly financialized world. Often, as neo-Gramscians such as Stephen Gill and Kees van de Pijl asserted, the transition towards neoliberalism relied on the consensual/coercive methods of 'new constitutionalism', using Regional Trade Agreements to lock in 'disciplinary neoliberalism' as part of a *passive revolution*.

Coercion was omnipresent in this class war. This was witnessed in its more overt form – Gramsci's *third moment* ("relations of military forces") – with the launching of the *Second* Cold War (1980–85). Reagan's military initiative was not just designed to help stimulate the economy and consolidate his HB (those linked to the Weapondollar-Petrodollar Coalition), like Truman's *First* Cold War it was directed at subordinate classes (e.g. NSC-68) and to reassert dominance over foreign elites: bringing the Allies back into the fold after the disasters of *détente* and disciplining the 'Third World', often by very violent means. Just how important the Cold War framework was for US hegemony became clear with the fall of the Berlin Wall when, despite Bush I's talk of 'peace dividends' and a 'New World Order', the State and Defense Departments would spend a decade searching for a viable th-thereat to substitute for the Warsaw Pact in its new Grand Strategy.

We saw how American hegemony reached its post-Cold War zenith under the Clinton administration: globalization euphoria, the Washington Consensus and the New Economy all served to reinforce the 'common sense' validity of neoliberalism/financialization, enabling the world's upper classes to enrich themselves (at the expense of those lower down the pecking order). Unfortunately, this optimism would prove transient. By the late 1990s, the internal contradictions of globalization and the neoliberal accumulation regime (e.g. increased global imbalances, rising inequality in social fragmentation, and household debt) were coming home to roost and profit rates started declining in the US from 1997. Although blowing speculative bubbles was considered an inevitable, and actually desirable side-effect of the financialized neoliberal regime of capital accumulation (with the Wall Street-Treasury-IMF [WSTI] Complex at the helm), the Long-Term Capital Management Fund (LTCM) crash in 1998 indicated that the 'heartland' itself could not immunise itself from contagion. Worse still, in March 2000 the New Economy ran aground with the bursting of the dot.com asset-bubble.

It was this context of economic and political malaise that the 'neocon' hegemonic project garnered support within the Republican Party, symbolised in Bush II's presidential primaries' success and the prominent positions occupied within the latter's administration. Apart from blowing yet another financial bubble (see below), Bush II's reaction to the US's failing hegemony, consistent with the New Right HB from which he emerged, was to augment authoritarianism at home – reviving *Red Scare*-style surveillance and curtailment of civil liberties under the PATRIOT Act and Homeland Security Act – and adopt a hawkish position abroad. Chapter 4 analysed the significance of this 'new imperialism': NSS-2002, the Iraq War, the WOT and even associated 'organic intellectuals' (e.g. Niall Ferguson, Max Boot, and Robert Kaplan). For many mainstream IR scholars and neo-Gramscians, the Bush Doctrine, the blatant disregard for international law, and human rights norms, and the resultant loss of 'intellectual and moral leadership', signalled the end of 'hegemony' in lieu of 'domination' or 'supremacy'.

Evidently, as befits the emergent materialist nature of the social world, politics is always shifting and each government's policies are contingent on historical processes. Compared to some of his predecessors, the Bush II administration displayed a greater reticence to be bound by multilateral agreements when they clashed with perceived national interests, and a tendency to over-rely on the *territorial* "logic of power", both to expand markets and guarantee on-going capital accumulation via the creation of a new *spatial fix*, and to further American geopolitical concerns in the Middle East. Nonetheless, it is important not to overstate these differences, as the Bush II administration largely maintained continuity and coherence with the established pattern of hegemonic governance and arguably fulfilling its hegemonic function. As even liberal internationalist, Thomas L. Friedman admitted, "the hidden hand of the market will never work without the hidden fist – MacDonald's cannot flourish without McDonnell Douglas".[4] Taken together with Hannah Arendt's observation – endless capital accumulation requires an endless accumulation of power – it was perhaps logically evident that a globalized economy needed a Global Leviathan with the military capacity to wage perpetual war on a global scale, as Dick Cheney envisaged. Despite liberal and neo-Gramscian interpretations, hegemony is more than just consensual power relations; at least for Gramsci, as set out in Chapter 1, it necessarily encompasses domination, with periodic recourse to militarism (Gramsci's *third moment*).

Similarly, the so-called neocon 'take-over' of the Bush II administration must be placed in context, harkening back as it does to the mid-1970s and consolidated under Reagan. Indeed, as Chapter 4 highlighted, the war on terror (WOT) shared very similar national and international objectives with Reagan's Second Cold War (e.g. consolidate HB, pump priming the military-industrial-complex (MIC)/security-industrial complex (SIC), reassert hegemony etc.). Extending Karl Polanyi and Hannah Arendt's ideas, Bush II's heightened authoritarianism can be understood as a rational reaction by the upper classes to impose social control over an increasingly individualised, fragmented society, torn apart by neoliberalism (a tendency repeated throughout the contemporary world order (WO).

Obama's arrival in the White House also helped to contextualise the Bush II administration. First, the enthusiasm that Obama's swearing-in generated amongst a broad section of the global elite – reflected in him being fast-tracked to a Nobel Peace Prize – may have been a comment on the unpopular nature of the previous administration, but it also demonstrated that US 'intellectual and moral leadership' amongst the world's elites still lay intact, despite the Iraq debacle. Second, despite his easy-going genial style and progressive liberal internationalist rhetoric, the 'deporter-in-chief' largely maintained and even expanded upon his predecessor's agenda, denoting the broad class agreement amongst American capital on the validity of Bush II's policies. Terminology such as the WOT might disappear from popular discourse under the Obama administration, but the Global Leviathan still remained committed to 'perpetual war', intervening in an increasing number of countries, albeit clandestinely, be it by special operation command (SOCOM), drones, cyber-attacks, or financial sabotage. There might have been a recognition in NSS-2010 of the existence of "other centres of power", but there was universal agreement amongst the American upper classes, unquestioned by either Obama or Trump, on the need to maintain US primacy, as emphasised in NSS-2015 and NSS-2017.

The final section of Chapter 4 set out to shed some light on the significance of the Global Financial Crisis (GFC). In the short term, ironically, the GFC actually reinforced US 'intellectual and moral leadership'. The American state (i.e. the Treasury and Federal Reserve) again could carry out its role as 'chief fire-fighter', acting as market and lender of last resort, 'pump priming' the global economy, reaffirming the dollar's centrality as the world's reserve currency, while offering global capital a safe harbour for its accumulated wealth in the form of treasury bonds (TBs). Yet in the medium to long term, the GFC might prove the tipping point for US hegemony.

It was not just that it demonstrated once more the glaring contradictions of a neoliberal financialized system of accumulation and investment/asset-bubble-blowing tendencies, but the scale of the havoc on the 'heartland' itself. Flooded by incoming foreign capital (resulting from systemic over-accumulation/exploitation), and beset by the ravages of neoliberalism (rising inequality, falling wages, debt, and alienation) American society was simply unable to carry out its hegemonic function as an engine for growth and 'consumer of last resort'. The capitalist system, arguably, was entering into one of Gramsci's 'organic movements': tantamount to the "terminal crisis"[5] of US hegemony, reflected in its diminishing capacity for 'intellectual and moral leadership'. In the short-term, there were clashes with the German-led eurozone over the correct fiscal response. But perhaps of even greater historical significance, the Communist Party of China (CPC) elite began to reassess the sustainability of its low-wage export-driven growth model and look for alternative locations to bury its surplus value in.

Chapter 5 was specifically dedicated to the 'challenge' posed to US hegemony by the meteoric rise of the People's Republic of China (PRC), bearing in mind Gramsci's criteria for assessing the power of a particular 'integral State' (i.e. 'state-society complex') within the inter-state system, as outlined in Chapter 1.[6] The chapter emphasised the huge geopolitical significance of China's global economic presence across the developing world and especially East Asia. And how increasingly, Gramsci's *first moment* (economic hegemony) was being reinforced by a burgeoning *second moment* (political hegemony) with the construction of multilateral institutions (e.g. Asian Infrastructure Investment Bank, New Development Bank, Contingent Reserve Arrangements, and Chiang Mai Initiative Multilateralized) designed, in keeping with Cox's analysis, to embed (Chinese) power relations and assimilate competing interests. Importantly, these organisations offered emerging countries alternative methods of financing (and progressively in yuan) than those serving US hegemony (and the WSTI Complex). Indeed, a testimony to the declining influence of Washington has been the US's *inability* to prevent such institution-building in the first place, having thwarted similar initiatives tabled by the European Union (EU) or Japan.

At the same time, we also observed that thus far CPC elite have been content for these institutions to 'shadow', rather than directly challenge, the established institutions of US hegemony (noticeably the Bretton Woods trio), of which the PRC remains an ever-increasingly active and influential member. American regime theorists hold out hope that the deeper China gets integrated into the US-led 'liberal rule-based international order' (LRBIO) – which to date has served its capitalist interests well – the costs of abandonment would prove far too great. Liberal internationalists warmly received Xi Jinping's speech at the World Economic Forum in Davos in 2017, in which the President emphasised the country's commitment to global free trade/investment, market liberalization/facilitation, and open multilateral trade.[7] Paradoxically, Trump's inward-looking "America First" policy has served to reinforce the PRC's image as a guardian of the LRBIO and on-going globalization.

Beijing, as we have seen, has consistently reiterated the idea that it has no world hegemonic ambitions and is happy to work within the LRBIO framework. Yet as argued throughout this book, the LRBIO (including respect for human rights) remains inseparable from US hegemony and American capitalism. Conforming to the *emergentist materialist* philosophy of science set out in Chapter 1, institutions are emergent out of underlying social structures. The sustainability of any particular regime ('surface hegemony') cannot indefinitely outlive 'deep' social structures ('structural hegemony'). It is reasonable to assume that over the medium to long term, the PRC will give greater support to those institutions which best help *reproduce* Chinese capitalism, which is liable to provoke a clash with the US.

The launching of the Belt & Road Initiative (BRI), we noted, potentially constitutes a serious challenge to US hegemony, both in its claim to be the motor of growth – offering a new infrastructure-based regime of accumulation – and with regards American long-standing geopolitical supremacy across Eurasia. Billed as a quasi-Marshall Plan, the BRI not only could offer Chinese SOEs a *spatial fix* to bury their surpluses and offset chronic over-capacity at home (consistent with the *territorial* logic of power), it promises to pull economies across the region within its economic and political orbit (the "connectivities") – e.g. Chinese tech companies investing in Bangladesh, Pakistan, Indonesia – like the American programme before it, help mould foreign SROP in line with the interest of Chinese capital, in accordance with Gramsci's *first* and *second moments*.

The scale of participation (over 70 countries, with a whole plethora of Western multinational corporations (MNCs) 'on board'[8]), resources mobilised ($900 billion in loans unwritten to date), and increasing institutionalised nature (bonds being issued via Shanghai and Shenzhen stock markets) are impressive. At the same time, as Chapter 5 indicated, one must exercise caution when offering prognoses on the future of the BRI. Serious questions still remain with regard to its functioning, profitability, and its interaction/compatibility with the PRC's own 'state-society complex'. The dynamics of the BRI, evidently, are contingent on internal class dynamics within China's underlying HB – albeit within a global capitalist system – hence the relevance of its on-going 'passive revolution' (see below). For the short to medium term, it appears reasonable to assume that EU and US will remain key markets for China, both for its exports and for its SOEs to acquire the technology and develop its brands.

As we saw in Chapter 5 the US's relationship with the PRC is highly complex. On the one hand, China is a key manufacturer/final assembler for a large percentage of its imported goods, forming part of a global production network which generates huge profits for American MNCs (e.g. Apple, Walmart, Intel, Target, and Nike). It also constitutes a colossal future internal market for its firms ('container of power') and remains the country's top creditor in terms of TB purchases and dollars hoarded. On the other hand, Washington blames Beijing for its balance of payments deficit (accusing it of currency manipulation and dumping) and is becoming increasingly concerned that 'American primacy' is being eroded by China's technological advancement/piracy, while denouncing the Asian power's growing regional militarism. This reflects a discernible split within US capital between its transnational corporation whose production-chains are dependent on the PRC, and keen to maintain the status quo, and uncompetitive or domestic-based businesses, who favour protectionism and economic nationalism. The latter Sino-sceptics are joined by the security establishment.

Obama's 'pivot to Asia', we noted, largely adhered to the Ikenberry-Slaughter 'carrot-and-stick' policy recommendations: (1) trying to accommodate China's demands, offering it the possibility to play a greater, privileged role within a US-led LRBIO, while pressing them to revalue the yuan; and (2) committing to the "strategic rebalancing" of the Asia-Pacific region by strengthening security arrangements with the PRC's neighbours in a quasi-Cold War containment policy (NSS-2015). Indeed, as Chapter 5 showed, the US has used its politico-military hegemony (the *third moment*) over East Asian countries to compensate for its ever-decreasing economic and political hegemony (the *first* and *second moments*) there.

In recent years, Washington has exploited legitimate regional concerns over China's rising economic and military might (most clearly demonstrated in its 'string of pearls' arrangement and territorial disputes) by linking up with conservative/nationalist social forces in East Asian countries to engage in a series of provocative actions (e.g. arms deals, anti-missile system installation, joint military exercises, and patrolling disputed waters[9]), driving a wedge between them and Beijing, therein seriously undermining any hegemonic ambitions the latter might harbour. Washington declares itself determined to take all measures to maintain its position as "system shaper" and to mobilise "all the instruments" of power at its disposal to check the PRC's assertiveness and guarantee "freedom of navigation operations" in Asia-Pacific (NSS-2017).

Despite its burgeoning military capacity and A2/AD strategy, to date, China has avoided direct military engagement in the area, aware of its counter-productive nature and of the US's absolute naval supremacy in Asia-Pacific. Moreover, as Chapter 5 underscored, the economic pull of the PRC is mitigating, to a certain degree, some of the territorial disputes, at least with regards to lesser Asian countries. Whether Chinese economic hegemony (*first moment*) and burgeoning political hegemony (*second moment*) are sufficient to realign East Asian politics towards a more Sinocentric orientation (including crucially South Korea and Japan) without military hegemony (*third moment*) remains to be seen. 'Anti-declinist' hawk Robert Kagan expresses the commonly held view in the Washington security establishment that the Global Leviathan must be prepared to resort to military means to prevent the latter occurring.[10] As American economic hegemony recedes and domestic society is torn apart by soaring inequality and class polarisation desperate times may call for desperate measures. Militarism is a blunt instrument, however. Even as part of a broad "balancing coalition" (e.g. the Quadrilateral Security Dialogue), and necessarily including Japan, the risks the US would run by entering into combat with China are considerable, spanning from 'imperial over-stretch' to 'mutually assured destruction'.

But although the first two sections of Chapter 5 focused on the PRC's global role, whether China would be able to replace the US as 'world hegemon', and the nature this would take, will ultimately depend upon how these global social forces interact with the dynamics of its on-going 'passive revolution' and underlying HB.

The spectacular economic ascent of the PRC and enrichment of the well-connected was born on the back of 'accumulation by dispossession', the commodification of land and labour, and super-exploitation of the workforce (many of them stripped of socio-economic rights). Squaring the circle of maintaining a 'wild west'-style capital accumulation model and polarised class society with a nominal *communist* state has proven difficult, witnessed in the increased wave of political protests and social unrest. Hitherto the CPC elite has opted for a nuanced strategy to deal with the challenge 'from below'. On the one hand, this has involved improving social policy (e.g. expanding welfare provisions, supporting minimum wage increases, and amending *hukou*) and introducing political and legal reform (e.g. the Labour Contract Law, limited democratic participation, and the 'war on corruption') in an attempt to assimilate them into their neoliberal hegemonic project (*trasformismo*). On the other hand, and especially acute under the *Caesarism* of Xi Jinping, the Politburo has stepped-up authoritarian rule, augmented population surveillance and heightened nationalism. As occurred in the US under Truman, militarism abroad was paralleled with militarism at home.

Since Wen Jiabao, the CPC has acknowledged the "unbalanced, uncoordinated, and unsustainable" nature of its economic growth model manifested in huge inequality, rural poverty, an underclass of migrant workers, the rural-urban divide, appalling pollution levels, and persistent investment bubbles. Xi's "Thought on Socialism with Chinese Characteristics for a New Era", unveiled at the CPC's 19th Party Congress in October 2017, pledged to tackle these problems improve the people's quality of life (e.g. fairer, less corrupt, more democratic, law-based, and "harmonious"). The aim, Xi announced, was to turn the PRC into a "moderately prosperous society" by 2020 *en route* a "great socialist country" by the mid-21st century.[11]

Though Xi once again promised China would never seek (military) hegemony or engage in expansionism, regardless of their developmental stage, Beijing is aware that any bid for (economic) hegemony, even at the regional level, depends upon the country becoming an engine of growth and the success of the "deepening reforms". Will China be able to avoid the 'middle-country trap', rise up the value-added chain (as Made in China 2025 aims) and to compete in the service and high-tech areas with the core countries? The internationalisation of the RMB and the functioning of the BRI are also important challenges facing Beijing. Again, these initiatives are being driven by social forces emerging from within China's evolving HB, but just how they will affect and be affected by the domestic class structure cannot be predicted. Fragmentation within the cadre-capitalist class cannot be ruled out, nor eventual class-conscious organisation and mobilisation amongst factions of subaltern groups.

Since world hegemony involves a country remaking the world 'in its own image' based on its SROP and FOS, it is likely that the WO under Chinese hegemony would have a very different hue to it than that under *Pax Americana*. Certainly, at the time of writing the strict authoritarian state-capitalist model operating in the PRC is a far cry from the democratic, egalitarian, and ecological version envisioned by Arrighi. A problem for Beijing also is that the Sino-centric cultural character of its 'state-society complex' does not lend itself easily to emulation abroad, clashing with the liberal universalism and Open-Door transnationalism hitherto considered inseparable from the exercising of world hegemony.

Culture, as Gramsci stressed, forms a vital part of 'intellectual and moral leadership', or political hegemony (the *second moment*). Clearly, the US has long exercised cultural hegemony (part of what Joseph Nye considers "soft power"[12]) over the Western world, extended globally following the end of the Cold War. Thanks to its dominance in popular cultural areas such as the performing arts, the entertainment industry (especially film and television), elite written press/magazines, social media, advertising, fashion, etc. the US can shape *ideas* – understood in the Coxian sense as "collective images of social order held by different groups of people"[13] – promoting liberal values and aspirations and, into the bargain, demand for American goods, services, and lifestyle.

Like the US before it the PRC has placed great importance on globalizing Chinese culture. Much of this typically takes place through the market – especially FDI – but while American cultural infiltration, as Gramsci observed, often took place within the nominal realms of 'civil society' – e.g. clubs, associations, and think tanks, such as the Young Man's Christian Association (YMCA), the Rotary Club, the Freemasonry, and later the Bilderberg Group, Trilateral Commission, and Heritage Foundation, etc. – the nature of its FOS means the PRC must rely more on overtly state-directed initiatives. The CPC, for example, has been busy setting up official media outlets around the world (e.g. Xinhua and China Global Television Network), financing over 520 Confucius Centres in around 140 countries to promote Chinese language and culture[14] (albeit with certain topics such as Taiwan, Tibet, and Xinjiang out of bounds), and subsidising foreign students' programmes. Again, at least for medium term, it appears reasonable to assume that US cultural hegemony will retain its attractiveness, judging by the number of CPC elites that send their children to be educated in the top American universities.

It is always notoriously difficult to identify the *exact* moment one finds oneself within any given historical process; in this case, whether we are now entering a period of hegemonic transition. As Bhaskar's stratified ontological model set out in Chapter 1 indicates, events (actual) emerge from the complex interaction of an unobservable underlying generative mechanism (real). Nonetheless, the evidence seems to suggest at the very least we are approaching what Gramsci termed "interregnum" a crisis created when "the old is dying and the new cannot be born" and in which "a great variety of morbid symptoms appear"[15] (e.g. global imbalances, protectionism/trade wars, geopolitical tensions, rising inequality, right-wing populism, heightened nationalism, migration crises, etc.). For world-theorists, such as Christopher Chase-Dunn, the demise of a world hegemon typically is followed by a fierce period of inter-state rivalry, reflected in economic, political, military turbulence, and war (witness the inter-war period between *Pax Britannica* and *Pax Americana*) as countries fight to prevent the devaluation of their capital.[16]

According to Arrighi, this period of systemic chaos will only end when new hegemon emerges victorious and establishes itself as the "headquarters" of the leading capitalist agencies and prepared to launch a new SCOA.[17] Working on the established template, it must also be a sufficiently large 'container of power' (i.e. bigger than the US) to satisfy global capital's needs to bury its surplus value (the 'consumer of last resort') and convert itself into the world's mass consumption society, par excellence. Evidently, businesses around the world are desperate to access the PRC's enormous internal market – estimated to have an urban middle class of around 780 million by the mid-2020s – and attract its FDI, students, and tourists (who now spend twice as much on luxury goods as Americans).

Herein lies the rub. With climate change and global environmental degradation already approaching critical levels, were the Chinese to consume at levels comparable to North Americans and European, the question of who exercises world hegemony might well turn out to be purely academic.

Notes

1 Gramsci (1971), p. 79.
2 Cox (1996a), pp. 98–9.
3 Harvey (1982, 2003).
4 Friedman (1999). See also Friedman (2000), pp. 443–4.
5 Arrighi (2010), pp. 221–2.
6 Gramsci (2007), Quaderni 13, p. 1598.
7 World Economic Forum (2017).
8 Examples of firms participating in BRI-related projects include General Electric, Hewlett Packard, Honeywell, Caterpillar, Citigroup, HSBC, Deutsche Bank, DHL, and BASF.
9 One could pose the question as to whether it is really necessary for the US 5th Fleet to carry out their 'routine military surveys' in the waters close to China's exclusive economic zone (EEZ). One could imagine the American reaction were China or Russia to hold nuclear aircraft carrier-led naval manoeuvres in the Gulf of Mexico, involving joint live-fire exercises with Cuba or carrying out amphibious landings in Mexico.
10 In a recent Brooking publication, Kagan explained:

> My attitude to China is, do well economically, but you cannot use your military to expand your power position in the region. Is that fair? No. Is there any justice in that? No. We get the Monroe Doctrine and you don't. That's just the way it is, I'm sorry.
>
> Quoted in Brookings Institution (2017)

11 China Daily (2017).
12 Nye (1990).
13 See Cox (1996a), pp. 98–9.
14 Confucius Institute Headquarters (2018).
15 Gramsci (1971), pp. 275–6.
16 Chase-Dunn (1998).
17 Arrighi (2008), pp. 233–4.

Bibliography

Arendt, H. (1966), *The Origins of Totalitarianism*, New York: Harcourt, Brace and World.

Arrighi, G. (2008), *Adam Smith in Beijing: Lineages of the Twenty-First Century*, London: Verso.

Arrighi, G. (2010), *The Long Twentieth Century: Money, Power and the Origins of our Times*, 2nd edn. [1st Edn. 1994], London: Verso.

Arrighi, G. & Silver, B. (eds.) (1999), *Chaos and Governance in the Modern System*, Minneapolis: University of Minnesota Press.

Brookings Institution (2017), "Avoiding War: Containment, Competition, and Co-operation in US-China Relations", *Foreign Policy at Brookings* (available online at www.brookings.edu).

Callinicos, A. (2004), *The New Mandarins of American Power: The Bush Administration's Plan for the World*, Cambridge: Polity Press.

Capgemini. (2017), "World Wealth Report 2017" (www.capgemini.com/wp-content/uploads/2017/09/worldwealthreport_2017_final.pdf).

Chase-Dunn, C. (1998), *Global Formation: Structures of the World-Economy*, 2nd Edn. Lanham, MD: Rowman & Littlefield.

China Daily. (2017), "CPC Stresses Socialism with Chinese Characteristics as Congress Opens, 18th October (available at www.chinadailyasia.com).

China Daily. (2018), "'Made in China 2025' Roadmap Updated", 27th January, (available online at www.chinadaily.com.cn/).

Clarke, R.A. (2004), *Against All Enemies: Inside America's War on Terror*, London: The Free Press.

Confucius Institute Headquarters. (2018), "Confucius Institute/Classroom" (available online at english.hanban.org/).

Cox, R.W. (1996a), "Social Forces, States, and World Orders: Beyond International Relations Theory" [orig. pub. 1981], in Cox, R.W. and Sinclair, T.J. (eds.), *Approaches to World Order*, Cambridge: Cambridge University Press.

Cox, R.W. (1996b), "Gramsci, Hegemony and International Relations: An Essay in Method" [orig. pub. 1983], in Cox, R.W. with Sinclair, T.J., *Approaches to World Order*, Cambridge: Cambridge University Press.

Duménil, G. & Levy, D. (2011), *The Crisis of Neoliberalism*, Cambridge: Harvard University Press.

Friedman, L.T. (1999), "A Manifest for a Fast World", *The New York Times Magazine*, 28th March (available online at www.nytimes.com).

Friedman, L.T. (2000), *The Lexus and the Olive Tree*, New York: Farrar, Straus & Giroux (Revised Edition).

Gilboy, G.J. & Heginbotham, J. (2010), "China's Dilemma: Social Change and Political Reform", *Foreign Affairs*, October 14th.

Gowan, P. (1999), *The Global Gamble: Washington's Faustian Bid for World Dominance*, London: Verso.

Gowan, P. (2009), "Crisis in the Heartland: Consequences of the New Wall Street System", *New Left Review*, January-February, 55; 5–29.

Gramsci, A. (1971), *Selections from the Prison Notebooks of Antonio Gramsci*, Hoare, Q. and Nowell Smith, G. (eds. and trans.), London: Lawrence & Wishart.

Gramsci, A. (2007), *Quaderni del Calcere: Quaderni di traduzioni (1929–1932)*, in Cospito, G. and Francioni, G. (eds.), Rome: Istituto della Enciclopedia Italiana, Quaderni.

Harvey, D. (1982), *The Limits to Capital*, Oxford: Basil Blackwell.

Harvey, D. (2003), *The New Imperialism*, Oxford: Oxford University Press.

Harvey, D. (2007), *A Brief History of Neoliberalism*, Oxford: Oxford University Press.

Ikenberry, G.J. (2002), "American imperial ambitions", *Foreign Affairs*, 81, no. 5, 44–60.

Ikenberry, G.J. (2004), "Liberalism and Empire: Logics of Order in the American Unipolar Age", *Review of International Studies*, 30, no. 4, 609–30.

International Monetary Fund. (2017), "People's Republic of China: Country Report No. 17/248" (www.imf.org/~/media/Files/Publications/.../cr17248.ashx).

International Monetary Fund. (2018), *World Economic Outlook, April 2018*, accessed 20th April (available online at www.imf.org/en/Countries/CHN).

Jacques, M. (2009), *When China Rules the World: The End of the Western World and the Birth of a New Global Order*, New York: The Penguin Press.

Kaplan, R.B. (2005), "How we would fight China", *Atlantic Magazine*, June (available online at www.theatlantic.com/).

Lee, C.K. (2008), *Against the Law: Labour Protests in China's Rustbelt and Sunbelt*, Berkeley, CA: University of Berkeley.

Li, C. (2013), "Rule of the Princelings", *Brookings Institute*, 10th February (available online at www.brookings.edu/articles/rule-of-the-princelings/).

National Security Strategy. (2010), *The National Security Strategy of the United States of America*, Washington, DC, May (available online at nssarchive.us/NSSR/2010.pdf).

National Security Strategy. (2015), *The National Security Strategy of the United States of America*, February (available online at nssarchive.us/wp-content/uploads/2015/02/2015.pdf).

National Security Strategy. (2017), *National Security Strategy of the United States of America*, December (available online at nssarchive.us/wp-content/uploads/2017/12/2017.pdf).

Nye, J.S. (1990), *Bound to Lead: The Changing Nature of American Power*, New York: Basic Books.

Osburg, J. (2013), *Anxious Wealth: Money & Morality among China's New Rich*, Stanford: Stanford University Press.

Polanyi, K. (1954), *The Great Transformation*, Boston, MA: Beacon Press.

So, A.Y. (2013), *Class and Class Conflict in Post-Socialist China*, Hong Kong: World Scientific Publishing Company.

Sum, N.L. & Jessop, B. (2013), *Towards a Cultural Political Economy: Putting Culture in Its Place in Political Economy*, Cheltenham: Edward Elgar.

van der Pijl, K. (2006), *From the Cold War to Iraq*, London: Pluto Press.

World Economic Forum. (2017), "President Xi's Speech to Davos in Full", 17th January (available online at www.weforum.org/agenda/).

Xi, J. (2015), "China Will Never Seek Hegemony, Expansion: Xi says", *Xinhua*, 3rd September (available online at www.xinhuanet.com/english).

Yuen, S. (2014), "Disciplining the Party: Xi Jinping's Anti-corruption Campaign and Its Limits, *China Perspectives*, 3 41–47.

Index

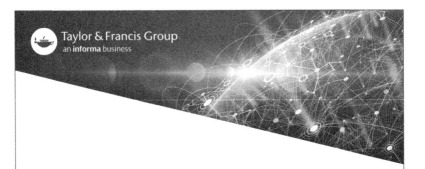

For Product Safety Concerns and Information please contact our EU
representative GPSR@taylorandfrancis.com Taylor & Francis Verlag GmbH,
Kaufingerstraße 24, 80331 München, Germany

Printed and bound by CPI Group (UK) Ltd, Croydon, CR0 4YY

01/05/2025

01858426-0003